STARS & STAR HANDLERS

Marilyn Monroe, and the "man in the shadow," agent Johnny Hyde, who loved her enough to move heaven and earth to obtain small but meaningful roles in *The Asphalt Jungle* and *All About Eve*—starting her career—before he died of a heart attack. *(Bruno Bernard/Globe Photos, Inc.)*

WHITNEY STINE

STARS
& STAR
HANDLERS

The Business of Show

ROUNDTABLE PUBLISHING, INC.
SANTA MONICA   CALIFORNIA

First Printing, 1985

Library of Congress Catalog Card Number—84-60759

PRINTED IN THE UNITED STATES OF AMERICA

This book is dedicated to the Agents, Managers, Publicists and other intrepid aboriginals of Hollywood and Broadway, whose names and deeds do not appear in these pages—not through oversight, but because of the slimness of the volume.

This overview can only examine the branches of the ancestral "family" tree. Each divergent limb, twig, and leaf is worthy of a book itself.

CONTENTS

Prologue, *1*

1—VAUDEVILLE & AMERICA'S FIRST AGENT, *5*

[Vaudeville • William Morris • Lee Stevens • Small Time • early booking agents • Keith-Albee • Annette Kellerman • Sir Harry Lauder • Abe Lastfogel • Marcus Loew • Martin Beck • William A. Brady • George Abbott • cabarets • flickers]

2—SILENTS WEREN'T GOLDEN, *21*

[Lillian Gish and A.F.I. 1984 Achievement Award • Gladys Smith & Maw Pickford • Uncle Tom's Cabin *• Mary Pickford • Lotta Crabtree • Elsie Janis • Cora Carrington Wilkenning • John R. Freuler • Charlie Chaplin • Adolph Zukor • Lillian Gish v. Charles H. Duell • lawyer Steuer • J. Boyce Smith • Francis Xavier Bushman • Klaw & Erlanger & Biograph • Red Carpet Treatment • Screen Players Rebel]*

3—FATHERS & BIG DADDIES, *39*

[Mary Astor & Otto Ludwig Langhanke • William Randolph Hearst & Marion Davies • Herbert J. Yates & Vera Hruba Ralston • Meshulam Riklis & Pia Zadora • Gloria Swanson • Cecil B. DeMille • Herbert Somborn • Joseph P. Kennedy • Ben Lyon & Hell's Angels *• Arthur Landau & Jean Harlow • Mae Murray]*

4—MOVIE MOPPETS, *55*

[Jackie Coogan • Skinner's Baby • Charles Chaplin • The Kid *• First National Studios • MGM • Arthur L. Bernstein • Pete Smith • Jackie Cooper & Norman Taurog • Coogan's guardianship & $4,000,000 • Wallace Beery •* Addams Family*]*

5—MCA IN CHICAGO: THE ORIGINS, *75*

[Dr. Jules Stein • William H. Goodheart • dance bands & vaudeville • Mae West • Vienna • Doctor Henry Gradle • rotating orchestras • Jule Styne • gangster Roger Touhy • Music Corporation of America • Musicians Union • Taft Schreiber • Guy Lombardo • Sonny Werblin • vaudeville in the 1920s • Nat Lefkowitz • George Burns & Tom Fitzpatrick • Will and Gladys Ahern]

6—AGENTS GAIN POWER . . . , *93*

[Myron Selznick & Lewis J. • Irene Mayer Selznick & David O. • Edward Small • Music Corporation of America in New York • E. M. Lester • Doris Cohen Jones • Radio • James Bacon • Paul Irving Lazar • Lewis Milestone & Jack L. Warner • Talkies • Howard Hughes • Frank Joyce • Ruth Chatterton & William Powell & Kay Francis & Constance Bennett • D. F. Zanuck • Barry J. Weitz • Milos Forman & Robert Lantz]

7—. . . AND MORE POWER, *115*

[Myron Selznick • Ben Hecht • Mrs. Patrick Campbell • Lillian Hellman • Harry Cohn & Clark Gable • Zeppo Marx & Leonard Spigelgass • Jean Peters & Carol Lombard • Jean Garceau • Louis Shurr & Bob Hope • Al Melnick • Frank Joyce • Leland Hayward • Fred & Adele Astaire • John W. Rumsey • Ben Hecht • Edna Ferber • Garson Kanin • Margaret Sullavan • Katherine Hepburn • Merle Oberon • Josh Logan & MCA • Charlie Rapp & The Borscht Belt]

8—THE HUNDRED-PERCENTERS, *133*

[Rhubarb • Gentle Ben • Clarence • Big Jim • Lochart's Elephants • Captain Luxford • John Kerr • Curly Twyeford • Couslon Glick • Pete & The Little Rascals • Rin Tin Tin • Hal Wallis • Darryl F. Zanuck • Bonkers and All My Children • Won Ton Ton • David V. Picker • Asta • Bill Koehler & Hal Driscall • Daisy • Lassie and Rudd Weatherwax • Chimps • Trusty Steeds • Colonel Tim McCoy • Gene Autry v. Republic Studios • Roy Rogers & Trigger • Dale Evans & Buttermilk • Swaps • Spectacular Bid & Shafter V. • Willie Shoemaker • Mark McCormack • Donald O'Connor & Francis • Hopalong Cassidy • Dr. Dolittle & Don Mc-Clennan]

9—MCA GOES TO HOLLYWOOD, *153*

[Music Corporation of America on the West Coast • The Wasserman Test • Fritz Lang & Harry Cohn & Sydney Buckman • Bette Davis • Clark Gable & Josephine Dillon • Mervyn LeRoy • Minna Wallis • Phil Berg & Bert Allenberg • George Chasin • Al Menascoe • Phil Berg • Alan Ladd & Sue Carol • June Allyson • Rosalind Russell & Frederick Brisson]

10—SELZNICKS AT THE TOP, *173*

[Gone With The Wind • Myron Selznick & David O. & Vivien Leigh & Laurence Olivier & The Burning of Atlanta • Ingrid Bergman • Intermezzo, A Love Story • Kay Brown • Selznick-Joyce Agency • Alfred Hitchcock & Joan Fontaine & Rebecca • Jesse L. Lasky & Adolph Zukor]

11—PACKAGES & PERCENTAGES, *187*

[Association of Talent Agents annual luncheons • Sandy Bresler • Phil Gersh • Martin Baum • Nina Blanchard • Robert Lantz • Ray Stark • Charles K. Feldman • Fritz Lang & Herman Mankiewicz • Follow the Boys *• Marlene Dietrich &* Just a Gigolo *• Bill Beedle & William Holden •* Golden Boy *• Ted Ashley & Famous Artists • Kinney National Services]*

12—HENRY WILLSON & TAB, ROCK, RORY, CHAD, TROY, RHONDA, ETC., *201*

[Henry Willson • Selznick-Vanguard Productions • Art Gelien & Tab Hunter • Roy Fitzgerald & Rock Hudson & Raoul Walsh • Lew Wasserman • Ingrid Bergman & Joseph Cotten • Joan Fontaine • Gregory Peck • Francis Durgin & Rory Calhoun • Marilyn Lewis & Rhonda Fleming • Robert Mosely & Guy Madison • Famous Artists • Troy Donahue • Alain Delon • Raymond Cramton & Chad Everett • Marie Wilson • Willson's funeral*]*

13—FROM PROMOTION TO PRODUCTION, *221*

[Charles Einfeld & the 42nd Street Special • Bette Davis & The Great Lie *•* Dodge City *•* The Fighting 69th *•* Sergeant York *•* Captains of the Clouds *•* Yankee Doodle Dandy *• Enterprise Productions • Edith Head •* Porgy & Bess *• Sidney Poitier & Martin Baum • Otto Preminger & Samuel Goldwyn & Sammy Davis, Jr. & Sportin' Life • Ingo Preminger • Song & Dance Man James Cagney & William Cagney Productions • Marge Zimmerman &* Terrible Joe Moran*]*

14—GOING INDEPENDENT, *235*

[Raymond Chandler • M. C. Levee & Paul Muni • Morris Stoller • George Wood • Johnny Hyde & Marilyn Monroe • The Asphalt Jungle *• James Bacon • John Bradford • Frank Capra & Glenn Ford & Abe Lastfogel & A Pocket Full of Trouble • Barry J. Weitz • Gary Marsh & Peter Weiss • the Valiant Independent Agent • Alan Carr • 1985 ten top agents]*

15—FAMILY AFFAIRS, *253*

[William Fadiman • Hollywood Leg Man • The Coogan Act • Baby Peggy • Dorothy North & Dennis the Menace *• Eddie Cantor • Mickey Rooney • Deanna Durbin • Max Baer, Sr. • Doris Day • Century Artists Agency • Marty Melcher & Jerome Rosenthal • court settlement, $22,835,646]*

16—STARS OF A DIFFERENT STRIPE, *267*

[Views of a retired agent • Victor Schertzinger • Gary Cooper • Eddie Anderson & Hattie McDaniel • Pat Morita & Dr. Haing S. Ngor • Bessie Loo • Lena Horne • Lew Leslie's Blackbirds of 1939 • Harold Gumm • MGM & Al Melnick • Lennie Hayton • Rex Reed • Harry Belafonte • Emmanuel Lewis & Webster • Lillian Schary Small • Walter Slezak & Edington & Vincent • Paul Kohner • Lana Turner • Joan Collins • June Wilkinson & dinner theaters • New York powerhouse agent]

17—MOGULS, MERGERS, & MAYHEM, *289*

[Jules Stein in California & the house on Angelo Drive • Betty Grable & Frank and Vic Orsatti • Rory Calhoun • CBS & NBC Artists Bureaus • Abe Lastfogel & U.S.O. Camp Shows • Bette Davis & John Garfield & The Hollywood Canteen • Frank Sinatra • Jules Stein & nepotism • William H. Goodheart retires • Hayward-Deverich Agency sells out • Berg-Allenberg merges with William Morris • James Stewart & Winchester '73 • Olivia De Havilland suit • Jules Stein resigns as president of MCA • the Boob Tube • Paul Gregory & Charles Laughton]

18—MCA & MONOPOLY, *305*

[MCA rents Republic lot • Rita Hayworth • Jennings Lang & Joan Bennett & Walter Wanger • Screen Actors Guild issues a waiver • MCA's Agents • Revue Productions • MCA acquires Paramount backlog • Justice Department shakes a big stick • Expansion continues • the Octopus withdraws its tentacles • MCA divests talent agency]

19—FLACKS & FLIM FLAM, *317*

[1984 Publicists Guild luncheon • Esmee Chandler • Harry Reichenback & the runaway virgins • Pine-Thomas and It Ain't No Sin • Russell Birdwell • David O. Selznick • Carole Lombard • Gene Autry • fan books • Louella Parsons • Jerry Hoffman • Dorothy Manners • Hedda Hopper • Sheilah Graham • Joyce Haber • Rona Barrett • Confidential magazine • Trade Press • The Hollywood Reporter & Daily Variety • Mike Connolly • Jack Bradford • the P.R. ladies • Maggie Ettinger • Helen Ferguson • Maidie Lyons]

20—FLACKS ACQUIRE CLASS, *339*

[Rogers & Cowan • Kathie Berlin • John Springer & Associates • Bobby Zarem • Lois Smith • Peggy Siegal • Sherry Lansing & Racing With the Moon • Marian Billings • Robert Osborne • Barry Lorie • Elizabeth Landon • Rob Friedman • Lloyd Leipzig • Ilene Feldman • Julian Myers • Renee Furst • David Epstein]

21—FAMILY AFFAIRS EIGHTIES STYLE, *355*

[Michael Jackson • the Jackson Five • Thriller *album • father Joseph Jackson • Frank M. Dileo • Ann-Margret & Roger Smith • Suzanne Somers & Alan Hamel •* Three's Company *• Las Vegas • Brooke Shields & Teri &* Sahara *• star salaries, TV and films • Marty Engels, Shirley Jones & Joe Landau • Anita Loos & John Emerson]*

22—CMA & ITS OFFSPRING, *373*

[Creative Management Associates • Freddie Fields & David Begelman • John Foreman • James Aubrey & Selena Meade • Shep Fields • Dan Welkes • Stephanie Phillips • Harvey Orkin & Sandy Lieberson in London • Franco Reggiani in Rome • CMA absorbs GAC • Henry Willson • Marvin Josephson Associates purchases CMA • Sue Mengers • Barbra Streisand • the New Producer • the New Agent • Jules Stein & Abe Lastfogel die]

Acknowledgements, *385*

Notes, *386*

Index, *394*

STARS & STAR HANDLERS

Orpheum
Los Angeles

ORPHEUM THEATER and REALTY COMPANY, Proprietors
M. MEYERFIELD, Jr., San Francisco, President.
Martin Beck, New York, Managing Director. Clarence Drown, Resident Manager.
PERFORMANCE EVERY AFTERNOON AT 2. EVERY EVENING AT 8.
MATINEE EVERY DAY

NOTE—The Order of the Programme is indicated by Annunciators Each Side of the Stage

Week Commencing Monday Matinee, September 16

A   SPECIAL CONCERT 2 AND 8 P. M.
ORPHEUM SYMPHONY ORCHESTRA
A. F. Frankenstein, Director
1. March—Militaire ....Franz Schubert, Op. 51, No. 1
2. Unfinished Symphony ....Franz Schubert
Allegro Moderato
Andante Con Moto

B   THE BRADSHAW BROTHERS
In an Act of Comedy Contortions

C   CESARE NESI
The Young Caruso

D   HARRY ARMSTRONG'S PLAYERS
In
"Squaring Accounts"
CAST:
Jeremiah Kilwait, a landlord..........................Richard Nesmith
"Sport" Conner, a newsboy..............................Verne Sheridan
SCENE—Kilwait's Office

E   W. C. FIELDS
The Silent Humorist

F   Novelty of The Age
DAYLIGHT MOVING PICTURES
MOTION VIEWS OF WORLD NEWS
A Feature of Note and Interest

G   Harmony and Comedy
Joe—VAN BROTHERS—Ernie
"Can Jimmy Come In?"

H   MRS. GENE HUGHES & COMPANY
Presenting
"Youth"
A Comedy Playlet by Edgar Allen Woolf
CAST:
Madame Cora Le Grand (Cora the first)................Mrs. Gene Hughes
Mrs. Cora Van Tassel (Cora the second)...............Addie St. Alva
Cora Van Tassel (Cora the third)....................Adele C. Potter
Cora (The Maid) ....Betty Swartz
Billy Weeks ....Bruce Elmore
TIME: The Present. PLACE: N. Y.

I   CHARLEY CASE
"The Fellow Who Talks About His Father"

J   DE WITT, BURNS AND TORRENCE
In Frank De Witt's Mirthful Creation
"The Awakening of Toys"
CAST:
A Jack-in-the-Box ....Frank De Witt
A Wooden Soldier ....Charles Burns
A Pierrot Doll ....Madge Torrence
Exit March—Waiting for the Robt. E. Lee.............Mur & Gilbert

No stamping of feet. No whistling nor hissing. Keep your feet off the seat in front. No smoking or lighting matches before leaving the theater.
Es Prohibido Fumar

MORTON L. COOK CO., PUBLISHERS, MAJESTIC THEATRE BUILDING.

(Courtesy of Variety Arts Theater, Los Angeles)

An early production of *The Red Mill*, with Fred Stone, Aline Carter, David Montgomery, and Ethel Johnson, at the Knickerbocker Theater in New York. *(Courtesy of J. Neyland collection)*

PROLOGUE

Formerly, they were called: *Jackals, Leeches, Toadies, Stooges, Parasites, Wastrels, Squeezers, Tapeworms, Boot-lickers, Flesh Peddlers, Ten percenters* . . .

Now, they are simply called agents.

Talent Agents.

They handle the stars.

Talent agents are as essential to the performing arts as the honey-bee is to the dandelion—but by nature are far more discriminative.

Unknown to the general public, but virtually indispensable to all phases of show business, agents exist in a subculture, mysterious shadow-figures who guide the destinies of everyone from Alan Alda to Agnes Ethel Zimmermann.

The stars of motion pictures, television, theater, records, videos, radio, rock concerts; the heros of the sports world *ad infinitum*, are controlled, manipulated, supervised, maneuvered, and guided by the powerful, unseen forces of the talent agent. Stars—behind the camera or the microphone or the catcher's mask; writers, producers, directors, and cinematographers, also employ agents. Like the luminaries for whom they create dialogue, instruct, photograph, and provide with other requisite services of an artistic or non-artistic nature, they are generally unable to place a value on their own talents. The agent is the middle-man, the go-between, the matchmaker; the "groom." It is a world without glitz. Amen.

This omnipotent wizard—who, like God, seems neutered—ruthlessly negotiates contracts, charmingly wins complicated percentage deals, doggedly ferrets out jobs in unlikely places, and offers allied services mainly concerned with the buck in the kick, lettuce, moola, the long green, the bread.

These magicians, while truly the *power* and the *drive* behind the artist/client, perform other sleight-of-hand duties that may include functioning as mother, father, confidant, banker, confessor, lawyer, pimp, psychiatrist, counselor, nurse, friend, and public relations expert.

Part of their job is to caress, pat, and massage the egos of their wards, who—insecure by nature—are often not performers by birth, but must be groomed and tutored into giving the impression that their talent, as well as their persona, is divine. Such are the highly specialized demands of the agent's chosen profession, that it is entirely possible that future agents will, themselves, employ agents . . .

It is said that these shibboleths have been, and are known as Jules of Stein, William of Morris, Myron of Selznick, Lew of Wasserman, Vic of Orsatti, Phil of Berg, Nina of Blanchard, Leland of Hayward, Minna of Wallis, M.C. of Levee, Robert of Lantz, Bert of Allenberg, Abe of Lastfogel, Paul of Kohner, Sonny of Werblin, Sue of Mengers, Martin of Baum, Ted of Ashley, Bessie of Loo, Martin of Baum, Ray of Stark, Freddie of Fields, Lillian Schary of Small, Henry of Willson, Dick of Shepherd, Mike of Medavoy, David of Begelman, Landau of Arthur, Charles of Feldman, William of Goodheart, and the many other knights and ladies who have briefly or longly toiled in offices on a Strip called Sunset or an Avenue named Madison.

When did this buying, selling and trading of flesh begin? The name of the first bonafide agent has been washed away in the tides of Atlantis, but surely predates Jesus Christ—the Deity most often called upon in debates between agent, client, and employer! But, the chasm that separates a *religieux* from an agent is not as wide, nor as deep, as it is imagined, when it is remembered that the stipend named in a client's contract is exactly the same amount traditionally rendered the church—a tithe of ten percent.

The question of who came first, the agent or the *artiste*, is more complicated than at first meets the eye. One theory—as good as any other—is that as the continental ice sheets were rising during the Pleistocene Epoch, a celebrated child was born, a beatific babe whose powers of imitation were so great that tribal members would often gather to watch him mime and hear him gurgle.

Did this diminutive demonstrator realize his own abilities for which *confreres* would pay tribute? Certainly not! But there *was* a shrewd sycophant who carted this genius from cave to cave to display him. Doubtlessly when the performance was concluded, and the frivolous freak was taking his bows, this "agent provocateur" extracted meaty ribs, sheaves of grains, fleshy roots, or other delectable viands from the audience as payment for watching the antics of his precocious protege.

Did, then, this impresario pile all the rewards at the feet of his bantam benefactor, or did he remove one small bone for himself? And who can say when this one small bone became a pile of silver shekels?

Variety, the "Bible of Show Business," might have headlined:

HOT TOT BOFFO B. O. IN STIX AMID HEAVY MITTS

Which translates: "gifted child is a box office success in the country, earning enthusiastic applause."

And, when this tiny titan returned to his cave, and began to distribute his loot among his fellows, surely there was one commendable curmudgeon who cautioned: "A few bones should be sequestered for such a time as when your tongue goes dry or a thorn becomes imbedded in your foot and you will no longer be able to bandy your buffoonery."

This mercurial misanthrope knelt and paid homage to his meal ticket, excessively praising his talent, and likening his features to those of the golden ass worshipped by the tribe. Then, just as ceremoniously, he grew humble and assumed an air of piety, for which his breed would become beloved. "Let me accumulate your bones," he entreated, "and later, when you have need of rich porridge, there will be good seasonings." Thus the Business Manager was born.

Centuries later (after the throne-side jester was banished from the courts for insulting the king once too often), when talented singers and dancers frolicked about from town to town, "showing off" for the edification of their peers, certainly one loquacious lackey was delegated to make the prior arrangements and beat the gong in anticipation of the arrival of the troupe. Thus the Advance Man came into his own, but he would have to wait for the birth of Gutenberg before he could be truthfully called a Press Agent.

In time, legal beagles also proved equally valuable to this eclectic menagerie, because it seemed there were always a few petty players who would swear upon a pile of papyrus that thus was so when it was not.

But the "main arranger" was an agent or a manager—terms now highly defined by law—because one so well versed in these special fields could extract one shank of lamb for acting as "manager" and another shank of lamb for acting as "agent." To this day, an Agent is defined as one who "solicits and negotiates employment," while a Manager "advises and counsels talent in all facets of career enhancement."

In time, the stipend for such revolutionary representation did become silver shekels. And, as the star of the performer/client reached ascendancy, so did the omnipotency of the agent. Content with being the supreme force behind-the-scenes, like Merlin of old, he chose the unfaltering orbit in which his clients spun to greatness—but he also sought to stem the tide when his comets would be in danger of losing their tails!

From the secluded citadels of big finance, while adroitly manipulating the chess pieces of the entire world of entertainment, these touchstones of power became the flesh peddlers of the business of show . . .

1

VAUDEVILLE
& AMERICA'S FIRST AGENT

Fred Allen
You can take all the sincerity in Hollywood and stuff it into a gnat's navel and still have room left for an agent's heart

Show business has a long history, but a short memory.

Faded and dim now, under layers of peeling paint and crumbling plaster, are the spectacular theater signs that once enlivened the sides of mammoth buildings across the width and breadth of America during the heyday of variety theater—vaudeville. Only faintly discerned are the once magical names of Keith, Albee, Frohman, Klaw & Erlanger, Belasco, Gus Sun, and Pantages—all meaningless to passersby more familiar with the impersonal Cinema I-II-III in the shopping mall and the efficient fourplex down the street. Yet, when vaudeville was king, these powerful entrepreneurs held the fate of variety theater in the palms of their hands—along with the gold coins their acts engendered.

All of these "presenters of stars" of the legitimate theater, vaudeville, and motion picture exhibition fame—who no longer conjure up memories of that "era of grandeur"—are gone, along with most of the performers from whom they made their millions. Dust also are the fabled theatrical agents of the period, William Morris, Jules Stein, Bill Brady, Harry Reichenback, George Wood.

To the young audiences of today, the famed stars of variety theater are forgotten: *Tanguay* could be a dance; *Fraganza* imported liquor, *Coquelin* a French compact car, *Weber & Fields* an advertising agency, *Vesta Victoria* an island, *Guy Bates Post* a cereal, *Conan* a barbarian, and *Bayes* is what dogs do at the moon.

Show people mourn the lovely Princess Grace of Monaco, but her fame in theatrical circles preceded by that of her uncle, the superlative comedian, Walter C. Kelly, "the Virginia Judge." Older fans may remember that before the Divine Miss M., there was the Divine Sarah.

Gone too are the 3,000 seat movie palaces of the 1920s, with their blazing marquees, studded with the names of half-remembered stars: Mary Pickford, Charlie Chaplin, Gloria Swanson, Lon Chaney, Nita Naldi, Rudolph Valentino. Yet, these names and countless others once were as famous as Joan Collins and her contemporaries on the boob tube.

From the days of vaudeville only three comedians are still performing: George Burns, Milton Berle, and Bob Hope, and they are Johnny Come Latelys.

About the origins of vaudeville says Marian Spitzer[1], "Although strolling players who sang and danced and joked for their supper were known in ancient Greece and Rome, the actual word vaudeville seems to have originated in fifteenth-century France. There, in the province of Normandy, is a spot called Val (or Vau) de Vire— the valley of the river Vire—where the inhabitants entertained one another nightly with ballads and satirical folk songs. Presently their fame spread beyond their own valley, and they traveled to other parts of France. In the course of time, *vau de vire* was corrupted to vaudeville.

"Some scholars maintain that the word first occurred in Paris with the singing of revolutionary songs, and that the phrase *voix de ville* (voice of the city) eventually became *vaudeville*. The earlier explanation is more commonly accepted. Regardless of its source, the word became international in character, and was first used in the United States during the mid-1800s. Some early American showmen found it too fancy for their tastes, preferring the word *variety*, but it caught on . . . ."

And as variety theater caught on, and more and more performers were drawn to the boards, it became apparent that while they might glow on the stage, their business acumen offstage was often appalling: stars could not bargain well for their services. It was time for a new profession to be born, people who *could* bargain for show people.

William Morris, the man who was the first agent in America, was born Wilhelm Moses in Austria in 1873. "He was a kid who couldn't talk English," wrote Joe Laurie, Jr.,[2] and who received very little schooling, who delivered papers before school and after supper clerked in a grocery store. In the afternoons he carried big bags of coal and delivered ice for just a few cents a day. To help support the family, he worked as an office boy on a cloak and suit trade paper, and by the time he was twenty, he was earning $15,000 a year via commissions by soliciting ads. They were about to put his name up as a partner, but the 1894 panic came and put the paper out of business, and with it, William Morris."

He was not considered particularly handsome, and he was of average height with an average build, but Morris was peculiarly suited to a branch of show business that was to achieve more and more prominence as the world turned: the *talent agent*. He was a booker of variety and vaudeville performers, and he had a "gold eye"—which was comparable to a musician with perfect pitch. He possessed an unfaltering instinct: he *knew* when an act was on its way up to the big time, or even on its way down to the small time. He *knew* when an act was in danger of falling apart even before astute theater managers realized the fact, and he could recognize talent four blocks away. But most of all, he had "the faith."

Laurie continued, "He always had a hankering to get into the business end of the show biz. To him it was a dream world with dream people, so different from the people in the cloak and suit business he knew. After being turned down by Mike Leavitt (a big showman at that time), Bill Morris swiped one of his letterheads and wrote to George Liman, who was the leading variety agent, telling him 'confidentially' that he was seeking a new connection. He got an appointment and told Mr. Liman that he had a lot of experience in the agency business and Liman, impressed, offered him $8.00 a week. Bill turned him down flat and finally settled for $9.00 a week. With the okaying of the salary, Liman gave him a list of acts and houses and told him to 'book 'em!'

"Bill got the office boy to tell him about the business, talked to actors and managers to get the lowdown (without tipping his mitt that he was a tyro), and in about a month was made general manager of the oldest variety agency in New York! (Sounds Horatio Algerish, doesn't it? But true.)"

And he was to remain Horatio. With his true sense of style, he created entire bills by "pacing" the acts, giving small-time theater managers a balanced show. Traditionally, the opening had to be a pantomime or animal act because the audience was still being seated. The star headliner traditionally appeared "next to closing." A typical small-time Bill Morris bill:

Andre the Clown
Torpedo Brothers
(jugglers)
Felix Lopez and Zelda Moore
(dance team)
M'liss McClure
(ragtime singer)
INTERMISSION

Larry Darby and Paul Davis
(comedians)
Maurice Debrow assisted by Alexandria
(magician)
Marilyn, David and Timmy Dorensky
(hit musical skit)
Madame La Tourette
(dramatic reading)
Jackie Hernden
(flannel mouth Irish tenor)
Afterpiece
(flashy—most acts)

However, all of the big-time theater managers selected and balanced their own acts, which were called for rehearsal on the morning of the opening. Only the star was certain of his spot on the show, but it was usual for other acts to be switched around. "Harry," the grizzled manager might say, "you take the second spot, and we'll open the second act with the Thorpe Brothers." Sometimes an act would be cancelled and replaced. These men knew their patrons. Audiences of upper Manhattan had different preferences from those of midtown or downtown.

"Flickers" had no proscribed length, but vaudeville acts fit into a time slot, and overtime—especially with musicians—was prohibitive. The manager timed the show, which was then "frozen." If the star took an extra curtain call, the exact length of that curtain call was subtracted from the next act.

But if Morris was happy representing acts, he was unhappy with the financial returns and dreamed of booking the big stars, whose big salaries guaranteed big commissions. Liman died, and his wife fired Morris, intending to continue the business herself, but she was in over her head. When Morris offered her four dollars for the furniture, she accepted, and he placed his own name on the door, quickly designing the logo that would become famous all over the show business world. The simply entwined "W" in William with "M" in Morris looked business-like and imposing even then. It was 1897.

At the turn of the century, Bill Morris began to enlarge the agency, employing several managers to help book talent which, depending on the policy of the theaters in question, might involve two-shows-a-day (later the killing five-a-day), full weeks, split weeks, and fill-ins for performers who were ill for one or two shows. One of the stars for whom he was able to obtain $3 a week, was the blond hoydenish Eva Tanguay, who later made the song *I Don't Care* famous, and who would later play the Palace for $2,500 a week. (After the stock market crash in 1929, when vaudeville bookings were difficult, Eva Tanguay had to "audition" her act for young managers, and it almost broke her heart.)

Five years later, Morris was booking twenty-nine weeks a year (most theaters were closed during the hot summer months), supplied talent to the houses of Hammerstein, Keeney, Poli, Proctor, Sheedy, Weber & Rush, Percy Williams, and others. He handled most of the vaudeville in New York. He could keep acts playing without a re-engagement, in different theaters in Manhattan for twelve weeks.

Many booking agents charged only five percent of what salaries they were able to drum up for their clients, others took what the traffic would bear: ten, fifteen, and in some cases twenty five percent. Favorite targets were foreign stars who wished to appear in America, and if there was a language barrier agents could negotiate their own terms. Some took *half* of the earnings! Because of such widespread chicanery, New York State enacted the famous "Law of 1910" (Chapter 700, Section 185, Paragraph 2):

The gross fees of licensed persons charged to applicants for theatrical engagements by one or more such licensed persons, individually or collectively procuring such en-

gagements, except vaudeville or circus engagements, shall not in any case exceed the gross amount of 5 percentum of the wages or salary of the engagement when the engagement is less than ten weeks; and an amount of 5 percentum of the salary or wages per week for ten weeks if a season's engagement constitutes ten weeks or more . . . .

"The backstage drama of show business, 1905-1913," Abel Green and Joe Laurie, Jr. wrote,[3] "was often more absorbing than the entertainment out front. In many respects it was pure melodrama—with Keith-Albee as dual villains in sideburns, and William Morris as the hero. Viewed today, the conflicts behind the proscenium seem rather like profane farce comedy . . . .

"Opposing Keith-Albee at every turn, worrying the fox from unexpected directions, rising up as often as he was crushed, was the amazing William Morris . . . Had he been less independent, less courageous, he would have ended up as an office boy for Albee, as so many of Albee's enemies did. When the old master couldn't beat them, he bought them out. But he could do neither with the indestructible William Morris . . . .

"One of Albee's first and major feuds was with Martin Beck, an ex-waiter who spoke seven languages, had impeccable taste in opera and music, and was not unaware of his accomplishments. In 1905, Beck was vaudeville king of the west. He controlled 16 to 18 theaters on his Orpheum Circuit chain . . . ."

In 1906, Bill Morris told *Variety*: "I remember some years ago when my office expenses were $200 monthly. Now they are $30,000. I didn't do it; it just naturally grew with the business."

Office expenses aside, Albee was still in his hair. He stepped up his efforts to acquire talent and booked Lily Langtry, "the Jersey Lily," comic singer Vesta Victoria, comedian Charlie Chaplin, and the song parodist Alice Lloyd. But at this time, his friend F.F. Proctor switched from booking Morris acts to doing business with Albee's United Booking Office, which threw Morris in a spin from which he almost did not recover. Keith-Albee could give actors contracts for thirty-four weeks on the road every year; Morris could promise only twenty.

In 1908, he told *Variety*, "Vaudeville has held up extremely well during the depression which has existed for over a year. In fact, all the variety forms of amusement (except summer parks) have passed through a period of depression in much superior form in the legitimate . . . That bespeaks an underlying strength which the 'higher theater' has not . . . ."

Laurie says:[4] "Bill was getting real big, when Albee stepped in and offered the managers membership in the United Booking Office, which charged commissions on acts for playing their own houses, and also split that commission with the managers of the U.B.O. It amounted to a lot of dough and was great bait. Bill Morris was making a quarter of a million a year on commissions; Bill didn't split commissions. So one by one the managers, whom Morris had helped make rich, left him to join the U.B.O., where they could partake of this unholy graft. With nothing to book, he incorporated for $500,000 and became a manager and also a deep thorn in Albee's side. Albee hated Morris but respected his showmanship! . . . ."

"Bill Morris," according to vaudevillian Will Ahern, "was always very certain that he got his rightful commissions and whatever else was due to him in life , but he never wanted anything that didn't belong to him. Almost nobody remembers that it was he who actually founded the Northwoods Sanitarium at Saranac, New York, in the mid-1920s, that's now called the Will Rogers Memorial Hospital, where show business people could go for treatment of tuberculosis. I knew a couple of vaudevillians who went there and everything was free. It was first called the Adirondack Tubercular Fund Northwoods Home, because it was located at Narraganset, New York. It eventually came under the jurisdiction of the National Vaudeville Association when Albee, who always had his finger in every pie, assumed control. When N.V.A. went down the tubes it was managed by the film industry, before the children's show business charity, the Variety Club took it over."

Bill Morris was coining money, but his income was considerably reduced when the Proctor and the Percy Williams circuits were sold to Albee, who was the cock of the walk.

"For a time, he booked special acts (Sophie Tucker was one) into Albee theaters," wrote Allen Churchill[5] "but with the appearance of the U.B.O. this too finished. Morris was a man who dreamed grandiose dreams, and acted on them. He now conceived the stupendous idea of getting Klaw and Erlanger to start a vaudeville chain in competition with Albee. To the young man's mingled delight and astonishment, Erlanger showed interest. Shortly Morris found himself in command of an outfit called United States Amusement Corporation. Klaw and Erlanger owned it, while the brothers Shubert functioned as quiet partners! Morris had been assured of unlimited funds for acts, as well as theaters in which to display them. 'Vaudeville by wholesale, that's what we're going to have,' he jubilated, envisioning a new dawn in the Golden Age of Vaudeville. Excitedly, he went to work putting the shows together.

"The initial collision between the two chains came in Philadelphia, where Morris presented a first bill at the Chestnut Street Theater. Some $5,000 worth of top talent was hurled into the fray by both sides. Morris offered a program headed by the Four Mortons, while Albee led with redoubtable Vesta Victoria. For his second show, Morris planned to spend $10,000, but at this glorious moment in his life—with dreams coming true—he began to detect a certain shiftiness in the eyes of Erlanger. Slowly it dawned on him that Klaw and Erlanger, as the United States Amusement Corporation, had built themselves up only to be knocked down—that is, bought out.

"They dared compete with Albee," Churchill went on, "only because they so completely understood his mania for monopoly. He would, they knew, buy opposition out at almost any price. Overtures had begun and meetings between Klaw, Erlanger, and Albee had taken place. The Syndicate insisted on one of the most peculiar deals of all time. 'A million-dollar profit,' was the cry. They proffered an itemized expense sheet of the short but expensive venture into vaudeville. Atop this they piled a cool million . . . ."

Bill Morris was left out in the cold, his dreams turned to dust, but he had two aces up his sleeve. One was Australian Annette Kellerman, who had achieved notoriety when she was arrested on a Boston Beach for wearing a "scandalous" one-piece swimsuit in 1911, and whom he consequently "discovered."

Miss Kellerman, fearing that he was not powerful enough to book her into major theaters, broke her contract and defected to Albee. She also had visions of appearing in the movies. (But when she did take that step in 1916 in a film entitled *A Daughter of the Gods* for Fox, she was a washout—although she appeared briefly in the nude, a titillating, if dubious distinction. Morris did Kellerman one better. He duplicated her act with a girl who had swum from the Charleston Bridge to the Boston lighthouse—fifteen-year old Rose Pitnof!

The other ace—and a far bigger star—was more receptive. British music-hall comedian, Sir Harry Lauder, who had been brought to America by booking agent Clifford C. Fischer to appear at Klaw & Erlanger's New York Theater in 1907, did not welsh on his deal with Morris, who upped his contract five-hundred dollars a week to $3,000.

Sir Harry knew what Morris was enduring, because he also knew tough times. Born in Portobello, Edinburgh, Scotland, in 1870, he had won a singing competition while still a child laborer in a flax mill. He had also worked in the coal mines for ten years, before getting his chance in show business by breaking into variety entertainment in 1900.

Wearing an impish grin, sporting a gnarled walking stick and attired in kilts, knee socks, and a tam o'shanter, Sir Harry's very appearance elicited chuckles from the audience. He wrote many songs which he sang in a pleasant, dry, comical manner, but his act was just as dependent upon the jovial attitude with which he spouted amusing monologues that "let his audience in" on the problems of drinking, his relationship with his "wee wifie," and the difficulties of his Scottish neighbors.

He had the rare gift of spontaneity—reacting as if a story had just occurred to him. As talented as he was, he instinctively knew that he belonged in variety theater where he alone could create his own special magic. He could never be confined to a set or appear in musical comedy.

His stock-in-trade was his Scottish and Irish songs, many of which he wrote himself. Fans loved to hear him sing the cheerful "It's Nice to Get Up in the Morning," the plaintive "Lass o' Killiekrankie," or the dramatic "Roamin' in the Gloamin'," which always brought down the house.

Morris knew that the future depended upon selling Sir Harry not only to the big towns but to the sticks, and conceived a massive publicity campaign that would justify his salary. He rented a private railroad car for the star, giving him every luxury. To Albee's horror, indeed, everyone *did* want to see the act, and Morris was grinning from ear-to-ear as he booked Sir Harry into a twenty-six day tour of fifteen cities that amounted to some fifty appearances, taking in $65,000 on admission prices of 50 cents to $2.00 a head.

Only in Washington did Albee triumph, but only briefly. When, Morris discovered that he was unable to book Sir Harry at any theater, he contacted the White House, knowing that Teddy Roosevelt had a soft heart for vaudeville. The president saw to it that a theater was made available for Sir Harry, and then showed up opening night. Albee, thereafter, drew in his horns and let the tour proceed.

Morris had difficulty keeping sub-agents. It was a difficult profession, did not earn a good salary, and men would leave after a few months to go on to better things. But in 1912, a fourteen-year old boy, a giant of five feet three, who had decided he had enough schooling and it was time to enter the business world, came to work at the agency. His name was Abraham Isaac Lastfogel.

A friend had given little Abe the name of two firms that needed office boys. One was a tailor shop, the other a theatrical agency. Abe thought that while the tailoring establishment was probably more reliable, the Morris office in Times Square was closer to his parents' tenement at Third Avenue and Forty-ninth Street. He had no way of knowing that he would end up heading the company that was to employ him.

Bill Morris hired him as office boy. E. J. Kahn, Jr.,[6] wrote in his two-part profile of Lastfogel: "A boyhood friend, now a monsignor in the Catholic Church, said a while ago, 'From the moment Abe entered the Morris office, it was to him like a vocation.' As a matter of fact, Lastfogel developed a steadfast veneration for William Morris, Sr. He has said that the highest compliment he can pay anybody is to say that the person reminds him of his late employer. Abe was an office boy only a short time. He soon became Morris's secretary, and by the time he was twenty-two he was treasurer of the agency. His youthful initiation and quick advance are responsible for an office tradition that occasionally bewilders people unfamiliar with the agency—taking on apprentices at an extremely early age and guiding them through the intricacies of the business . . . ."

With the agency coffers enriched by Sir Harry's tour, Morris' head was turned toward vaudeville houses again. Although blacklisted by the U.B.O., he knew dozens of acts that were also out-of-favor; booking programs was not to be a problem. And he always had an eye out for newcomers. He bought the lease on the Boston Music Hall which Albee, in a rare oversight, had neglected to renew. He then refurbished the old American Theater on Forty-second Street in New York, where he offered 22 acts of vaudeville. Theaters in Chicago and Brooklyn were acquired, and he was back in business—with a vengeance! Under constant pressure for years, he neglected his health, yet he plunged on in his quest to best Albee.

Marcus Loew, who had made a fortune in strategically-placed real estate—and co-owner with David Warfield of some small-time theaters and nickelodeons—offered to go in with Morris in a new concept of presenting vaudeville *and* motion pictures on the same bill. On the very brink of success, however, Morris became ill. Convinced the grim specter was in the wings, he sold out to Loew, but kept his personal management company, even though Sir Harry was the only name still under contract. Miraculously, his health improved and he brought the old Scotsman back for a series of "farewell" tours, laughingly called "much adieu about nothing" because stars were famous for their sign-off tours. Morris regained strength scouting around for other artists to represent; he was soon back in business.

Adding to Morris' woes, however, was powerful entrepreneur Martin Beck. Now he offered real competition by luring the international star, Madame Sarah Bernhardt, to America in 1912.

Because of an agreement with his arch-enemy Albee, Beck was supposed to stay west of Chicago, but he soon branched out and hit his opponent where it hurt most: in New York. He built the Palace Theater at Broadway and 47th Street, which opened on Easter Monday, March 24, 1913, and in time became the finest showcase of top talent in the country.

But, when a Morris deal fell through for Beck to purchase six Percy Williams houses, Albee promptly bought them; Morris Meyerfield, Jr., sold his seventy-five percent controlling interest in the Palace, and Beck was hoisted with his own petard, with Albee in control. Outsmarted, Beck then went over to Klaw & Erlanger to produce and direct legitimate theater.

In 1913, all casting offices—including Morris'—were quite similar in appearance and almost identical in operation. Writer/director George Abbott, who started out as a stage actor, described

William A. Brady's casting office in his autobiography:[7]

"John Cromwell, who later became a first-rate Hollywood director, was in charge of the casting. Hopeful actors might wait for an hour, sitting, standing, until when the room was full, Cromwell would come out and we would all line up. He would go right down the line saying, 'Nothing. Nothing. Nothing.' And then once in a while, 'You wait.' Or if it was a friend, 'Hello, Ed, sorry.' An actress might start to tell him of her theatrical experience, or an actor would start to say he thought he was right for a certain part. Cromwell would move right on without waiting for the end of the sentence.

'Sorry...nothing...not a thing...sorry.' Sometimes the actors would even take hold of his sleeve to delay him, but he would move impassively down the line until he had cleared the room. At the time I thought that he was cruel, but I know now that it was an act of self-defense. His heart would break if he considered each case individually, and he had to protect himself . . . .

"All casting in those days of 1913 was done by interview, in the office. The system now in general use—and which, I think, I was first to innovate: tryouts by reading for parts—was unheard of . . . ."

So came the actor's nightmare, the hated "cold reading," where a script is thrust into the hands of the startled actor, who is asked to interpret a character about which he knows nothing. Toward the end of 1916, there was one of those strange enigmatic turn-arounds in show business that frequently occur for no logical reason. There was a subtle shifting of public likes and dislikes. Broadway seers pointed to the world situation: the possibility of war, the Bolsheviks, Wall Street, the length of women's skirts, the cost of beer, a hot summer, a humid autumn, a cold fall, and the scarcity of new talent. Such predictions were (and are) commonplace in the world of entertainment. Although provocative, they did not signify what was actually taking place. One word, *cabaret*, was the answer.

For a headliner to be approached by an agent to perform in a "restaurant" was considered insulting and degrading. A restaurant dispensed food and drink, a theater dispensed entertainment, and the lines of demarcation could not have been more tightly drawn. Tales of San Francisco's Barbary Coast joints, where entertainers in the Gay Nineties had sung and danced, were still within memory, as were the dance hall "hostesses," nothing more than "soiled doves," from Abilene to Virginia City, who had given a bad reputation to the mixing of whiskey and music.

To a vaudevillian, a Proscenium Arch was the Holy Veil that separated the audience from runny greasepaint, wardrobe that had seen better days, and various tricks of the trade rightfully hidden behind the footlights. The stage was pure illusion, created out of a carefully formulated pattern of what was sure fire and what was not. If stars stopped the show cold or bombed, the apron set up a comparatively safe psychological barrier from the howling mob.

How could entertainers perform unselfconsciously in close proximity to the audience? Each song, each bit, each gesture, was scaled to be seen from a respectable distance. Up close, what was funny or touching in long-view perspective would be obviously larger than life. No performer wished to appear a caricature. Even obvious farce-comics had worked years to perfect a seemingly unstructured act to great effect. From ten feet away, what would be left of their "gems" except the bare bones of shtick?

Small room acoustics were also troublesome to the eardrums of a singing star who was accustomed to projecting—belting out a song—to the upper reaches of "nosebleed heaven." Accustomed to an audience of fifteen hundred souls, how could they tone down to a gathering of 150? Besides, band members were supposed to be in the orchestra pit, not strung out behind them on the stage.

But, when Morris ran up against these arguments, all of which he understood better than his clients, he would hit his desk and shout, "Scale down! Scale down!" Could he have seen a Las Vegas in the future? "This cabaret business will be with us a long time. Knuckle down and re-work the act."

Whenever he brought up a choice booking at a posh cabaret—like Reisenweber's, or Joel's, or the Blue Hour, or the Ted Lewis Club—all of which paid good money, he coldly reminded his temperamental wards that vaudeville had begun in outdoor cafes in Europe and made the switch to theaters, and not vice versa!

Even the agent's most haughty clients were charmed by his little speech—as well as the enormous sums of money he was able to extract for their new acts, scaled-down to the size of the room!

Headliners like Sophie Tucker made headlines at cabarets like Reisenweber's.

Show business was changing in 1918, and as flickers became a respectable art form with D.W. Griffith and Charlie Chaplin, more and more heads turned toward Hollywood—the land of the locust as well as the lotus.

BLACKOUT: 1914

New Husband

Honey, I just saw a line in front of the *Majestic* for your new picture *Laurie, Scrub Girl*. Your *name* is on the marquee above the title! Do they have permission to do that? Let's look at your contract.

Female Star

Never read it all the way through, but I get two-hundred dollars a week that goes up to two-hundred and seventy-five dollars in two years.

New Husband

There's no billing clause in this contract. All the terms are in favor of the studio, and if you're supposed to make eight pictures a year, how come you made nine last year?

Female Star

Gerda got pregnant, and couldn't do *Phoebe*, so I took her part. She's really a swell person . . . .

New Husband

She didn't *pay* you, did she?

Female Star

No . . . But the studio was very grateful and gave me a case of champagne.

New Husband

My God! A case of champagne! Do you realize that you made only one thousand, one hundred seventy-four dollars and fourteen cents per picture last year?

Female Star

You figured that in your head? You're so smart. I'm ashamed to admit I only went to the third grade.

New Husband

Honey, you need someone to take over your business affairs. You'll start out by coming down with a virulent case of Alhambra fever.

Female Star

What's that?

New Husband

That's a disease that you'll have until we work out a new contract giving you five-hundred a week, and me two-hundred as your manager. This is only the beginning, honey, only the beginning!

Film producer Charles H. Duell's lawsuit against Lillian Gish could have resulted in great damage to her career, but she courageously went to the press with her story. *(Whitney Stine collection)*

Gladys Smith, who later became Mary Pickford, may have looked like an angel, but had the brains of a C.P.A. *(Whitney Stine collection)*

2

SILENTS WEREN'T GOLDEN

Star
But I want to go out and play like other kids.
Mother
There will be plenty of time for playing after you make your first million dollars.

Agents perked up their ears. If stage stars were to make feature films for road-showing in theaters, rather than the usual one-reel, twelve-minute "turns" exhibited in vaudeville, salaries were obviously going to be accelerated commensurate to the length of the feature. Why not arrive at a stipend based on the footage? But both stars and producers scoffed at the idea. Agents were shown politely to the door. Then they suggested that a salary in keeping with the price of the road-show ticket would solve the problem. Or, how about a percentage of the gross on each theater? Stars were willing, but the producers rejected the idea. What? Give the stars a financial interest in the film ? Never. Agents were not-so-politely shown to the door.

Producers held long conferences alone with the players. Obviously, agents were interested only in whatever commissions could be obtained on the spot, and were not concerned with the long-term careers of their clients. Why, the producers argued, be saddled with a parasite? Performers had long made their own deals with stage producers; why not trust film producers as well?

Agents argued that stars could not adequately discuss their own worth; it was embarrassing, and besides, performers were artists unschooled in proper business procedures. At this point, agents were unceremoniously thrown out of the offices, with orders to the receptionists that the producers were "not in" to the scum!

Later when films were made in Hollywood, the producers arranged for first class accommodations for their stars. Pullman berths and private compartments; hotel suites filled with flowers for women and cases of scotch for the men; cartons of Fatima cigarettes, lavish wardrobes; personal servants, chauffeured limousines—all to be had for signing a contract and acting before that black box. What performer could resist such an artfully planned ego trip? And the salaries offered for three or four weeks' work was phenomenal—$25,000 or $30,000, which seemed stratospheric to stage stars accustomed to eight performances a week at $400. Thus, when Klaw & Erlanger (who were first to list their programs by "in order of appearance" to cut out billing fights) made a deal with Biograph for their top stage successes to be brought to the "silver screen," the "spoiled star" syndrome began. Stage stars were coaxed west to appear in "those terrible flickers," or as Ethel Barrymore put it, "the tape."

Producers, hungry for famous stage names, figuratively rolled out the "red carpet" for Broadway stars. The famous term had been created by Lily Langtry, who had insisted in 1907 that a rug runner be laid from her dressing room to the stage to keep the hems of her gowns clean. The only color available was red! The amenities used to induce legitimate stage stars west were envied by the players who made their livings solely by appearing in films. Broadway stars were equally impressed by these "movie stars" who not only knew the mysterious art of acting "before the box," but were accustomed to rising at dawn and working until sunset— or beyond.

The only compensation for this strange, exotic life was the paycheck at the end of a week. It also seemed ironic that the faces of these film players were known in every hamlet in the country, while the stage stars were only recognized by a comparatively few theatergoers.

When questioned about the differences between acting on the stage and performing in films, Mary Pickford remarked succinctly: "We get to look pretty all the time—and we never have to learn lines!"

The truth of her comment lasted some twenty years—until the motion picture industry switched from silent to talking films. But in 1984, when the American Film Institute honored eighty-eight year-old Lillian Gish with its Life Achievement Award, (March 1, 1984, which was televised April 17), the general public, who had never seen her act at the peak of her screen career, saw excerpts from four touching silent performances: *The Birth of a Nation* (1915), *Way Down East* (1920), *Orphans of the Storm* (1922), and *The Wind* (1928).

Her acceptance speech noted that D. W. Griffith was fond of describing silent movies as the universal language mentioned in the Bible. "We in the audience write all the lines, so none of the characters say anything that displeases us." It was a sentiment that might also have been uttered by another of the stars from Hollywood's early days—Mary Pickford.

It was a matter of necessity that all of the famous leading ladies of the silent screen were teenagers. Their youth had not only to do with the lack of flattering lamps—sunlight was used mostly, and the primitive film of the era showed every wrinkle—but grinding out twelve or fifteen films a year under the most adverse conditions required good health and excessive energy. Many a fourteen-year-old played women of twenty five or thirty. Any female over that age was considered a "character woman." And many screen stars were "through in pictures" as their third decade approached

Whereas few child stars of the 1920s to the 1980s eased into adolescence and then into adult roles, while keeping their following, the foremost child player of silent pictures (and the first star to be billed in films) never escaped the child image, first as "Baby Gladys Smith," and "Little Mary," then "The Girl With the Curls," and finally "Mary Pickford."

Tiny (about five feet tall), blond and dimpled, her screen personality was tempered with a touch of acerbity that saved her films from being mawkish and saccharine. But due to a public that would not accept her as an adult, Mary Pickford, although it was personally frustrating, continued to play teenagers as late as 1927 at the age of 34!

Two years later, she made her talkie debut in *Coquette* sporting a shingled blond bob, where she played an adult so well that she won an Academy Award, but the public was unconvinced. After three other talking pictures, with diminishing returns— including *The Taming of the Shrew* with her husband, Douglas Fairbanks, which received a small release—she left the screen. She later said that she never officially retired, but assumed that she would do other pictures, but the right property never came along. For decades, she held court at her magnificent home, Picfair, on Summit Drive in Beverly Hills, happily married to Buddy Rogers. A recluse for many years, she was briefly glimpsed when she won an honorary Academy Award in 1975. Columnist May Mann, one of the few people whom she continued to see, convinced her to be filmed for the ceremony. Propped up on a settee, looking very tiny and extremely frail, with the camera a discreet distance away, she said her thank you. She died in 1979.

Born in Toronto, Canada, April 8, 1893, Gladys Smith started acting in earnest at the age of five—at her own suggestion—in the local Valentine stock company, after which she toured for eight years with mother, sister Lottie, and brother Jack in melodramas, such as *Uncle Tom's Cabin* in which she played Little Eva.

While her timing in the theater was astute, her timing in real life was faultless. Scheduled to be going over lines in New Jersey, she barged into a New York theater in the midst of a rehearsal of *The Warrens of Virginia*. Famed producer David Belasco was in a snit because of the unprofessional acting ability of a child in the show. Feeling the hand of fate on his shoulder, Belasco looked down into that innocent face, gave her the part, and changed her name to Mary Pickford.

After playing that role on Broadway for three years, she again barged in where an angel might fear to tread, this time the Fourteenth Street Biograph Studios, where D. W. Griffith was shooting a one-reeler, *The Lonely Villa*. Like Belasco, Griffith was enchanted and promptly offered her an extra part at five dollars for each day that she worked.

Pickford was her own best agent: She looked D. W. in the eye, "I'm worth ten," she announced flatly. Surprisingly he gave in— probably taken aback that a such an angelic-looking child of sixteen had such an excellent business sense. She inherited her shrewdness from "Maw Pickford," who was expert at wrangling extras on contracts and was not above counting the house to see how many people showed up at a given performance, gleefully pointing out to producers that her daughter was coining money for them.

Maw Pickford was the prototype for Stage Mothers, though she was not the first. Mary Anne Crabtree's flame-haired daughter Lotta quickened the hearts of the Gold Rush forty-niners in San Francisco as she sang her plaintive ditties, after which Mary Anne stooped to pick up the coins with which the enthralled spectators had all but pelted her infanta. Another arch-mother was Jenny Bierbower, whose tiny child, Elsie Janis, grew up in show business under her severe, but lucrative management. The protective Jenny was always present, and when Elsie Janis entertained the troops during World War I, her mother was right there with her—a stone's throw from the trenches. During her days as a silent picture star and a mature monologist in vaudeville, mother hung on, indeed so tightly that Janis never had the courage to marry until her forties, after her mother was dead. The marriage to a much younger man did not last, and Elsie Janis spent her remaining years a recluse. She died at the age of 67, in 1956.

However, for the remainder of Mary Pickford's career, greed often took precedence over artistic ability: she was determined to be the highest paid female in films. Soon, she was making $40 a week, after she left D.W., escalated in seven years to $4,000 at Famous Players. But Mary was unhappy. She wanted more—at least as much as the fabulous $12,000 per week that Mutual Film Corporation was paying Charlie Chaplin. Beneath a demure demeanor, Pickford had an unfaltering gaze that gave the impression she knew what others were thinking. She had a certain quizzical facial expression that made her employers feel they were exploiting her. Not for nothing had she played Little Eva to so many Simon Legrees!

Eyeball-to-eyeball no outsider could act as a better go-between than Pickford. Adolph Zukor once said of her: "There is no doubt about her tremendous drive for success and the cash register nature of a segment of her brain." But in 1916, with several producers vying for her services, she was in a quandary. It was at this point that, quite by chance, "America's Sweetheart" acquired a friend whose name sounded like a woman novelist—Cora Carrington Wilkenning. A scenario agent, Cora was a live wire who sold a series of articles bylined by Pickford to the huge McClure newspaper syndicate. They were ghosted by Frances Marion, who had written several Pickford vehicles. Cora made a fabulous deal: Pickford was paid $24,243.30 from 1915 to 1918—sixty percent of the gross sales. For varying sums, she also endorsed such diversified products as Pompeian massage cream and automobile radiator caps. According to *Variety*, she was making so much money that her taxes in 1918 were $300,000!

Whether Cora Carrington Wilkenning was officially Pickford's agent is beside the point (it became a matter for the courts to decide); she did act in her behalf. Mary had made a handshake deal with Zukor with a drawing account around $4,000 a week and a fifty percent participation in a Mary Pickford-Famous Players Corporation. With this knowledge, Cora called upon Mutual's John R. Freuler, Chaplin's mentor, and paved the way. As Terry Ramsaye told it:[1] "Then Miss Mary went down to the Mutual offices with the green carpet and the red mahogany and sat right where Chaplin had sat before her. Inevitably that Chaplin deal came into the conversation.

" 'I think,' observed Freuler with typical deliberation, as he reached into his breast pocket, 'that we might make Miss Pickford happy yet. You might sign a contract with this pen—it is the one Mr. Chaplin used.'

"Freuler flourished the big Waterman. Perhaps it was in preparation for this gesture that he had bought it from Chaplin's attorney.

" 'But before I offer any figures,' Freuler continued, 'I must consult our exchanges and some of the exhibitors to see how much your pictures would be worth.'

"Mary tapped the floor with a petulant foot. She did not like that. She felt the whole world knew what she was worth.

" 'You see,' Freuler went on, ignoring the storm in Mary's eyes, 'my investigation may show that you are worth a great deal more than I would venture to offer, off-hand.' "

It became known in the industry that Mutual was investigating Pickford's grosses. Ramsaye continued:

"Mrs. Wilkenning, the agent, was still looking for a chance to stir up new bids for Pickford. The report came up Broadway by way of Wall Street that 111 Fifth Avenue, the office of the American Tobacco Company, was seething with millions and motion picture ambitions. It was reported that Benjamin B. Hampton, vice president in charge of advertising, was about to head a big money invasion of the film field.

"Hampton was interested when Mrs. Wilkenning called. There were conferences in her office. Pickford and Hampton met there. Mary seems to have been a bit hesitant, now that she was face to face with a step that might break her long and profitable connection with Famous Players. Hampton wanted to talk certainties and insisted on something tangible upon which to base his contemplated promotional efforts."

Pickford sent him a note saying that she had made up her mind to leave Famous Players, and he gave her an option at a thousand dollars for thirty days—time enough to form a corporation that would ensure a drawing account of $7,000 a week and fifty percent of the stock.

Cora blithely informed Zukor of the arrangements. Needless to say he was furious: to him a handshake was a handshake, and he did not wish to lose Hollywood's most box-office-worthy star, and neither did other companies who contributed to the Famous Players program. There was gossip concerning mergers of several companies. Pickford was the center of a beehive, and whoever came up with a deal to distribute her films would wear the beekeepers hat.

Bankers offered Zukor $1,500,000 for his stock in Famous Players, which he refused. Cora brought William Randolph Hearst and Pickford together, but the meeting came to naught. Realizing that she was the queen pin, Pickford did not renew her option with Hampton, and was courted by Albert E. Smith of Vitagraph, who planned to enlarge his company to the tune of $25,000,000 which would include an offer of $10,000 a week for Mary. But a dispute arose, and the deal soured.

Freuler then stepped in with a contract that surpassed everything offered so far: Pickford would have fifty percent of a new company (later Artcraft Pictures Corporation), with an automatic $10,000 a week draw and a $150,000 bonus for signing the contract. But the tenacious Zukor was not to be downed, and that handshake haunted him. After several political ploys within the company, he offered the Pickford Film Corporation terms that Pickford finally accepted a guarantee of $1,040,000 for two years, paid in increments of $10,000 per week; half the profits from her pictures, and a $300,000 bonus to be paid as earned by the films. In addition, she was to be paid $40,000 for the 26 days that she had not been on the Famous Players payroll!

Other concessions in the detailed contract provided that not only was her name to be emblazoned in large type in advertisements for her pictures, but no one else was to be given billing; train transportation was to be provided to and from California; an automobile was to be placed at her disposal outside Manhattan; she was to be given her own motion picture studio, and last but not least, she was to have approval of story, cast, and all technical personnel. It was the sweetest deal to come along in the short history of Hollywood, comparable to Chaplin's contract, and she was the most powerful woman in the industry. Pickford was not the first woman in films to get a percentage of her pictures; that distinction goes to Australian Nellie Stewart, who received 1000 pounds sterling and a percentage of the gross in 1911 for starring in *Sweet Nell of Old Drury*.

After making thirteen pictures on her contract, Pickford was lured to First National, which had just brought Chaplin into the fold on an eight two-reel picture deal, agented by brother Sydney, with a guarantee of $1,075,000.

Maw Pickford got into the act this time, instead of Cora, and earned $50,000 for herself by agenting a better deal for her daughter: $250,000 for three features, and later the possibility of an extra $300,000. Zukor was beside himself; he offered Mary $260,000 to *stay off* the silver screen for five years!

Not only was Mary insulted, but she was dissatisfied with the First National contract. It was not surprising therefore, two years later, when Chaplin, D.W. Griffith, and Mary Pickford, and her new husband Douglas Fairbanks formed United Artists Corporation to release all of their own pictures. The major film studios were shocked at this show of combined star power. A classic line was then uttered that has come down in film annals. Richard Rowland, head of Metro Pictures Corporation, expostulated: "So, the lunatics have taken charge of the asylum!"

Fifty years later, Darryl F. Zanuck would make that same comment about agents becoming the kingpins of Hollywood.

In 1912, Mary Pickford had brought a girl about her own age to D.W. Griffith who would become his biggest star. Her name was Lillian Gish. He directed her in the box office successes *The Birth of a Nation* (1915), *Hearts of the World* (1918), *Broken Blossoms* (1919), and *Way Down East* (1920).

But, when Griffith over-extended himself financially after the success of *Orphans of the Storm* (1922), Gish signed a solid contract with Inspiration Pictures, Inc., on September 1, 1922. The deal called for twenty-four pictures to be filmed between then and January 31, 1930, with a starting salary of $1,250 per week and to escalate to $2,500 per week, besides a percentage of the gross. The deal sounded sweet indeed, but Gish was to enter a period of her life when headlines across the country would challenge her career. The camera perfectly captured the delicate vulnerability of Lillian Gish, but there were those connected with her private life and her film work who took advantage of this very same quality.

Inspiration Pictures was headed by Charles H. Duell and Boyce Smith. Duell was a lawyer and a colorful character. A member of an old Knickerbocker family and a relative of Elihu Root, he had been a good friend of Theodore Roosevelt at the time of the Bull Moose campaign and had once been treasurer of the New York Republican Committee. Married to former actress Lillian Tucker, he appeared a kind sort of man and quickly gained Gish's confidence. There was also a somewhat baffling clause in her contract that spelled out that, if Gish were to marry, Duell could terminate the pact twenty days after the vows if he decided to do so. He produced two films for her in Italy, *The White Sister* and *Romola*, both released by MGM.

With time, Gish began to have misgivings about Duell's intentions. When he asked her to sign over all the profits from *The White Sister*, she did not know what to do. She noted in her autobiography:[2] "I had been seeing a great deal of Charles Duell, who was my lawyer, producer, and financial advisor. He also suggested that he become executor of my estate. I often signed papers that he brought me, relying on his word that they were for my benefit. But I began to have the uncomfortable feeling that he was taking over my life. Looking back at that period, I realize that he thought of me as a valuable piece of real estate with the lease about to run out . . . .

"After *Romola* was finished, I received a diamond ring from Duell, but it was charged to the company as a gift for finishing the picture. And before long I returned it to him. A short time later, when he seemed deep in financial problems, he proposed to me."

It appeared to her that Duell was an opportunist and that his view of the union was a business arrangement. She told him she would not consider marriage. Inspiration Pictures was dissolved on January 31, 1924, and Duell bought her contract for $50,000.

D.W. Griffith had once told Gish that one of the requisites of being a motion picture star was that her private life must be like that of Caesar's wife—above reproach—and that one touch of scandal would be the end of her. She had taken his advice to heart. But when she told Duell that she had decided to see a lawyer, he threatened to ruin her. She realized that, although loath to call attention to herself in public, she had no choice. She personally presented her case to leading newspaper publishers, showing the damning contracts and documents so that the subsequent trial was covered without scandalous implications.

The New York Times announced on January 31, 1925:

LILLIAN GISH SUED
BY FILM PRODUCER

Charles H. Duell Seeks to Prevent Her From Acting Under Direction of Others

STAR CONDEMNS CONTRACT

Her Attorneys Call it Tyrannical and Say That She is to Wed Duell is Presumption

Lillian Gish, star of the screen, was made defendant yesterday in a suit filed in Federal Court by Charles H. Duell, who seeks to prevent the star from making motion pictures except under the contract that he has with her.

Later the article reported: "Time and again, after Mrs. Duell obtained a Paris divorce on the ground of desertion, the engagement of the President of Charles H. Duell, Inc. to Miss Gish was reported. And every time there were mutual denials. In fact, only yesterday attorneys for Miss Gish characterized as 'wholly unwarranted presumption' the intimation that Mr. Duell hoped to win the favor of Miss Gish's hand."

The summons and complaint of Duell had been filed in the United States District Court by his attorneys, Duell, Anderson & Duell, of which firm his brother Colonel Holland Duell was a member. Duell contended that a film called *The Outsider* was scheduled to start production at MGM in December of 1924, but Miss Gish had come to New York instead of reporting to the lot. A hearing was scheduled for February 9 before Federal Judge Augustus N. Hand, on an order to show cause why an injunction against the star should not be granted.

Attorney Louis S. Levy, of Chadbourne, Stanchfield & Levy, represented Gish in court. The article continued: "...the firm issued this statement: 'This latest move is part of a design to force Miss Gish to support Mr. Duell. The experience of Richard Barthelmess and of John King is only repeated in Miss Gish's experience with Mr. Duell. Each of these outstanding artists has found it impossible to live under his business arrangements. Miss Gish's situation discloses, in our opinion, the worst conditions of the three.'

"Mr. Duell assumed to act as her lawyer, her trustee, her manager, and at the same time to contract with her as the executive head of a company to produce her pictures. She started with a fairly intelligent contract. It was between her and Inspiration Pictures, Inc., a highly responsible, first class corporation. Her work was done faithfully and well. And yet, after two years during which Mr. Duell constantly whittled down her rights and from time to time took this and then that advantage from her, she suddenly finds herself ostensibly yoked to Mr. Duell's personal company, though Inspiration Pictures, Inc., is entirely released from obligation."

The trial dragged on through February and March, with several red herrings introduced by Duell, one brought up on Valentine's day revived an incident of undeclared jewels found in Gish's luggage when she had arrived from Italy. "This stirred Max D. Steuer, her attorney, to anger," dutifully reported *The Times*. "He called the allegations of the affidavit 'foul slanders' and promised that if Lillian Gish 'never works again she is not going to work for Charles H. Duell.' The jewels, involving a necklace said to have been worth $6,540, were later turned over upon payment of $12,000. Mr. Rennie (her brother-in-law) brought the money to the Customs House, and in claiming the gems he said that they had not been declared because of forgetfulness."

On March 7, Duell retained Colonel William Hayward, former U.S. District Attorney to defend him on a perjury charge. On March 11, Rennie was cleared of a disorderly conduct charge brought by Duell, for lack of evidence. On March 12, Federal Judge Goddard denied Duell's petition to restrain Gish from working for another company.

On March 25, *The New York Times* reported the happenings of the preceding day:

LILLIAN GISH OPENS
LAW SUIT IN PERSON

Nibbles carrot as Her Lawyer Describes Her as Helpless in Business.

"WOULD SIGN ANYTHING"

Was under Domination of Duell Counsel Asserts, in Attack on Producer's Contract.

There was almost as much attention given to the carrot, which she nibbled because of nervousness, and the recapitulation of her past as there was to the issues. Colonel Duell called it "a contract jumping case." He said that Gish had done very well by the contract, and that *The White Sister* had a $1,500,000 budget, claiming that she had been paid $250,000 in salary.

Mr. Steuer remarked to the judge, "Now it may be, your honor, that it will be necessary for Miss Gish to testify in this case and I should like to tell you something about her. Probably you have never come in contact with a mentality so uniquely lacking in capacity to read or even to analyze a document, or understand figures. Although she is without a peer as an actress on the screen, she would sign anything that anyone, Mr. Levy or myself, for instance, asked her to sign . . . ."

He said that, at the time of the contract, "Miss Gish had implicit faith in the producer—he was a god in her eyes." He added that Duell had drawn up wills for the Gish family in which Duell was sole executor."

On March 26, *The New York Times* noted:

MISS GISH AT TRIAL
A STUDY IN EMOTION

Registers Pleasure as Lawyer Scores, a Frown at Talk of Engagement.

FIRST-DAY CARROT MISSING

*Testimony Shows Duell Held Star's
Securities and Made Himself Executor of Sisters' Wills.*

The courtroom overflowed, as crowds tried to get a glimpse of Gish, who was dressed demurely in a dark blue serge suit. With "two strands of hair falling on her shoulders, she looked more like a schoolgirl than a movie star." It was revealed when the only witness of the day—her former lawyer George W. Newgass—was called to the stand, that he had had business dealings with Duell while under retainer for Gish.

Her contract called for $2,500 a week for *Romola*, and 15 percent of the gross receipts over the $565,000 cost of the film. It was further revealed that Newgass had advised her to consent to raising that amount to $700,000 before she would receive profits, thereby costing her $60,000. He also admitted that he acted as broker in financing Duell, Inc.

J. Boyce Smith, former secretary for Inspiration Pictures was called to the stand on March 26. Under cross-examination by Steuer, he admitted that Duell had sought to reduce Gish's salary from $2,500 per week to $2,000, and in fact had issued her first check for the latter amount, which was only rectified when she returned it to the company.

On March 27, Judge Mack was forced to clear the room of spectators because of the hordes waiting to see Gish, admonishing: "This isn't a theater!" Smith was again cross-examined at great length and then Duell's secretary, Blanche C. Brigham, took the stand to confirm that Duell intended to get Lillian to sign a waiver for $42,000 about the time that Inspiration was facing liquidation, and that he "wanted half of it." When Gish did not sign, her salary was withheld.

Duell took the stand on March 30, and for some following days much time was spent discussing the "unofficial" engagement of Gish and himself, as well as his continued advice about money affairs. The next day, being questioned by Steuer, he turned out to be such a poor witness that Judge Mack warned him against himself. He was finally forced to admit that he was practically her only counselor on the profit waiving.

Duell did not heed the judge's advice. On April 1, he again behaved badly in court, and Steuer did not fail to make the point that he was a sort of Jekyll and Hyde in acting both as Gish's employer and her personal counsel. As her employer, Steuer contended, he schemed to "gouge" her out of money due under her contracts, and acting as counsel, advised her to accept the "gouging." As far as the engagement went, Steuer recalled that Duell had once hired lawyers to sue a newspaper for announcing the engagement, giving them a note signed by Lillian that read: "I am not engaged to be married to Charles H. Duell or any other man." It was also brought out that a check was issued to Lillian when there were insufficient funds in the bank, and that the entry in the checkbook was altered to appear that the check was given out when due, and not three days later.

On April 3, *The New York Times* noted on the front page:

COURT HOLDS DUELL ON PERJURY CHARGE: QUASHES GISH SUIT

Judge Mack Dismisses Film Producer's Action and Declares He Defrauded Star.

CALLS HIS TESTIMONY LIES

Brings Surprising and Dramatic End to Case With Stinging Address From Bench.

DEFEATED MAN IS STUNNED

Leaves Under $10,000 Bail— Later Lays Plight to Fact He is "World's Worst Witness."

"Had it been a motion picture that was being played in the Federal Court," the article stated, "the scenes could not have moved more swiftly nor the audience have been more surprised. Within the brief space of fifteen minutes the court had been opened, the judge had ascended to the bench, the case had been dismissed.

"Duell had been told that instead of being the accuser he should have been the accused, and then he was charged with perjury, threatened with disbarment, for he is a lawyer, forbidden forever from appearing in the Federal Court, held in $10,000 bail for the action of the Grand Jury and finally paroled in the custody of his brother, Holland Duell, who is his counsel . . . ."

In her memoirs, Gish stated: "Charles Duell lost all of his money on the lawsuits he brought against me; he was disbarred from practicing law. I was told by lawyers that I could have had him put in prison for a year. But I did not want revenge, only freedom from contact with such a man, which I finally gained. I might point out that Duell died in 1954 and is not to be confused with other persons named Charles Duell who have achieved prominence in other fields . . . ."

The triumphant coda to the long and trying lawsuit occurred on April 14, 1925, when Lillian Gish signed a contract with MGM to make six pictures that guaranteed the sum of $800,000, with creative approval. She made several stunning films, including *The Scarlet Letter* (1926) and *The Wind* (1929), both directed by Victor Sjostrom. She left Hollywood after *One Romantic Night* (1930) and later remarked, "I had made all the faces I could make."

But male stars, like heart-throb Francis X. Bushman (born 1883) fared somewhat better than the women stars. Bushman, however, was unable to sustain his popularity, and ended up doing very small roles when the big money days were over.

Fred J. Balshofer, one of the founders of Quality Pictures Corporation, and Arthur C. Miller, spoke about the year 1915 and Francis X. Bushman:[3] ". . . who was married and had five children, was idolized by women. He was a sculptor's model and had won 'the most handsome man' contest sponsored by *Ladies World* magazine before he became an actor at the Essanay studio in Chicago. He was over six feet tall, with dark curly hair, and was a strikingly handsome, virile-looking man in his early thirties. Bushman always appeared as if he had stepped out of a fashion plate.

"The night following our arrival in Chicago, I signed him to a contract while he, Beverly Bayne, his leading lady at Essanay, William Aranson, his manager, and I were having dinner together at the College Inn, a night club in the Sherman Hotel. The contract was for two years; it called for him to star in a series of films for Quality Pictures at seven-hundred and fifty dollars per week, plus a percentage of the profits. The pictures were to be made in my Hollywood studio, but Aranson explained that Bushman could not very well leave Chicago before paying off some of his debts. I gave him a personal check for ten thousand dollars as an advance against his share of the profits, which, in fact, guaranteed the validity of the contract. I thought I had him figured out and, true to my expectations, I'll be damned if he didn't plank down about half of the advance on a special maroon-colored Marmon automobile the very next day . . . ."

Bushman was not the first male star to receive a percentage of the gross of his pictures: playwright James O'Neill, according to *Movie facts and feats*, a Guinness record book by Patrick Robertson:[4] ". . . played the wronged Edmond Dantes in Famous Players' maiden production *The Count of Monte Cristo* . . . . O'Neill had played the part on stage no less than 4,000 times over a period of 30 years and was both too old (65) and too ham for the screen version, but Daniel Frohman knew that his was the name which would draw theatergoers to the cinema and he offered the star 20 percent of the net profits as an inducement. Returns were undermined by a rival Selig version of the *The Count of Monte Cristo*, but the Famous Players version eventually grossed $45,539.32 of which O'Neill received $3,813.32."

Bushman went on to MGM and became a big star in derring-do roles like Messala in *Ben Hur* (1926), but his popularity waned in the late 1920s. He lost his fortune in the crash of 1929, afterward going into several businesses, including selling antiques in a store in Hollywood. He ended up in supporting roles, (notably as Bernard Baruch in *Wilson* (1944), and King Saul in *David and Bathsheba* (1951). His last screen appearance was in *The Ghost in the Invisible Bikini* (1966)—the year he died at 83. He, too, had made all the faces he could make.

BLACKOUT: 1916

Male Star
I'm exhausted. I've made six pictures this year.

Studio Head
Just do *Jim's Romantic Moment*, then you can go to Catalina for a week before starting the next one.

Male Star
But, you know that Charlotte and I are going to be married. I want a proper honeymoon. A week is not enough.

Studio Head
All right, then, take two weeks, but the marriage must take place on Catalina. The press will never find you there.

Male Star
I still don't understand your insistence on absolute secrecy.

Studio Head
If your fans—who are primarily female—find out that their hearthrob isn't single, and therefore theoretically available, how long do you think your popularity would last?

Male Star
But, my acting . . . .

Studio Head
It's not your acting, my friend, that women come to see, it's your he-man physique and your profile!

Male Star
I still think . . . .

Studio Head
We are not paying you to *think*. Don't you know that every woman in America wants to go to bed with you? And they don't want to fantasize about a married man!

Mary Astor's father, Otto Ludwig Wilhelm Langhanke, handled her finances, and collected her four-figure paychecks until her second husband pointed out the inequity. *(Courtesy of Warner Bros.)*

Gloria Swanson, the first "clothes horse" of the movies, had a career that lasted from silent pictures to television. *(Whitney Stine collection)*

3

FATHERS & BIG DADDIES

Female Star
All I seem to do nowadays is sign checks. What are they all for?
Father
Shut up and do as you are told!

A classical example of a female star mismanaged by an overly zealous father was the case of Lucille Langhanke, who was fourteen in 1920. A more appropriate name—Mary Astor—was devised by producer Jesse Lasky and columnists Louella Parsons and Walter Winchell. She was to make 109 feature films, retiring finally after *Hush, Hush, Sweet Charlotte* in 1964—a career that spanned forty-five years. Troubled with a heart condition, she has lived for many years at the Motion Picture Country Home in the congenial atmosphere of stars and technical personnel who have also retired and wish to live among "their own."

The product of a doting mother and a rapacious father, who had first wanted her to become a concert pianist, the starstruck Lucille had entered two *Motion Picture* magazine contests, at twelve and at fourteen, and made the Honor Role both times— which meant her photographs were published in the rag.

On the second occasion she was selected the winner, and famed portrait photographer Charles Albin approached her for a sitting, very much taken with the young girl's large brown eyes, long curly, molasses-colored hair and flawless complexion. She was five feet five and one half inches tall, in an era when leading men were only an inch or two taller. He took several breathtaking photographs that did full justice to her curiously mature beauty.

And it was at Albin's studio that Astor met Lillian Gish, who was so impressed that she personally directed a very long screen test to show D. W. Griffith, but he decided not to use her. The reason was revealed many years later, when Lillian told Astor that the great director had not placed her under contract because of her father. Griffith, an old hand at stage mothers and fathers, had said at the time, "That man's a walking cash register. I could never mold this child into an actress with him on my neck all the time."

In a 1972 autobiography,[1] Astor said of her father, "Otto Ludwig Wilhelm Langhanke deserves a book of his own. My feelings about him are still quite ambivalent, and in my mind he still comes on very strong. He is there in the residue of anxiety when I dream; whenever I discuss my work in movies, he is there as a prime mover. He is my scapegoat, my apology when I try to rationalize my behavior. I should be free of him now, but such a powerful personality is difficult to shrug into oblivion."

She continued: "If he were a character in a movie I would cast a blending of Yul Brynner and Erich von Stroheim. Ambitious, intense, a great deal of Prussian pompousness, a longing for luxury, a deep appreciation of beauty, sentimental about music, Christmas trees and sunsets, cold in his family relationship. And totally impractical. I wish he had transmitted his energy and ambition to me genetically, instead of using me as a channel. He was a rebel, who rebelled against anything new, who got stuck in his own century. His idealism was heady stuff. I respected, loved and feared him. I gave him the devotion one might lay at the feet of a guru. I followed his lead blindly. But eventually his lead was so confusing that I became somewhat like a neurotic mouse in a maze. A mouse that learned to think and feel and resent . . . ."

Otto Ludwig was a high school teacher from Quincy, Illinois. He gave up his profession to manage his daughter, thinking that he might also write scenarios. It was through this ambition of Langhanke's that Astor's first opportunity arose. Taking along the Albin shots, he set up an appointment with Harry Durand of the Famous Players-Lasky story department to try to sell his English translation of *Elga* by Suderman. Durand was not interested in the German story, but was very taken with the Albin photographs of Astor, which he had asked to see.

As a result of Durand's interest, Astor was given a six-month contract with Famous Players-Lasky. Her first bit (in *Sentimental Tommy*) was cut from the final version of the film, but a still photograph of her was used in the billboard advertisements. Then she did *The Beggar Maid*—kissed by Reginald Denny—a two-reeler that brought the famous painting by Burne-Jones to life, and in it she was billed *above* the title.

With Mama on the set, fussing with her costumes and makeup, and Daddy taking care of her finances—for she was now under a lengthy contract with Famous Players-Lasky—she made six feature-length movies and six two-reelers in New York. Her parents never let her out of their sight, and she was dependent upon them for everything. As hard as Astor tried, Otto Ludwig was seldom pleased. Then in April, 1923, a month before her seventeenth birthday, Astor came to Hollywood to make *Beau Brummel*, on loanout to Warner Brothers with the great John Barrymore who taught her a great deal about acting and breath control. He did not teach her about love until two years later, before the start of *Don Juan*. The romance developed into a torrid love affair, with the silent but tacit understanding of her parents, who managed to leave them alone for six hours a day of "coaching" at the Ambassador Hotel, where Barrymore was staying.

By this time there was enough money for an expensive house on Temple Hill (jointly owned by Astor and her parents), a Pierce Arrow motorcar, and a chauffeur named Parker. When she married a wealthy director, Kenneth Hawks, sound pictures were oncoming. Fox, her studio at the time, arranged a sound test and dismissed her voice as "almost masculine." Otto Ludwig, who still collected her paychecks and gave her an allowance, was advised that if the studio picked up her option, she would be expected to take a 50 percent cut in salary. Astor notes in her memoirs: "My father turned them down. 'We'll wait until they come to their senses,' said he. I was the one that did the waiting. And it was the last time my father represented me. Hawks had heard of the interview, and of the reputation my father had with other producers for being high-handed and pompous. They didn't like doing business with him, not just because he was tough but because he was totally unreasonable, uncompromising. Hawks advised me to get an agent, and he had the unpleasant job of informing my father that none of the producers would ever admit him to their offices again . . . ."

Hawks did get an agent for his wife, but nothing happened until she appeared opposite Edward Everett Horton in a legitimate play,

Among the Married. She received five offers for talking pictures, her voice now being called "low and vibrant!" During the run of the play she made two films, but—on January 2, 1930—Hawks was killed in a plane crash while shooting scenes for a film he was making.

Still grief-stricken, she filmed her first talkie, *Ladies Love Brutes*, after discovering that there was no money in the bank account—Hawks having lost everything in the recent stock market crash. Although Otto Ludwig wanted her to cut expenses and move back to the Temple Hill house, Astor refused to give up her independence. Her parents lived in the lap of luxury, with two cars, a housekeeper, and gardener. Her four-figure paychecks went to Otto Ludwig, and she was still given a small allowance. This changed after she married Dr. Franklyn Thorpe, who pointed out the inequity of the arrangement and told her father that henceforth she would take care of her own finances. She was free of him at last—but not psychologically.

Years passed, picture followed picture, star roles gradually turning into supporting parts. She finally won an Oscar for supporting Bette Davis in *The Great Lie* (1941), in which she played a concert pianist. She took the ill Otto Ludwig and wife Helen, who now lived quietly in Lancaster, California, to a matinee showing. She reported: "Since before my father had decided I was to be a movie star, he had ambitions for me to be a great pianist, somehow in his faltering mind when he saw me playing the piano in the picture he was almost tearfully proud that I had achieved so much. He kept commenting about my tempi and fingering and the way I made the melody *sing* Disturbed, I tried to explain that it was a dubbing job, that I really wasn't playing, but he merely shushed me. I couldn't have disillusioned him if I'd wanted to. I had finally 'pleased Daddy' . . . ."

Aside from the anxious fathers who have moved heaven and earth to promote the careers of their offspring, other males of the species have done likewise for their lady loves. Books have and will continue to be written about this phenomenon, which often has more to do with libido than talent. Sometimes these Men of Influence have been agents, often managers, frequently lovers, occasionally husbands, and almost without exception moneyed. But they have *always* been older. Since the days of the great impresarios of the theater, three such men stand out among many: William Randolph Hearst, Herbert Yates, and Meshulam Riklis. If not particularly wide-eyed, their *vis-a-vis* had two elements in common: youth and blond hair. The exceptions were Norma Shearer, who wed MGM bigwig Irving Thalberg, and Bella Darvi who made a fool out of Darryl F. Zanuck, president of Twentieth Century-Fox.

Hearst was 54 when he met former Ziegfeld beauty Marion Davies, age twenty at the time of her film debut in *Runaway Romany* (1917). Throughout some 44 films, from *Cecilia of the Pink Roses* (1918) to *Ever Since Eve* (1937), Hearst masterminded her career, using his vast newspaper empire to acclaim her star status and praise her performances. Lovers for 34 years, they would have married if his Catholic wife had given him a divorce.

Beautiful and talented, Davies was born with a business brain, but Hearst never permitted her to grow as an actress. Until she retired at the age of forty, he cast her in roles where she wore long blond curls, big hats, and miles of white ruffles.

In 1941, Herbert (Papa) Yates, age 61, head of Republic Studios was very taken with Czechoslovakian athlete Vera Hruba (Ralston), age 22, Sonja Henie's runner up in the 1936 Olympic Games ice skating event. After her first film, *Ice-Capades* (1941), her 25 films were mostly supervised by Yates, from mysteries like *Storm Over Lisbon* (1944) to westerns like *The Fighting Kentuckian* (1949). He often hired expensive leading men to co-star opposite her. After they married in 1952, her productions grew more lavish, and the box-office returns less gratifying. He (and she) retired from the business in 1959.

Unlike Hearst, Yates strove to expand Ralston's limited dramatic range, instead of starring her in skating films like *Lake Placid Serenade* (1944), in which she excelled.

Meshulam Riklis, at age 49 a multi-millionaire tycoon (owner of the Riviera Hotel in Las Vegas, Dubonnet Wines, and other concerns), married Pia Zadora when she was seventeen. In show business since she was seven years old, Zadora appeared on stage in *Applause, Fiddler on the Roof*, and *Dames at Sea*; on television as a spokesperson for Dubonnet; as pin-up in *Oui* and *Hustler* magazines; in Las Vegas as a performer at the Riviera, and on film in *Santa Claus Conquers the Martians, Butterfly, Lonely Lady*, and *Voyage of the Rock Aliens*.

Pia Zadora, a witty lady, has won awards at the Tokyo Music Festival, completed a video with Jermaine Jackson in the spring of 1984, and yet may strike pay dirt.

Sixty-six years ago, another witty lady was about to get her big break in silent pictures. The year was 1918, the girl was Gloria Swanson.

She had just finished a film at Triangle when Oscar Goodstadt, the casting director at Famous Players-Lasky, telephoned to inform her that Cecil B. De Mille would like to have an interview with her when she had time. They made an appointment.

Swanson had seen impressive offices before, but was unprepared for the magnificent set-like atmosphere of De Mille's suite, which was complete with stained-glass windows, a huge sofa, and a collection of ordnance on the walls. His desk was situated on a riser, reminding her at once of a throne.

De Mille was extraordinary looking; bald and open-faced, he had a scowl that could send extras on the set running, and his gaze could stop an elephant at fifty feet. He always wore riding breeches and boots—his trademark (and he was still wearing them thirty-two years later when he appeared as himself in her film, *Sunset Boulevard*).

He was reported to be tyrannical on the set, yet could be warm and friendly at home or with friends. However, he was a perfectionist and probably recognized that same trait in Swanson. On that first meeting, he took her hand and led her to the sofa, giving her all his attention. He remarked that he remembered her from a Mack Sennett picture, telling her that he wanted to cast her in a film he was preparing. He asked what sort of a contract she had at Triangle, and when she replied that she was free, he wanted to know who represented her. She answered that she did not have an agent and that, since she was almost nineteen, her parents did not handle her business affairs. His ears perked up. He was also interested in the fact that she was born under the sign of Aries—the twenty-seventh of March.

Although Swanson did not have a contract with Triangle, she had accepted a raise of fifteen dollars after finishing her first picture for them—and thereby hung the tale.
my first picture with Mr. Conway, but nothing came of it. They gave me a fifteen-dollar raise, that's all.' "

When Triangle called two days later, asking Swanson to report to work, she told them that she was going to work for Cecil B. De Mille. As it turned out, the fact that she had accepted the raise implied that she had a verbal contract. The Triangle lawyers presented their case to an impartial arbitrator at the Motion Picture Association, who ruled against Famous Players-Lasky, consequently she was forced to sign a contract with Triangle.

After several ridiculous war potboilers (*Secret Code, Wife or Country*) that embarrassed her, Triangle was having financial problems and agreed to let her out of her contract. De Mille replaced his leading lady in *Don't Change Your Husband* with Swanson. The contract with the studio was signed a month later. It provided a starting salary of $150 a week which would escalate to $350 per week by December 5, 1920. On January 21, she received a $50 a week raise. She made *For Better or For Worse* and the smash hit, *Male and Female*, as well as *Why Change Your Wife* and *Something to Think About*.

Swanson was by this time divorced from actor Wallace Beery. In 1919, she married Herbert Somborn, president of Equity Pictures, who read her contract and grew upset. He explained that the studio had the option for two additional years, and that the $50 raise would be subtracted from her paycheck beginning in 1920! With her name on the marquee of theaters all over the land, he assured her that she was important enough to be earning ten times what she was getting.

Somborn contacted a lawyer who agreed that the contracts were completely one-sided, binding Swanson but not the studio. When she became pregnant, she went to Jesse Lasky to explain that she would be unable to work because the baby was due in October. She was of the opinion that her contract, which would expire in January, was invalid anyway.

The contract was finally worked out, with Swanson doing the negotiating (consulting with her husband). She would make $2,500 a week for four pictures a year, escalating to $7,000 during the fifth year, plus amenities such as a star bungalow on the lot and musicians on the set. In the meantime, she discovered that her husband's money was tied up, and she was expected to foot the bills—starting with their honeymoon suite at the Alexandria Hotel in Los Angeles!

By 1923, Swanson was known as "the clothes horse of the motion picture industry." Her fantastic wardrobes for every film brought multitudes of shop girls into theaters all over the country, just to see her in yards of lace and lame and velvet, ermine-trimmed trains, and hats that framed her magnificent facial bone structure.

Separated from her husband, she was having a romance with director Marshall Neilan, another Aries, when in March she learned Somborn was suing her for divorce on the grounds of adultery with *fourteen* men, including Cecil B. De Mille, Adolph Zukor, and Jesse Lasky! Claiming that he had, in effect, agented a contract worth over $3,000,000 over three years, he was demanding a settlement of $150,000. It was pure and simple blackmail.

De Mille invited her to his house for a meeting. "I'm not afraid to fight," she told him angrily, "and I'm sure I can win. This is irresponsible mud-slinging. Why, Mr. De Mille, you're on that list yourself. You know it's a pack of lies. And poor little Mr. Zukor. Now, really." He reminded her that Mickey Neilan was on the list too. She agreed to think about it for a day, and as De Mille saw her out the door, a telegram was delivered. The message was from Will Hays, head of the censorship office that the studios had set up to govern themselves, stating that the Swanson matter had to be settled out of court, because it was not only her career that was endangered but the reputation of the Hollywood motion picture industry as well.

However, she was able to settle with Somborn for $3,000 in cash, and weekly payments of $500 were deducted from her paycheck until an additional amount was obtained. The studio also stipulated that she would make one more picture for them, since they had paid out the cash. A new contract contained a new clause— dealing with morals.

A short time later, Swanson found herself seated next to Will Hays at the head table at an industry banquet. She paid little attention to him. He finally asked her why she was ignoring him, and she brought up the telegram. He knew nothing of the incident. It then dawned upon her that Lasky and De Mille had tricked her. When she confronted Lasky, he admitted the ruse, saying that fighting Somborn in court would have ruined her career.

When Swanson's contract was nearing an end in 1925, she was approached by United Artists; Douglas Fairbanks, Mary Pickford, and Charlie Chaplin wanted her to join them, which meant purchasing 100,000 shares of preferred stock, sharing in profits from other UA films, plus producing her own pictures, and taking the "middle-man" earnings for herself. The offer was too good to turn down, although Lasky kept upping his offer to re-sign with Paramount, finally reaching the sum of $22,000 a week. On July 15, she signed the agreement with UA.

In 1927, Swanson then embarked upon her first independent film. *The Loves of Sunya* was an important picture which would mark the debut of the new movie palace in New York, the Roxy Theater, March 11, 1927. She had by this time divorced Herbert Somborn and married the Marquis Le Bailly de la Coudraye, whom she had met in France at the time of the filming of *Madame Sans Gene* in 1924.

Joseph P. Kennedy, head of FBO (Film Booking Office), and the father of seven children, came into Swanson's life over dinner late in 1927. They had been brought together by Robert Kane of Paramount, who thought Kennedy (a banker) might put some money into her films.

Kennedy evinced interest not only in financing Swanson's next picture, but in handling all of her business affairs. She gave him *carte blanche* to look into her files, which were examined with great care by two of his men; the upshot was that they took over her business matters. Kennedy dissolved her old company and formed a new corporation in Delaware—Gloria Productions. She wrote in her memoirs:[2] "In two months Joseph Kennedy had taken over my entire life, and I trusted him implicitly to make the most of it. He insistently kept all business negotiations in my name confidential and secret. E.B. Derr handled the paperwork through the FBO office in California, and Pat Sullivan signed the checks . . . . Whenever Joe was in Hollywood, he was there as head of FBO-RKO and the manager of Pathe, never visibly as the boss of Gloria Productions . . . ."

Inevitably, a romance developed between Swanson and Kennedy, who was deeply involved in her new picture, eventually called *Queen Kelly*, directed by Erich von Stroheim. The picture was rife with trials and tribulations, especially during the African sequences, because of great difficulties with the director over the story line. Long over-schedule, filming was finally halted with $600,000 down the drain.

Swanson's next film was in 1929 and a talkie, *The Trespasser*. It was a big hit, and she was nominated for an Academy Award. She went to London for the premiere of the film, and somehow was able to keep her dignity, even though she and the Marquis were on board the same boat with Kennedy and his wife. Rose Kennedy was most gracious; if she knew that her husband was involved with Swanson, she never indicated it.

The following year, Kennedy gave playwright Sidney Howard a Cadillac for coming up with a new title—*What a Widow*—for his inamorata's next feature, which had been called *The Swamp*. When Swanson discovered that the automobile had been charged against her personal account, she said casually over dinner one night: "You gave Sidney Howard the car; I didn't. He thanked you for it, not me. So I think it's only fair that you pay for it." Kennedy almost choked on his food and left the room. She never saw him again. A few days later she received a letter from Derr, informing her that he was returning his power of attorney, and guaranteeing he had never used it during the calendar year of 1930. When Kennedy returned to the East, he claimed that he had cleared millions while he was in the motion picture business, and to have made Swanson financially well-fixed, but Waykoff told her that money-wise she was far from wealthy.

Swanson noted in her autobiography: "I had been living a life of royalty, but I had been paying for it out of my own earnings. When we went through my books, we found such interesting items as Sidney Howard's car, and a fur coat that Joe Kennedy had given me as a present, not to mention more substantial items like the private bungalow Joe had built for me on the Pathe lot. As the auditing proceeded, the figures began to tell the oldest story in the world. Moreover, the accounts were in an impossible tangle. It would take a year to sort them out, and it soon became clear that the Kennedy offices would provide no help in the matter.

"I hired lawyers and accountants, and they all confirmed what Irving had told me to begin with: I had some property and lots of possessions, but I also had two children and a career that had been badly tarnished of late. It was imperative that I go back to work immediately and start recouping some of my recent losses . . . ."

Swanson's film career did not recover, and the glory days were over, even though she made six films between 1931 and 1941. She took a fifth husband, wealthy William Davey, but the marriage lasted only a little more than a month.

But in 1950, she made the most memorable film of her career, *Sunset Boulevard*, for her old studio, Paramount, creating the role of Norma Desmond, a star of the silent screen who wants desperately to make a comeback with the help of a young screenwriter, played perfectly by William Holden. Erich von Stroheim played her butler and ex-husband, and Cecil B. De Mille played himself. She won her third Academy Award nomination for the role. She continued to work in many fields into her sixties and seventies, painted, sculpted, appeared in all of the media, including Broadway in *Butterflies Are Free*, and wrote her best-selling memoirs. Looking glamorous in a red-fringed dress, which showed trim legs, she even danced the tango with a bevy of young men on the *Carol Burnett* television show in 1973, where she also sang a song and performed in a skit, impersonating Chaplin, just as in *Sunset Boulevard*. In 1976, she married her sixth husband, William Dufty, a writer seventeen years her junior.

Gloria Josephine Mae Swenson Beery Somborn, Marquise de la Falaise de la Coudraye, Farmer Davey Dufty died quietly on April 4, 1983, in New York. All the press people remembered her famous line in *Sunset Boulevard*: after being told by her young man, "You used to be big," she retorted, "I am big—it's the pictures that got small!"

But the young Swanson, in her most breathless and passionate early roles, never approached the pure animalistic sexual quality of Jean Harlow.

A co-player of Harlow's, Ben Lyon, still handsome in his mid-seventies, one of the stars of *Hell's Angels* (1930), and widower of Bebe Daniels, sat on the sofa in the living room of Bob Chatterton's Intimate Cinema in North Hollywood and briefly talked about his days as a leading man in Hollywood. When asked about *Hell's Angels*, he laughed. "It was a heck of a picture; it seemed to me that it was in production for *years*. It started out as a silent, you know, then when sound came in Howard Hughes re-shot the scenes with the principals for the microphone. He kept most of the dogfight footage and added sound to it."

He laughed heartily. "I had two leading ladies, first was Greta

Nissen, a Scandinavian, who was very nice but had a heavy accent, and she was replaced by Jean Harlow, who had a kind of flat voice, but a terrific personality. Hughes was thinking about dubbing Greta's voice, and probably would have, but dubbing was still kind of tricky, and then when he met Jean—well, I guess sparks flew— because they paid off Greta and hired Jean.

"We had the same agent, Jean and I, a peachy little guy, Arthur Landau—small in stature but big in heart. Although she was pretty inexperienced, our director James Whale got a performance out of her.... Landau was sort of like Lana Turner's agent in *The Bad and the Beautiful*, sentimental and proud."

Jean Harlow, born Harlean Carpenter, March 3, 1911, in Kansas City, Missouri, had come to Hollywood in 1927 with her mother Jean and stepfather, Marino Bello. She was an extra in a few films like *Moran of the Movies* (1928), and appeared in several Hal Roach comedies the same year, including Laurel and Hardy's *Double Whoopee*, and it was later on the Roach lot that Landau had discovered her.

Hughes offered Landau a three year contract for Harlow, $1,500 for six weeks work in *Hell's Angels*, $250 a week when she was working, and $200 when she was not, and yearly raises of $50 a week. After the picture was finished, Hughes loaned her to Universal for *Iron Man*, and to Warner Brothers for *The Public Enemy*, with James Cagney, at $1,500 a week; to Columbia for *Goldie, Platinum Blonde*, and *Three Wise Girls* for the same amount; to Fox for *The Secret Six*; and to MGM for *The Beast of the City* at $1,750 a week. Hughes was making the profit, and Landau was helping Harlow meet her bills.

Although Harlow's reviews were not good, her popularity was mushrooming. With six pictures released from April 1931 to March 1932, her fan mail was steadily increasing, and the fan magazines had taken notice of her. It was the time for Landau to move when Irving Thalberg of MGM indicated that he wanted to buy out her contract with Hughes, but would not personally negotiate with him.

In *Harlow*,[3] Irving Shulmans's intimate biography (with a great deal of material supplied by Landau), the author reported: "A week of telephone calls at last prompted Hughes to meet with Landau, and the short agent told the tall producer that he was no longer prepared to finance Jean's career; if Hughes would not star her in a picture or sell her contract, supporting her, Mama Jean and Marino Bello would become the responsibility of the Caddo Corporation. Solemnly, Arthur showed Hughes an accountant's itemized statement of Jean's indebtedness to the Landau office and pointed out that Hughes was big enough to be liberal. As always, it was a matter of moment and place, of speaking to Hughes at a time when he was bored enough to find diversion in magnanimity, and he generously agreed to sell the Harlow contract to MGM studios for a hundred thousand dollars. There followed two desperate weeks of negotiation, and at last Hughes accepted sixty thousand dollars and the right to use Jean in two pictures within five years at the salary she was receiving from MGM."

The contract with MGM was signed: $1,250 a week for the first year; $1,750 for the second year, escalating to $5,000 a week beginning with her seventh year. If she was to be paid two weeks a year, instead of the usual forty, the studio would take up options for an eighth and ninth year at the same salary as her seventh year. MGM agreed to pay for her secretary, hairdresser, maid, car and driver, and for her picture wardrobes.

There were many stories circulated about her platinum hair, but according to the late makeup expert Gene Hibbs, it was Helen at Westmore's Beauty Salon who, while preparing the dye—which in those days was an exact art—was apparently distracted while mixing the ingredients, and the preparation turned Harlow's hair into that striking white-blond shade that helped make her famous. She had to be at the studio for a luncheon, and she was so ashamed of her hair that she wore a turban, which became unwrapped. The rest is history.

Arthur Landau remained her agent, close confidant, and friend during the remaining five years of her life. Harlow died of cerebral edema at the age of 26 on June 7, 1937. Glamor photographer George Hurrell, her favorite portraitist said of her: "She wore her extraordinary beauty like a dress; she was casual and fun-loving, and she always gave so much of herself whether she was just chatting on the set or posing before my camera lens. I preferred to photograph her in white."

Mae Murray, the blond and beautiful silent film star/dancer who lived the good life and died broke, gave a touching description of stardom in her memoirs: "You could say we were like golden dragonflies over a swamp. We seemed to be suspended effortlessly in the air, but in reality our wings were beating very, very hard, very, very fast, so fast they were invisible . . . ."

BLACKOUT: 1914

New Husband
Anyone with half a brain can see that the kid's got talent running out of her ears. Look at the way she smiles! I'm going to take her to see Mr. Griffith.

Mother
But the set is over-run with all those peculiar-looking characters.

New Husband
They're only actors, great people. It's the costumes that make them look so strange. There's a lot of money to be made in pictures.

Mother
Where will you put the kid while you're roustabouting?

New Husband
The wardrobe lady is a friend of mine, she'll keep an eye on her.

Mother
But she's so young, barely thirteen.

New Husband
Well, Lillian Gish is eighteen, Mae Marsh is nineteen, and they started out real young. Now they play women in their thirties. Film makes everyone look older.

Mother
I don't know if Ethylene wants to be an actress.

New Husband
Sure she does! All kids love to act.

Mother
You say there'd be a lot of money involved?

Jackie Coogan, "The Kid," made $4 million, but when he reached his majority, there was only $535,932 left in the kitty. *(Whitney Stine collection)*

Jackie Coogan and his lawyers. Left to right are: Frank P. Doherty, Coogan, William M. Rains, and Albert L. Denney. *(Whitney Stine collection)*

4

MOVIE MOPPETS

Wallace Beery
"So whaddya gonna do with the Kid's money?"

Jack H. Coogan
"Every penny the boy makes I'm putting away for him."

The most appealing male child star of the silent era was Jack Leslie "Jackie" Coogan, born October 24, 1914, in Los Angeles, who became famous as a tousled-haired, blondish ragamuffin with baggy trousers and an oversized cap.

An offspring of vaudevillians John H. and Lillian R. Coogan, he was to the 1920s what Shirley Temple would be to the 1930s, Margaret O'Brien to the 1940s, Natalie Wood to the 1950s, Jay North to the 1960s, Rickey Schroeder to the 1970s, and Emmanuel Lewis to the 1980s—a money-making charmer with no brattish overtones. He had a wide, dazzling smile that lighted up his face, and when his expressive brown eyes filled with tears, lumps automatically rose in the throats of audiences all over the world.

At the age of twenty months, he made an unexpected debut in vaudeville, when he "shimmied" out of the wings of the Riverside Theater on Upper Broadway in New York City, in the middle of his father's turn. John H. saved the situation by having him join in an eccentric dance step. Thereafter, he was part of the act.

He appeared in his first film at age three—*Skinner's Baby* (1917) for Essanay, and the next year he went on the road with John H. in a popular revue, starring swimming champion Annette Kellerman.

In the spring of 1919, Charlie Chaplin—who had honed his tramp characterization, the Little Fellow, to the edge of genius—caught Jackie Coogan in the Kellerman revue. The child was doing a satirical impression of the famous dramatic actor, David Warfield, at the Orpheum Theater in Los Angeles. Chaplin was captivated by the cherubic five-year-old, seeing something of himself at the same age, an orphan dancing for pennies on the streets of London. Impressed with the boy's unaffected personality, he promptly went backstage.

Out of his tramp costume, Chaplin was a good looking, rather dignified thirty-year-old man, and it was a moment before Jack H. recognized him. At first, the father assumed the actor was interested in him, but it finally dawned on him that Chaplin wanted to meet the boy. Chaplin shook hands with Jackie and complimented him profusely. Before Chaplin waved goodbye, he called cheerfully, "We shall have a meeting."

As Chaplin drove back to Beverly Hills, a story-line for a picture was already forming in his mind. In his biography[1] of Chaplin, Theodore Huff wrote: "The inspiration for Chaplin's comedies came from incidents or characters observed in everyday life. A visit to a department store suggested *The Floorwalker*; observation of firehouse routines led to *The Fireman*; meeting Jackie Coogan inspired *The Kid*; encounters during his trip around the world furnished ideas for *Modern Times*, *etc.* All of his films are built on real backgrounds or people, with the slight twists which render them funny or pathetic."

Enthusiastic about the boy, Chaplin was dismayed to hear through the grapevine that comedian Fatty Arbuckle, who had also caught the act, was negotiating with John H. , but then was relieved to learn that it was the elder Coogan in whom Arbuckle was interested. When the Kellerman revue went on hiatus, Chaplin invited the Coogans over to his studio, a Tudor structure on the corner of La Brea Avenue and Sunset Boulevard, to watch the filming of a two-reeler, *A Day's Pleasure*, to be released by First National. He placed young Coogan in several crowd scenes to familiarize him with the hubbub on the set—the actors, the technicians, and especially the camera.

Chaplin knew that, for the story that he had in mind to work, a close relationship had to be established between the child and himself, because they were to share equal footage. He was not known for his generosity in writing meaningful parts for other performers in his tramp films, and his motives in this case were not altogether altruistic. Accustomed to releasing four to eight two- or three-reelers a year, he had lately run into a paucity of comedic ideas.

Also, he felt it was time to break into feature-length films that would permit time to more fully develop the plot. Hitherto, he had scarcely had time to set up a series of sight gags, and no room to introduce meaningful, supporting players who could have added texture and contrast to his character. He was at the point in his career where he needed someone to "play against." He had appeared in only one long picture, *Tillie's Punctured Romance* in 1914 for Keystone, which Mack Sennett had directed and Marie Dressler had stolen.

"Jackie Coogan was an unusually bright youngster," Huff asserts, "and had some acting experience, but still required careful training for the demanding scenes he had to perform before the camera. The training itself called for patience, tact, and the infinite charm Chaplin was capable of. Coogan came to adore his mentor, and the affection is communicated on the screen. Possessed of a decided personality—the kind that registers well—the child acquired an unfailing ease before the camera."

The scenario, which Chaplin generously named *The Kid*, was filled with the sort of drama that early-1920 audiences took to their hearts: a poor artist's wife abandons a baby in the backseat of a limousine, with a note: "Please love and care for this infant child." The limousine is stolen, and the thieves place the child near a garbage can in an alley of a disreputable neighborhood. A tramp discovers the baby, and when he tries to pass off the child, which no one wants, he takes the tiny bundle to his garret. Five years later, the Kid and the Tramp are discovered working an old scam: the child breaks a window with a rock, and the tramp comes along and is paid for his services as a glazier.

Inconsolable at abandoning her baby boy, the now-rich mother salves her conscience by performing charity work. She and the Kid meet when he is injured by a bully, and she returns him to the tramp. The doctor reports the case to the authorities when he realizes that the tramp is not the Kid's real father, but they escape when officials from the orphanage call at the garret. The doctor shows the note left five years before to the mother. She offers a reward for the return of the Kid, which is claimed by the owner of a flophouse where the Tramp and the Kid are passing the night. The mother picks up the child, and the tramp returns home, where he falls asleep on his doorstep. He has an allegorical dream and, awakened by a policeman, he is taken to a mansion where he is welcomed by the Kid and his mother.

The dream sequence was referred to in the *National Board of Review*, 1921, January/February issue: ". . . . take the Chaplin vision of heaven. (To be sure, the sub-title labels it 'Fairyland!') A slum street, suddenly festooned and garlanded and all the people wearing white wings tacked on to their otherwise unchanged clothing. They have not changed at all in any other respect, except that they can fly about ludicrously on invisible wires: a cross between a cabaret and a children's ball. The people fight and envy just as before, and a policeman with wings has to enforce brotherly love with his pistol! What an ingenious travesty on our easy beatitudes . . . !"

According to British film historian Kevin Brownlow,[2] "For Jackie Coogan, the film was the experience of his life. He still talks about it with delight. Chaplin was immensely kind and considerate, and his direction of the boy was one of the miracles of the movies . . . ."

"The Chaplin studio was unique," Brownlow quoted Coogan. "And as he was the only producer on the lot, we had the whole place to ourselves. Sometimes we wouldn't turn a camera for ten days while he got an idea. And when he got an idea, he brought it all together in his mind. He was a brilliant man. Everybody in the motion picture business or any of the arts should be terribly envious of this man because he had it all. He could originate it, he could facilitate it, and he was a director; he later scored all of his own pictures—he had the ability to get the most out of people.

"Here you've got a little boy, a waif, he's adopted without the benefit of the law, and he gets sick and the County Orphanage man comes and says, 'He has to go to the hospital. Are you the father?' And he says, 'No . . .' And they try to take me by force to the workhouse, which was practically condemning a child to death in those days.

"I can remember him explaining what he wanted me to do. He

started to dramatize it—I saw it in my mind's eye. He was a marvelous story-teller, and he put it on an intensely personal basis, so that when he said, 'Camera' and then 'Action!' and the Welfare Worker threw me into this truck, that's when the dam broke. I was really gone. I was tore up. 'I want my daddy!' I was hysterical. If you are going to portray someone being hysterical, you'd better get yourself hysterical, or it's as phony as a three-dollar bill. You've just got to let everything go. It's just like vacuumizing yourself, just letting everything out. In a grown person, I would say frustrations; in a child, I don't know what was let out. But I know I just felt hollow. My head was like a bell that was ringing."

Yet, for a time it seemed that the picture, which took a year and a day to film, would be held up, and might never be released. Terry Ramsaye[3] relates: "*The Kid* was completed in the midst of Chaplin's first domestic crisis, when attorneys were seeking a settlement with Mildred Harris, the first Mrs. Chaplin.

"There was the prospect that the negative of the unborn *The Kid* would be attached on an alimony claim and Chaplin hurried East with it. In New York the process servers pursued Chaplin and his comedy from hotel to hotel and up and down and about. Meanwhile, the negative, for safe-keeping, was continuously in transit in a meandering taxicab, with Carlyle Robinson, Chaplin's press agent, riding on guard over the treasure.

"When the chase pressed too close the film-laden taxi leaped convenient state lines, into New Jersey, into Connecticut, up hill and down dale across bridges and ferries. Those tin cans contained a world of laughs and a fortune for Chaplin. They came to rest at last in far-away Utah where the state laws prevent attachment. Chaplin there caught his breath and cut his comedy in peace while the lawyers negotiated in Los Angeles . . . ."

Continues Theodore Huff: "Jackie Coogan made a great personal hit and was hailed as the best child actor yet seen on the screen. Endowed with naturally expressive features and profiting from Chaplin's coaching, he became adept in screen pantomime, playing scenes with wonderful feeling. For this film Jackie Coogan deserves equal honors with the star; each scene together belongs equally to both . . . . *The Kid* is characterized by genuine pathos—a 'picture with a smile, perhaps a tear.' A single misstep might have made it mawkish but no such misstep was made."

The Kid, released by First National in January 1921, was called a masterpiece, and became an immediate box office champion—to the tune of $25,000,000, a million of which Chaplin kept. It made Coogan a hot star property. John H. gleefully signed a six-picture contract at the studio for the services of his son, which started with *Peck's Bad Boy* (1921) and ended with *Circus Days* (1923). Probably the most memorable film was *Oliver Twist*, in which Coogan played The Artful Dodger opposite Lon Chaney's malevolent Fagin.

With a bonus of $500,000 and sixty percent of the profits on Jackie's films, John H. was then lured from First National to Metro by Marcus Loew, the theater exhibition magnate, who had recently acquired the Culver City studio.

Coogan's first film under the new contract, which had Hollywood all agog was *Long Live the King*. It was "Produced under the personal supervision of Jack Coogan, Sr.," and Jackie played the engaging little prince, Otto of Lavonia. John H. was determined to keep his son "unspoiled" so he gave him $6.50 a week allowance, indicating that he would have access to all of his money when he attained his twenty-first birthday in 1935.

By this time, Coogan had acquired a business manager, Arthur L. Bernstein, who counseled John H. about investing the growing fortune. In 1923, Coogan made *A Boy of Flanders*, the second of a long string of hits for Metro, and thereafter appeared in two or three films a year.

In 1924, Coogan went on an extensive Children's Crusade publicity tour of the United States on behalf of 70,000 orphans in Palestine, Syria, Greece, and Armenia, for the Near East Relief, which included an audience with the Pope, who presented him with a silver medal containing the papal arms in gold. At home, a new company was formed: Jackie Coogan Productions, Inc.

In 1925, Lillian R. Coogan produced a baby boy, Robert, an appealing child who went on to appear in several MGM films, including two Jackie Cooper pictures, *Skippy* and *Sooky*, in 1931. But he never achieved the stardom or the popularity of his brother, although patrons were drawn by his name.

At this time, there was speculation around Hollywood concerning the lifestyles of the parents of various child stars. This had been brought to a head when child actress Mary Miles Minter sought to recover her estate at her majority, and received almost nothing. No one was surprised when Walter Winchell noted in a column that, when Jackie's mother turned away a caller with the excuse that her son was "with a private tutor," the caller retorted: "Don't ever teach him arithmetic, because someday he's going to wonder where all of the money has gone to."

Publicity man Pete Smith organized a huge campaign to take advantage of the cutting of Coogan's Buster Brown long bob, at age twelve. The event was duly recorded for posterity in a film called, *Johnny Get Your Hair Cut*, filmed in 1926.

At the threshold of adolescence, Coogan's salad days were over, and after his first talkie was released in 1927, he left MGM. Seeking to bridge the age gap, Paramount starred him below the title in *Tom Sawyer* (1930), with Mitzi Green. The advertisements showed the full-length photograph of the somewhat pudgy youngster holding a copy of the Mark Twain book under the legend:

"THE KID" Grows Up ! Now He TALKS for the First Time!

The ad department could not resist showing a small photo cut-out from *The Kid*, with the line in small type, "The most popular Boy in the world as The Kid of Charlie Chaplin's great picture." Coogan made one more film the next year, *Huckleberry Finn*, but The Kid, no longer a kid, had lost his audience. And on the horizon was another Jackie—Jackie Cooper, who had the same sort of appeal and who would inherit his mantle. As adults they actually appeared in two movies together, *Kilroy was Here* (1947) and *French Leave (1948)*.

In January 1932, John H. and Lillian R. obtained a dismissal of an earlier petition for guardianship, based on plans to establish a trust for the preservation of their son's estate. On May 4, Jackie was injured in a car accident, which took several lives—John H. , who was driving; juvenile actor Junior Durkin, who had appeared in the Tom Sawyer-Huck Finn movies; Charles Jones, manager of the Coogan ranch in San Diego; and actor/playwright Robert J. Horner.

The day before Coogan reached his majority, October 24, 1935, Lillian R. gave him a check for $1,000—and stopped his allowance. John H.'s will left everything to his wife, who assuaged her grief by marrying Arthur Bernstein on December 31, 1936. After this marriage, no moves were made by the stepfather to make an accounting of the estate or transfer any money the young Coogan had earned.

While attending the University of Southern California, Jackie received his allowance of $6.50 per week, lived with his parents in Van Nuys, and made *Home on the Range* (1935) for Paramount.

Meanwhile Coogan had fallen in love with starlet Betty Grable, with whom he performed a long shagging dance sequence in *College Swing*, filmed on the Paramount lot. After their engagement was announced in November 1937, an irate Lillian R. telephoned Mrs. Grable and admonished: "If Betty thinks she is marrying a rich boy she is very much mistaken. He hasn't a red cent. Jackie is a pauper."

Coogan married Grable in November 1937. In financial straits, he filed a suit that would have industry-wide repercussions. *The New York Times* noted on April 2:

MOTHER IS SUED BY JACKIE COOGAN

Film Actor Charges She and Stepfather Are Withholding $4,000,000.

DEMANDS AN ACCOUNTING

Los Angeles Court Names Temporary Receiver and Orders a Hearing April 20.

"Jackie Coogan," the newspaper noted, "known as the 'kid' of motion pictures is 'broke,' and has been deprived of his life's earnings of more than $4,000,000, he charged today in a suit filed in Superior Court against his mother and stepfather, seeking an accounting.... Judge Emmet H. Wilson appointed a receiver for all the 23 year-old actor's assets, and those of his mother and stepfather, Mrs. Lillian R. Coogan Bernstein and Arthur L. Bernstein. The order specified that no blame was attached to Mr. Coogan's late father, John H. Coogan....

"The complaint demands that the court enjoin Mr. and Mrs. Bernstein from selling or disposing of any property in their possession, including the assets of Jackie Coogan Productions, Inc., and of

Coogan Finance Corporation, pending a hearing set for April 20 before Judge Wilson . . . .

"Mr. Bernstein through his attorney, Charles J. Katz, denied all the allegations and said that he would contest the suit.

" 'All these charges are absurd,' declared Mr. Katz, 'the young man is suffering from a hallucination. He has received everything that he is entitled to and more.'

"Mr. Bernstein and Mr. Katz denied that Mr. Coogan earned $4,000,000, declaring that the amount was considerably less.

" 'His mother was entitled to all his earnings up to the time that he became of age,' Mr. Katz said . . . ."

Regarding the suit, the article detailed: "In a statement issued tonight Mr. Coogan said, 'It was the only course I could take. I have waited patiently for some time for my mother and Mr. Bernstein to make an accounting to me of my property. I owe a duty to my wife and to myself not to wait longer. It is a course I deeply regret to take. It is my intention at all times to see that my mother and my little brother are amply provided for. If my father had lived no controversy of this sort would have arisen.' "

For the next few days the allegations flew back and forth:

On April 12, Mrs Coogan declared that she was deeply hurt by the accusations in the suit. "He and I have always been so close," she said, "and there never was any trouble between us. I am sure he has been misguided by outside influence. He says he has nothing and that I refused to give him any part of the estate. No promises were ever made to give him anything."

Coogan counterattacked with, "All I know is that I earned millions of dollars and don't have anything now, while my stepfather is rolling in wealth. Two times last winter I went to the Santa Anita race track and sat in the $1 seats, but I could look up and see my stepfather in the clubhouse with the rich people. I made my bets at the $2 window and he was making his bets at the $100 window. That's how it's been with everything else. Mother said that it was all hers and Mr. Bernstein's and that so far as she is concerned, I would never get a red cent."

On April 15, Coogan's lawyers obtained a court order to allow Los Angeles County Sheriff officers to crash the electrically controlled gate to serve papers on Lillian R. and Mr. Bernstein, who had eluded the process servers for three days. They were subpoenaed to give a deposition in court on the 18th.

Three days later, Lillian R. tearfully told the court: "There are two reasons why Jackie has not shared in his estate. First, is that the law makes minors' earnings the property of their parents. Number two," and she broke down on the witness stand, "Jackie was a bad boy, a very, very bad 20-year-old boy, who couldn't handle money. His father told him, 'If you had money, you'd go completely haywire in two months.'"

What she had meant when she referred to him as a "bad boy" was that he had gotten drunk once after flunking out of college. The next day, she filed an affidavit in court declaring her son earned only $1,300,000 in the movies and in vaudeville instead of $4,000,000 as he claimed. She also claimed that he had earned between $30,000 and $40,000 in the last two years.

Coogan stated he had received a check for $500,000 after his parents had the guardianship dropped in 1923. He further maintained that his lawyers were searching for another will, "I'm certain that Dad prepared another will later than that admitted to probate."

Jackie responded on April 20 by filing an affidavit in Superior Court, charging that his mother had made a number of inconsistent and contradictory statements under oath in her deposition given in his suit for an accounting of his earnings. He stated that his mother's assertions that she never intended to set up a trust fund for him, and that he never had an estate were not true, because she had been appointed guardian for the estate. He emphasized that, later, she and his father obtained dismissal of the guardianship because they anticipated creating a trust for the investment and preservation of his estate.

Superior Judge Emmet H. Wilson, in a court order the next day, maintained that before he would approve of any theatrical, radio, or motion picture contract for a minor, the parents or guardians must agree to establish a trust fund into which would be deposited by the employer at least one-half of the salary of the child. He declared that the accumulated money could be paid to the child when he attained majority, or in installments after that age as the parents should direct. He referred to a 1927 law giving judges the authority to approve contracts for minors, virtually making the court guardian of the child.

Coogan stated that he was waging a fight to establish protection for other screen children, including his little brother. His attorneys said that Coogan was not fighting for a part of the money he earned, but for all of it. It was his contention that he should be the one to decide how much to give his mother, not vice versa.

On April 22, Lillian R. won a court delay until May 2, to come up with an accounting of her son's assets. She was also granted permission to change some of her earlier statements regarding the plans she and John H. had had to establish the trust.

Wallace Beery, the gruff-voiced actor, made an appearance on Jackie's behalf, saying: "Not once, but many times, Jack Coogan told me that he had never used or intended to use a cent the boy earned. 'Every penny the boy was making was being put away and saved for him,' Jack said on several occasions."

Betty Grable also appeared on the stand and repeated that Lillian R. had told her mother that Coogan was a pauper.

After the delay, Lillian R. testified that she could not remember the guardianship petition. "It may have been a technical, legal procedure at that time. For two years after he was of age, Jackie remained with me, and not until he married Betty Grable did he leave home. It isn't reasonable to believe that a boy who found home life as unpleasant as Jackie now tells, would have stayed at home, particularly when he was earning $30,000 and $40,000."

In a related story, the parents of Bonita Granville, Bobby Jordan, and Dickie Moore announced that trust funds had been set up for their children, but they would seek legal opinion to see whether the provisions were adequate. It was hoped that a standardized agreement for guardianship of movie children might be widely adopted by the film industry.

It is interesting to note that Bernstein had not given all of his attention to Coogan. He once waved a check for half-a-million dollars in the face of Shirley Temple's mother. Gertrude Temple told writer J.P. McEvoy, "He told me he had just got this for Jackie and we ought to let him handle Shirley, because we didn't know anything about the picture business and we would certainly be cheated if we didn't let him take care of us. Practically every agent in town had been after us, and we didn't know which way to turn. Bernstein talked and talked until we were dizzy and then, in desperation, we called our family doctor and asked him to come over and advise us, because he was the only professional man we knew . . . ." Actually,

Shirley's father was a banker and handled her finances very well. She received her millions when she reached twenty-one.

On April 2, Lillian R. surrendered to John Biby, the receiver of her son's trust, a 7-carat diamond platinum ring, purchased by John H. for $25,000, and a diamond-studded platinum pocket watch given to Coogan several years before, which he said his stepfather had appropriated for his own use.

The New York Times reported on April 27:

COOGAN'S "MILLIONS" DWINDLE TO $535,932

Actor's Stepfather Owes the Production Company $42,821—Cash Assets $1,785

Jackie Coogan who is waging an accounting suit against his mother and stepfather, learned today that even if he wins all they have, he will get only $535,923 of the millions he earned as a child actor.

The article also reported, "The fact came out in an inventory filed with the county clerk today, made by a receiver for the assets of Mr. and Mrs. Arthur L. Bernstein. The report also declared that there were $3,950.61 in delinquent taxes against the property for the second half of the current year and there was only $1,785.91 in cash.

"The inventory shows that Coogan himself owes Jackie Coogan Productions, Inc., $171.96 in sums expended in his behalf. His mother owns gross assets of $39,443.57, the report continued, and her indebtedness consists of $7,500 in notes to a bank, secured by 400 shares of stock of General Motors and Loew's. Also, although she has four bank accounts in different names, she has only $519.57 in cash.

"Bernstein was shown to have gross assets of $2,635, but owes the Coogan Production Company $42,821 and the Coogan Finance Company, $6,031.82. A beer distributing agency, owned by Bernstein, owes $1,730.25 to the Coogan Finance Company."

The receiver reported finding no evidence of any illegal activities by the Bernsteins. The Production company was described as acting as a sort of "family budget system," and had assets of $696,304.30, but only $535,923.70 in net assets although it was legal owner of the Bernstein ranch , the 17-carat diamond ring, and two Rolls Royce automobiles.

On May 2, Judge Emmet H. Wilson overruled Bernstein, the demurrers to the accounting suit, confirming the appointment of a receiver and granting a preliminary injunction preventing disposal of any Coogan or Bernstein assets. He also emphasized that allegations of undue influence on Bernstein's part must be carefully considered by the court. Lillian R. said the several hundred shares of stock included in the report had actually been purchased with her own money.

Jackie Coogan was very proud of one major victory for the child stars who would follow; the Child Actor's Bill was passed on May 4, 1939, which allowed the court to approve contracts submitted by a guardian to insure that one-half of a child's earnings were placed in trust until the age of majority was reached, with an accounting of all other monies to be supplied to the court. This Bill became known as "The Coogan Act." As late as the 1970s, Coogan was seeking to have the law upgraded, because television utilized many child players.

On August 16, 1939, the Los Angeles Supreme Court approved a final settlement of $252,000, of which the Bernsteins were given half. Coogan was stunned that $126,000 was all that was left of $4,000,000.

After the settlement, for all intents and purposes, Jackie Coogan's main career was over. Although he made a couple of films and appeared in vaudeville, he never officially retired. Betty Grable and he were divorced in 1939, with financial troubles cited as a major factor. Two years later he surprisingly made up with Lillian R. and Bernstein, and moved back into the Van Nuys ranch house.

He went into the armed services in World War II, married Flower Parry, a showgirl, and when they were divorced, married singer Ann McCormack. His third, and last, wife was dancer Dodie Lamphere.

Beefy and balding, he went into several other businesses, including selling used cars and working in an army surplus store. He was one of the first stars to enter television in the late 1940s, and for seven years he appeared on Mike Stokey's *Pantomime Quiz*. Occasionally a director would bring him back for a small role, sometimes playing heavies, and as movie historian Leslie Halliwell noted he "found work hard to come by in the sixties unless he was willing to make an ass of himself." Then, at the age of fifty in 1964, he suddenly achieved new fame, playing the grotesque-but-lovable Uncle Fester in the hit TV series *The Addams Family*, which lasted from September 1964 to September 1966. Occasionally, he appeared in films. In 1973 he reminisced at his home in Palm Springs: "Other kids went to see Babe Ruth," he said, giving that smile that still lighted up his face. "Babe Ruth came to see me!"

Coogan died of a heart attack at sixty-nine, March 1, 1984, in Santa Monica Medical Center where Dodie had taken him. He was said to have had one regret—that he had never told Charlie Chaplin how much he really cared for him.

But in 1930, there was another Jackie around the corner. Jackie Cooper never made the millions that Jackie Coogan did not enjoy. When, at the age of nine, he was cast in the title role of *Skippy* (1930) at Paramount (his mother had brought him to a "cattle call"), the studio discovered he was already under contract to Hal Roach, where he was one of *Our Gang*. They borrowed him for the picture for $25,000, while he received his usual $50 a week. Cooper would become as famous for his crying scenes as Coogan had been.

Skippy was directed by Cooper's uncle, Norman Taurog. While on location in San Bernardino, the first crying scene happened to be scheduled at the end of a difficult day. The director called for quiet on the set so that Cooper could concentrate on his emotions. His grandmother told him to be a good boy and cry, but the tears would not come.

In his autobiography,[4] he revealed: "Taurog had a temper. He was a short man, and he peered over his glasses, and that—all the kids on the picture had come to recognize—was a bad sign. This day he peered, and he screamed, and he hollered. He shouted that it had been a mistake to have hired me (I knew I had been hired first, but I wasn't about to dispute him), and he called me a 'lousy ham actor' (the first time I had heard that phrase), and he told his assistant to start getting the standby kid ready to replace me."

Still no tears. Instead Cooper became angry. "It was an

impasse," Cooper continued. "As I waited, I saw a new figure on the set, another kid dressed exactly as I was dressed, in the Skippy costume. Evidently they had gotten the spare costume—they always have two of everything on a set, in case the original is rendered unusable for any reason—and quickly put it on one of the other kids. It was Robert Coogan, Jackie's kid brother, a couple of years younger than I was. The idea that they would give my part to another boy was enough to make me very sad very quickly . . . .

"I knew there were two more big scenes coming up when I would have to cry. By then I understood how they had tricked me the first time and I was sure that they were going to trick me again. So I was determined that when the time came, I would cry by myself."

Still there were no tears. Prior to the start of *Skippy*, a friend of Cooper's mother had given him a small dog. Well-behaved and obedient, the animal was tied to Cooper's chair on the set.

"But that dog was suddenly a *cause celebre*," Cooper wrote. "Norman vented his wrath upon him. He said the dog was a nuisance, disturbing everybody on the set, making him nervous."

Taurog remarked that he was going to take the dog to the pound, but mentioned that if Cooper cried for him, he could probably get to the pound before they put the dog down. "I smelled a rat," Cooper continued. "This was the trick they were trying to use to get me to cry. I didn't dare risk a smile, but inwardly I congratulated myself for being too smart for them. This one wasn't going to work. I stood there and watched as my grandmother took the dog, untied him, carried him out. She said she was going to put him in the car and drive to the pound."

He heard his dog yelp and realized that she had pinched him. Cooper became so angry that he went into a tantrum and threw anything he could get his hands on.

"Norman said okay," he reported, "that was the end. If I didn't stop that immediately, he said, he'd have the policeman—there was always a security guard on the set—shoot my dog. I said he didn't have the guts. Norman nodded to the security guard. I saw him draw his gun out of the holster, and watched him as he went in the same direction my grandmother had gone with my dog.

"The set was deathly still. I couldn't see them. Then I heard a single shot. It echoed a moment. Then total silence."

Cooper could visualize his dog, bloody from that one awful shot, and began to sob so hysterically that the emotion was almost too much for the scene. Taurog quieted him, saying that perhaps the dog had survived the shot and if he calmed down and performed the scene as required, they would see if the dog was still alive. He did the scene.

"Later, of course, I found my dog totally unharmed," Cooper said, "and Norman and Nonnie and the security guard grinned at each other, proud of that little trick they had pulled . . . ."

That night, Cooper could not eat, vomited, could not stop crying, and could not sleep. A doctor was summoned who gave him a shot.

Cooper had one more crying scene to do and didn't know what they would try next. His mother solved the problem the way it should have been solved in the first place. She set Cooper down and explained what the scene was all about in detail.

And as she spoke about the emotions he was to feel, and *why*, he began to cry honest tears, and he performed the scene in one take. "And," Cooper said in his book, "most people who remember *Skippy* at all remember that scene the clearest. Taurog received all the credit for it, of course." But Cooper earned an Academy nomination for the film in 1930.

He next moved to RKO/Pathe for *Donovan's Kid* for the same salary, but when he went to MGM, for *The Champ* and other films, the studio paid $150,000 for his contract. His new pact started out at $1,300 a week for the first year up to $4,000 a week for the fourth year. His mother spent $1,600 a month to support him, assets were a thirteen year endowment policy listed at $50,000, $8000 in cash. But he would make an extra $7,500 to $10,000 a week appearing in vaudeville.

The years passed, he grew into older roles as a teenager and became an adult, making more pictures at other studios, doing personal appearances, and finally tackling Broadway. After he came back from service in World War II and demanded a final accounting of his monies, he discovered with some shock that he had assets of about $150,000. Between 1930 and 1942, he estimated that he had averaged about $1,500 a week, besides radio and vaudeville appearances, which totaled somewhat over $1,000,000.

Unlike other stars whose popularity had vanished and who could not find work, Cooper plunged into stage work and finally television, acting and directing and eventually ending up as the head of Screen Gems, a producing company. He made other fortunes, directing dozens of individual episodes of TV series like *M*A*S*H*, several movies for television, and feature films.

As Louis B. Mayer, head of MGM once noted, "The only thing wrong with child stars is that they grow up!"

Jesse L. Lasky signs the contract giving Ruth Taylor, *left*, the role of Lorelei Lee in *Gentlemen Prefer Blondes*, by Anita Loos, *right*. Standing are John Emerson and Hector Turnbull. *(Gene Robert Richee/Paramount Pictures)*

BLACKOUT: 1922

Male Star

They wouldn't let me go. I sang four encores, was on twenty-two minutes . . . .

Agent

I didn't get your name.

Male Star

Morrison, Johnny Morrison. You know, "Little John."

Agent

Little Johnny?

Male Star

Yeah, LITTLE JOHN. Songs and patter.

Agent

Refresh my memory.

Male Star

You took me on three weeks ago, and got me a split week at the Bijou in Omaha, remember?

Agent

You sing tenor?

Male Star

No, I'm a baritone. I sang *Under the Bamboo Tree.*

Agent

Oh, sure I remember now. You wore a coolie hat! I don't have any bookings. Tenors are hard to place in the Midwest.

Male Star

But I'm a BARITONE!

Agent

Well, baritones are hard to place in the Midwest.

Male Star

I would have been held over, but the manager had already booked this baritone who . . . .

Agent

. . . . sang *Under the Bamboo Tree* and wore a coolie hat? Right? Crissakes, book into an amateur night!

Gladys and Will Ahern perform their famous Ramona "controlled waltz" dance at the Scala Theater in Berlin in the winter of 1938, also shown live over German television. *(Courtesy of Will and Gladys Ahern)*

5

MCA IN CHICAGO: THE ORIGINS

Vaudeville Star
I'm so popular in Havana, they're going to name a cigar after me.

Agent
Yeah? I sure 'n hell hope it draws better than you do!

The Music Corporation of America was destined to be the largest purveyor of talent that the world has ever known. It was founded in Chicago in 1923 by Jules C. Stein and William H. Goodheart. They booked dance bands in the beginning but not magicians—*they* were the magicians that made it all happen.

Julius Caesar Stein, destined to become the most famous talent agent of them all—and the least known to the public—was born April 2, 1896, in South Bend, Indiana. The son of Lithuanian immigrants Louis M. and Rosa Cohen Stein, who owned a dry goods store, "Little Caesar" had impressed upon him at a young age that the family lived on the small percentage earned on the difference between the wholesale and the retail price. It was a lesson that he put to good use years later, when he handled the lion's share of show business talent.

The extraordinarily poised and self-contained "Little Caesar" was more than a precocious child who took mandolin instructions because Rosa had been talked into buying the instrument from a salesman. The boy liked music, and sax and violin lessons followed. (Fifty years later he joked, "I played a schmaltzy fiddle," and would sometimes prove it at small parties.) Before he was ten years old, he had organized his first backyard band, composed of schoolmates. Soon, he was accepting small paying engagements at birthday parties and bar mitzvahs.

Small of stature and slightly built, "Little Caesar" was not handsome in the conventional sense. Eyeglasses imparted a scholarly look more suited to a concert violinist than an orchestra leader, or the talent agent that he was to become. The band had such a full calendar that the thrifty and enterprising Stein organized another band to take care of the spill-overs. Louis R., impressed with his son's zeal, admonished: "You're going places, Jule. Always *think big*. I never did."

But Stein's ambition far outstripped being a violinist/conductor. During the summers of 1911 and 1912, he attended nearby Winona Academy. At sixteen, with earnings accumulated so frugally, he somberly announced to his family that he was going to prep school in West Virginia, and would form a band to take care of his expenses. Soon, he had three bands touring the area, for which he collected his usual fee. He paid his musicians less, pocketing the difference. It was the same principle that Louis R. utilized in his general store: marking up wholesale merchandise. Stein was peddling flesh.

The next year, he enrolled at the University of Chicago, from which he graduated after two years with a Ph.B. His tuition was paid by proceeds from a new band and the "cut" received from booking other bands.

Show business was only a means to an end. It was his overwhelming ambition to become a physician, but it took eighteen months of heavy band booking before he had saved enough money for medical school.

He met many interesting people in those days, including an unknown entertainer named Mae West. He provided the back-up for one of her small-time vaudeville engagements. He told Michael Pye:[1] "She was just starting out, a voluptuous, attractive woman. She was one of the first white women to shimmy . . . . I used to take her down to the black joints and she learned to shimmy there . . . ." Stein would remain friends with West for over sixty years.

He returned to the halls of academe in 1917, entering the Rush Medical College in Chicago, from which he graduated in 1921 with an M.D. degree (also having done time as a reserve officer in the Army Medical Corps). Dr. Stein looked longingly at the expensive automobiles tooling down Lake Shore Drive, and an occasional Rolls Royce caught his eye—what he would not give to drive such a car!

At this time the field of Ophthalmology was expanding, and Dr. Stein decided to take a post graduate course at the Eye Clinic at the

University of Vienna. (He had started his residency at Cook County Hospital before he went abroad.) After the war, Austria was in a state of shock. Having been ruled by the Hapsburgs from 1440 to 1918, the former Austria-Hungary had been split into Hungary, Poland, and Czechoslovakia, with the Slav lands south of the Danube joining Serbia to form Yugoslavia.

Dr. Stein was relieved not to be connected with show business in these countries, where eight languages were spoken. Although music was a universal language, the thought of booking bands under such conditions was overwhelming. What kept him going was the knowledge that the respectability of the medical profession, and its promise of a large income, was finally within his grasp.

Living in Vienna was expensive; there was no "side work" for a lonely Jewish boy. Although he returned to Chicago with a more mature perspective on life, he was down to $300. But with the dawning of the Jazz Age, there was more money than ever to be had from booking bands—even with Prohibition.

Composer Jule Styne, age 19, met Dr. Jules Stein in 1922 at a Musician's Union hall. And Dr. Stein asked Jule Styne, who played good dance-band piano, if he would like to work a summer resort.

In his biography of Jule Styne, Theodore Taylor, wrote:[2] "Jule played with the Stein band that summer at Miller Beach, Indiana, and soon learned what other musicians had known for several years: young Dr. Stein was a much better booker than he was a violinist. They couldn't wait to get him off the stand whenever he visited. Dr. Stein never improved his musicianship.

"For 'sweet' bands of this type, the main booker in the Chicago area in the early twenties was Edgar Benson, who took a third of the musician's earnings as his commission. Enterprising Dr. Stein had a theory that more money could be made; that the assorted horn, fiddle and piano players would be a happier lot if the agent only charged ten percent. Later on, Jule met him one night in La Salle, Indiana. The doctor, wearing a fur-collared coat, already looking successful, said, 'Would you believe that band made thirty thousand in thirty nights? I made three thousand. Mickey Rockford, a five-foot-two bodyguard, was with him, holding the money satchel. Mickey had a gun . . . .'"

Resuming his residency at Cook, age 26, he teamed up with a

gregarious twenty-year-old pianist, temperamental William R. Goodheart, Jr., a student at the University of Chicago. They formed a new band and went back into the booking business. Billy was born with the facility of knowing what would sell, whom he could promote, and what the public would buy. He realized that show business had more facets than the crown jewels of England.

Although Dr. Stein was making a little money from the bands, he still had his eye on medicine. He was despondent after Harvard and Johns Hopkins had turned him down for advanced opthalmological studies because he lacked credits in organic chemistry. But then came the welcome news that the famous eye surgeon, Dr. Harry Gradle, was looking for an assistant. Stein took the position, which unfortunately paid only $50 a week.

Seeing patients during the day and playing with the band at night left no extra time, yet he managed to finish a paper, "Telescopic Spectacles and Magnifiers as Aids to Poor Vision," published in 1924, and widely distributed by the famous Zeiss Optical Company as an instructional manual. This work brought him a certain amount of fame in medical circles, but little money. As if he was not busy enough, he signed up for a five-year stretch as a first lieutenant in the Medical Officers Reserve Corps of the United States Army.

That same year, capitalized with $1,000, he and Billy—who had dropped out of college—opened a one-room, one-dollar-an-hour booking office, with a secretary and an addressograph machine on Jackson Avenue. Reminded of his father's advice to "think big," Doctor Stein and he contemplated the Radio Corporation of America, which had been formed two years before. He believed that the founder, David Sarnoff, had the right idea. "Just think, Billy," he said, "no matter who is connected with RCA, it's the corporate body that everyone will remember; the designation has style and class. If we name our company Stein and Goodheart, what will happen when we die?" They decided on the name of the Music Corporation of America for their new firm.

Looking at the impressive letterhead, Dr. Stein nodded solemnly. "One day, Billy, I'm going to drive a Rolls Royce and have a seat on the New York Stock Exchange."

Billy laughed, "And I'm going to make a million dollars and retire at the age of forty!"

Both men were to achieve their wishes—and far more. Their dream was just beginning.

Dr. Stein's trained analytical eye told him that there was a giant need for reorganization in the procedures of band booking. A sedate hotel offering afternoon tea dances employed a mellow sounding orchestra, heavy on violins, while a dance emporium that catered to the younger set highlighted jazz, with more percussion. Bands finding a niche stayed in the same location for the season. Yet business was falling off; it seemed that each new speakeasy that opened took clientele away from them.

From personal experience, Dr. Stein knew that most band leaders bought standard sheet music, which resulted in very similar sounds. He hired musical arrangers, so that each band would have a distinctive sound. He went to the hotel managers. "Don't you see?" he urged. "You'll get more return trade if you rotate orchestras."

Rotate was the magic word: a first for the music business. Managers found that Dr. Stein was right: their clientele doubled, and they were ecstatic with the new arrangement.

The musicians were happy, hotels and clubs were happy, indeed there was only one group who was *not* happy, according to Murray Schumach:[3] "Locals of the musicians union did not like this: it cut employment for home-town musicians. Mr. Stein, a member of the union and a delegate, refused to budge. Other unions went after him. Bombs were tossed into restaurants where his bands played. Waiters went on strike. Mr. Stein continued to fight. When he learned that many thousands of persons were listening to an orchestra on radio crystal sets, he booked it—and his profits multiplied. Union officials offered him 'protection,' for a fee. 'I wouldn't give them a penny,' he said. Then Roger Touhy, one of the most dangerous gangsters of the Prohibition Era, demanded a cut. Mr. Stein was warned he would be killed if he did not leave town. He refused even to hire a bodyguard. Instead he took out a $75,000 insurance policy against kidnapping.

" 'They tried to muscle in on me,' he recalled icily. 'I never let them in. I had the guts of a fool.' "

He also convinced managers in certain locations to book bands for one night only, on the theory that dance aficionados would return much more frequently if they had access to different kinds of music. As Music Corporation of America booked more small bands, the office force was increased with the addition of Jules' brother Bill, who had studied to be a lawyer, but who also played sax and who acted as road scout. He constantly checked attractions all over the Midwest.

Hitherto, the bandleader had been responsible for purchasing train tickets to make certain that sidemen made the gig, and the booking agents had been given their commissions at the start of the engagement. Now it made sense for the agency to book the band, receive the money, deduct a percentage—far greater than the 2½ percent that the vaudeville syndicate allotted agents—pay the band members, arrange for train tickets and hotel accommodations and perform various "hand holding" chores, leaving the bands to do what they did best—make music. The musicians were happy because of more bookings; the band-buyers were happy because of increased patronage that often resulted in "sold out" signs being placed in their foyers, and Jules and Bill Stein and Goodheart were happy because business was flourishing. But they were on the road so much that their office was understaffed.

One summer day, a very young man named Taft Schreiber, who played sax, came into the office looking for a job. "Come on in," said Dr. Stein, "we need an office boy." He sent Taft to night school and then day school, then both, so that he could finish his education.

What distinguished Jules Stein from other booking agents of the day was *education*. He was intelligent, while they were smart; he was sagacious, while they were shrewd; he was astute, while they were crafty; he was conservative, while they were flamboyant. But, above all, he had developed a charming authority while administering to his medical patients. Band-buyers and hotel managers believed what Stein said, and he never lied.

He spoke of his days at Dr. Gradle's office in an interview with Michael Pye:[4] "I had a young assistant and he'd ring up about bookings while I had a patient in the chair. I'd be saying 'Can you read that?' and speaking down into the 'phone at the same time. We had Hushaphones then—boxes round the speaker—so nobody could hear what you were saying."

He would continue the conversation while conducting the examination "Yes, book the band in Freeport, or Kankakee, or Des Moines . . . ."

Rotating bands began to acquire a following, hotel managers

and band-buyers called to inquire not only about future bookings but an exclusivity in their area. Obviously it was a good practice to do business with MCA, an organization that could provide all the talent required at a price that management could afford. Clubs and hotels were continuously supplied with bands streamlined to their patronage all year long.

Business increased to the point where Stein was forced to reassess his own value to the company. He was weary of working double shifts, and there was none of the excitement of performing before an audience, or the thrill of making an exceptionally good deal. He asked Dr. Gradle for a year's sabbatical, promising to return to the practice as soon as additional personnel could be trained at the agency.

But the music business was booming, and the income of the most famous ophthalmologist paled in comparison to the amount of money to be stripped out of the music business.

"The Coon-Sanders Kansas City Nighthawks had a midnight broadcast from Missouri," Stein revealed to Joyce Haber:[5] "They had listeners all over the world. They didn't know who I was when they played a roadhouse called the Lincoln Tavern in 1924. But I pestered them to go on a tour of one-night stands. They finally said, 'Okay, if you pay us $10,000.' I didn't have the $10,000. I went back to them and said, 'I'll give you $2,000 when you sign the contract and the rest when you go on tour. . . . My trick was to ask for 50% in advance when I booked them. I got enough to pay them the rest. I made $10,000 in one month . . . ."

He was unable to keep his promise to Dr. Gradle: Dr. Julius Caesar Stein became simply Jules Stein, agent. Very soon, he had that Rolls Royce, but it would be some years before he got his seat on the stock exchange.

Bill Stein *schlepped* from one club to another, signing talent by gut feelings. First-class hotels required top talent, for which band-buyers were prepared to pay big bucks, but second-class markets had to be content with less expensive newcomers, while lodges and dance halls could afford only minimum fees for one night stands. He signed all types of bands. MCA was never at a loss to provide musicians for whatever the traffic would bear. Early on, as much care was taken in booking an Elks club in Fishtail, Montana, as later would be expended providing talent for the Blue Room of the

Roosevelt Hotel in New Orleans. In both cases, the efforts paid off with repeated engagements. It seemed logical that if MCA was going to represent a band, that band should be loyal to him and not accept any outside appearances. Therefore, Stein pioneered exclusive contracts not only with the performers that MCA handled, but also with hotels and nightclubs.

In fact, as the years passed, he bought other businesses so that he could supply his customers with everything from glassware to booze. "Why waste your valuable time with vendors," he would say in that persuasive way of his to hotel managers and club operators, "when we can take care of all your supplies with one telephone call?"

Competing agents were aghast at what they regarded as monopolistic practices. Although they muttered and fretted, they had to admit that Music Corporation of America was extremely efficient in handling all of their client's needs. Not only was MCA expert at booking attractions fifty-two weeks a year if need be, it was also able to demand high salaries.

Music Corporation of America was run as a very successful business. As one of their agents once said, "We are not set up as a human relation counselor. We are not father figures, and we prefer not to become involved in the personal lives of our clientele." In that sense they differed from the usual agent, who was often considered "family" to his clients.

Taft Schreiber spoke to Haber about his employer: "I remember back in the '20s in Chicago when he had a Rolls, and drove around with a raccoon coat and muffler and pince-nez glasses. He did it because it was the thing to do. He was a modern guy, and he's always kept up with the age . . . .

"He was a hellava bachelor, the girls were always attracted to him. He lived in the most fashionable '20s hotel, the Lorraine, and was always a fellow of great taste. He started to go to Europe right after school and the war. He more than delegated in business. He believed in making people part of the thing. We were his associates; he wasn't the boss . . . ."

Stein was encouraging to his sub-agents, but he was a devout believer in constructive criticism. He would show the men the ropes on the road, then let them alone. But he was an omnipresent force and would counsel if need be. Reading their letters, he would often say that they used too many "I's," cautioning them to be more humble. He would advise newcomers, "You cannot compete with the people you handle, so don't try! Modesty is by no means an underrated virtue."

On the road one day, Bill Stein dropped by Music Box Restaurant in Cleveland, where Guy Lombardo and his Royal Canadians were playing three shows a day. Since the reputation of the place had never been sullied by a police raid (as a speakeasy), station WTAM had installed a radio wire so that the band could broadcast.

Impressed with the fact that the band played slightly out of tune, which resulted in a very lush sound that immediately identified them, Bill came back several times trying to represent them, but to no avail. Lombardo was wary of agents, and he had never heard of Music Corporation of America. With the usual enthusiasm reserved for musicians that he wanted to sign, Bill promised Lombardo that he would "introduce him to the big time." Lombardo remained sanguine.

Goodheart also visited the roadhouse. As it turned out, he and Lombardo shared the same birthday—June 19, 1902. But the resemblance ended there. Goodheart was brash and quick-tempered (more so as he grew older); Lombardo was quiet, dignified, and sedate (less so as he grew older).

Guy Albert Lombardo, the son of an Italian immigrant, came to the United States from Canada in 1924, with his composer/sax player brother Carmen. Like Jules Stein, Guy had been a child violinist who had organized bands in his teens.

When Lombardo and his Royal Canadians moved to the Blossom Heath Club in Cleveland, Bill pestered him with telephone calls. Music Corporation of America had signed the famous Kansas City Coon-Saunders band, The Nighthawks, and put them on the road to turnaway business.

"It was Jules Stein who innovated the lucrative and killing one-night stands," Lombardo stated in his autobiography.[6] "His milieu was basically the Midwest and he would take a band and book it for weeks, playing a different town every night. With Coon-Saunders, he had expanded the operation, nationwide, and the commissions were piling up . . . ."

Jules Stein came to Cleveland himself, and invited Lombardo to his hotel for a meeting. Music Corporation of America's reputation had grown since Bill and Goodheart had first contacted the orchestra, and Lombardo was now intrigued with the operation.

"He was an elegant young man," Lombardo recalled, "poised and self-confident, and he told me he was about to open an office in New York. 'We're just starting and it's going to take me a while to get the lay of the land. But the thing I have uppermost in my mind is that I'm going to bring Guy Lombardo and His Royal Canadians to New York as my big attraction. I think you guys are so good you're going to make it big and the other bands are going to line up to be represented by MCA.' "

Thereupon an historic contract was signed, which would later be disallowed by the Musicians' Union. No contract, before or since, contained such outrageous terms: the pact would remain in force until Music Corporation of America made one million dollars in commissions! But Lombardo never regretted it, and on one of his traditional New Year's Eve telecasts playing "the sweetest music this side of heaven" in the middle 1970s, a sedate, mellow, smiling Stein, now retired, appeared in a segment with Lombardo, commemorating their long association. It was a touching moment—two elderly men who had known each other for over fifty years, reminiscing about the old days.

When Stein found good manpower, he paid well. "Find the man with character and capability," he once said, "who can do the job better than you can, provide the rewards, and let him run."

Before Stein brought Lombardo to New York for a record breaking gig at the Roosevelt Hotel Grill, he was booked into the Granada nightclub in Chicago, where the radio program brought in customers in droves. This resulted in a Decca recording contract. As hundreds of thousands of radios were sold, stations needed to fill up untold hours of air time and turned increasingly to music, a field that was slowly being dominated by MCA.

Lombardo wrote, "Jules Stein would make sure, however, that he never booked us in a town that had no broadcasting facilities. Especially on a Monday night, when we were heard coast to coast on the Robert Burns show. He had mapped out an itinerary that would remain virtually unchanged until 1933. We would play the Roosevelt from October to April, including two remote broadcasts a week and the commercial program on Monday. From April to

June we were on the road, with a large number of dates on campuses. For the summer we played a Long Island roadhouse, the sumptuous Pavilion Royal in Valley Stream. In September we usually played theater dates and then back to the Roosevelt."

MCA was always looking for new manpower, and during Lombardo's second year with Music Corporation of America, Stein provided a band-boy, a brash Rutgers graduate, David Werblin, whom everyone called "Sonny." It was Sonny Werblin's job to set up the bandstands, make travel arrangements, and collect fees from the entrepreneurs who had booked the band. "Sonny was to work with MCA from 1932 to 1965," Lombardo explained. "The lessons he was to learn on his first Lombardo tour would help him earn a vice-presidency of the company in 1951. With Jules Stein, he would become one of the most powerful men in show business; he would be summoned by David Sarnoff to provide television programs for the NBC network.... Yet Werblin would probably be better known as the owner of the New York Jets, who signed Joe Namath, than as one of the most astute minds in the entertainment industry. He remains today one of my closest friends . . . ."

Werblin gave up the Jets in 1968. At that time he happened to be a neighbor of Johnny Carson at the United Nations Plaza. Apparently the proximity of such a stellar talent nudged Werblin's show-business instincts. He got together with Carson to form Raitan Enterprises, which produced the *Tonight Show*, renting it back to the network for a weekly stipend. The arrangement continued until 1972, when Werblin left the company.

With MCA firmly entrenched in Chicago, the William Morris Agency still reigned supreme in New York City. Nat Lefkowitz joined the Morris office as a controller in 1926, and in 1928 became a CPA. Lefkowitz was born in Brooklyn, on July 24, 1905, attended public schools, and graduated from CCNY School of Business. "I was fired from my first five jobs after graduation," he remarked years later, "and wasn't sure I would stay with the sixth—which was Morris. In 1938, I received my Masters degree from Brooklyn Law School and was admitted to the N.Y. bar, by then I knew that I had found my niche." Lefkowitz was like all of the other Morris executives—he never had a contract with the company. He was a modest, unassuming man who guarded his privacy and was much liked by confreres. He was also a disciplinarian and established a dress code, frowning upon even a suggestion of flamboyant appearance in his men. He stayed with the organization until his death on September 4, 1983.

In the late 1920s, the routine of various band playdates was much the same in all parts of the country, but there were vastly different modes of operation between the East and West Coasts and the Midwest concerning vaudeville. Theaters in San Francisco and Los Angeles often depended upon vaudeville headliners out of Chicago, although some small-time booking was done locally. One traditional departure was the division of the split-week. In New York, Chicago, and points between, Monday through Wednesday made up the first half of the week, while Thursday, through Sunday made up the last half. However in California, the second half began on Wednesday.

Agents who were unfamiliar with this procedure would send acts west on a late train Wednesday night. To their horror, performers would discover upon arriving on Thursday that they had been listed as a "no show," and another act had replaced them. This was tantamount to being cancelled for drunkeness, or being replaced because their act was falling apart.

The unreliability of an act could spread quickly. The manager's report listed the misdemeanor, and it might take weeks for the "front office" to realize that the performer had not known about the difference in booking practices, and therefore should not be held responsible. It was the opinion of many theater managers that, since they were troupers, they should have known better; they should have picked up the information in the vaudevillians' underground.

To vaudevillians all over the country, the phrase to "play the Palace" meant only one Palace—in New York City, the ultimate playdate. Thousands of stories belong to that famous New York house. Of the 1927 era, George Burns wrote,[7] "Well, you're not going to believe this, but it's true. Gracie and I were playing the Palace Theatre in New York, and at that time the hit musical was *Show Boat*. It was produced by Charles Dillingham and he was putting together the cast for his London production. He came to the Palace because he was considering us for the Eva Puck and Sammy White parts. Puck and White were the comedy leads in *Show Boat*, and this would have been a tremendous break for us. But when I found out Dillingham was in the audience I got so nervous I forgot to check out which way the wind was blowing. So when we did our act my cigar smoke went into Gracie's face. The next day our agent, Tom Fitzpatrick, got a wire from Charles Dillingham. It read, 'The team of Burns and Allen I'll pay $500 a week. For the girl alone I'll pay $750.' As you've probably guessed, the London *Show Boat* sailed without us.

"As long as I've mentioned Tom Fitzpatrick, I'd like to tell you a little anecdote involving him. Tom Fitzpatrick was one of the top vaudeville agents. He handled a lot of good standard vaudeville acts, such as Jack Benny, Barry and Whitledge, Block and Sully, Will Mahoney, Swift and Kelly, Burns and Allen, and many others. Tom was very religious, and one of the kindest, warmest, most considerate men I ever met. In those days it was the practice of the various acts to go into their agent's office to find out if they were booked somewhere. But Tom was so soft-hearted he couldn't tell an actor that he had nothing for him. It was just impossible for him to say, 'You're not working next week.' So when you came into his office and there was no job, Tom got very nervous and started opening and closing drawers of his desk like he was looking for something. He just couldn't bring himself to face you. The minute he started that bit you knew you were laying off. And because he was such a nice man and you didn't want to hurt his feelings, you'd back out of his office and quietly close the door . . . ."

In the 1980s, George Burns was one of the only vaudevillians still working steadily and making millions via films, television, Las Vegas, and autobiographical books.

Will and Gladys Ahern, contemporaries of Burns and former headliners in vaudeville, came into the Vine Street Brown Derby restaurant.[8] (The Brown Derbys had been built by Gloria Swanson's second husband, Herbert T. Samborn, partly financed by Jack L. Warner, and had long been a hangout of the acting profession.) Will and Gladys blinked a bit from the sunshine reflected off the sidewalk outside, and the maitre de ushered them to their usual booth. Will was in his late seventies, and Gladys was a bit younger. He was a portly white-haired gentleman who looked more like a banker than an actor, and she was still beautiful, trim, and chic looking. They made a striking pair.

Will was a bit flushed. He had just appeared in the Los Angeles production of *Guys and Dolls* with Milton Berle, and had practically stopped the show with his second act number. Both kept busy on stage and in television, and had appeared in Johnny Carson's *Sun City Scandals '72*. Between jobs, Will—who was still on the National Board of Variety Artists—could be seen everyday at his Rainbow Rehearsal Studios up the street, at the corner of Vine and Yucca. They also attended the Comedy Club, housed in a large building on La Brea Avenue, with a full stage where ex-vaude-villians gathered along with ex-members of the Ziegfeld Follies, to entertain and "keep up the act." Gladys headed the Musettes, an organization that helps veteran entertainers.

Robert Dwan, in an article about the show business couple in the Calendar section of the *Los Angeles Times*, described their act: "Will appeared in a comedy cowboy outfit, did rope tricks and told jokes. Gladys spoke with a Mexican accent, did a toe dance inside a spinning rope to the tune of 'Alice Blue Gown.' They sang Western ballads and danced the Charleston and the Black Bottom. Will used a derby hat with a swivel to spin a rope on his head, and his big finish was a spectacular acrobatic Russian dance. It was simply 12 minutes of pure entertainment, compiled from what they could do best and what pleased the audience most. Their genius was in making these diverse numbers come together in a cohesive act . . . ."

They had not yet ordered lunch when Gladys' face lighted up, and she launched into the topic for the interview. "Vaudevillians were—and are—a people apart. There's nobody quite like us. We were raised in the theater, and we all had great fun. Of course there was work and practicing and work and more practicing, because sometimes a trick would take three years to perfect, but the camaraderie between acts was something else!"

"Yes," Will put in, "once you had conceived an act it was yours for life. Gladys and I have been doing our rope trick for fifty years, and it's still a crowd-pleaser! I pity the performers who play Las Vegas and then do their act on a talk show for scale." Will continued seriously, "Everyone in the country has seen the act for nothing, and that means over-exposure."

Gladys ordered a Cobb salad. "We always checked *Variety* to see who was appearing with us on the bill, and we'd think: Oh, that's great, we'll be in Cincinnati and eat at that Chinese restaurant that had that great won ton soup! Or we'd meet an act on Broadway and

47th Street and say, 'Hey, we're going to be appearing together in Washington, D.C., where are you staying?' And we'd agree to meet. We were like one big, far-flung family getting together for the holidays.

"Of course, we'd pull each other's leg occasionally. I remember I met Clara Barry when we were playing Orpheum-time, and she enthused: 'Wait till you play Sacramento! Boy, do they have a plush house. Don't worry about a thing. The dressing rooms are the last word. This stage is out of this world. Go right to the theater from the station and rehearse your act.'

"Well, we couldn't wait to get to the theater from the depot. And what did we find? It was the most broken-down house we'd seen in years. The dressing rooms had no light to speak of, and the stage was so small that Will fell into the orchestra pit on the opening show! But this sort of experience was not par for the course, and we gave Clara 'what for' when we ran into her again."

"Many vaudevillians have criticized Keith-Albee," Will remonstrated, "and with good cause, I understand from some of the old timers in the business. But by the time we came along, most of the in-fighting that had taken place between vaude houses before the first World War was long past."

"Yes, to us, Keith-time was the best," Gladys reminisced, "and the theaters were great. In Boston we had three rooms backstage— a sitting room, a dressing room, and a bath. There was an elaborate Green Room to greet guests, and there was also a kitchen and a nursery. We'd all look after the kids when their parents were on the stage."

"Yes," Will chimed in, "and remember the opening of the Palace in Cleveland? Keith brought in a special train from New York with the Astors and the Vanderbilts. And what a show we gave them! There were a lot of classy things about playing Keith-time. Of course, many acts didn't like their terms, but work was steady. One nice thing, though, was that the railroad men always came backstage with timetables, wanting to know where you were headed next. We'd give them the tickets and our luggage was sent to the boarding houses. We'd look up the nearest tea room in the classifieds, because they always had the best food. I remember having dinner in a cute little place in St. Louis once, and the date pudding was the best I'd ever eaten. I couldn't resist a second helping. A lady

came over to our table and whispered, 'You must be performers—
you eat so much!' The lady was Trixie Fraganza."

"Although we preferred hotels," Gladys put in energetically,
"we did stay in a couple of famous boarding houses. One was Mrs.
Sparrow's in Baltimore, and another was in Youngstown, Ohio,
where George Burns and Gracie Allen always stopped. But this was
in the twenties, and I've always been glad that we came along in
show business at that special time."

"Yes," Will agreed, "We didn't really have it tough like they did
in the old days when there was no decent transportation and
managers often made it difficult for the acts. We learned a great deal
about people in general when we played so many theaters over the
years. Down south, the audiences were a little slower on the pickup,
so we had to give them a little more time. In Pennsylvania, West
Virginia, and parts of Ohio with the steel workers, the populace was
eighty percent foreign, so we re-worked some subtle jokes, went
more into pantomime. Boston, Philly, Chicago audiences were very
quick and used to snappy pickups.

"I remember an agent named Carrells, a wonderful, homey sort
of guy, who worked out of the North American Building on State
Street in Chicago. He became our mainstay, because he could
promise fifteen or twenty weeks, then six weeks on the Electric Circuit in St. Joe, Joplin, Coffeeville .... Carrells always stuck by his
word, not like some agents today whom you couldn't believe if they
were part of your family! He was a gentleman. Five percent. He got
us $175 a week for the act, but jumps were short by—no long trips.
In those times, Gladys and I could live very well on six dollars a
day."

Will grinned, "But of course, the highlight—the very top— was
playing the Palace. There was nothing to touch that prestige. The
last time we played there was with Ted Lewis. I remember the date
well—July 10, 1928." A faraway look came into his eyes. "But
after that, I toured with *Good News* and was on Broadway with Ed
Wynn in Ziegfeld's *Simple Simon*, while Gladys joined my brother
Dennis on the Orpheum Circuit in the West. Then we went to
Europe again, vaudeville died, we toured the troops during World
War II, came back with our act on television in the 1950s—full circle again."

Gladys sighed, "But, it's still show business!"

BLACKOUT: 1933

Agent

Good morning. I hope I didn't get you out of bed. I waited until eleven thirty. I understand your contract is coming up for renewal. These are very perilous times, what with theaters closing all over, and I know Louis B. will insist you re-sign under the same terms. I can get you a better deal.

Female Star

My brother Jamie handles all my business affairs.

Agent

Believe me, I admire your loyalty. He handles only one star, you, while I have seven of the biggest names in the business. I've gotten more money and bigger concessions for all my people than any agent in this town. I feel it's time you had story, co-star, and director approval.

Female Star

Will you split your commission with Jamie?

Agent

Hell no! There can be no "under the table" deals.

Female Star

Frankly, and this is off the record, Jamie doesn't want me to re-sign. He wants to personally produce my pictures. We'll set up our own financing organization. He wants complete artistic control. In fact, he's just written a script that sounds scrumptious .... I play a twenty year old. I'd love to be photographed in Technicolor. Did you see *La Cucaracha?*

Agent

Yeah, the color was beautiful. But let me tell you something, Toots, the major studios hold all the cards. You'll spend all your money and then won't be able to release your picture. All the good people are under contract and you can't get a decent box office co-star. If you're going to play a twenty-year-old, you must hire the best cameraman and makeup .... Hello? Hello? Hello?

Jules Stein (right background) with bandleaders, including Louis Prima, Jan Garber, Lawrence Welk, and Freddie Martin, outside the Music Corporation of America's building in Beverly Hills. *(Gene Lester/Saturday Evening Post/The New York Public Library, Astor, Lenox & Tilden Foundations)*

Kay Kyser and Jules Stein cooking up a deal. *(Gene Lester/ Saturday Evening Post/The New York Public Library, Astor, Lenox & Tilden Foundations)*

6

AGENTS GAIN POWER . . . .

Pat O'Brien
Good morning, Myron. Did you win at poker last night?

Myron Selznick
Yeah. (muttering) There goes the son-of-a-bitch who collects the other ninety percent of my commission!

If William Morris seemed destined to be an agent from the very first, a most unlikely candidate was Myron Selznick (original name Zeleznik).

At age 27, he was brash, hard drinking, and brawling. He settled somewhat uncertainly in Hollywood in 1925. Good looking in those days, he was a big, stout man with the Selznick distinctive coarse hair, but he had small, penetrating eyes that would shift nervously about when conversation veered away from the only subject he knew well—motion pictures. He had produced several films for his father, and then had gone to England to make *The Passionate Adventurer* for Gainsborough, with Clive Brook and an old girlfriend, Marjorie Daw (whom he was to marry January 23, 1929). While in London, he met Alfred Hitchcock, who was an art director and serving several other capacities, and their fates would be entwined later in Hollywood.

Also in Hollywood at that time was probably the first agent to produce motion pictures there: Edward Small. Born in Brooklyn in 1891, he was an actor and impresario who had come to Los Angeles two years before Myron Selznick arrived. Small co-produced his first picture, *Passion's Pathway* (1923), followed by five other melodramas. Later, in 1932, he would form Reliance Pictures, distributed through United Artists, and eventually come to specialize in such adventure films as *I Cover the Waterfront* (1933) and *The Last of the Mohicans* (1936). In 1938, he would form Edward Small Productions, making *The Man in the Iron Mask* (1939) and many others, ending his career with the exploitation film, *The Christine Jorgensen Story* (1970).

Selznick had come to the West Coast with his 55-year-old father, Lewis J., who, as head of Selznick Pictures in the East, had gone broke and barely avoided bankruptcy three years earlier. Adolph Zukor, William Fox, and other film moguls who had refused to book his product into their large chains of theaters had drummed him out of business.

Ronald Haver, in his magnificently produced paean to David O.,[1] speaking of the Zukor/Fox relationship with Lewis J., put it succinctly: "These two men, with whom he had less than cordial relations, were delighted to see the disappearance of the Selznick name from Broadway's electric signs. They were not alone. Lewis J. had alienated many important and powerful men, and his collapse was as complete as it was sudden; it seemed to both Myron and David that everybody in the business had ganged up on their father, maneuvered him into bankruptcy, then turned their backs on him, refusing to help him get back on his feet and in some cases even actively working against him."

It was very difficult for the boys to see their father humbled. It was also a psychic shock for David O., who had been given every advantage, because there was not enough money left to pay bills, and he was not accustomed to creditors and lawsuits. The family was forced to move from Park Avenue to a three-room flat where Mrs. Selznick performed all household tasks. A strong, valiant woman, she did not seem disturbed by her husband's defeat.

Myron, however, deeply resented the collapse of his father's empire and would never—throughout the remainder of his life— forget those movie moguls, who he was convinced had ruined the family name. "Largely through Myron's lust for revenge," Haver concluded, "the family events of 1924 were to have unforeseen and unsettling effects on the film business over the next twenty years."

Lewis J. was currently involved in a scheme with an outfit called Associated Exhibitors, which needed pictures to distribute, but with his reputation, he was turned away from many doors. Of Myron Selznick, Irene Mayer Selznick, daughter of Louis B. Mayer, and David O.'s wife-to-be, wrote:[2] "Myron was compact, a man of few words, subtle, yet cynical. He was balding at an early age and, what's more, wore glasses, an unlikely portrait of a Lothario and an athlete, both of which he was .... Myron was both astute and talented. He was a big shot—or at least he had been, and he still felt like one, which made it awkward. He knew a lot about making pictures and had produced a great many for his father, beginning in his late teens. His father had such inordinate confidence in him that he had turned over the entire production of films to him. Of course, he couldn't get a job on that level, and he was damned if he would compromise much . . . ."

In Hollywood, Myron Selznick, broke and despondent, felt like a fish out of water in a land of relentless sunshine. He looked back fondly on his college days at Columbia University when Lewis J. had given him an allowance of $1,000 per week (David O. received $750). He was forced to borrow money from actor Owen Moore and other pals from New York.

Myron Selznick and David O. shared a small two-room apartment with Lewis Milestone, a writer who had started out as a film cutter, and producer Bennie Zeidman, neither of whom had money. When the Associated Exhibitors deal went sour, David O. went to Florida with his father to try to muscle in on the land boom and create a motion picture studio, leaving Myron Selznick on his own.

Myron felt helpless; yet he was determined to get even with the studio heads who had caused his father's downfall. Although their studios were huge and commanding, the moguls themselves were not. Lewis J. had been a jeweler before becoming a film producer, and the other fathers of the industry had similar backgrounds; few were educated: Samuel Goldwyn had been a glove seller, Adolph Zukor a furrier, Sam Warner a mechanic, Albert Warner a soap salesmen, Jack L. Warner an illustrated song slide singer, Harry Warner a film exhibitor, Jesse L. Lasky a cornet player, Harry Cohn a trolley bus driver, Carl Laemmle a bookkeeper, William Fox a garment cutter, and Louis B. Mayer a junk dealer.

On the positive side, he knew contracts forward and backward, had a discerning eye for story material, appreciated and understood creative people, intuitively grasped difficult situations at a glance, and could spot a phony at a furlong and a half—all qualities necessary for success in Hollywood.

On the negative side, he bored easily, found very few picture people amusing, always wanted to be on the move, could "talk a good story," was frequently insolent, and drank too much.

He was floundering about, not knowing which way to turn, playing tennis during the day and carousing at night. During this time both "Uncle Carl" Laemmle at Universal and Bernard Fineman at Paramount turned him down for jobs: the name Selznick was anathema in Hollywood.

Myron Selznick was finally given a chance to produce a film, which no one remembers today, called *The Arizona Whirlwind*, then Joe Schenck hired him to produce *Topsy and Eva* (1927), with Vivian and Rosetta Duncan, from their stage success. The project was doomed from the beginning because the sisters were in their late-twenties and could not maintain the illusion of youth: every wrinkle showed. Of trying to portray youth on the screen, Lillian Gish recalled:[3] "The camera was heartless; it exaggerated. I remember John Barrymore's once saying, 'If you stay in front of that camera long enough, it will not only show what you had for breakfast, but who your ancestors were.' "

Meanwhile, Lewis Milestone not only was writing adaptations but directing pictures at Warner Brothers for $400 a week, and Bennie Zeidman had a producer's job at Paramount. They rented a house at the beach, a few doors from Louis B. Mayer's abode, and asked Myron Selznick to move in with them. "Come and stay with us, David," Selznick urged, when his brother came to town. "I'm not working either, something's bound to turn up for either you or me, or maybe both."

At this point, an incident occurred that opened up a brand-new field in Hollywood, one in which he would excel, one that would provide him with the sweetest—and the most savage—revenge on those very people who had brought down the House of Selznick in New York. He became a talent agent.

David O. Selznick was far more imaginative than his brother, if not as bitter about their father's financial collapse. He decided to fight fire with fire and make the name of Selznick stand for the finest in motion picture production. He was an aggressive, dark-haired man with big shoulders and big teeth, truthfully resembling Theodore Roosevelt, whom he sometimes impersonated at costume balls. On brother Myron's insistence, he came to Los Angeles.

Breaking into film production was not easy, and although Lewis

J.'s former partner, Louis B. Mayer, did not want him at MGM, David O. petitioned bossman Nick Schenck (for whom he had once performed a favor) to give him a job at the studio. The only position open was that of a "reader" in the story department. He was starting over on the bottom rung.

He went to work at MGM in October 1926 (on two weeks probation) and made himself useful in various capacities until Irving Thalberg, chief of production, fired him a year later for "insulting behavior." (Uninvited, he had boorishly burst into the executive dining room and violently disagreed with Thalberg on how *White Shadows in the South Seas* should be shot.)

Undaunted, David O. left the den of Leo the Lion for the Adolph Zukor jungle at Paramount, offering his services on the same terms as MGM. Again, he did extremely well, but felt his story acumen and creativity were not being properly utilized. Meanwhile, to the consternation of many enemies all over town, not the least of whom was Mayer himself, David O. fell in love with Irene Mayer, Louis B.'s protected daughter, whom David O. had met at the beach three-and-one-half years earlier. They were married in April 1930, which resulted in the oft-quoted quip: "The Son-In-Law Also Rises."

The marriage bed had scarcely cooled when David O. asked David Sarnoff, head of RCA (which had purchased RKO), for a job. Within two years, he was head of production. Then Mayer surprisingly asked David O. to come back to MGM; Thalberg was very ill, and someone with talent and chutzpah was sorely needed. He accepted. The reason, according to Bosley Crowther,[4] was that he remembered what Lewis J. had told his mother on his death bed: "Tell Dave to stick to his own people; the only people you can depend on are your own."

In the short span of seven years, David O. was on top of the Hollywood heap. He became more brilliant, more ingenious, more aggressive, but he possessed one indispensable and saving trait: he had an instinctive sense of good taste. He knew how to write, to direct, and to produce, as well as to stimulate the creative juices of others. He began his own company in 1936, Selznick International (how he gloated over the "International!"). Three years later, he immortalized the name of Selznick by making the classic *Gone With the Wind*, which copped eight Oscars.

At the age of 37, he had made his masterpiece, and he would suffer the same fate that 26-year-old Orson Welles would two years later with Citizen Kane—neither would ever top his own achievement.

Meanwhile, back in New York. When Music Corporation of America opened a branch office in the Paramount building on Broadway in 1928, New York nightlife was tough to crack. Jules Stein was a totally different type of person from the usual uneducated, loud-mouthed ten-percenter who dressed in plaid suits, smoked enormous cigars and waved diamond pinkie rings. Agent E.M. Lester encountered Jules Stein, (who was commuting between Chicago and New York) on Sixth Avenue, and snarled, "We don't bother you guys in the Midwest, why in hell are you spending the money to set up here? You're babes in Gotham showbiz politics. No bandleader will touch you guys with a ten-foot pole!" Stein's reply is unrecorded, but having braved the Al Capone political machine in Chicago, it is unlikely that he was impressed.

Stein, whose eighteen-hour days left little time for romance, finally married at 32 on November 16, 1928. His bride was the beautiful Doris Cohen Jones, a native of Kansas City, Missouri. The union, in the true sense of that word, was to last 52 years. A supportive woman of wit and culture, Doris Cohen Jones Stein was to produce two daughters by him, become a stunning companion, and establish a reputation as a celebrated hostess. Five years later, when he opened posh, paneled offices in the Oriental Theater building in Chicago, she presented him with an eighteenth-century writing desk and a breakfront, which were to travel with him to various offices and, upon his retirement, move permanently to his home on Angelo Drive in Hollywood.

Stein developed a love for antiques for two reasons: one was esthetic (the beauty of the woods and the magnificence of the designs could not be denied) and the other was monetary (the pieces were excellent investments). Years later, after the MCA offices around the world had been furnished with rare pieces, he could actually see their assets growing! The corporation also owned fifty percent of Stair & Company, in New York, one of the largest purveyors of antiques in the United States, and the Incurable Collector, as well as having ten percent interest in the huge Mallett's in London, from which came most of the furniture.

Depression-ridden America took to free radio like a nail to

wood, and Stein provided package deals for radio similar to the ones he had set up for nightclubs and hotels. The agency hired *all* talent—star, guest star, backup singers, orchestra, announcer, scriptwriter, and producer—and then sold the entire program to a sponsor who, before MCA packaged shows, had to deal with advertising agency show packages. The advertising agencies often found themselves at a disadvantage because they were unable to put together deals with the MCA stars that appealed to the sponsors. Sometimes, they were priced out of a program, because MCA could sell a similar package cheaper, since it had all the talent under contract. (It was just such tactics like hiring talent from themselves that finally brought the Justice Department down on MCA.)

Stein was never idle a moment. He had no outside interests, did not play golf or polo or go skeet shooting, his reading tastes ran to non-fiction, and only later would he read an occasional script. His mind was always working—in three-quarter time. Meanwhile, Billy Goodheart, whom Leland Hayward once referred to as the "greatest agent of them all," was champing at the bit. His bouts of temperament were increasing around the office. He was reported to have a cabinet filled with bismuths and aspirins. When he was in a foul mood, underlings suffered. Early on, Sonny Werblin, who started out as his office boy, was often the brunt of Goodheart's blasts. After seeing that his pencils were sharpened and his inkwell filled, Goodheart would break the leads and spill the ink and scream abuse that his desk was not even taken care of properly. He was often irascible and associates had a difficult time keeping their tempers when he raged.

In those halcyon days between the two wars, MCA systematically began to sign the cream of the crop from virtually every section of show business, building an empire second to none. Its tendrils circled the earth.

David G. Wittels[5] noted that by 1934 Music Corporation of America's annual profit was over $1,000,000, and "That was not Stein's only source of income, however. He continually preached security to his band leaders, urging them to buy huge annuities and insurance policies. When they saw the wisdom of his advice, he sold them the policies through an insurance agency tie-up which he beforehandedly had arranged. When they needed automobiles, Stein stood ready to serve them, having taken over two automobile agencies. If they needed batons, fancy stands or other paraphernalia of classy bands, Stein could supply them through a company that he owned. Nor did he leave them to the tender mercy of strangers if they decided to buy homes or invest in other real estate. In the nest of companies fathered by MCA there was at least one real estate firm . . . .

"People who hired his bands found him just as accommodating. He had foreseen the close of prohibition and had bought up bonded-warehouse liquor certificates. After repeal he went into the liquor business on the side. He also formed a company dealing in novelties. The result was that when night clubs and dance halls bought bands from MCA, they could also get liquor, fancy stirrers for highballs, streamers, confetti, gay hats for gay customers, souvenir ashtrays, and even admission tickets—all in one neat transaction."

James Bacon, the Hollywood columnist, was a junior at Notre Dame University during the middle-thirties, and he was named music chairman of the junior prom. The class wanted Benny Goodman and his orchestra to play for the event. Bacon recalled in an article:[6] "By this time Benny and his great musicians, Harry James, Ziggy Elman, Gene Krupa, Teddy Wilson *et al*, had moved to the Congress Hotel in Chicago. I went up there to sign Goodman for the prom.

"Benny was excited about the idea. He had never played a college dance date with his new band, and he was thrilled that the first one would be Notre Dame. 'I'll call my booker to come over right away,' said Benny.

"The booker, of course, was Jules Stein, who told me right off that he was a Notre Dame fan because he was from South Bend. Then we talked money: 'Benny will cost you $3,500, plus $750 extra to replace him here at the Congress.'

"I was crestfallen and so, if his long face was any criterion, was Benny. I argued with Jules that we were in the middle of the Great Depression and the Notre Dame junior class couldn't come up with that kind of money . . . ."

Bacon had to settle for Bernie Cummins' band, and was in his words, "considered a bum by my classmates because I didn't come home with Goodman." But Bacon came to Hollywood, and did become a friend of Stein's years later.

Although MCA and William Morris would become the giant

agencies of the motion picture business, and Jules Stein and Abe Lastfogel eschewed ostentatious behavior either in themselves or their employees, other agents received reams of publicity about their raffish lifestyles. Primary among this breed was Paul Irving Lazar, also known as "Swifty."

Paul Irving Lazar was born March 28, 1907, in Stamford, Connecticut. After taking a law degree from St. Lawrence University, he went into practice. When he won a suit against MCA, he was asked to join their legal department. He was not the eccentric figure in those days that he later became. He began booking bands (Jimmy Dorsey, Gene Krupa, and many others) into nightclubs. A small, compact man, a few inches over five-feet, he always seemed in a hurry. He was successful and he liked the agency business.

However, he had an innate love of the written word, and he decided to go out on his own as a literary agent, and that was the field that made him famous—or vice versa. Bald, gnome-like, always sartorially resplendent, he began to amass an impressive impressionist art collection, which he displayed in opulent surroundings. Pianist/wit Oscar Levant once described Lazar as "The Jewish Onassis of Beverly Hills—the only man to ride down Wilshire Boulevard in a yacht."

He did not earn his nickname of "Swifty" until the middle 50s when Humphrey Bogart bet him that he could not ferret out five deals for him in 24 hours. Lazar won, and has been "Swifty" ever since.

He arranged many literary coups over the years, including the selling of Richard Nixon's memoirs for what eventually brought in about $2,000,000, then arranged the David Frost/Nixon television interviews for another large figure. Lazar told Wayne Warga:[7] "I'm an agent, not a politician. If a book is available, I sell it. If *Mein Kampf* was available I'd sell it. I'm not even a Republican. I've been a Democrat for 50 years. Mr. Nixon didn't care so I don't see why anybody else should care."

Later in the interview he revealed, "My feeling is that you have a better chance to sell something before it is exposed to the public or critics. Especially since nobody reads much, anyway. What you do is tell it with some embellishment—it's usually better that way than the story you're selling, anyway—and you've got a deal. The greatest fun is to sell something you don't represent at all."

Lazar continued: "I once suggested to Harold Mirisch that he buy *West Side Story*. He asked me why I thought so. I told him why. Then he said, 'Who do you represent?' 'You,' I said. And he paid me a fee. If I like something I'll go out and sell it. I usually manage to get paid anyway. I've never met Alistair MacLean, but I've sold all of his books to the studios. His publishers asked me to do it. I never met Colette but I bought *Gigi* for Metro for $300,000. I will also put my own money up for something I think is worthwhile. It's great fun to work with wonderful things.'"

Bi-coastal, Lazar and his wife Mary, a brilliant hostess, live in a spacious mansion in Trousdale Estates, Beverly Hills, with paintings and *objets d' art*. They also spend several months in their elegant New York apartment, and he has offices in Los Angeles, New York, Paris, and London, though he is essentially a one-man operation.

He represents, or has represented, Maxwell Anderson, Lauren Bacall, Noel Coward, George Gershwin, Lillian Hellman, Ernest Hemingway, Vladimir Nabokov, Cole Porter, Artur Rubenstein, Neil Simon, Arthur Schlesinger, Irwin Shaw, Truman Capote, and Theodore White, among many others. He has sold such properties as *The Sound of Music, The Thorn Birds*, and *The Fifth Horseman*.

In an amusing book, Kenneth Tynan,[8] star confidant, wit, and critic, wrote: "July 14, 1977: There is a dinner party tonight at the Beverly Hills home of Irving Lazar, doyen of agents and agent of doyens. The host is a diminutive potentate, as bald as a doorknob, who was likened by the late screenwriter Harry Kurnitz to 'a very expensive rubber beach toy.' He has represented many of the top-grossing movie directors and best-selling novelists of the past four decades, not always with their prior knowledge, since speed is of the essence in such transactions; and Lazar's flair for fleet-footed deal-clinching—sometimes on behalf of people who have never met him—has earned him the nickname of Swifty.

"On this occasion, at his behest and that of his wife, Mary (a sleek and catlike sorceress, deceptively demure, who could pass for her husband's ward), some fifty friends have gathered to mourn the departure of Fred de Cordova, who has been the producer of NBC's 'Tonight Show' since 1970; he is about to leave for Europe on two weeks' vacation. A flimsy pretext, you may think, for a wingding;

but according to Beverly Hills protocol, anyone who quits the state of California for more than a long weekend qualifies for a farewell party, unless he is going to Las Vegas or New York, each of which counts as a colonial suburb of Los Angeles.

"Most of Lazars' guests tonight are theatre and/or movie people; e.g. Elizabeth Ashley, Tony Curtis, Gregory Peck, Sammy Cahn, Ray Stark, Richard Brooks. And even Fred de Cordova spent twenty years working for the Shuberts, Warner Brothers, and Universal before he moved into television. The senior media still take social precedence in the upper and elder reaches of these costly hills . . . ."

"The clue to longevity and happiness is primarily your work," Lazar told Enid Nemy in an interview,[9] "It comes before your wife, before everything. It's a challenge, it's me against the world and I've beaten them at it . . . . If you keep moving, they ain't going to get you. You won't get hit with a hunk of pie with a brick in it. If you stop, somebody is going to get you . . . . I like people in action . . . . People who stand still are liable to get run over by people like me."

Which might also have been an axiom of Myron Selznick when he first became a talent agent in 1926. It was "a decision," wrote Irene Mayer Selznick, "that I believe ruined his life. He loathed every minute of it, even though he had a brilliant success. He had been inadvertent. His best friend in New York had been a Selznick star named Owen Moore, once married to Mary Pickford, and the best-dressed man in films. Owen, remarried, now was an MGM star and was having contract trouble, and Myron, an old hand, told him how to handle it. Owen could only carry out the first stage of the plan and appealed to Myron, who went in and got all that Owen wanted—and plenty more. It was done in nothing flat, and Owen was floored."

Meanwhile, as it happened, Selznick's first client was not a film beauty, but his erstwhile host, Lewis Milestone. Jack L. Warner had signed the writer/director to a new contract at the same salary. When Milestone studied the agreement later, he was dismayed to learn of the demands and refused to work, whereupon the studio sued for breach of contract. Furiously, Milestone filed for bankruptcy.

Selznick was well aware of what being "broke" meant in the film community. His mind was fresh with the memories of his own father's humiliating financial problems, plus the fact that Jack L. was taking advantage of his friend, whose talent directing and adapting *Seven Sinners* and *The Cave Man* (1925) had made money for Warner Brothers.

Thinking that he could intercede for Milestone, he contrived to meet Jack L. on the tennis court, but Warner was adamant. "Sure, I'll withdraw the suit," he said breezily, "but it's still $400 a week."

"Millie is very gifted," Selznick replied. "I almost fell out of my seat at the preview of *The Cave Man*. It's one of the funniest pictures I've ever seen."

"Yes, it has its moments," Jack L. agreed, "but the $400 stands."

"It's not enough!" Selznick cried indignantly, words that would become a litany during the bargaining of every contract he ever negotiated.

As Selznick was stomping away he ran into B.P. Schulberg, an associate producer at Paramount, who asked if he knew where Millie was. Myron pointed him out on the tennis court, and left in a huff.

When Milestone come home that evening with a one-picture deal on a low-budgeter, *The New Klondike*, Myron was incredulous. "How much are you getting?" was Selznick's first question.

Milestone beamed, "$750 a week!"

"It's not enough!" Selznick cried, after which he advised, "Just cool your heels, Millie, this picture and *The Cave Man* will both be released about the same time, and if the reviews are good, every studio in town will be clamoring for your services, and you'll be able to get a lot more money."

Neil McCarthy, the nimble-witted attorney for Howard Hughes, saw the films and was impressed by the comic touches. He warily approached Selznick. "We have a comedy scenario, *Two Arabian Knights*, that's just up Milestone's alley. It's going to be an 'A' production. Have a talk with him."

Selznick puffed up like a pouter pigeon. "He's expensive," he announced. "After these two pictures he's worth $2,000 a week."

"Impossible!" McCarthy exclaimed. "But Howard might go for half that."

"It's not enough!"

"$1,250, then."

"I'll tell you what," Selznick said, "Hughes appreciates talent. Let's split the difference."

McCarthy nodded coldly. "I'll get back to you."

But it was Howard Hughes who called Selznick that night. "You've got a deal," he said. "Tell Milestone to be at the studio tomorrow morning."

Selznick could hardly contain himself to break the good news.

Milestone was shocked. "My God, did you say $1,500 a week? Without you, this would have never come about. What do you want out of the deal?" Selznick paused; lawyers were paid a stipend for their services. A manager was a sort of high class secretary, but if an agent could get clients more money as easily as he had been able to do for Millie .... He made a fast calculation. "How about .... ten percent?"

"Fair for you, fair for me," Milestone replied happily, "let's seal the bargain. Let's go have a drink at the Montmartre."

Selznick happily acquiesced—he never turned down the opportunity for a drink.

The more he thought about becoming an agent, the easier it seemed. He knew from experience, having been head of Selznick Pictures, that most agents were simply leeches, syphoning away a portion of their client's salary—and for what? The agents he knew in New York wore plaid suits, used "dis" and "dem," talked out of the side of their mouths, and were not to be trusted. Hollywood agents entered through the back gate of the studios and waited in the outer office until they were called. They were at the bottom of filmland society, and not really socially acceptable.

Selznick meant to change all of that. In the first place, while he had a New York accent, he was educated. Certainly, no one could accuse him of not knowing anything about the business. And he knew these men with whom he meant to deal, he saw them occasionally at parties and even played poker with several film executives. Over at MGM when Howard Strickling, publicity aid to Pete Smith, heard about Selznick's deal, he stuttered, "P-P-Putzy t-t-ten p-p-percenter!"

With $150 a week automatically coming in, Myron Selznick began to look around town with an eye to taking on other clients. He

really wanted to make pictures, but until he got a production deal, he would see how much he could gouge the studios as an agent.

In October 1927, Warner Brothers had introduced sound pictures with their Vitaphone system, used on Al Jolson's *The Jazz Singer* and several short musical subjects. There were not enough theaters yet wired for sound to fully book their first 100 percent talkie, *The Lights of New York*, which was turning away business wherever it played. If the industry capitulated to sound, which Selznick felt was inevitable, the studios would be clamoring for stage actors with good voices, and those stage actors would need someone to represent them in Hollywood.

Selznick knew that tough times lay ahead, but he had a scrappy personality: he was not to be intimidated by a glove seller or a junk dealer.

He fully realized that, although star salaries were thought to be high by people outside the profession, considering the possible grosses of a picture, the weekly stipends were not out-of-line. In many cases, they were small compared to the returns.

Film people were not noted for their business acumen; many were counseled by husbands, wives, lovers, mothers, fathers or any family member who might be handy at the time. Few even had lawyers until they sued or were sued. The studios took full advantage of this situation.

One of the first men that Selznick had met in Hollywood whom he had genuinely liked was dapper Frank Joyce, the brother of star Alice Joyce. Their personalities were complementary: Frank was quiet and soft spoken, and looked very much like the hotel manager that he had been. Selznick was brash and loud, with a demonic streak. However, the men seemed to be together often, frequenting the same haunts and invited to the same parties.

Aware that Frank had a good business brain and managed his sister's business affairs, while sharing a cab one midnight, going home from a party and quite drunk, Myron leaned back and said, "Frank, my boy, let's set this town on its ear and open a talent agency."

Frank did not know if it was Selznick talking or the Black Label whiskey. He replied, "Sure, sure, anything you say." But surprisingly, Selznick called the next morning, full of plans. Frank still did not know if the idea had merit. He had a good reputation, and being connected with a Selznick could have its drawbacks. However, he was not making all that much money and he figured that he had little to lose.

Selznick had been courting Marjorie Daw for some time: they were married on January 23, 1929, in New York, at the office of the city clerk. There was no money for a big wedding, and neither of them actually wanted one. They returned to Hollywood, moving into the apartment house on Franklin Avenue where his parents and David O. lived.

The Selznick-Joyce Agency opened without fanfare, but the timing was opportune.

Lewis J., who often groused about the old days, reminded Myron about the difficulty they had experienced holding on to stars. In those cut-throat days in New York, producers often raided other producers' stables of players.

"During the long transition period from silents to talkies," wrote noted scriptwriter Frances Marion,[10] "little attention was paid by the studios to the rising power of the agents, who were like hunters stalking their prey. Astute men, facile talkers, their minds uncluttered by any problems beyond their well-organized units, they impressed talented individuals with the need for protection 'against the greed of the producers.' Myron Selznick was the most dominant figure among these agents, and he had been trained by his father in every facet of movie-making. Myron's knowledge of the picture business, his persuasive approach, made even the well-established artists, though confident of their future, willing to part with ten percent of their salaries and sign long-term contracts with him.

"At first, the studios rebelled against dealing with 'those Shylocks,' but soon they realized how helpless they were to protest; they needed certain stars, directors, actors, and writers and had to negotiate through the agents that represented them. Salaries began to climb higher and higher. Columnists reported that stage actors brought from New York and England were paid $5,000 or $6,000 a week, and mentioned that the deals had been consummated by such-and-such agency. This naturally caused unrest among some of the current contract-holders who had signed with the studios before the agents had come to their defense. As a result, the ones who had expressed relief not to have their heads chopped off when sound came in now chafed at seeing outsiders stealing part of their glory. 'Actors,' said Irving (Thalberg), 'are like children. No matter how many gifts are under the Christmas tree, they always want the ornament on the top.' "

But in 1929 there were still many unwritten laws in the industry, the most important of which was that stars employed by one studio would not be lured away by another studio when contracts were running out and new pacts were about to be signed. Thus, the stars had no bargaining power, and everyone knew what amount was on everyone else's paycheck every Friday night.

Selznick discovered that the contracts of Kay Francis, William Powell, and Ruth Chatterton were due to expire at about the same time over at Paramount. He made it a point to run into these three stars socially, which was easy to do as Irene was a superior hostess (she and David O. entertaining frequently). It was most natural that Myron should be at table.

Ruth Chatterton, Selznick found, was happy with her films at Paramount, especially *Sarah and Son*, which David O. had produced, and which received an Academy Award nomination. But she was unhappy with her salary, which was minuscule compared to what she thought she should be getting. William Powell and Kay Francis were appearing in *Street of Chance*, which David O. was producing, and both felt underpaid.

Myron Selznick knew that MGM, Fox, Columbia, or United Artists would honor the "gentleman's agreement," but he turned his tail toward Burbank and Warner Brothers. That studio was making so much money from Vitaphone pictures that they had bought out the new First National Studios (which had a string of theaters) for ten-million dollars cash. With an outlet for their films, stars of first magnitude were badly needed. He didn't think the brothers would have qualms about besting their brethren. He asked for an eleven o'clock appointment, knowing that Jack L. would have to get an okay on any deal from his brother Harry in New York. With the time difference between coasts, he wanted to be sure that Harry was still at work.

Jack L. received Selznick, if not with open arms, at least at the door of his office, which was reached through a curved driveway off Olive Avenue, rather than through the front gate. But it was a triumph for Myron just the same.

They exchanged tennis scores: then Jack L. told a couple of terrible jokes, and at last they got down to business. Jack L. could be charming when the occasion demanded. This was not such an occasion. "Okay, Myron, what have you got for me?" he asked bluntly, expecting to hear about the availability of one star, but his eyes popped open when he heard the names. He laughed out loud, all but rubbing his hands together and twirling his mustache until he heard how much money Selznick was asking—$6,000 each per week for Chatterton and Powell, $4000 for Francis!

Jack L. somewhat nervously agreed that it would be nice to have Chatterton at his studio; they didn't have an actress with her prestigious stage background. Yes, he had always admired Kay Francis, who was a clothes-horse, and yes, if Bill Powell was unhappy with the stories they had given him at Paramount, he could have story approval. However, he hedged on the money, but he needed the stars, even if it meant giving them 25 percent more than they were getting. He excused himself and called his brother Harry in New York. He came back and took the deal.

The men shook hands, and Selznick was at the door before he turned and gave the stinger: "By the way, Jack, Connie Bennett gets ten weeks off from Pathe/RKO, enough time to do two pictures for you. There's nothing in her contract that says she can't, and anyone who's played poker with her knows what a good business brain she has. It'll cost you 150 G's per picture."

Jack L. gave him a hard look. "Why didn't you tell me about this before I made the call to New York?"

Selznick grinned, feeling the power of the moment. "Connie Bennett is worth a dozen long distance calls!"

Selznick was fond of Constance Bennett for several reasons. She came from a distinguished, five-generation acting family. Her father was the terrible tempered stage actor, Richard Bennett; sister Barbara had acted in films in 1929 and 1930, sister Joan was just becoming an important leading lady, and her divorced mother, Adrienne Morrison, who been a stage actress in the late 1920s, had taken up a most difficult profession: she was partner in the Pinker-Morrison Literary Agency in New York, and had negotiated many plays for stage production. Myron admired her intelligence and spunk, which she had passed on to her daughters.

Constance was not only a beautiful actress but a shrewd negotiator. Jack L. took her services for two films. One was *Bought*, a prophetic title—at $30,000 a week a new high in Hollywood. The next year, he paid a cool $150,000 for four-and-a-half weeks work, and she insisted he also pay Myron Selznick's fee and the income tax on her salary! "I'm a businesswoman, not a philanthropist," she quipped. After the contracts were signed, sealed, and delivered, Selznick's phone did not stop ringing. He was soon driving a sleek Duesenberg up and down Sunset Boulevard.

But although the major stars in Hollywood were becoming acutely aware of the importance of being represented by astute agents, little was written about their power. In 1935, Darryl F. Zanuck, who had left Warner Brothers to form Twentieth Century Fox (and was very aware of what salaries agents demanded for their star clients to come over to his small studio), gave his impressions of talent agents in an article:[11] "There are arguments both for and against agents of any kind. However, the same rain that brings smiles to the farmer brings pneumonia to the man who gets his feet wet. There are times when I would gladly heave a brick through the Joyce and Selznick windows. At other times, I could fall on an agent's neck and weep with joy. It all depends on whether he is doing something for me or simply 'doing' me . . . . A good agent is an undeniable boon; a bad one is an evil in disguise . . . ."

Forty-nine years later, Czech-born director Milos Forman, in presenting an award for outstanding achievement in the agency field to his agent Robert Lantz at the fourth annual luncheon of the Association of Talent Agents at the Beverly Hills Hotel spoke of how, during the last twenty years, he had changed his entire life, including nationality, home, and the language his mother had taught him, but had never changed his agent.

When F. Murray Abraham was awarded his Best Actor Oscar for *Amadeus* on March 25, 1985, he thanked Robbie Lantz for introducing him to Milos Forman who had also won an Oscar for directing the same film. Reporter "Tush" noted in weekly *Variety*[12] that "Lantz urged agents to greater self esteem. He observed that among many in his profession, 'agents is not a nice word; we should be representatives.' He quipped that some agents become less respectable, not by practicing their own calling, but by becoming producers and studio executives . . . ."

BLACKOUT: 1938

Female Star

So in 1918, I went out to Wilshire Boulevard—there was nothing there except bean fields—and bought a twenty-acre parcel. My husband at the time said: "You're out of your mind! Who the hell wants to build there? Look at what happened to Harry Culver, never made a dime on real estate." My husband said he knew all about land values. You've heard of the suckers who bought the Brooklyn Bridge? Well he *bought* a piece of Catalina Island, only he didn't know someone else owned it! When I fell on my derriere after sound came in, I moved into the penthouse of one of the hotels I owned, and I sold that land on Wilshire for a million and a half dollars, which I invested in several office buildings. Other stars of my era worry about sustaining their images in badly-paying supporting parts. Let them. I live *now* the way they used to live before *they* had to move into rooming houses a couple of blocks off Hollywood Boulevard!

When agent Leland Hayward married client Margaret Sullavan, one wag wired: "Congratulations on getting the other ninety percent!" *(Courtesy of Henry Willson collection)*

Agent Louis Shurr with client Cornell Wilde and Wilde's wife Jean Wallace. *(Courtesy of Marvin Paige's Motion Picture and TV Research Service)*

7

. . . AND MORE POWER

Male Star

It's traditional to give thank-you's in connection with Academy Awards, but I'm still not speaking to my co-star; the director and I fought bitterly. We had three cameramen, I had to rewrite the script, and I haven't heard from my agent since my wife left me. Frankly, I deserve this Oscar, because I did it all myself!

Myron Selznick continued to handle a few top writers. Ben Hecht recalled,[1] "His work of vengeance changed the Hollywood climate. It doubled and quadrupled the salaries of writers, actors and directors—myself among them. Myron making a deal with a studio head was a scene out of Robin Hood. He was not only dedicated to the task of bankrupting the studio, but ready to back up his sales talk with fisticuffs if the discussion went not to his liking. Brooding in his tent after a sortie on a major studio, Myron would chortle, 'I'll break them all. I'll send all of those thieves and four-flushers crawling to the poorhouse. Before I'm done the artists in this town will have all the money . . . .'

"My first dealing with Myron involved going to work for Howard Hughes. I told Myron I didn't trust Mr. Hughes as an employer, and would work for him only if he paid me a thousand dollars every day at six o'clock. In that way I stood to waste only a day's labor if Mr. Hughes turned out to be insolvent.

"Myron was pleased with my attitude and put the deal over with dispatch. The work I did for Hughes was a movie called *Scarface* . . . ."

Myron Selznick was always on the look-out for stage actors from New York who might have a career in Hollywood. He had seen thirty-two-year-old Pat O'Brien on Broadway, and liked his outgoing Irish personality. When O'Brien was going into rehearsal for *Tomorrow and Tomorrow* on Broadway, Howard Hughes offered to pay director/producer Gilbert Miller $10,000 to release him for the film, *The Front Page*. O'Brien jumped at the chance to come to Hollywood and work for $750 a week, more than double what he had been earning in the theater. He recalled in his autobiography:[2] "One evening, a strange little figure wandered onto the set, a sort of tough Jewish leprechaun. He looked a little high as he turned to me.

" 'Who's your agent?'

" 'I haven't any.'

" 'You have now, sweetheart—but I won't take a dime from you until I improve your present deal.'

"I said, 'You've got yourself a deal, whoever you are.'

" 'Selznick. Myron Selznick.'

"That was the birth of my actor/management deal with Selznick. A great team of studio screen-makers: Myron Selznick—driving, demoniacal, self-destructive; and Frank Joyce—shy, quiet, the proverbial smiling partner. They were the first agents to demand huge salaries for actors, the pioneers of special deals, the makers of respect for talent."

While Selznick most often handled young people, he was not above signing oldsters if he was aware of their reputations. He met the 65-year-old, legendary Mrs. Patrick Campbell at a party in 1933. She had been the original Eliza Doolittle in George Bernard Shaw's *Pygmalion*. Having heard of her fabled stage performances since the age of nine, Selznick was eager to be her representative. Lewis J. had told of the brilliant effect that David Belasco had contrived for her in the stage hit, *The Heart of Maryland*—swinging on a huge bell-clapper. Adding her to his client list would bring a touch of old world class, but she had made only one film in 1930 for First National and her swinging days were over.

He was prepared for a sweet *grande dame*. A *grande dame* she was, sweet she was not; she had the tongue of a viper. She immediately endeared herself to a great many young men-about-town who appreciated acidic wit and mannerisms more appropriate to London's West End. Her fabled beauty gone, she was now stout and henna-haired, the only quality remaining from her great career being her still-magnificent voice which could boom out at the least-opportune moment.

When Selznick introduced Mrs. Pat to Sid Grauman at a premiere at his Chinese Theater, she burbled, "Howjado. Your fly's undone!" Unfortunately her comment was uttered in a momentary lapse of conversation and wafted out over the airwaves. Similarly, she ruined her chances of bigger parts at MGM when dining with the Thalbergs. Lillian Hellman wrote in her memoirs[3] about loaning $300 for Mrs. Pat to splurge on a dress for the occasion. Hellman asked if the actress had made a good impression. Mrs. Pat replied, " 'No duckie, and I don't think I'll get it .... I was doing rather splendidly at first. And then, well, it's true isn't it, and that's the important thing. I said to Mr. Thalberg, 'Your wife has the most beautiful little eyes I've ever seen.' "

None of the casting directors in town knew or cared who Mrs. Patrick Campbell was. Indeed, few had ever heard of *Pygmalion*, but Selznick finally wrangled a few supporting roles for her. Sir Cedric Hardwicke, no mean wit himself said: "Her manner grew more regal as memory faltered." Her films were *Riptide* and *Outcast Lady* at MGM, *One More River* at Universal, and *Crime and Punishment* (1935) at Columbia. But the pickings were slim and she returned to England, dying a pauper. "If she had behaved," Selznick said, "she could have done all those roles that fell to Dame May Whitty."

Ben Hecht himself had been forced to turn agent at Paramount in order to get a loan repaid. He had just written a gruesome crime melodrama, *Underworld* (1927), when his old writing buddy Herman Mankiewicz borrowed $10,000 from him "for a few days," which stretched into considerably longer. Hecht finally resolved the impasse by confiding his problem to the Front Office. He asked that "Mankie" be given a $500 a week raise, which the studio would deduct from his wages to repay the loan. The Head agreed, paid Hecht the entire $10,000 in a lump sum, and Mankie became the highest-paid writer at Paramount—on paper!

There was also another important leverage for absolute control of studio contract lists. If a star at a major studio misbehaved (demanded more money, control over scripts or asked for director approval), it was easy enough to loan him or her out to Poverty Row producers who were eager to get stars for film properties. Stars would complete terrible pictures under terrible conditions and then return home, chastised and obedient, accepting their next assignment without complaint.

Occasionally this device backfired, as in the case of Clark Gable who was kicking up his heels at MGM in 1934, wanting more money. As a disciplinary measure, Louis B. loaned him to Harry Cohn at Columbia for Frank Capra's little bus comedy, *It Happened One Night.*

Gable was demoralized: he showed up at Capra's office to pick up the script, so drunk he could barely walk. But the picture had repercussions no one had seriously considered: it earned five Academy Awards—Best Picture, Best Actress, Best Actor, Best Writer, and Best Director. It also set the underwear industry on its ear. When Clark Gable exposed his naked chest in the famous "Walls of Jericho" undressing scene, all would-be Gables all over America refused to wear undershirts.

"Gable was grinning ear-to-ear at the Academy Awards that year," recalled screenwriter Leonard Spigelgass.[4] "I had hoped to interest the studio in a story I had written about a prizefighter, perfect to cash-in on Gable's new bare-chested look. No one at the studio would even talk to me about the project. I think Louis B. Mayer was embarrassed about the whole business, and Cohn and Capra at Columbia had made a fool out of MGM to his way of thinking. Gable's stock was very high. Later I went briefly into the agency business, working for Zeppo Marx who had left the four Marx Brothers act, a guy of many talents. I would not say that one of those talents was agenting, and I was certainly more comfortable with a quill in my hand than a feather on my nose, which gives an idea of the sticky position agents had in those days. One story making the rounds was that Zeppo, who could be a scrapper, should be called 'Socko' after an altercation with a fellow-reveler at the Trocadero Night Club!"

Gummo retired from the act early on and was replaced by Zeppo, who played the foil and/or romantic lead in their plays on Broadway and in their first five films—*The Cocoanuts* (1929), *Animal Crackers* (1930), *Monkey Business* (1931), *Horse Feathers* (1932), and *Duck Soup* (1933)—after which he left the act.

In a letter of resignation to Groucho he said, in part, "I am sick and tired of being a stooge. You know that anybody else would have done as well as I in the act. When the chance came for me to get into the business world, I jumped at the chance. I have only stayed in the act until now because I knew that you, Chico and Harpo wanted me to . . . ."

Zeppo's talent agency thrived, and although he had acted as

business manager when he was with the act, he only handled one deal for his brothers after he left: wrangling $250,000 at RKO in 1938. When Groucho, who could be sarcastic, criticized him for not getting an additional $100,000 he threw up his hands and said "That's it!"

Zeppo was also in the business of manufacturing airplane parts. With engineer Albert D. Herman, he invented an electric wristwatch that monitored the heartbeat of the wearer, emitting an alarm if the beat was too rapid or too slow. He was married twice: to Marion Benda in 1927, by whom he had a son, Timothy, and to model Barbara Blakely in 1959 (who later married Frank Sinatra).

When Zeppo died at eighty-two on November 30, 1983, in Palm Springs, the general public was sanguine: he was remembered vaguely as the "un-Marx Marx brother," the "handsome one" who played straight. He was the last surviving brother: Chico died at seventy-five in 1961; Harpo at seventy-six in 1964; and Groucho at eighty-seven and Gummo at eighty in 1977.

"One of the stars that Zeppo wanted to represent," Spigelgass remembered, "was Carole Lombard, because her comedy timing was inborn, but he couldn't lure her away from Myron Selznick."

Lombard had met Myron through Frank Joyce's sister Alice. Since Carole was a hard worker and accepted a wide variety of parts (showgirl, gold digger, princess, clothes horse, sophisticate, dancer), Selznick was able to up her salary at Paramount.

Carole Lombard was born Jane Alice Peters, October 6, 1908, in Fort Wayne, Indiana, moving to Los Angeles in 1914 with her mother and brothers after her parents divorced. While she was attending Virgil Elementary School, neighbors Al and Rita Kaufman reportedly brought her to the attention of director Alan Dwan who featured her in the Fox picture, *A Perfect Crime* (1921).

While Mrs. Peters was not the typical, overbearing type of stage mother who hung around the studio and fetched and carried on the set, she and Lombard were very close. When they were not together they spoke on the telephone at least once a day for the rest of their lives.

From the beginning Lombard was beloved by film crews, because she was unpretentious, always in high spirits, and used colorful expressions—as at home on the waterfront as in a film studio. She loved to have a good time. Later, when she became a star, she became noted for playing expensive practical jokes.

After appearing with cowboy Buck Jones in *Hearts and Spurs* ("We *both* had title parts!" she quipped), she was in an automobile accident that left an almost invisible scar on her cheek. Her option at Fox was not picked up. After being off-screen for a year, she went to Mack Sennett for $50 a week to do twelve two-reel comedies, shot between 1927 and 1929. She always gave credit to Sennett for developing her stylish comedy timing.

Her co-star in *No Man of Her Own* (1932) was Clark Gable, whom she would marry in 1939. On the set one day she presented him with a twenty-five-pound ham with his picture plastered on it— everyone broke up with laughter.

Lombard was rapidly gaining a madcap reputation in Hollywood. Her scatological language somehow seemed natural rather than crude. No one took offense, because she was naturally funny. "To be called 'a son of a bitch' by Carole was in itself a compliment," Paramount still-photographer John Engstead once said. "She would go to any lengths to pull off a joke, but they were never cruel or at someone's expense that she did not know. It was a compliment to be on the receiving end of one of her sallies."

She was a rarity in Hollywood, a beautiful comedienne. Film critic Pauline Kael wrote that her "talents were not the greatest, but her spirits were, and in her skin-tight satins she embodies the giddy, absurd glamour of the Thirties comedy."

When her contract ran out in 1936, Selznick negotiated a new, revolutionary pact with Paramount that brought her $150,000 each for three pictures a year, plus the freedom to free-lance. He then sold her to David O. for three pictures at $175,000 each. She received the best reviews of her career for the hilarious Technicolor farce, *Nothing Sacred* (1937), with Fredric March. That year, she was the highest-paid star in Hollywood, earning a hot $465,000.

Not a man easily amused, Myron Selznick always laughed uproariously at her practical jokes. He thought nothing of it when she dropped off her newly-signed contract at his agency one day. After a month, her lawyer called and asked if the check was in the mail.

"What check?" Selznick asked innocently.

"You'd better look over your contract with Carole Lombard," came the terse reply.

The agent removed the contract from the file and discovered

that Lombard had had one page re-typeset in the exact font, chang-ing the wording so that she, Carole Lombard, was entitled to ten percent of Selznick's earnings instead of the other way around! The story was gleefully repeated all over town—it was rare that anyone was able to get away with anything on Myron Selznick. He took the ribbing in a rueful, good-natured way. Finally, she called him up. "Don't you know that I love you, you old fart?"

As the 1930s ended and his business grew, Selznick employed more sub-agents, drank increasingly, and eventually neglected even Lombard. She began making her own deals and choosing her own scripts. Her marriage to Clark Gable was considered a perfect match.

In 1941 Lombard made *To Be or Not to Be* with Jack Benny for United Artists release, a comedy-drama that has aged well over the years (and been reconstituted less successfully by Mel Brooks and Anne Bancroft in 1984). They played a Polish Shakespearian act-ing couple, and the action took place in Warsaw on the eve of World War II. The film had not yet been released when Lombard, her mother, publicist Otto Winkler, and all hands were lost when their plane crashed into Table Rock Mountain, thirty miles southwest of Las Vegas, Nevada, on January 16, 1942. She was returning from a successful war-bond selling tour, having raised $2,107,513 worth in Indianapolis alone. Selznick was devastated by her death.

Lombard's former business manager, Jean Garceau—who worked for Gable nineteen years after Lombard's death—recalled[5] how hard the actress worked to make Gable happy, and how her office was always the center of activity:

"They were always in there. It was busy and fun, and it was never a dull moment.

"Her biggest problem was dealing with Gable's more frantic female fans.

"I had a file I called my 'mad woman' file, just letters that were so crazy, wild and sexy . . . . terrible, terrible letters."

Gable's most prominent feature, his jug-handle ears, were never even noticed by Mrs. Garceau, who says Gable was more hand-some in person than on the movie screen.

"He really was the glamour man of the world. His walk, that's what I remember . . . . Just let him get up and walk around and that's when the charm, the electricity started. All those years with him I never saw those ears."

One of the New York agents Myron Selznick admired was Louis Shurr, who handled many variety artists and stage people such as Lou Holtz, Bob Hope, William Gaxton, Bert Lahr, Victor Moore, George Murphy, and Ken Murray. "Shurr was one of New York's colorful figures," noted William Robert Faith in his biography[6] of Bob Hope, "a shortish (five-foot-five), beak-nosed go-getter who drove around in a chauffeured limousine, usually accompanied by one or another supertail showgirl who would be wearing a mink coat that Louis loaned all his girls . . . .

"Shurr was dubbed 'Doc' by his Times Square clients and friends because he had been successful in salvaging a few troubled Broadway shows during their out-of-town tryouts. Shurr had noticed Hope in *Ballyhoo*, had caught his act at both the Palace and the Capitol and was, of course, familiar with *Roberta*. He was vigorously touting Murphy for a film contract, and he had the conviction that Hope, too, would ultimately make it in the movies."

But before Shurr and his sidekick Al Melnick wrangled the big contract at Paramount, Pepsodent toothpaste dropped the *Amos 'n' Andy* radio show and signed on as sponsors of the Bob Hope Show. Hope had acquired agent Jimmy Saphier (who would be with him for 36 years until his death in 1974), who specialized in radio, and press agent Mack Millar (who would handle him until he died in 1962). Saphier's proposed contract, to start in September 1938, gave Hope $3,000 per program, to escalate to $5,000 per program for 1944. Shurr undertook to represent Hope in films, but was not able to get much money for his first feature film, *The Big Broadcast of 1938*, because his client was an unknown in movies. However, Hope made fourteen films in the next five years, and by 1942 Melnick had wrangled a one-picture deal at Goldwyn (*They Got Me Covered*) at $100,000 and a percentage. Paramount gave him the same for *Let's Face It*—and the big money days were ahead.

(Inside jokes were the rage in Hollywood in the 1930s. On one occasion, in *The Gold Diggers of 1933*, Shurr's name appeared on the "insert" of a glass door, under the title of "secretary.")

In March 1935, Frank Joyce died. With the quiet, well-mannered partner out of the picture, Selznick had no one to place a damper on his wilder schemes; he became even more ruthless, and strangely unapproachable for an agent. He called the shots now and producers swallowed their pride, kowtowing when they needed one of his clients and knowing that no matter what amount was first offered, they would be greeted by the explosive, "It's not enough!"

If Myron Selznick was one-of-a-kind in a town whose middle name was nepotism, Leland Hayward was a total original in a hackneyed society. Later, many agents tried to copy not only his suave manner but also his style of dressing, which was foreign to the Hollywood of wild-colored sport shirts and loafers. Some ten percenters even went so far as to hire decorators to refurbish their offices like his, but none ever quite succeeded in matching his manner, his dress, or even the way he conducted business. He had *elan.*

Although Selznick did not look for another partner, the debonair Leland Hayward, who made frequent trips back and forth to New York, served as a good sounding board. He brought to the agency an "open mind," a contrast to the family small-town atmosphere of Hollywood, which was practically incestuous.

Hayward's daughter, Brooke wrote[7] of him, "His appearance was at odds with his profession. Tall and thin (hair parted debonairly in the middle when he was younger—graying and close-cropped like grass later on, a trademark in time), with an air both haggard and elegant, he strolled in white flannels and yachting sneakers through the corridors of the major studios of a Hollywood that had never seen anything quite like him before. The prevailing notion was that agents were a breed apart, somewhat declasse, that they all had foreign names, like the Orsatti brothers, or spoke with heavy Russian-Jewish accents and came straight from handling vaudeville acts on Broadway. Father captured Hollywood's imagination by inventing a new style; he was an outrageous Easterner who wore linen underwear and came out on Wells Fargo. It was said that his office was the first in Beverly Hills ever furnished with antiques, and that his manner of dress—Eastern college—influenced Fred Astaire and changed Hollywood fashion. Fred was, in fact, his first client . . . ."

At 24, Hayward had been fired from his press agent job at United Artists for using his influence to plant items in newspapers about pretty actresses he happened to meet. This was fine with the girls, but not his bosses, who wanted him only to publicize them. He had produced a few pictures at First National, which won no honors—he was to say frankly in later years that they "stunk."

If anyone had told him that he would become a talent agent, he would have accused them of being drunk. "All the agents I know," he was fond of saying, "started out in some other business. Did you ever hear a little boy say, 'When I grow up, I want to be an agent?'"

It was 1926, and Leland Hayward had not been in town very long and was hunting some night life when he stopped into the Trocadero nightclub. He had a drink with the owner of the Trocadero, commiserating with him over the empty house. "I'd pay three or four thousand a week to get an attraction to pull in the crowds," the proprietor remarked. "Someone like the Astaires, for instance. "

The Astaires were currently doing great business in a revival of their 1925 hit, *Lady Be Good*, in Los Angeles. Hayward jumped up from his seat and drove over to the theater to make the offer. He knew that Fred and his sister Adele were from Omaha, and he was from Nebraska City. That was his opening gambit. The Astaires gulped and accepted the offer of $48,000 for twelve weeks work, and Leland made $4,800 on the deal. It was easy money, he thought.

Next, he called upon John W. Rumsey, head of the well-known literary agency, the American Play Company in New York, and offered his services. "If you let me work out of this office and half the commission on any of your client's plays or books, I'll work like hell!"

He was very persuasive, and it was a deal that Rumsey never regretted because Hayward sold $3,000,000 worth of properties and talent to Hollywood in one year. He jumped aboard the bandwagon of talking pictures—the studios were re-tooling for sound—and began signing up actors and writers by the dozen, keeping them satisfied by performing all sorts of personal services that had never been done by an agent before.

He made so much money that he had purchased a one-third interest in the company. In 1932 he made another offer to Rumsey, "I'll give you my stock in the agency," he said magnanimously, "but I want all of my clients." When Rumsey agreed, Hayward established his own company. Realizing that he could not be on two coasts at the same time, he formed an association with Myron Selznick. Together, they set precedence for high salaries. They lured stars from one studio to another when new contracts were to be signed, successfully breaking the old tradition of studios not bidding against each other for players.

Ben Hecht once reported that the first and most important of his agents was Leland Hayward, who had launched himself as a ten-percenter by taking a manuscript from his desk in Beekman Place—one that Hecht had discarded as unfit for publication—and selling it to Metro behind his back. The manuscript was a short story eventually produced as *The Green Ghost*, directed by Lionel Barrymore.

"Leland's immediate demand for a cut of fifteen hundred dollars startled me," Hecht wrote,[8] "it was the first time such an inroad into my earnings had been attempted. I hurried indignantly to the Metro office in New York and insisted on an extra fifteen hundred dollars for my story, and sent this added boodle to Leland. Thereafter, I became reconciled to paying over great sums to men who seemingly did nothing but notify me they had secured a task for me which either I did not want or had already finished.

"Leland had become an agent out of a boyish veneration for writers. This mood deserted him early in his agent's career. He became disdainful of writers and easily irritated by them. He said that they had disillusioned him—'So help me God, they're more hammy and hysterical than even actors, and more ungrateful ....'

"He was always more perked up over my refusing to do a movie chore than over my having done it. A good part of my reputation as a troublesome fellow in Hollywood was based on Leland's happy pronouncements to the studio caliphs—'You can't get Hecht. He read the story and thinks it stinks. I tried to argue with him, but all he said was you haven't got enough money to get him to do such kind of crap.' "

Hayward handled Ernest Hemingway, Edna Ferber, Charles MacArthur, Gene Fowler, Donald Ogden Stewart, Howard Lindsay and Russell Crouse, Lillian Hellman, and Dashiell Hammett.

Concerning Edna Ferber, Garson Kanin remembered[9] that Leland Hayward ".... struggled with the financial aspects of the deal he was about to make for her successful novel *Saratoga Trunk*. Miss Ferber had spent some three years writing the book, and now it appeared that she would be taxed on what she made from the book in a single year. This seemed blatantly unfair, but nothing could be done.

"Hayward came up with an idea that has been copied many times since. Instead of selling the property outright to Warner Brothers, he decided to lease them the rights for a period of ten years, at so much a year. It was a brilliant idea and has worked well ever since."

Hayward's romance with Katharine Hepburn started after he negotiated her salary at RKO for *Bill of Divorcement* (1932) at $1,250 per week. When he married actress Margaret Sullavan, also a client, a wag sent him a telegram:

CONGRATULATIONS ON GETTING THE OTHER NINETY PERCENT

Concerning the affair with Hepburn, Gary Carey wrote:[10] "Hayward's professional relationship with Kate had taken a romantic turn at about the same time as *Morning Glory*. No one knows how serious their alliance really was (Hepburn has never discussed it), but many people feel that, next to Spencer Tracy, he was the most important man in her life. She found him fascinating—as did nearly everyone. Tall, slender, and handsome, Hayward was a complex, moody man, ruthless in business dealings, sophisticated and fastidious about his pleasures, totally unpredictable in behavior . . . .

"A voracious reader and passionate brain-picker, he could converse intelligently on practically any subject, no matter how esoteric; his range of interests was wide, and besides being the greatest agent of his day, he was also a crack pilot, camera fanatic, art connoisseur, card shark, man's man, and a lady-killer. Hayward was fickle in his affections. All during his romance with Hepburn he had a harem of girl friends; actress Margaret Sullavan gave Kate her stiffest competition."

Merle Oberon peeked out from under a wide-brimmed red hat in the garden of the Beverly Hills Hotel in 1977 and recalled:[11] "Leland was an absolutely fascinating man, and one of the most charming men I've ever met, and he had a face that just glowed with enthusiasm. Oh, he was a salesman! Ernest Hemingway called him the best agent in the world. He was a rarity in Hollywood because he was well-bred. He knew what fork to use, had gone to Princeton and had a very extensive vocabulary—all of which astounded the other agents whose families had come over on the boat. Today, one would say he had 'class.'

"I always say that a man can be judged by his wives—Leland's were all spectacular: Maggie Sullavan, a wonderful actress with a voice no one could ever forget, who had been married to both Hank Fonda and Willie Wyler; Slim, a cover girl and a beauty who had been married to Howard Hawks; and then Pam Churchill, who had been married to Sir Winston's son. I always felt by the time these ladies married him, they had been well prepared for a very hectic life. But with everything, he was a good father to his children, whom he adored."

Albin Krebs noted:[12] "Many of the producers never forgave Mr. Hayward for signaling the beginning of acting and writing talent-raids among all the major studios. Notable among the Hayward haters was Louis B. Mayer of Metro-Goldwyn-Mayer, one of the most powerful men in Hollywood. This did not bother Mr. Hayward, however, in fact, some years later he rubbed things in by persuading his client, James Stewart, to buck Mr. Mayer's effort to get him back on the M-G-M payroll after the actor's World War II service. At Mr. Hayward's urging, Mr. Stewart maintained, successfully, that his service time applied to his contract. The court decision made it possible for many others to abrogate their studio contracts on the same grounds . . . ."

Legends have sprung up about Hayward, many having to do with his acute telephonitis. Writer George Axelrod called him "the Toscanini of the telephone." Edna Ferber, lunching with him at the Brown Derby in Hollywood, became so distraught after he accepted four calls that she not only pulled the phone out of the wall and threw it on the floor, but also added his plate of food! German director Fritz Lang once remarked, "A telephone should have been attached—like a penis—to his body."

Apparently Hayward had underground contacts who informed him about the whereabouts of those whom he wanted to reach. He once located Josh Logan in a remote Cuban village, where he had gone with scenic designer Jo Mielziner to take photographs as inspiration for the backdrops of *Mister Roberts*. Logan still does not know how Hayward found him or discovered that the village had a phone. He once routed Henry Fonda out of the steambath in a hotel at which he was not registered, and ferreted out Jack L. Warner in a villa in the South of France for which he had signed the lease only that morning.

During his last active years, as Hayward became more reclusive, most of his dealings were by long distance telephone. It was said that, unless a client was making at least $3,500 a week, he would not accept their calls.

Finally, when he decided to get out of the talent business, he approached Music Corporation of America. He had a meeting with Jules Stein, who had known him for years but had never realized just how extensive—and well-rounded—Hayward's client list actually was until they got down to discussing figures. Stein admitted that MCA's list was secondary to Hayward's.

MCA bought him out, and Hayward went back to New York to produce plays. His first production was *A Bell for Adano* (1944), followed by Pulitzer Prizewinner, *State of the Union* (1945), *Mister Roberts* (1948), and *Call Me Madam* (1950), *Wish You Were Here* (1952), *Gypsy*, *The Sound of Music*, and *Goodbye Charlie* (1959), and *A Shot in the Dark* (1961). His last play, an Off-Broadway effort, *The Trial of the Catonsville Nine* (1971) was produced just before he died.

Incredibly, he also found time to produce movies—*Mister Roberts (1955), The Spirit of St. Louis* (1957), and *The Old Man and the Sea* (1958).

Leland Hayward and his broadway ilk—before television became an "audition ground"—occasionally went to the famous resorts in the Catskill Mountains to scout working talent. Between Decoration Day and Labor Day, a mass exodus of vacationers, principally from the New York area, trekked to the 500 hotels and 3,000 bungalows featuring every recreational facility imaginable. This lineup of stars appearing at the various hotels would not be unusual:

Nevele: Tony Martin
Concord: Jerry Lewis
Pines: Ritz Brothers
Brown's: Judy Garland
Laurels: Billy Eckstine
Grossinger's: Eddie Fisher
Raleigh: Sammy Davis, Jr. (The Will Mastin Trio)

This so-called "Borscht Belt" was extremely lucrative for performers, who were often booked season after season. Milton Berle, Red Buttons, Sid Caesar, Jack E. Leonard, and Zero Mostel were especially beloved. Big-name headliners could earn from $1,500 to $2,500 a night. Before the heyday of Las Vegas that was a great deal of money indeed. In 1966, show business people earned a total of ten-million dollars from these resorts.

Perhaps the most famous booking agent in those days, according to Joey Adams,[13] was Charlie Rapp, who began his career at age twelve when he wrangled a play-date for his apartment-house superintendent's boy soprano. The fee was $10, which he split with his client.

Rapp came to the mountains in 1938, after booking club dates in New York during the winter. His friend Lou Brandt, who owned the Sagamore Hotel at Lake George, became a client, as did Joe Novack of the Laurel Country Club. When the William Morris Agency ceased booking the Totem Lodge because of a cutback in budget, Rapp became the golden-haired boy. Soon he was booking the Arcady Country Club and the Youngs Gap Hotel and on his way to becoming a success in the Catskills. Other agents were Al Perry, Joe Sweig and the only gentile among the group, Pete Larkin.

Rapp had a booking plan that made a great deal of money for him: he would buy a star for seven days for a guaranteed amount, then book the act for one night stands at seven different hotels. For instance, he would pay comedian Henny Youngman $2,500, selling him to the Tamarack for $1,000 on Saturday night, lower the price to $750 at the Raleigh on Sunday, and during the week he might take $500 for Wednesday night at the Laurels and make deals for the rest of the week. "But," Joey Adams commented, "if there is no demand for Henny on Monday night, he'll sell him for a pound of sauerkraut to the delicatessen on the corner."

The four Mark Brothers in *Duck Soup; left to right*, Chico, Zeppo, Groucho, and Harpo. Zeppo left the act to become an agent. *(Courtesy of Paramount Pictures)*

HOOT
GIBSON
in
'PAINTED
PONIES'
UNIVERSAL JEWEL

BLACKOUT: 1948

Cowboy Star

After the war, my career was washed up. Cowboy pictures were as dead as the Dead Sea. I put Old Jim—you remember, "the most intelligent horse in the movies"—out to pasture, and I had put some money away and was doing nothing but playing a few holes of golf in Palm Springs and flying to New York once a year to see a few new shows. One day this uppity TV kid came along. He looked about twelve years old, but was clever as hell. He knew that I owned a slew of my old features, and he said, "Hey, old timer, let's release 'em to video."

I agreed, and we packaged thirty-nine and do you know what? They were so popular the kid said, "Let's shoot some new ones if you think you can still get on a horse." I didn't take offense, because I knew a lot of tricks that the kid didn't. I saddled up Old Jim, who was still game, and called a couple of my old sidekicks who had acted with me in most of my pictures, and who weren't working either, and we shot several scripts up at a place called Valquez Rocks so that the backgrounds would match when we cut in a lot of the old footage—cattle drives, canyon chases and trick-riding stuff. None of us had changed all that much, and we matched wardrobes to our old shots.

In two years I was so famous I couldn't go into a grocery store without the kids swarming all over me, asking for my autograph. And Old Jim and I started making personal appearances at fairs again. Here I am, sixty years old, more popular than I ever was in the old days. Talk about fate. Imagine, an old geezer like me a multi-millionaire—at this stage of the game!

For the Rex Harrison giraffe-riding scene in *Dr. Dolittle*, trainer Don McLennan and a dozen other men guide the animal—enclosed in a special chute on rails—forward behind the brush. *(Courtesy of 20th Century-Fox)*

"Our Gang" with their trustworthy mascot, "Pete." *(Whitney Stine collection)*

8

THE HUNDRED-PERCENTERS

Trainer

You think I make a lot of money with Geraldine? By the time I pay for boarding, food supplements, vet bills, gas to drive out to the ranch and visit her twice a week, there's not much left. She hasn't worked in fourteen months. Strawberry roans are out this year.

It is an old but true axiom that motion picture and television actors would rather take a beating than work with animals and children, who can steal scenes with the lift of an ear or a toothy smile. Not only must human performers guard against being upstaged by animal performers, but the logistics involved in filming the simplest scene can be exhausting and often unrewarding.

But the filmic exploits of Rhubarb the cat, the feats of Flipper the porpoise, the lumberings of Gentle Ben the bear, the antics of Clarence the cross-eyed lion, and the sundry animals immortalized by Disney from squirrels to mice, frolic over the television tube to high ratings.

The appeal of animal performers is universal; in vaudeville, so-called "dumb acts" were usually included on every bill and were resented, particularly if they were earning more money than human performers—which was sometimes the case. They were also a headache—and a footache—to human performers, especially those who had to follow! Pity the poor act that appeared on the heels of an animal that had made a mistake on stage: the turn could finish before the audience quieted down. The hilarity greeting a recitation of the "out, damned spot!" sleepwalking scene from Macbeth can only be imagined.

One of the most famous acts was the dancing bear, Big Jim. He performed the same routine for many years, and his trainer changed the name of the dance to whatever craze was currently in vogue: Jim waltzed, fox-trotted, bunny-hugged, tangoed, shimmied, charlestoned and black-bottomed. Lockhart's Elephants were also a crowd-pleaser, but probably the most durable were the "drunken dog acts" such as Charles Barnold's, which made $1,000 a week in 1907. Often special booking agents handled animal acts. Their talents may have had to be trained, groomed, and fed, but at least they did not talk back!

"The earliest Hollywood agents were the Hundred Per Centers," wrote Alva Johnson.[1] "[They] came into being in 1914 when Cecil B. De Mille and Jesse Lasky were making their second feature-length picture, *The Ghost Breaker*, with H.B. Warner. In one scene Warner was supposed to be in a dungeon with plenty of rats. As De Mille was getting ready to shoot the scene, he demanded to know where the rats were. The property man said there were no available rats in Hollywood. He had searched high and low, and couldn't find any."

De Mille told him that there better be rats, and plenty of them, the next day.

"The scene was shot satisfactorily. The rats were small, but numerous and chummy. Some of them trotted over to the prisoner, sat up on their haunches and started to lick themselves. White spots appeared on them. The property man had negotiated with the owner of a pet shop for the rent of a troupe of tame white rats and had painted them with lamp black. The pet-shop man became the first Hundred Per Center, or agent who owns his clients in fee simple. There are agents for almost every known animal . . . ."

Aside from occasional rats for specific scenes, the creatures were not used again for mass effect until *Willard* (1971), with Ernest Borgnine, when a young boy makes the rodents do his bidding. As the human star of the picture Ernest Borgnine was offered a percentage but took a straight salary instead—much to his regret when the picture made a mint.

The kind of annuity that all animal trainers dream about is a film or television series, but the work is terribly difficult because each dog, cat, mouse, or bird must have a double or stand-in, and must be capable of constantly learning new tricks.

In the 1930s and 1940s agent Captain Luxford handled

penguins, for which he received $25 for the ordinary kind and double that for a star like Pete, who was endearing in *The Man Who Came to Dinner* and *My Favorite Blonde* (1942).

The only non-human creatures to win an Academy plaque (1948) were the extraordinary birds in Ken Murray's *Bill and Coo*, in which artistry and patience blended in a novel and entertaining use of the medium of motion pictures. Now they have annual Patsy Awards for the top animal performers of the year.

John Kerr, who ran Animaland in Long Beach, supplied a large number of animals including Carmichael, a tarantula who bugged Johnny Weissmuller in a Tarzan film. Curly Twyeford was the person the studios called when they needed birds. Coulson Glick supplied tigers and leopards—one of which was understudied by a Newfoundland dog, groomed and made-up to resemble the star cat. The Korda brothers were introduced to a large dog in a lion suit, with facial makeup so real that it frightened everyone. It was used for scenes in *Jungle Book* (1942), with Sabu. William F. Donohue, owner/trainer of Uno the Mule, made as high as $1,250 a week. Uno was not only famous for his unique hee-haw, but his extremely accurate kick.

Just as appealing as the various moppets that peopled the long-running *Our Gang* one-reel short-subjects was mascot Pete, the white dog with a black ring around his right eye, played by several canines over the span of the 22-year-old series. In most of the tiny plots he was required to do no more than sit about on his haunches appearing photogenic, or run after the gang, but occasionally a bit of action depended upon his active participation. His close-ups, like those of leading female stars, were shot early in the day when he was fresh and alone with his trainer, to be cut into the action filmed later. He is still to be seen on television in some one hundred shorts under the umbrella title of *The Little Rascals*. Jackie Cooper made $50 a week (Pete made more!) while he appeared in several of these shorts from 1929 and 1930, some silent, some sound.

Cooper recalled in his autobiography:[2] "The dog in the *Our Gang* shorts impressed me more than the other kids did. I loved that dog, and one of the great events of my childhood career occurred the weekend Pete Stringer, the man who owned the dog, let me go home with him. To stay a whole weekend with Pete and his dogs was my idea of glory and paradise combined . . . ."

The idea of using a white dog with a black ring around the eye originated with Nipper, the RCA dog with a similar configuration, whose likeness was featured on all His Master's Voice recordings, and extensively used in advertising. Nipper was winningly portrayed in Paramount's *The Emperor Waltz* (1946), in which Bing Crosby played a phonograph salesman whose dog had a romance with a French poodle named Fifi, owned by Duchess Joan Fontaine. But TV's *Tales of a Gold Monkey* (1983) did the genre one better by having the hero/pilot's white dog wear a black eye *patch*!

But biggest canine star of them all was Rin Tin Tin. Warner Brothers' most valuable asset, "the dog" began in France during World War I when an American serviceman, Leland Duncan, found a German Shepherd and her five pups in the wreckage of a bombed airfield. He brought one of the males—Rin Tin Tin, named after the good-luck dolls that pilots placed above primitive instrument panels in their planes—back to Los Angeles, teaching him to perform tricks and to obey voice commands with the hope of getting motion picture work. The dog was intelligent and clever, but had a bad disposition.

In his autobiography,[3] Hal Wallis (later Head of Production for Warner Brothers but in 1922 in charge of publicity) related: "My job was to make the dog internationally famous, and also hide his true nature.... Rin Tin Tin first made his name at a dog show at the Hotel Ambassador in Los Angeles. His picture was published in the *Los Angeles Times*, and Jack Warner signed him to a contract. I took him on a sixteen-week tour across the country. Almost human, he was able to pick up a coin with his nose and put it in a cup, jump up and down on a stool, and count to ten with his paws. I publicized his repertoire of tricks and even arranged a biography to be published. Lee Duncan and Rinty, as the dog was known, went to countless hospitals and sanitariums, cheering up patients. Duncan even taught him to bark in ragtime—a very popular feat . . . ."

"Rinty" had made one feature when he was brought to Warner Brothers, which was having difficulty meeting payroll. This condition was corrected with the help of young writer Darryl Francis Zanuck, who concocted stories built around the dog's gregarious personality. (" . . . . with superhuman effort," Zanuck wrote in a script, "Rinty shakes the bull [dog] off of him, clamps his own fangs on the dog's neck and throws him upwards out of scene.") Rinty reached stardom as an intense, effulgent, inventive, obedient, brave, valiant, trustworthy, intelligent canine, and in performing countless stunts in nineteen films earned Lee Duncan some five million dollars.

"Zanuck's first Rin Tin Tin picture," his biographer, Mel Gussow noted,[4] "a wild yarn full of desperate perils and incredible un-dog-like feats of daring, was about a dog's slavish devotion to his master—which is what could be said about all Rin Tin Tin features. About all that changed were Rinty's stunts and the setting.

"Zanuck had genuine admiration for the dog. 'Rin Tin Tin could do anything,' he said, 'or rather Rin Tin Tins could do anything.' Actually there were about five or six Rin Tin Tins at one time—one for long shots, one for close-ups, one to play the gentle parts, one to fight. Another could jump and do terrific stunts. Another had marvelous eyes . . . ."

When Warner Brothers introduced talking pictures with *The Jazz Singer*, which featured several lines of dialogue along with Al Jolson's singing, all performers under contract took microphone tests to gauge how their voices recorded. Rin Tin Tin was lined up with several Warner beauties for a publicity stunt, and it was finally judged that his voice was in the middle decibel range, which made his bark esthetically pleasing!

No publicity gimmick was overlooked—even in the romance department. He and his German Shepherd mate, Nanette, were a hot "item" and Rinty was even photographed muzzle-to-muzzle with the bitch for *Photoplay* magazine!

In his book on the coming of sound,[5] Fitzhugh Green discussed the sound dilemma: "Taking away the director's voice made quite a difference to one actor, Mr. Rin Tin Tin or 'the dog,' as he is usually known on the lot. They decided to make a talking picture starring Rinty. They wanted his pants and barks and growls and pawings on the door and all that sort of thing.

"But 'the dog' had always followed the special directing of his owner, a tall, athletic, gray-haired chap named Duncan. 'Stop!' 'Lie down.' 'Speak.' 'Go right.' 'Go left.' 'Growl.' 'Sick 'em.' The dog, with almost supernatural understanding, would answer every demand, his eyes fixed on his master, working as hard as he could to do the thing well.

"Now, during the Vitaphone sequences, Duncan couldn't use his voice anymore. Would they be able to make the picture? Duncan thought so. He began working with Rinty, simply using ges-

Gene Autrey and Champion. *(Courtesy of Republic Pictures)*

Gene Autrey in 1950 and his plane, which he piloted to and from location and on personal appearance and radio tours. *(Photo by Cronenweth/Columbia Pictures)*

Ray Milland and the title actor on the set of *Rhubarb*. *(Courtesy of Paramount Pictures)*

Rin Tin Tin, "Rinty," was one of the meanest dogs in the movies—off-screen. *(Courtesy of Warner Bros.)*

tures; motioning right, left, stopping him, beckoning him on. The dog responded marvelously! They were able to get him to do anything they wanted to without saying a word."

Animal trainers have followed Duncan's example to this day. Rin Tin Tin's first talkie was the all-star, two-strip Technicolor extravaganza, *Show of Shows* (1929), which featured every star on the Warner lot. Rinty played a master of ceremonies and introduced a number with a series of barks!

Beginning in 1930, Rin Tin Tin even had his own radio program, a fifteen-minute Saturday show, sponsored by Ken-L-Ration. On NBC for three years, it then switched to CBS for his last year. Rinty did his own distinctive barking and growling, but the rest of his pantings and pawings were provided by human mimics. Twenty-four years later, in 1955, Milk Bone brought "the dog" back on the Mutual Network for a half-hour Sunday show that lasted one season. The German Shepherd—still up to his old tricks of saving everyone on the block—was now owned in the series by a small boy named Rusty.

Usually the radio writers shamelessly included a plug for the sponsor near the end of each program. After a difficult stunt Rusty would chirp: "Okay, Rinty, you've earned your Milk Bone!"

When the original Rinty died in 1932, a eulogy was printed in *Photoplay*. Similarly the famous cat Bonkers, a regular performer on the television soap opera *All My Children* received what amounted to an obituary in the April 19, 1984 edition of *The Hollywood Reporter*, when Alan L. Gansberg reported Bonkers' demise: "He was owned and trained—if one can train a cat—by Jacqueline Babbin, the producer of the series . . . ."

Every day, Bonkers arrived on the set with his owner-trainer at noon, participated in the dress rehearsal, took a break during which time he was groomed, and then performed in the actual taping of the show. He was not paid a salary but worked for carfare, always taking taxis. Gansberg reported that the feline star was survived by Babbin and Azzie.

Rinty's "son," Rin Tin Tin, Jr., starred in several early talkies. In 1976, a movie spoof of dog pictures, *Won Ton Ton—the Dog that Saved Hollywood*, featured a galaxy of cameo star roles and a Rin Tin Tin look-alike, a German Shepherd named Augustus (Gus) von Shumacher playing the title role!

About Gus, producer David V. Picker said:[6] "What we do is use our main lead dog—who's in 99% of the picture—for all the major scenes. Then, if we don't get all the coverage we want, we move on, and the dog works with the second unit to pick up the rest of the material. It does make it a little more complex. But I must say with all the fears and trepidations we had going in, Gus has turned out to be an absolutely wondrous animal. We've had a minimal amount of problems. As a matter of fact, although not on this picture, there have been pictures where I would have preferred to have Gus over some of the actors I've worked with!"

Another famous canine star of the '30s and '40s was Asta, the feisty wire-haired fox terrier owned by Myrna Loy and William Powell in the MGM *Thin Man* series, the ancestor of the dog who played the same role in the Peter Lawford-Phillis Kirk TV series ten years later. Trainer Bill Koehler worked with the dog in the series, as well as with the animals in another TV sitcom, *Please Don't Eat the Daisies* (1965-1967). Koehler, with partner Hal Driscall, was with Disney Studios for 21 years, where they worked with Sam, the sheep dog in *The Shaggy Dog* (1959), the great dane and the spider monkey in *Swiss Family Robinson*, and the Irish setter in *Big Red* (1962), among others. Koehler also trained Bullet, Roy Rogers' dog. In 1965, Koehler picked up the Patsy Award for his cat Syn, the best animal performer for *That Darned Cat*.

Another famed canine, Daisy (a male who played females), barked to fame in some fourteen Penny Singleton-Arthur Lake *Blondie* films (1938-1950) and was even billed as "Daisy" in *Red Stallion* (1947). He had such marquee value that he starred for seven years with Ken Murray in the 1940s in his *Blackouts*, at the El Capitan Theater in Hollywood. Later, the dog Benji exhibited some of Daisy's charm, particularly in *O Heavenly Dog*, (1980) when Chevy Chase is murdered and reincarnated as a dog, so he can solve his own murder—Benji ran away with the picture!

To find the right dog for *Lassie Come Home* (1942) filmed from the famous book by Eric Mowbray Knight, MGM advertised for a "cattle call"—or in this case a "dog call" to be held at Gilmore Stadium at 3rd and Fairfax in Los Angeles. After a reported three hundred dogs were eliminated from the competition, which turned into a howling, barking, canine convention, Director Fred Wilcox called dog-trainer, the late Rudd Weatherwax, to bring a selection of collies to the studio for screen tests.

Still none of the dogs seemed quite right. However there was one left in the station wagon outside—a cull that had been given to Weatherwax to settle a ten-dollar debt. He was named Pal, and his screen test was remarkable: he seemed to embody all of the qualities needed for the role, plus he looked beautiful in the camera lens. It was not unusual for males, which are supposed to be more photogenic, to portray female dogs (of the long-haired variety, obviously) in films, so Pal became the most famous female impersonator of his day.

Lassie and his progeny (sixth generation now) and various stand-ins made a fortune for Weatherwax, who died in early 1968. The dogs continued working intermittently in a series of Lassie films, the last of which was *The Magic of Lassie* (1978), co-starring MGM alumnus James Stewart.

Once tabbed by a reviewer as "Greer Garson in furs," Pal even provided the bark for a radio series when Lassie was airborne in 1947, and his son Laddie appeared in the long-running *Lassie* TV series (1955—1974), also recording the famous bark for an animated TV series from 1973 to 1975. Ephraim Katz reported[7] that, "While in New York for personal appearances on the stage of Radio City Music Hall the dog stayed in a $380-a-day suite at the Plaza Hotel."

Canines and felines, popular as they have always been in films and on television, must share their fame with the simians. In a wry piece in *TV Guide*, Laddie Marshack wrote,[8] "At his peak— or, if you prefer, his apex—C. J. the orangutan was making $500,000 a year for starring in his own NBC series, *Mr. Smith*, and merchandising his name. C. J. was born in the Dallas Zoo and purchased by Ralph Helfer, one of Hollywood's top animal trainers. Before long he was making movies with the likes of Clint Eastwood and Bo Derek. His series was cancelled, but C. J. is unperturbed. Where there's Hollywood, he figures, there's a vine . . . ."

The making of the many Tarzan films, with trained jungle animals doing "turns" would take several volumes to detail. It was not unusual for Cheta the chimp to have the ending all to herself, performing an outrageous stunt in medium close-up. *Bedtime for Bonzo* (1951), starring Ronald Reagan, is now a cult film for obvious reasons and is popular on the rented video cassette circuit.

But literally towering above all screen animals were the trusty steeds of the cowboy stars. The first screen cowboy was kinetic Gilbert M. "Bronco Billy" Anderson (born Max Aronson) who made the historic *The Great Train Robbery* (1903). As a co-founder of Essanay Studios, riding several different horses, he filmed some three-hundred-odd one-reel Westerns. Bronco was the only cowboy to receive an honorary Oscar as a "motion picture pioneer, for contributions to the development of motion pictures as entertainment." The award was made in 1958—38 years after his retirement!

Other horses became as famous as their riders: stone-faced William S. Hart's Fritz, ascetic Ken Maynard's Tarzan, debonair Tom Mix's Tony, austere Buck Jones' Silver, stalwart Rocky Lane's Blackjack, plaintive-voiced Tex Ritter's White Flash, and affable Bill Boyd's Topper.

When director James Cruze was planning to make *The Covered Wagon* for Paramount in 1922, he contacted Colonel Tim McCoy who supplied the Indian extras for the film and acted as technical adviser. McCoy had supposedly lived with the Sioux Indians for a time. Film life appealed to McCoy, not only as an actor, which he became in Zane Grey's *The Thundering Herd* (1923), but as an authority on Western and Indian lore. He often joked that he was the only government-appointed agent in Hollywood!

On the other hand, twenty-year-old Gene Autry was "discovered" in 1927 by Will Rogers, who caught him strumming a guitar while he was supposed to be working as a telegrapher in Chelsea, Oklahoma. Rogers suggested that Autry go to New York and get a job "singin' and playin' " on radio. It was not too much later that Autry and dispatcher Jimmy Long wrote "That Silver-Haired Daddy of Mine," which became identified with him in those days as much as "Rudolph, the Red-Nosed Reindeer" did much later. In the years ahead, although not able to read music, Autry would record some three hundred numbers, most of which he wrote himself.

He cut hit records, appeared on the radio on *The National Barn Dance*, and eventually ended up in Hollywood—or in his case North Hollywood. In his autobiography,[9] he tells it this way: "The minor league studios like Monogram and Mascot were taking a bath. So it happened one day that a man named Nat Levine, owner of Mascot Pictures, was in New York trying to raise money for a

Ken Maynard shoot-em-up. Levine had specialized in Saturday morning serials, such as *Burn 'em Up Barnes*, and one with Clyde Beatty, the wild-animal trainer.

"Levine met with Herbert J. Yates, who owned American Records and Consolidated Film Labs, a processing plant that later became part of Republic Studios. The way it worked, whenever Yates invested in a movie he got the contract for processing the film. He probably developed the prints of ninety percent of the pictures then being made in Hollywood.

"It seemed clear to Herb Yates that the Western movie needed a shot in the arm. He discussed it with Moe Siegel, then the president of American Records, and they agreed that the straight, action Western was a thing of the past. So they met again with Levine, and Yates said, 'Nat, I'll give you the money, but on one condition. We have a fellow who sells a helluva lot of records for us. He's on the radio in Chicago, on a national hookup. Does the 'Barn Dance.' Nat, it would be worth your while to take a look at Gene Autry."

And the Horse Opera was born. The kids who attended the Saturday Matinee had a new idol, their own Gene "Autery," who was clean livin', wore a white hat and gloves, carried a guitar as much as he did a shootin' iron, and never (well, once!) kissed the girl for the fadeout. The kids felt certain that he kissed his horse Champion. He went on to explain in his memoirs, "Let me dispose right now of a malicious rumor that has haunted me all my life. I did not kiss my horse! We may have nuzzled a little, but we never kissed. Never. I can take a joke, but it bothered ol' Champ."

For *Tumbling Tumbleweeds* (1935) Autry used multiple-track recording for the first time with the title song; mixing the track on discs, he was able to sing both the lead and the tenor, creating his own harmony. It is an established practice now on tape, made popular by Les Paul and Mary Ford in the 1950s (Mary had earlier appeared on his radio show).

Gene Autry, turning out films to the tune of one every six weeks, made 93 features from 1934 to 1953, before he turned to television where he cranked out 91 more. His Flying "A" Productions was responsible for other hit series: *Annie Oakley, The Range Rider,* and *Buffalo Bill, Jr.* His horse, the third of the Champions, had his own show, *The Adventures of Champion*.

In the 1930s, just as Mae West and Deanna Durbin saved their respective studios (Paramount and Universal) from bankruptcy, so did Autry's pictures save Republic. But in 1937 Autry discovered while on the road that Papa Yates was heavily into block-booking. In order for a theater owner to book an Autry picture, he was forced to take the entire studio film output. Autry, who was making $40,000 a year for seven or eight pictures, furiously confronted Yates, demanding not only that this "package deal" business be eliminated, but also that he be given a fair share of the profits from his films. Failing to get what he wanted, he went on suspension.

Having already announced the next Autry picture, *Under Western Skies*, Yates cast Leonard Slye, who had been going under the name of Dick Weston, in the lead. And Roy Rogers, a new singing cowboy, was created.

The studio obtained an injunction against Autry working anywhere—even on the road. A new contract was eventually worked out at $10,000 a picture, escalating to $20,000 over seven years. But from his films and personal appearances in 1941 he made $600,000.

Over the objections of the studio in 1942, Gene Autry enlisted in the Air Force, where he remained until after the hostilities ceased. Since his contract had run out during the war he assumed he was a free agent, but Papa Yates thought otherwise and was determined to add the years in service to the end of the contract. Gene realized that he was not only fighting for his own livelihood, but for every other actor who had gone into the military. He hired Martin Gang, the brilliant lawyer, who filed the landmark case against Republic. Autry won the case in Los Angeles, but the studio appealed. While awaiting the decision of the Supreme Court, Gene and Yates got together and made a deal: for a percentage of the profits, he would make five pictures. If Gene won the case he would have his freedom, if not he would finish the contract on the studio's terms.

The Supreme Court upheld the case, and Gene incorporated himself and went to Columbia Pictures to become a hot property all over again, with his faithful sidekick Champion. His radio show *Melody Ranch* had a huge audience, and he made a fortune on the road.

In 1978, Gene's corporation—Golden West Broadcasters—owned four radio stations, KTLA television station, a national agency selling radio-time, a ten-acre movie and television production center, and the California Angels baseball club. Plus, on his own he had the Gene Autry hotel complex in Palm Springs and many other enterprises. Yet it was Champion who achieved a distinction that could not be claimed by any other horse in the world: he has his hoofprints in the concrete in the forecourt of Grauman's Chinese Theater in Hollywood—alongside the bootprints of his master.

But perhaps the best remembered of the latter-day Western stars is winsome, squinty-eyed Roy Rogers (wealth estimated at $100 million from shrewd investments). Billed as "The King of the Cowboys," he assumed Gene Autry's mantle at Republic while Autry was in the service. Rogers came to California in 1929 as an itinerant peach picker, and played bits in many Western pictures. He formed the popular singing group, "The Sons of the Pioneers," with whom he appeared on Los Angeles radio and later in films. In 1947 he married Dale Evans, who became his leading lady. Like Gene Autry, they made a fortune on the road. After Westerns had run out at the box office, he also turned to the tube.

The Roy Rogers Show on TV (1951-1964), starred Rogers as "King of the Cowboys," Evans as "Queen of the West," and featured Trigger, Evans' horse Buttermilk, a diner cook, Pat Brady's jeep Nellybelle, Rogers' dog Bullet, and The Sons of the Pioneers, as well as the saccharine themesong, *Happy Trails To You.* A variety-type program, *The Roy Rogers and Dale Evans Show* lasted only from September 29 to December 23, 1962.

Rogers had his faithful horse, Trigger, "The Smartest Horse in the Movies," and Trigger, Jr., stuffed for posterity, and the remains, along with Bullet and Buttermilk, are on display at the Roy Rogers and Dale Evans Museum in Victorville, California.

Rogers told Bob Thomas of the Associated Press, March 10, 1984: "…. you can't find horses like Trigger to work with. They just don't have the speed, the maneuverability, the response to the rein. They threw away the pattern after Trigger.

"Roy Rogers and Trigger became one during the days when we were making pictures. In the beginning whenever I went on the road, people would ask, 'Where's your horse?' Trigger retired in 1958 and died in 1965 at the age of 33. In all the years we worked together, he never once fell. There were other cowboys in pictures who weren't so lucky. Like Bob Randall who took a fall and broke his neck."

Later in the interview, posing before the rearing Trigger, Dale explained: "I saw a photograph of the funeral of Man o' War, and there he was in a beautiful, satin-lined coffin. I thought that would be the way for Trigger to go. But when he died, Roy insisted that he was going to be stuffed and put in the museum. I was so angry, I said 'All right, but when you go, I'm going to have you stuffed and placed on top of Trigger!' "

Roy added: "I told her just make sure I'm smiling."

Other riders of celebrated horseflesh—the diminutive jockeys, all the way from Santa Anita to Tanforan, from Churchill Downs to Hollywood Park—have big agents. The jockeys are actually "booked" on the various mounts for the day, which leaves them time to concentrate on winning their races and eliminates time-consuming business arrangements that may involve riding some twelve to sixteen horses per week.

In a Willie Shoemaker interview,[10] Kevin Brass related: "Of his first Kentucky Derby win, riding the legendary Swaps in 1955, he says: '[Eddie] Arcaro was aboard Nashua. Swaps was ahead the whole way, then Eddie came around on the turn. I asked Swaps to run and he beat 'em by a length . . . .' "

"His second Derby win with Tommy Lee in 1959: 'I had a chance to ride Sword Dancer, who I had ridden in the Derby trial the week before. I told Harry [Silbert, his agent] that I would rather ride Sword Dancer because I thought he was going to win the Derby. He said, "You can't, because I have already obligated you to Tommy Lee." As luck would have it, I beat Sword Dancer by a nose. If I had my choice, I would have been on the other horse . . . .' "

While horses are sleek and dramatic, jackasses are solid and comic. From 1946 to 1956, Donald O'Connor portrayed Cadet Stirling opposite Francis the talking mule, in seven money-making features: *Francis Goes to the Races, Francis Goes to West Point, Francis Covers the Big Town, Francis Joins the WACs, Francis in the Navy,* and *Francis in the Haunted House.*

Four years later, TV got on the talking-horse bandwagon with Mr. Ed, "the playboy horse of Los Angeles," starring the equine and Alan Young. The show ran until 1966, with one of the most hilarious segments being the guest appearance of Mae West who traded double entendres with Mr. Ed, the voice of which was provided by former cowboy star, Rocky Lane.

What differentiated Francis and Mr. Ed from the Jerry Fairbanks Paramount short-subjects of the Thirties and Forties, *Speaking of Animals*, was that both horses moved their mouths in such a way that they actually seemed to be talking, while the animals in the shorts were required to perform no elaborate tricks, because their moving mouths were animated "cartoon-style."

With Autry and Rogers, it was simple enough to tailor a story around musical numbers. But for longevity, no cowboy can top Bill Boyd, who played romantic heros in silent and early sound films and who parlayed his white-haired Hopalong Cassidy character through countless Westerns, from 1935 to 1948. After that he became a hero to a new generation, through TV syndication of 54 of his old films which he had been wise enough to acquire. He also filmed twelve new pictures, which he produced himself.

Twentieth Century-Fox's *Doctor Dolittle* (1967)—which "did little" at the box-office—was produced by Arthur P. Jacobs and starred Rex Harrison. Starting out with a budget of $12,000,000, it ended up costing $19,000,000 (which included $300,000 for Christopher Plummer when the studio thought Harrison was bowing out). The 58 day shoot in England alone, under terrible weather conditions, included building a central television antenna for the town of Castle Combe, where Doctor Dolittle supposedly lived, so individual antennas could be removed from rooftops.

"Another problem was the training of the animals befriended by Doctor Dolittle." John Gregory Dunne wrote.[11] "Months before shooting began, hundreds of animals had been selected for training at Jungleland in Thousand Oaks, California. Because of the strict quarantine laws in the United Kingdom, two sets of animals had to be trained, one for shooting in Hollywood, the other for shooting in England. All the principal animals in the cast—Jip the Dog, Polynesia the Parrot, Chee-Chee the Chimpanzee, Sophie the Seal and Gub Gub the Pig—had doubles. Pigs grow so rapidly that Jacobs had to replace Gub-Gub every month with a new and properly-sized porker, and both Chee-Chee and Jip had not one but three backups.

"Simulating sound-stage conditions, the trainers at Jungleland constantly flashed lights on the animals and moved among them so that they would not get skittish when finally confronted with the high-powered arcs and the hundreds of people present on the set. Six months were devoted to teaching Chee-Chee the Chimpanzee how to cook bacon and eggs.

"On Stage 20 at the studio, Doctor Dolittle's study was constructed in anticipation of the fact that few of the animals were housebroken. The floor was slightly tilted and fitted with a drain so that it might be hosed off easily. In all, Jacobs spent $1 million simply to train, house, feed and transport the animals . . . ."

Animal trainer Don McLennan, along with co-owner Roy Cabot of Jungleland, supervised the animals used in the film, and it turned out to be a mammoth undertaking. Paid by the week, McLennan eventually walked away with $35,000 in salary because of the innumerable production delays that pushed the film over schedule. "Not all of the delays were caused by the huge variety of animals on the set," McLennan—a wiry, compact man—related at his brother's house in Upland, California, in January 1984,[12] "but Rex Harrison was not only skittish about working with certain species, but complicated scenes involved musical numbers and split-second timing with the animals and birds coming in on cue. Harrison talk/sang the songs 'live' with piano accompaniment, and the orchestra was dubbed in later. It was a nerve-wracking business, where anything could— and did—go wrong."

McLennan, equipped from birth with nerves of steel, had grown up on a farm with horses, and started out in show business as a trick rider with the Clyde Beatty Circus in 1944, having served overseas in a cavalry parade platoon. A member of the William Boyd *Hopalong Cassidy Show* that toured Hawaii in 1947, he had performed stunts "under the belly and over the top," shoulder and tail stands, straight cruppers and many variations of cartwheels. He had also toured with dog, chimpanzee, and elephant acts with various circuses. With his wide background, he was peculiarly suited to the job as head animal trainer for the movie.

The most complex scene—actually the prologue to the film, to be projected on the screen after the overture but before the animated cartoon titles—sounded simple in the script. It called for Harrison, dressed in a frock coat and top hat, to nonchalantly ride a giraffe through a jungle. For six months McLennan worked with the giraffe, first teaching the nervous animal to tolerate a human being on its back, which was in itself no mean feat. Giraffes, unlike horses, cannot be taught to respond to reins. Yet the ride through the jungle had to appear effortless, since all animals respond naturally to Doctor Dolittle, who converses with them.

The scene was finally rigged so that Harrison would be seen riding the giraffe behind some shrubbery, the height of which was determined by an ingenious structure. This apparatus was actually a padded chute mounted on rails, with an opening at each end. The giraffe was coaxed to go in one end and pause while Harrison was helped onto its back.

When the director yelled "Action!" McLennan—hidden by the shrubbery—coaxed the giraffe forward while other men, also unseen, pushed the chute forward on the rails as the giraffe ambled along with the debonair Harrison astride. What looked so simple and unaffected in the camera took the combined efforts of a dozen men, and required numerous takes. "It was one of the most difficult undertakings I've ever been involved in," McLennan said, "and one of the most satisfying when I saw it on the screen."

But the preview audience in Minneapolis did not respond to the film, and cutting was in order. It was unanimous that the prologue slowed down the action, but the scene could not be cut because a photograph of Harrison riding the giraffe had been used in advertising and promotional material.

After much discussion, the studio placed the scene—with new dialogue to explain the action—in a sequence where Doctor Dolittle travels through the island jungle to the sea coast. It was a logical way to include the scene, and it was hoped that the audience would not notice that Harrison was dressed in different clothing in the giraffe scene.

When McLennan watches the movie today, all he can think about is the difficult training of all the animals; humans definitely take second place.

BLACKOUT: 1931

Band Leader

With the Depression so bad, I'm afraid that vaudeville theaters are going to cut way back on prices they pay headliners. Better book me for a long tour at my usual $7,000 a week while you can.

Agent

Don't be an ass. Vaudeville and movies are still the cheapest entertainment the public can buy. I've just raised your price to ten grand a week, and the contract's in my pocket.

Bette Davis, seen here in *The Old Maid* (1938), was the first
Hollywood star to sign with Music Corporation of America.
(Courtesy of George Hurrell)

9

MCA GOES TO HOLLYWOOD

Female Star
Guess who carries a Gucci handbag, subscribes to Women's Wear
Daily, *got good reviews directing a movie, loves to travel, and made
$300,000 last year?*

Starlet
Barbra Streisand?

Female Star
No, my agent!

It was inevitable that Music Corporation of America would
make the trek westward to Hollywood.

The organization had opened an office in Los Angeles in 1932,
but it handled mostly radio. Jules Stein rented a house for a short
while in 1936 to look the town over. "No one knew who I was," he
later remarked, "and the people in the motion picture industry were
very cold." But he felt that when the studios returned to musical
films, business would pick up considerably because he had—or
would have—under contract such talent as Louis Armstrong, Les
Brown, Bob Crosby, Tommy Dorsey, Lionel Hampton, Harry
James, Sammy Kaye, Gene Krupa, Ted Lewis, Vincent Lopez, Guy
Lombardo, Louis Prima, Artie Shaw, Jack Teagarden, Bob Wills,
and many others.

MCA had groomed a young man who would become a key
force in the motion picture industry in the mid-1930s. His name was
Lew Robert Wasserman, whose first job at age twelve was selling
candy in a burlesque house. At 23 he was managing a Cleveland

nightclub, when Bill Stein offered him the job of National Director of Advertising and Publicity at $60 a week. Although it meant taking a cut in salary he joined MCA in December 1936, five months after he had married Edith Beckerman, a clerk at the May Company. During their first six months, money was so tight they shared a Murphy bed.

"When we married," his wife told *Women's Wear Daily*, "we didn't talk along the lines of wealth .... We wanted success, certainly, and I knew he was ambitious. But I never thought of him as an empire builder. In the 1930s all you worried about was where your next dollar was coming from. We were Depression Kids ...."

Austere, tall, thin, and handsome, Wasserman worked like a Trojan, becoming a vice-president of MCA two years later. In 1940 he was named vice-president of the motion picture division. He would become one of the most powerful forces in the country. In a cover profile on Lew Wasserman in the March 1985 issue of *California* magazine, Susan Deutsch noted:[1] "The true scope of Wasserman's influence is hard to measure; his impact on the entertainment industry is only a part of it. His political advice has been solicited by Jack Kennedy, Lyndon Johnson, Jimmy Carter, Governors Brown (both Sr. and Jr.), senators, congressmen and an endless variety of state legislators. In 1952, at the behest of the mayor of Los Angeles, Wasserman drove in an unmarked car into Watts to help quell the riots. In industry strikes, his rumored presence at the bargaining table is enough to give hope to both labor and management that a settlement is in sight. Moreover, had not the interests of Ronald Reagan and Lew Wasserman converged in 1952, it is reasonable to speculate that the incumbent President might otherwise be just another aging actor looking for work ...."

Every contract negotiated contains a story, and one of the most famous concerned beefy Harry Cohn, the vulgar, loud-mouthed head of Columbia Pictures. Co-starring with Cohn in the story is screenwriter/producer Sydney Buchman, one of his top men. Supporting players were Lew Wasserman and Louis B. Mayer.

Buchman was an artist who had written many top pictures, including *Mr. Smith Goes to Washington* (1939), with Jimmy Stewart. He had written and produced *A Song to Remember* (1945), with Cornel Wilde and Merle Oberon among many others. At the height of his powers, Buchman wanted a new deal wherein he would receive $100,000 to write and produce one picture a year, plus fifty percent of the profits. Cohn counter-offered with $50,000 and fifty percent for *two* pictures a year.

The men reached an impasse; neither would give in. Buchman let his current agent go and hired Wasserman. As Bob Thomas told the story,[2] "Wasserman telephoned Cohn with the news: 'I'm representing Sidney Buchman.'

" 'The hell you are,' said Cohn.

" 'Well, I am, and he's leaving your lot,' Wasserman announced.

"Cohn maintained a stony silence with Buchman. Meanwhile, Wasserman was lining up a contract for Buchman with Louis B. Mayer, who was eager to have him work for MGM. After a week Cohn buzzed Buchman and asked him to come to the office. Cohn asked about the MGM deal, and Buchman explained it to him. As they talked, Cohn received a telephone call from his wife.

" 'I got a dirty bastard in my office,' Cohn said.

"When Mrs. Cohn learned he was speaking of Buchman, she insisted that he come for dinner at the house that night.

" 'She's killing me on this thing,' Cohn explained. 'She keeps telling me I'm making the mistake of my life.'

"The evening at the Cohn residence was strange and silent. After dinner, Cohn followed Buchman out to his car and seemed not to want him to leave. Finally he asked where they had gone wrong in their relationship, and Buchman reiterated what he wanted.

" 'It's too late. I haven't the face to tell Wasserman and Mayer that I can't take their deal. They'll think I've been stringing them along, trying to get the terms out of you. There's only one way to do it; you've got to call Wasserman and Mayer and explain to them what happened. You may have to ask Mayer to do it on a favor basis.' "

Cohn swallowed his pride, made the calls, and Buchman stayed on the Gower lot.

Because Wasserman judged the scripts that the studios submitted to his clients, Jack L. Warner, who was not fond of agents and barred MCA from his studio for a time in the late 1940s, used to quip, "Well, we passed (or flunked) the Wasserman Test!"

Music Corporation of America's entry to Hollywood had come about in 1938 through band leader/singer Harmon Oscar

Nelson, who was married to Bette Davis. Nelson was handled by Lester Luisk, whom Stein hired, and the wooing of Davis began in earnest.

After Stein signed Davis—who had just won an Academy Award for *Jezebel* and was going into her big box office years—it was only a matter of time before other stars got on the bandwagon. Warner Brothers players John Garfield, Errol Flynn, Ronald Reagan, and Jane Wyman came in, and the rush was on. Soon MGM's Clark Gable, Greta Garbo, Van Johnson, Myrna Loy, and James Stewart joined the fold, along with Paramount's Paulette Goddard, and David O. Selznick's Joseph Cotten.

Theater clients would include Barbara Bel Geddes, Carol Bruce, Mildred Dunnock, Buddy Ebsen, Celeste Holm, Victor Jory, Fredric March, Dorothy McGuire, Ethel Merman, Dame May Whitty, and many more. Among nightclub clients were Victor Borge, Carl Brisson, Hildegarde, Dwight Fiske, and Jerry Lester. Later, Music Corporation of America via its pension fund for employees also invested in Broadway plays like *Dear Ruth*, written by client Norman Krasna, which bowed on Broadway in December, 1944, at a cost of $40,000 and went on to gross over $1,000,000. Stein also invested in *State of the Union*, produced by MCA vice-president Leland Hayward, who had just sold his agency to Stein.

There was a saying in Hollywood that "sooner or later every major film star would end up at MCA"—which was not far from wrong. One of the last holdouts was Clark Gable.

Gable had played his first "important" small part in Pauline Frederick's 1926 West Coast stage production of *Madame X*. But the 25-year-old actor had attracted scant attention, except from his leading lady, with whom he was having an affair although he was married to Josephine Dillon, the woman who had discovered him.

It all began for "the Big Lug" in Portland, Oregon, in 1923. Miss Dillon was a somewhat dowdy but interesting actress, 39 years old, who earned a B.A. at Stanford University in 1908. She had gone to Oregon from Los Angeles to operate a theater group, and Gable's fiancee, actress Franz Dorfler, recommended that he enroll.

Miss Dillon was a fine teacher and an inspired drama coach. She perceived there was something about this tall, over-sized clumsy oaf that made women sit up and take notice. Gable had a devil-may-care attitude that was totally winning. He confessed that he had wanted to become an actor ever since he had seen a production of *The Bird Of Paradise* in Akron at the age of fifteen.

It was Miss Dillon's business to scout for talent, and Gable was not without some stage experience; his first job in the theater was as a backstage call-boy, and he had performed some comedy parts. There was about him a wonderfully open, vulnerable quality, and he was so masculine! Due to a variety of manual jobs—from tool-dresser on oilwells in Bigheart, Oklahoma, to lumberyard work in Silverton, Oregon—Gable had acquired a brawny physique. He had a big head on bigger shoulders and a small waist, a body that called out for tailored clothes, which he would not be able to afford for many years.

Whether or not her interest in him was sexual at that first meeting is unknown. Nevertheless, as his studies continued—as unlikely as it may seem—a romance did develop. He all but forgot about Franz. (She turned up in 1935, working as a domestic for his agent, Bert Allenberg, and testified on his behalf in a trumped-up paternity trial.) His taste now was for older women, who would become legion: among them, leading ladies of the stage Jane Cowl, Pauline Fredericks, and later young Joan Crawford who also mothered him to an extent. There were many women in his life, always one at home to come home to if he chose, because he needed "looking after." (Even when he married the love of his life, Carole Lombard, he called her "maw" and she called him "paw.")

Under Miss Dillon's tutelage he lost his lanky gait and developed a confident walk; she taught him how to turn his whole body instead of twisting at the torso; she made him practice throwing his shoulders back and carrying his chin at a slightly higher angle so that his short, bull neck would not be as apparent.

She lectured him upon the importance of keeping his face serene, not to grimace when he spoke, which emphasized his dimples. With time and effort she was able to eliminate several annoying mannerisms which, she was sad to note, gradually crept back after their divorce and he became famous. Gable was a willing pupil: his thirst for knowledge was great, and he listened and obeyed every direction. It was only later that the schoolmarm/student relationship palled. Being an actor was the most important goal in his life. And he wanted to go to Hollywood.

Miss Dillon taught him to use his big, work-scarred hands as an asset by not calling attention to them, although he was always conscious that they were there—like a bunch of bananas—and she advised that he perform with a sober expression, because his teeth were bad. Later she paid to have his two front teeth pulled and replaced with gold caps, which he painted white for stage roles. Realizing that he had what amounted to a grammar school education she gave him books to read, and coached him incessantly on pronunciation and projection. She sought to lower his voice, which became high-pitched when he became excited.

"You're an actor, Clark," she would say again and again, "and audiences pay money to not only hear the lines but to understand them! You can't give any sort of performance until you can speak with complete authority." He read aloud for her constantly, and, under her prodding, his diction improved to the point where he lost his rather nasal Ohioan regional accent. He became interested in Shakespeare, and read the classics. She taught him how to give a "cold reading"—necessary for auditions, where actors were cast on the strength of reading lines without proper study.

Miss Dillon's work with him had only just begun when she decided to improve her finances by returning to Hollywood and opening another school for movie hopefuls. After working in a stock company, Gable came to Los Angeles in the summer of 1924. They were married December 18. The marriage—some said a loveless one—lasted until April 1, 1930. Those were six years of bit parts in movies, doing various plays in touring companies with one three-month run on Broadway with *Machinal*, years in which Miss Dillon's coaching came into fruition for Gable. He became an assured, polished performer with star quality.

During those six years he had lived everywhere but home. He was now seriously involved with a divorcee, 44-year-old Ria Langham, a Houston socialite with five children. (Three of her own and two stepchildren. They would marry March 31, 1931, in a formal white wedding.) After a couple more plays came the turning-point—*The Last Mile*, with Gable playing a killer named Mears, which opened at the Majestic Theater in Los Angeles on June 7, 1930.

As producer/director Mervyn LeRoy described the event in one of his autobiographies:[3] "The curtain went up. On the stage is a jail scene, showing cells. A man was standing there, his hands up on the bars, just looking. He was the most powerful-looking man I had ever seen. Before he opened his mouth, you knew he was going to be good. Merely the way he stood there had authority. Just the way he moved made you forget it was only a play. It was real. I shall never forget it.

"I could hardly wait until the show was over to go backstage and see him . . . . I pushed through the crowd and said: 'I want to see Mr. Gable.' It was difficult to get through, because he had three agents, but I finally reached him.

" 'I'm Mervyn LeRoy,' I said, 'I'm from Warner Brothers. I want to make a test of you.'

" 'I'd be highly honored,' he said.

"He came out to Warner Brothers and I made a test of him for the part of Joe Massara in *Little Caesar*, which I was about to direct . . . ."

LeRoy showed the test to Jack Warner and Darryl Zanuck and begged them to cast him in the picture, but they replied that his ears were too big. LeRoy commented, "Today Warners would give a great deal just to release Gable's ears."

The most formidable thing about Gable in those days was his motion picture agent, Minna Wallis, who had discovered him in *The Last Mile*. She had opened a talent agency with a bright woman, Ruth Collier, capitalized with a thousand dollars borrowed from Myron Selznick.[4]

Minna told Gable he couldn't be filmed with painted-over gold teeth, and he went to a dentist who performed the necessary extractions, providing him with a masterful partial denture that was undetectable on the screen. Because of a long upper lip, he later added a flattering mustache which distracted attention from the slight bulge of the plate.

He made a screen test at MGM, at the insistence of Lionel Barrymore with whom he had appeared in *The Copperhead*. The test turned out to be ridiculous. For some reason he was photographed in a South Sea costume with a flower behind his ear. "Why on earth," Howard Strickling, head of publicity, said later, "anyone would draw attention to his ears is beyond comprehension, or even why they bothered to test him in that absurd costume is anybody's guess. It had nothing to do with my department."

When Warner Brothers turned Gable down for a contract,

Wallis took him to MGM in December 1930, after she had convinced Pathe to cast him in *The Painted Desert*, with William Boyd. She then persuaded Warner Brothers to use him in a small part in *The Night Nurse*, with Barbara Stanwyck, but he did not create a stir. The studio, planning to use him as a heavy, signed him to a twelve-month contract at $650 a week. Gable had always been tight with his money, and now he began to save assiduously.

In the meantime Josephine Dillon still continued to coach actors, sometimes referring to Gable bitterly, sometimes tenderly, depending upon her mood. She made only enough money to be able to get along. By the late 1950s she was almost destitute.

Minna Wallis continued to handle Gable until after Frank Capra, who had directed Gable in *It Happened One Night* (1934), showed a print of the picture to his agents, Phil Berg and Bert Allenberg, who were impressed and wanted to handle him. Lyn Tornabene wrote:[5]

"Berg went to Ruth Collier and Minna and said, 'We'll give you twenty-five thousand for Gable's contract.'

"That's Phil Berg's story.

"Minna Wallis says, 'Not true. Not true at all. I wish it had been. Money never entered into it. Clark and I talked it over thoroughly. Then I talked to Bert Allenberg who was a darling man—used to golf with Clark—and we decided that's what he wants, that's what he can have.

" 'Well, I was just a woman. This was a big organization. I was upset; can't say I wasn't hurt. But Clark was the one to be considered. And if he had stayed with me, he would have been unhappy no matter what I did, and I probably couldn't have done the things Bert Allenberg did for him. Bert worshipped him, and he was crazy about Bert.'

"Phil Berg insists money was exchanged. 'We didn't steal clients,' he says, 'we bought them. In fact, I was the one who *started* buying contracts.'

"Whether Clark was bought, stolen, or given away, he signed with Berg/Allenberg, but remained a friend of Minna's all his life. Rumors still persist that they were lovers, but proof of that is as impossible to produce as the check that passed from Berg to Wallis. 'It was a relationship that is difficult to explain,' Minna says, 'I adored him, just adored him. He was sweet and wonderful to me always.' "

Wallis went on to say that Gable, George Brent, John Barry-more, and Errol Flynn looked upon her as a mother figure.

" 'I remember one night he [Gable] came here for a dinner party. We were playing cards or something and he said, 'Minnie, who's that handsome guy in that picture over there?' I said, 'That was you, twenty years ago.' He loved to tease me: he was my friend . . . .' "

But Wallis remained his lifelong friend, even sending him books during his last days in the hospital.

When performing on the stage, Gable had relied on techniques that Miss Dillon had taught him. He had performed capably, but he was an actor as much born for film as was Bette Davis: it was their medium. The basic secret of Gable's success was that a certain inherent sexuality came over stridently in the camera, a quality not always apparent on the stage. Women moviegoers fantasized that he would literally sweep them off their feet and carry them to the boudoir (as he did Vivien Leigh in *Gone With The Wind*), where he would be brusquely tender, but dominate them completely. (In fantasy, with Gable, it was always the missionary position.)

With all of Gable's great charm and sexual presence, it was surprising that other men did not find him a threat; instead they wanted to emulate this big, rugged guy. He was a ladies' man and a man's man. Outside of matinees, equal numbers of men and women attended, enjoyed, and were influenced by Gable's films.

He continued to save and invest his money when he became "The King." The end of his big box office years at MGM included *Boom Town* with Lana Turner, *Comrade X* (1940) with Hedy Lamarr, *They Met in Bombay* with Rosalind Russell, *Honky Tonk* (1941) with Lana Turner, and *Somewhere I'll Find You* (1942) with Turner again.

His marriage to Carole Lombard ended with her death in January 1942. Grief-stricken at 41, he went into the Air Force as a private, coming back to MGM in 1945 a captain, bringing with him the Distinguished Flying Cross and the Air Medal.

Like many Hollywood stars who had gone into service, his career was never quite the same after the war. He was paunchy, middle-aged, and his face had its share of wrinkles. Phil Berg did what he could for him; Gable's salary was $525,000 a year. He made a succession of twenty mediocre films, from *Adventure* (1946) with Greer Garson to *It Started in Naples* (1960) with Sophia Loren. Often his leading ladies were young enough to have been his daughters.

He married twice again. The marriage to Lady Sylvia Ashley lasted from 1949 to 1951, when they were divorced. With Kay Williams Spreckles, whom he married in 1955, he seemed to recapture some of the personal happiness of the Lombard days.

Agent Phil Berg retired in June of 1949, and Gable never spoke to him again. Berg sold out to Allenberg, who merged with the William Morris Agency in December, taking Gable with him.

Gable continued making pictures, but it was not the same without Berg. After meeting the austere but personable George Chasin, Gable decided to cast his lot with MCA. Chasin told Gable that Hollywood was changing; the way to keep money was to establish a foreign residence for eighteen months and make films in Europe. Chasin looked into the Gable contract, which was about to run out at MGM, and after many complicated maneuvers Gable left for Europe on May 6, 1952. While there he shot *Never Let Me Go* with Gene Tierney in England, *Mogambo* with Ava Gardner and Grace Kelly in East Africa, and *Betrayed* with Lana Turner in Holland. He returned to Hollywood on December 13, 1953, his exile over and his 23-year tenure at MGM finished.

George Chasin wrangled $400,000 and ten percent of the gross at Fox for Gable's participation in *Soldier of Fortune* with Susan Hayward, and *The Tall Men* with Jane Russell. He then formed a company that included Jane Russell and her husband Robert Waterfield, called Russ-Field Gabco Productions, under which he produced *The King and Four Queens*.

Chasin did well by his client, but much of the magic was gone from the Gable performances; although still rugged-looking he appeared older than his age, and he continued drinking and smoking.

In 1960 Gable was ready for retirement when Chasin sent him a highly articulate, but rather strange script—Arthur Miller's *The Misfits*. Gable was wanted to play the role of a penniless cowboy, Gay Langland, who captures wild mustangs for slaughter. Marilyn Monroe, Miller's wife, was to play the fey romantic lead. The offer was $70,000—more than Gable had ever made on a single picture. He was still hungry for money.

As Barry Norman noted:[6] "Gable was at breakfast with Al Menasco, a wealthy businessman and his closest friend, when the producers arrived to find out whether he would play the part or not. As he went out to spring on them what he thought would be his unacceptable demand for the extra 250,000 dollars, he said to Menasco: 'This won't take long. Keep my coffee warm.' He was away for more than half-an-hour and returned, according to Menasco with a bemused expression on his face. All he said was: 'They took it.'"

Chasin, who also handled Monroe and Miller, was a realist; he had a clause in Gable's contract that, if shooting should go over the specified schedule, the actor was to be paid $48,000 a week extra. He was also to receive ten percent of the gross.

Gable arrived on the sandy desert location in Nevada and started work on July 1. He did all of his own stunts involving the horses, which actors twenty years his junior would have refused to do. There was delay after delay. The last shot was completed at Paramount on November 4, and the film was finally wrapped. He was totally exhausted. The only bright incident occurred on location when his wife told him that she was pregnant. At sixty he was to be a father, and he was delighted.

On November 16, 1960, Gable died in the hospital having suffered a heart attack ten days before.

On February 2, 1961, *The Misfits* was released. It brought Gable his best reviews since *Gone With The Wind*, but it failed to make money.

On March 20, 1961, Gable's son John Clark was born.

Josephine Dillon was remembered in his will. Gable gave her the modest house on Landale in North Hollywood, where she had lived for so many years. Gable had gone out like the King he was, but he could not take that last million dollars with him.

On the other side of the spectrum from the "Big Lug" image was the "Frozen Face" persona of Alan Ladd, who also eventually ended up with MCA.

When *This Gun For Hire* opened in May 1942, starring Alan Ladd and Veronica Lake, the public saw a new type of star—an anti-hero, an unsmiling, expressionless tough guy, steely-eyes shaded by a hat, and a tense, compact body encased in a trenchcoat. It seemed that Alan Ladd was born with a gun in his hand. That was the image. The public would never see the relaxed pleasant, rather religious, kindly father that he was in those days. There was a dignity and a sweetness about Ladd that would last all of his life.

Audiences realized that they were looking at a new star. Although Ladd had appeared in small roles in dozens of films, all they could see in him now was "Raven"—the stony-faced killer. The public also assumed that he was taller than five-feet-five, an illusion created by casting Veronica Lake (five-feet-two) opposite him. Ladd and Lake made an exciting team, the handsome, terse man and the beautiful, laconic woman. However, the chemistry that came over on the screen was not as apparent on the set. Actually, the star of the picture was supposed to be Lake, who had garnered wonderful reviews in *Sullivan's Travels* (1941) opposite Joel McCrea, but it became Ladd's picture because he was creating a new screen character.

Alan Ladd was born in Hot Springs, Arkansas, in 1913. His family moved to North Hollywood three years later. He was an athlete in high school, then took a variety of jobs trying to break into show business—he worked on a newspaper and in a gas station, operated a hot dog stand, became a lifeguard, and was even a grip at Warner Brothers. His first bit was in *Once in a Lifetime* (1932).

Ladd was one of the very few bit players to become a major star. In all probability, he could not have bridged the gap but for the tenacity of agent Sue Carol. She had been born Evelyn Lederer in October, 1903 (or 1907, or 1910), of a prominent Chicago family. She had a beautiful heart-shaped face, and her figure had an exciting soft look. While on vacation with her mother in Los Angeles after a divorce from her first husband, she became a starlet, and was introduced by actor Nick Stuart, whom she later married, to casting director Joe Egli at Fox. Her name was changed to Sue Carol (Lederer, she was told, was "too Jewish!").

Her first film was *Slaves of Beauty* (1927), (appearing as one of the slaves) and her last film was *A Doctor's Diary* (1937) at Paramount. Having divorced Stuart in 1934, she married writer Howard Wilson in 1936. A sensitive performer, Carol realized that Hollywood stardom was not the sum-total of a great career, and she had an undeniable maternal instinct. With her first-rate motion picture connections, good friends suggested that she go into the talent business.

"Not only are you pretty," agent Henry Willson told her, "but you've got brains! Because you know the business so well and also know everyone worth knowing in town, it's a logical step. The only other female agent of note is Minna Wallis, and your contacts are different from hers."

"But I can't ask my friends to switch over to me!"

"You don't need to," Willson replied affably. "You know what to look for—go out and discover new talent."

In 1938, with Bruce Shed, she opened an office in the Talmadge Building on Sunset Strip. The partnership lasted barely a year. When Shed left, Sue Carol and Associates and the Sue Carol Theatrical Agency came into being.

Of the meeting of Sue Carol and client Alan Ladd, Beverly Linet wrote:[7] "There have been many versions of what happened next. In the most recent one—probably the closest to the truth— Sue recalled: 'Someone said I should listen to a radio show that had a talented fellow on it who was so versatile that he played two parts—an old man and his grandson. I was intrigued, and tuned in. That was the first time I heard Alan's voice. I thought he was remarkable. I had no idea what he looked like or what his personality was like. I didn't know a thing about him except that he was a good radio actor and I wanted to meet him, so I phoned the station and asked him to drop by the office.'

"And Alan told it this way: 'She thought I'd be sixty years old. We were both glad I wasn't.'

"Sue's first impression would be indelible: 'He was very shy, but he had a wonderful smile. His eyebrows and his eyelashes were pitch-black over level green eyes which were deep and unfathomable—an actor's eyes. He was for me.' "

She did not disappoint him. She brought up the name of Alan Ladd constantly. During the next two years, he was cast in more than twenty pictures, playing everything from a seasick passenger in *Rulers of the Sea* at Paramount for $250 a week to the British flyer in *Joan of Paris* at RKO for $750 a week. Bigger checks came from radio work; he was considered to be a reliable actor who could play any age, and he often appeared to advantage working with such stars as Bette Davis.

Carol was married and the mother of a child, Carole Lee. Ladd had been married for five years and had a boy, Alan Ladd, Jr. (who would one day be president of Twentieth Century Fox studios, and then after several shuffles along the main power line would become head of both MGM Films and United Artists Corporation on March 13, 1985). No one in Hollywood could pinpoint exactly when the business relationship turned into a romance between Carol and Ladd.

Said Henry Willson, "I'd seen male agents make a fool of themselves trying to get their girlfriends—who had large breasts and little talent—parts in pictures; but with the shoe on the other foot, Sue was completely opposite. She was never foolish. With Alan she knew that she had something to sell—she had an instinct about talent. As far as the romance angle, I think they were both in love long before either one realized it, and they were very right for each other. I don't think it ever bothered them that she was so much older.

"She was not a driven woman; she kept her femininity," Willson continued, "but she was persistent and she had him up for every role in town. She would actually cut his price for larger parts, because she wanted decent film on him. She was as certain of his talent as Johnny Hyde was later of Marilyn Monroe's—but there was one great difference. Sue was there to enjoy his fame when it came, Johnny Hyde was dead . . . ."

Ladd received his divorce in July of 1941, and Carol obtained her freedom in March 1942. They were married twice, once in Mexico on March 15, then again (to be certain the ceremony was legal) in Santa Ana on July 22.

Now happily married, Carol decided to give up her agency. She did not need the money, and she thought vaguely that she might go into interior decorating. Also, she felt it would be awkward if she continued to handle her husband. He would be in the big league, and she felt a more influential contact would be helpful to his career. She also needed an ally that would bolster Ladd's self-assurance.

Although confident of his ability as an actor, he was haunted by the fear that he would be a flash-in-the-pan and end up in bit parts the way he had started. While he was not parsimonious, he saved saved and invested his money wisely, becoming a multi-millionaire through stock investments and oil wells, owning an office building on Wilshire Boulevard, an estate in Holmby Hills, two ranches, a house, and—to his great joy—a hardware store in Palm Springs. Carol and he would have two children of their own: Alana, born in 1943, and David, born 1947.

But with his inward insecurity he began to drink, socially at first, and then heavily. Alcohol would be his undoing, as it was with so many stars.

Music Corporation of America was interested in representing him. However, Carol had known Bert Allenberg for years, and she made a deal with him whereby she would receive half of the agency commission of ten percent. Years later, MCA would become Ladd's agent.

By 1951 Ladd was making $100,000 a picture, which was raised $50,000 plus ten percent of the gross when he left Paramount for Warner Brothers in 1952. At Paramount he became the big star that Carol had envisioned. If his leading ladies were taller than he, as was usually the case, in scenes where they were standing together he was either perched on a box, or they were standing in slit-trenches. Some of his films almost had to be "choreographed"— nothing new in Hollywood, since many leading men were short—so that his vis-a-vis was sitting while he was standing, or vice versa. Long shots were avoided while they were standing side by side.

He made 46 pictures after *This Gun for Hire*, but he will probably be remembered best for *Shane* with Brandon de Wilde, Jean Arthur, and Van Heflin, for which he received the best reviews of his career. Brilliantly directed by George Stevens and shot on locations in the Grand Tetons, the picture made some $9,000,000. He was back in the top-ten box office stars, the first time since 1947.[8]

In 1956, June Allyson made *The McConnell Story* and fell in love with him. In her memoirs,[9] she related: "Sue .... never left the camera area, I was told. She watched every scene and every shot— and all shots had to favor Alan, even to the detriment of his leading lady ....

"I had said that I didn't worry about those things—I just concentrated totally on the person I was involved with in the scene and left the professional cameraman to handle the rest. If they wanted the back of my head, so be it.

"And then I was given the final warning. Alan was a very cold and distant man, they said.

"Again I said, 'Don't worry. I'm there to do a job, not hold a tea party.'

"I gathered from my first day of working with Alan Ladd that everything I had been told was true. Sue was indeed giving all kinds of suggestions and orders and Alan wasn't opening his mouth ....

Sue did his talking and he merely listened impassively . . . ."

Ladd did warm up emotionally, but Allyson intimates that they were never intimate.

His films during the next eight years were mostly disappointing. He had produced *13 West Street* in association with Columbia Pictures, and had made an abortive film in Italy, *Horatio*, finally released in the United States as *Duel of Champions* in 1964. Some called him a defeated man.

He then played Nevada Smith in what amounted to a supporting role in his last film, *The Carpetbaggers*, with George Peppard, Elizabeth Ashley, and Carroll Baker. The picture, a return to the lush productions of the old days, was ironically shot at Paramount, where he had not worked in a decade. To the studio's credit he was given the star treatment, including a large dressing room. The film was released on July 2, 1964, and made money, but the critics took little notice of Ladd.

Alan Ladd was found dead in bed by his butler on January 28, 1965. The cause of death, according to doctors, was accidental—a reaction to a combination of depressant and ethanol.

Wearing black with a dark veil, Sue Carol, accompanied by her children Alana and David, attended the funeral services at Forest Lawn in Glendale. Although ten years older than her discovery, Sue Carol had outlived him . . . . something, it was said, that she had never even considered.

Rosalind Russell was a latecomer to the fold of MCA. At 21, having graduated from the American Academy of Dramatic Arts in 1929, she was first handled in New York by the Chamberlain Brown Agency. She was booked into the summer stock season of 1929 and 1930 at Saranac Lake, where she appeared in 26 parts in as many weeks. She played on Broadway in *Garrick Gaieties* (1930) and *Company's Coming* (1931), but was discovered by a Universal Pictures talent scout while appearing in a "subway circuit" play, *The Second Man.*

Russell had great bargaining powers, which never left her. In her memoirs[10] she noted: "Gazing at the man from Universal, a representative from that other planet, I told myself to act large. You have to act large with these people, or you're dead, I silently advised Rosalind, then I spoke. 'I want seven hundred fifty dollars a week.'

"The Universal man wasn't offering half that, so I went home.

"By the time I reached the apartment, the phone was ringing. 'Let's talk some more,' said Mr. Universal.

"I knew I had him.

" 'You don't know anything about me,' I said, 'and I don't know whether I can act in films. I don't even know whether I want to. But I'll tell you what I'll do. I'll go to Hollywood and you can test me. You can test me every day for two weeks. You'll pay my fare both ways, my hotel expenses, and a hundred dollars a test. If you think I'm worth it after you see the tests, you'll sign me at seven hundred fifty dollars a week. If you don't like me after you see the tests, I'll come home.' "

While Russell was still doing the tests at Universal, actress Charlotte Wynters, married to actor Barton MacLane, suggested she do a test at MGM. The test was excellent, but at that point Universal decided to give her a contract. Since she preferred MGM, she and Charlotte formed a plan. When Russell went to be interviewed by Junior Laemmle, the head of Universal, she would make herself look tacky, wearing good clothing, but everything a bit off-key. She made her hair stringy, spoke through her nose, looked unhappy, and frequently mentioned her mother. With great relief, Laemmle gave her a release. She promptly went home, washed her hair, bathed, changed clothing, and went to MGM.

Russell was content to play "the other woman" in many of her early films, and was frequently loaned out, as in *Craig's Wife* (1936) at Columbia. But she was at her best in *The Women* (1939) with Norma Shearer and Joan Crawford, in *His Girl Friday* (1940) with Cary Grant—a remake of *The Front Page*, for which Howard Hawks changed the male part of Hildy Johnson to a woman for her. Seven years and 27 pictures later, she went out on her own to freelance, the wisest move of her career, even though Louis B. Mayer offered her $7,500 a week to stay.

In 1941 she had married Frederick Brisson, who had been introduced to her by Cary Grant. The wedding took place in Solvang. Four years younger than Russell, he was born March 17, 1912 in Cophenhagen, Denmark, the son of actor Carl Brisson. He was an associate producer and publicist on his father's last two British films, and was the advance man for Moss Empires, Ltd., an organization that owned all of the legitimate theaters in England. He produced *Moonlight Sonata*, with Ignace Paderewski, and became a junior partner of Frank W. Vincent.

Brisson, by the time of his arrival in Hollywood, had several famous clients, but declined to take over the agency when Vincent retired. He wanted to get into the production end of both films and theater. He produced a number of New York shows, including *The Pajama Game* (1954), *Damn Yankees* (1955), *Under the Yum-Yum Tree* (1960), and *Coco* (1969).

One Sunday in early 1954, Russell called Doris Stein to discuss a costume ball. The conversation turned to career matters, and Russell laughed. "I've handled everything myself for quite a while, but I'm thinking about doing a musical version of *My Sister Eileen* in New York, and I suppose I should have an agent. Is Jules home?" And that is how Russell became a client of MCA, beginning with *Wonderful Town*.

Many middle-aged actresses envied Russell because Brisson produced starring vehicles for her during slow periods in her film career. However, he was not connected with her greatest critical successes, *Picnic* (1955) and *Auntie Mame* (1958). He produced only five of her films: *The Velvet Touch* (1948), *Never Wave at a WAC* (1953), *The Girl Rush* (1955), *Five Finger Exercise* (1962) and her last film, *Mrs. Polifax—Spy* (1971), which required careful photography because her arthritis medication caused her face to swell.

When Russell died on November 28, 1976, she was home with her husband just the way she would have wanted it . . . .

BLACKOUT: 1939

Female Star

But how can I be broke? I make eighty-five thousand a picture, and my radio take is twenty-two thousand!

Manager

It's easy. Income tax takes a big bite. Then there's the yacht. I begged you not to buy it . . .

Female Star

It was James who wanted the *Empress* to run back and forth to Catalina on weekends. He made the trip twice if I remember. Since the divorce, it's been in dry dock.

Manager

That's another thing. It cost you twenty thousand and two years alimony to get rid of dear James. Then you're sending your sister's two boys to Amherst. Your mother's expenses are high since she had the stroke and has to have a nurse. Your older brother is into you for eighteen thousand five. Your sister has never paid you back for the downpayment on her house in Riverside. The apartment house on Elmhurst Drive has six vacancies.

Female Star

Thank God, Clarence has money. At least he will go fifty/fifty with me when he moves in . . . I think we'll elope to Acapulco. With this marriage I don't want a lot of publicity.

Manager

Clarence's Dunn & Bradstreet rating is not very high, you know. He has alimony on two past wives, and his kids are in school in Switzerland. His dad is in a rest home. I don't think you can count on him very much in that direction. How about cutting down on the cars? You've got a Cadillac, a Rolls, and your housekeeper is driving a Bentley.

Female Star

That housekeeper, as you call her, is my cousin.

Manager

So a cousin should drive a Bentley?

Director Alfred Hitchcock, *right*, **and Joan Fontaine on the set of** *Rebecca.* *(Courtesy of Henry Willson collection)*

10

SELZNICKS AT THE TOP

Charlton Heston
*Even in movies, all the various crafts and professions involved in film
are usually drawn very maliciously and pejoratively. But of all the
professions involved in film, the one that is usually represented most
unfavorably is that of agents. They're usually presented as lying,
hypocritical, cheating, totally tasteless men who wear checked suits.
I, in fact, am not much of an expert on agents, because I've only had
one in my whole career.*

George Chasin
Thank you.

By the late 1930s both Myron and David O. Selznick were at the
top of their respective Hollywood heaps. Although there were no
corpses littered about, there may have been a few bruised egos,
because the brothers were ruthless in their determination to set the
town on its ear.

David O.'s production of *Gone With The Wind* would use many
of Myron Selznick's clients, including George Cukor as director,
Ben Hecht as one of the writers, and Thomas Mitchell as Scarlett
O'Hara's father. But Myron was unhappy that all of the actresses
tested for the part of Scarlett O'Hara—Jean Arthur, Diana
Barrymore, Anita Louise, Paulette Goddard, Lana Turner, Joan
Bennett, Tallulah Bankhead, Edythe Marriner (later Susan Hayward), and the rest were handled by other agents (with the exception
of his client Frances Dee, who had been eliminated from the
running earlier).

A public favorite for the role was Bette Davis. There had been
talk of teaming her with Errol Flynn (neither were Selznicks clients),
when the book had been optioned in galley form by Warner
Brothers, where both stars were under contract. However, when

Jack L. had told Davis—who was raising hell after a series of terrible pictures—that he had a wonderful part for her, she retorted, "I bet it's a pip!" and stormed out of his office.

When David O. purchased the book, there was some talk about Warner Brothers loaning Davis and Flynn as a team, throwing in Olivia De Havilland for the part of Melanie. However, Davis was adamant about not playing opposite Flynn, and Selznick was not enthusiastic about the idea either. But everyone agreed that De Havilland—a Myron Selznick/Leland Hayward client—was a brilliant choice for Melanie.

It was unanimous that Clark Gable was the perfect Rhett Butler, and it would be a big coup if Myron could come up with an equally ideal Scarlett. He did not give up hope; David was volatile, and it might be that another client would be tested and win the role.

In 1938, Myron was busy selling David O. clients for other pictures—Carole Lombard for appearing in *Made for Each Other*, Fredric March, Billie Burke, and Roland Young for *The Young in Heart*, and Edna Best for *Intermezzo: A Love Story*. And other deals going all over town. Still, the role of Scarlett haunted him.

He represented both Laurence Olivier and Merle Oberon, who were doing *Wuthering Heights*. While director William Wyler was demanding retake after retake on that picture, Vivien Leigh was having a passionate love affair with Olivier (although he was married to actress Jill Esmond, and she to barrister Leigh Holman). When Vivien Leigh made a quick trip to Hollywood from England, she had more than amour on her mind: she wanted the part of Scarlett! Time was short, because she had to be back in the West End for a stage play.

Leigh had a crucial meeting with Myron. At 25, she was one of the great beauties, with her brown hair, delicate complexion, green eyes, and slim figure. To Selznick she was the embodiment of all Southern womanhood—until she opened her mouth. Then she became indubitably British. This was a great drawback for Scarlett, and Myron hesitated to introduce her to his brother.

One of the high points of *Gone With The Wind* was the burning of Atlanta. Rhett, driving a horse and wagon, rescues Scarlett, Melanie, and her newborn baby, along with the slave, Prissy. The wagon scenes, using doubles, were to be filmed in long and medium shots against the conflagration, with the eventual players, in matching shots, to be cut in later. Before filming of the actual picture, as an economic measure, it had been decided to burn a collection of old sets (including the wall and gate from *King Kong* and the *King of Kings* Jerusalem facade), all equipped with appropriate false fronts so that new sets for the picture could be constructed on the forty-acre back lot at Selznick International.

Many important industry figures had been invited to witness the spectacular fire, which was to take place on Saturday, December 10, 1938. Seven Technicolor cameras had been assembled to shoot the action from every possible angle. In addition to the large number of people who had been invited to witness the event, the Los Angeles fire department was there with 34 pieces of equipment in case the fire got out of hand.

As the flames leapt upwards, turning the Culver City sky into a blazing inferno, the massive sets crashed and the Atlanta munitions warehouse exploded in a spectacular fashion.

At this point, Myron Selznick arrived with the usual ace up his sleeve—in this case an English ace. He was not without drama, this man; he had planned an effect that he thought would be quite stunning.

Laurence Olivier in his autobiography[1] recalled: "Myron picked us up in a car that evening, and we headed due south to Culver City where, on the old Pathe lot, David was burning forty acres of ancient exterior sets for the fire in Atlanta. Three times we saw the horse and wagon drive through the flaming archway of the barn, with the same double for Gable each time but three different types for Scarlett; after the last passage through, a wire was pulled and the roof of the barn fell in a flaming crash. (Flames are obligingly easy things to cut on, so the three Scarletts were readily interchangeable.) The shooting over, no attempt was made to extinguish the fire, and by its light I could just make out the figures of George Cukor, the original director and devoted friend, and David, whom I also knew well from our business differences in 1932.

"I looked back at Vivien, her hair giving the perfect impression of Scarlett's, her cheeks prettily flushed, her lips adorably parted, her green eyes dancing and shining with excitement in the firelight; I said to myself, 'David won't be able to resist that.' I retreated, leaving the field to Myron; David and George were approaching and Myron stepped towards them. He indicated Vivien and said, 'David, meet Scarlett O'Hara . . . .' "

In a magazine piece entitled "Discovering the New Ones"

(1941), David O. wrote: "Before my brother, Myron, Hollywood's leading talent agent, brought Laurence Olivier and Vivien Leigh over to the set to see the shooting of the Burning of Atlanta, I had never seen her. When he introduced me to her, the flames were lighting up her face.... I took one look and knew that she was right—at least right as far as her appearance went—at least right as far as my conception of how Scarlett O'Hara looked. Later on, her tests, made under George Cukor's brilliant direction, showed that she could act the part right down to the ground, but I'll never recover from that first look."

Vivien Leigh received only $20,000 for her role as Scarlett O'Hara in *Gone With The Wind*. David O. told Olivier: "I'd be the laughing stock of all my friends if I paid her any more, an unknown, a discovery, for such an opportunity."

David O. was not famous for paying large salaries to the actors he cast in his films, a famous case being that of Ingrid Bergman.

Kay Brown, talented talent scout and story editor of David O.'s New York office who had brought GWTW—and many other properties—to his attention, was enthralled with the beautiful star of a Swedish picture, *Intermezzo*, dealing with a world-famous violinist with the seven-year itch who has an affair with his daughter's piano teacher. Miss Brown pestered David O. about this actress, Ingrid Bergman, finally working out a deal with her Swedish agent Helmer Enwall for her to remake the picture in the United States. Brown would remain Bergman's lifelong friend, eventually becoming her agent and introducing her to Lars Schmidt, her third husband.

David O. put Bergman under wraps with dialogue coach Ruth Roberts, to improve her English, while starting the publicity wheels turning about his "new star, whose natural beauty was so spectacular that she did not wear makeup." Myron Selznick assumed that Bergman would sign with him, but she chose Charlie Feldman instead.

As it happened, Bergman made only two films for David O. under her seven year contract: *Intermezzo: A Love Story* (1939) and *Spellbound* (1945). He loaned her to other studios at ever-escalating prices, while she received contract pittances.

About *The Bells of St. Mary's*, in which she played the nun, under Leo McCarey's direction at RKO, and opposite Bing Crosby's priest, Bergman says in her memoirs:[2]

"I went to see Selznick. The same old dialogue took place: It wasn't good enough. It was a sequel. Why waste my talents ... etc., etc. 'But it *is* good enough,' I said, 'I know it's good enough. And I want to play it.'

"David looked me straight in the eye, the very serious, great film producer, and asked the dynamic question: 'What are you going to do while Bing Crosby is singing?'

" 'I'm going to look at him,' I said, 'That's all. I don't have to do anything but look at him.'

" 'Look at him? You're a great actress and you're just going to look at him?'

" 'I shall register radiance, adoration, perhaps perplexity.'

"But of course David argued very well. Finally I was in despair, and David, naturally, seeing he'd won now, thought he would shift the responsibility for my not getting the picture to Leo McCarey.

" 'If you're so keen, I'll talk to McCarey about terms.'

"In other words he'd ask so much they couldn't possibly afford to have me. So he started off by doubling my normal rental fee.

"And Leo said quietly, 'Okay, yes.'

"Then David—who rented Selznick International studio space from RKO—said, 'And I shall want a year's studio space—free.'

" 'Okay, yes.'

" 'And I shall want rights to *A Bill of Divorcement* ....'

" 'Okay, yes.'

"Now David was taken a little aback by all this, and he had to think very quickly about what he should ask for next. So he managed to think up two more properties owned by RKO and each time Leo said, very politely, 'Okay, yes.'

"And finally David asked, 'Do you really want to pay out all this to buy Ingrid Bergman?'

" 'I'm so happy that Ingrid is for sale,' said Leo ...."

After the initial shock wore off, stars became accustomed to hearing themselves discussed in much the same terms as one might bargain for a prize-winning milk cow or a thoroughbred bull— probably the beginning of the term Flesh Peddler. David O. , in his way, was a talent agent *par excellence.*

Said Ingrid later in the same book about David O. : "He had such enormous enthusiasm, and such enormous energy. He really burned his candle at both ends. Of course he rented me out for large sums as soon as I returned to Hollywood, and a lot of my friends said, 'What an interesting agent you have. The roles are reversed. He gets ninety percent and you get ten percent . . . .' I laughed about it. I didn't really mind. I'd signed a contract. I earned a lot more money than I ever had in Sweden. David didn't know I was going to be successful any more than I did. If he could make money renting me out, good luck to him. We made some great pictures and I loved working . . . ."

Coming up on David O.'s slate of pictures was *Rebecca*, Daphne du Maurier's gothic romance, which he had purchased in 1938 after the book was a success in England, and before it became a phenomenal best seller in the United States. He thought the role of the shy second wife, who had no actual name in the book, was perfect for Carole Lombard, and that the part of Maxim de Winter, twice her age and troubled by the death of his first wife, was ideal for Ronald Colman.

With his client list[3] growing, Myron Selznick remembered Alfred Hitchcock fondly from his *Passionate Adventure* days in England, but he was aware more of his latest directorial efforts, *The Lady Vanishes* and *Jamaica Inn*—the latter also from the pen of du Maurier. He suggested to David O. that it might be wise to bring Hitchcock to America. His touch might do for the brooding, suspenseful story. He sold Hitchcock to Selznick International for a steep $40,000 a film.

Selznick was delighted when David O. decided to use Laurence Olivier as Maxim, aware that he could squeeze his brother for a great deal of money for the actor. However, this casting opened a kettle of herring because Vivien Leigh became determined to play the wife. She came directly from the set of *Gone With The Wind* to make a test, but just as she had been sensationally cast as Scarlett, she was wrong for the second Mrs. de Winter.

Loretta Young, Anne Baxter, and Margaret Sullavan tested, but the part went to Joan Fontaine, who turned out to be the right choice; she was brilliant, if underpaid. Fontaine wrote in her memoirs,[4] in a chapter entitled Human Bondage: "There was a time when an agent had only two or three special clients. He advised them, kept in touch with the latest films on the production agenda, schemed, pushed, planned, haggled . . . . I can't remember a film agent trying to get a role for me or finding a suitable assignment and going after it. I've had many agents during the course of my career. As affable as they may have been, wining and dining me, sending lavish presents on Christmases and birthdays, to my knowledge not one of them has ever suggested me for a specific role.

"David O. Selznick was 90 percent brighter than the 10-per-centers. He gave his contract players a percentage of the salary he got for them on loan-out to other studios, and pocketed the rest. Ingenious. I was under a seven-year, exclusive, fifty-two week contract to him. As I remember, at the beginning my salary was $250 a week. If he took eight weeks to shoot *Rebecca*, I was then paid only $2,000—regardless of the fact that the film was a financial bonanza for Selznick. My yearly salary of $13,000 was increased only slightly by semi-annual raises during the seven years.

"Although I made no other films for him personally, D.O.S. made huge profits by loaning me to other studios. For example, my last film under the Selznick contract was *The Emperor Waltz* for Paramount. D.O.S. received $225,000 for my services. I received $75,000—minus my agent's commission . . . .

"Studios also encouraged the actor to buy a large house, several cars, and to hire servants—perhaps to purchase a yacht or race-horses. This was considered necessary for the star's 'image.' It also brought him to heel very quickly when the studio applied pressure. If it did not, the trick was to submit a horrendous script, which the actor would be forced to turn down, thereby putting himself on layoff. Many a dreadful part has been played by an actor whose financial affairs were such that he dared not refuse. Many an actor has ruined his career by taking such assignments . . . ."

But Myron Selznick, who had once concentrated solely on building the careers of his clients and besting the film moguls in the process, began to delegate more authority to his sub-agents, who indeed wanted to take over the agency. But Selznick would have none of it, even though he was neglecting some of his best people. His drinking worsened during the early war years—Bob Thomas related:[5]

"No amount of argument from his brother, his clients, or his friends, could dissuade Myron from his relentless consumption of whiskey. His alcoholism became accepted as part of his pattern of life. Studio bosses maintained bars in their offices, primarily for the use of Myron Selznick. As soon as he entered to negotiate a con-

Adolph Zukor and Jesse L. Lasky review blueprints for a new studio on the Paramount lot on Marathon Street in Hollywood in 1927. *(Courtesy of Paramount Pictures)*

Myron Selznick at age 45, shortly before he died in 1944. *(Courtesy of Marvin Paige's Motion Picture and TV Research Service)*

Leslie Howard and Ingrid Bergman in *Intermezzo: A Love Story*, her first American film. *(Henry Willson collection)*

tract, he went directly to the bar and poured himself a drink. There was no evidence that negotiations were made easier by Myron's indulgence. But the executives feared that Myron would be much tougher without a drink.

"He refused to discuss his drinking with anyone, including his own brother. Rarely did he indicate the inner torment that caused him to drink. Once he disclosed to Loretta Young that many nights he crawled into his mother's bed and cried himself to sleep—'me, a grown man!' When Miss Young asked the nature of the unhappiness that caused him to drink, he replied, 'I don't know.'

"Some of Myron's close friends theorized that his sorrow stemmed from the complexity of being a Selznick in the movie industry . . . .

" 'My brother is the only man in history to make a fortune from revenge,' said David Selznick. Indeed revenge had motivated Myron's drive for power in Hollywood. But now Myron had humbled the men who had ruined his father. What was left for him?

"He did not enjoy the agency business. Beyond the wielding of power there was nothing creative in peddling other people's talents. Those moments in Myron's youth when he was overseeing the production of five movie studios, when stars and directors and writers were seeking his guidance and support—those were the golden times of Myron Selznick's life. Then he was creating, building, seeking new vistas of entertainment. He was directing the destiny of his father's entertainment empire—and he failed.

"Lewis J. Selznick had pushed his gamble too far, and Adolph Zukor and the other giants had closed in on him. Myron still harbored the nagging thought that if he himself had managed production with greater brilliance, the name of Selznick might never have been dishonored."

Yet Myron was well aware that the dynamic David O. had the powerful personality and the artistic, creative talent that he lacked, and was also imbued with the *discipline* to carry off his projects brilliantly. Even the pictures that lost money later on, *Portrait of Jennie* and *A Farewell to Arms*, were more unfortunate story choices than anything else; the production values and the David O. flair remained. More often than not, his dogged interference with scriptwriters, directors, cameramen—and all facets of production—improved the pictures and brought acclaim to himself.

Throughout the fall of 1943, Myron Selznick was not in the best of health. He grew increasingly critical of his brother, especially when drinking. He wrote a diatribe on 18 November, which David O. answered five days later. The reply was printed by Rudy Behlmer in *Memo From David O. Selznick*:[6]

"I have your note of November 18 about your dealings with me and with our studio. I never thought I'd have to go through this argument with you again, but since you asked for it, I suppose I'll have to take the time.

"First, let me say that there is not a single instance . . . . on which you ever favored me or us either on making a deal or on salary . . . .

"You know perfectly well that Carole Lombard did not leave you because of anything to do with us, and that on the contrary, she took the position up to the day of her death that she would rather work for me than for any other producer in town, and she persisted in this attitude all through her difficulties with you and beyond these difficulties. You also know that you stuck me for the highest price ever paid for Carole Lombard on any deal you or anybody else ever made for her, either before the pictures she did for me, or after them. In fact, it was one of the laughs of your own staff and of everybody else in town as to the extent to which you stuck me on Carole Lombard and on others, including Freddie March, whom I also paid the highest price he has ever received in his career, either before or since . . . .

"There is perhaps no better proof of the accuracy of my statements than Alfred Hitchcock, one of the cases you have tried to use in the past to prove the 'trouble' you have been in with your clients as a result of us. Both Dan [O'Shea] and myself did everything possible to keep Hitch from signing with other agents, and to this day he has signed with none. Only the other day Dan took the occasion to point out to Hitchcock again, and as he has done often before, that your office sold Hitch to us at a price which we discovered to our horror subsequently was much higher than he had been quoted at, to every other studio in town, all of whom were not interested . . . .

"Far from losing any clients from us, I am so sick and tired of hearing this completely unfair statement that some day I'd like to sit down with you and show you the long list of clients that you got through us, and others that you retain because of us . . . ."

He closed with:

"I think one reason why you lose so many people is because you are such an extraordinarily bad judge of who are your friends and who are not . . . .

"Also, nevertheless, and with love, David."

Myron died at Santa Monica Hospital on March 23, 1944, of complications following internal bleeding: portal thrombosis. Although only 45 years old, his body was that of a much older man. Clients, including Pat O'Brien, were pallbearers. The simple eulogy, written by Gene Fowler, was read by William Powell.

Jesse L. Lasky, now an independent producer, was one of the first to hear of Myron's death, and he placed a call to Adolph Zukor in New York. Although Lasky had been fired during the depression and no love was lost between the two men, death surmounted all obstacles.

"Myron's dead," he said simply.

The old man sighed deeply. "It's not enough!" he cried, and hung up the telephone.

BLACKOUT: 1956

Female Star
You can't tell me that I'm so far down on my luck that I have to accept a tiny role in another star's picture!

Agent
But it's a cameo!

Female Star
A cameo is something that is worn around the neck and if it's too tight, it can choke you. My name has always been above the title!

Agent
But this cameo routine is fashionable now. Everyone's doing it. Remember, practically every role in Mike Todd's *Around the World in Eighty Days* is filled with big, big names.

Female Star
That is different. It's a fun thing to do for Mike, but in this picture I have only three scenes.

Agent
But what three scenes they are! A youngish woman in the first, then a gay divorcee, and last an embittered old woman—a time span of forty years. This is the sort of role that could revive your career in a big way. It's a showcase. European stars are not too proud to accept small roles—it's not how many "sides" there are or the "screen time," but the *content*.

Female Star
If I did agree to do this picture—and I'm not saying I will—what kind of billing could be worked out?

Agent
How about a "special appearance by . . . ." 25 percent size?

Female Star
No. If I do it, I want "Also starring, in a special appearance by 'my name' in italics, 75 percent size, directly under the title—*and* enclosed in a box!

Vera Zorina, with chorus boy George Raft to her left in a dance number from Charles K. Feldman's all-star production of *Follow the Boys. (Courtesy of Universal Pictures)*

Ground-breaking ceremonies for the new "Burbank Studios" included, *left to right*, Burbank's Mayor Robert Swanson; vice-president and treasurer of Columbia Pictures S. H. Malamed; the Chamber of Commerce's Miss Hollywood, Lanita Kent; Los Angeles Mayor Sam Yorty; and the head of Warner Brothers, Ted Ashley. *(Whitney Stine collection)*

11

PACKAGES & PERCENTAGES

Nurse
(sympathetically)
Take it easy now. Just a little more, and you'll have given your pint of blood.

Star
(guffawing)
Don't forget to send ten percent to my agent!

It seemed that the speeches and the awards would go on forever. The event was the Association of Talent Agents fifth annual awards luncheon at the Beverly Wilshire Hotel, February 27, 1985. Agents Sandy Bresler and Phil Gersh were honored with the Distinguished Agents Awards.

Bresler, whose award was presented by actor Leslie Nielsen, said, "I'm flattered not because I'm a quote hot-shot agent representing good people, making great deals, but as an agent for this organization . . . . as a member of this board and what has been accomplished." He was alluding to the efforts made to promote professionalism among its members.

Gersh, picking up his award from presenter director Arthur Hiller remarked, "Agents deserve this recognition and it makes me proud to be a part of this profession." He went on to say in a lighter vein that his award was probably based on his 40 years in the business.

In 1984, on February 17, *The Hollywood Reporter* in covering the fourth annual affair, noted: "Hollywood agents, stereotypically cast as parasites, sharks, *etc., etc.,* had their image redeemed

Wednesday as Los Angeles officially declared Feb. 15 to be Talent Association Day, in honor of the 'professionalism and integrity' that agents have brought to Hollywood."

Honored were Martin Baum, Nina Blanchard, and Robert Lantz. The M. C. Levee Award—named for a famous agent of the 1930s and 1940s—was given posthumously to Charles K. Feldman, accepted by his wife, Jean Howard. (Abe Lastfogel won the award in 1983).

It was pointed out that Feldman, who began his career as an assistant cameraman for director John Ford, had three hundred clients, including Richard Burton, Marlene Dietrich, Greta Garbo, Marilyn Monroe, and John Wayne, and helped map out the careers of Lauren Bacall, Kirk Douglas, and Lizabeth Scott among others.

Producer and former agent under Feldman, Ray Stark, presented the award, commenting that his mentor had taught him everything he probably knew, "when to lay back, when to soft sell, when to zing in." He said that Feldman had told him, "You're very rarely right in this business, so when you are, make the most of it."

Stark had been one of the new breed of agents at Famous Artists. A Rutgers man, a journalist and publicity writer after World War II, he handled radio writers, then became a literary agent with clients like Ben Hecht, Thomas B. Costain, and John P. Marquand before going to work for Charles Feldman. (He left to go into film production in 1957, organizing the Seven Arts company with Eliot Hyman, and producing independently in 1966.)

The talent agent accolade was long overdue. Charles K. Feldman had been Hollywood's first agent/packager. Although stars like Charlie Chaplin and Mary Pickford often produced and starred in their films under their own production banners for release through studios or formed their own company, agents were not actually involved in the deals.

And although David O. Selznick did indeed put talent packages together *en passant*, which he sold to other studios, his name—other than "by arrangement with David O. Selznick," pertaining to his loan-out stars—was not included in production credits. He may have dictated mountainous notes to the executives on each of these ventures, but he had no legal status after he had sold the package itself.

Stories told about Charles Feldman became famous. One incident that involved client/wit/raconteur Herman Mankiewicz is still retold with great glee in Hollywood circles.

"Charlie," said director Fritz Lang in 1975,[1] lounging in the hillside garden of his estate on Summitridge Drive in Beverly Hills, his mascot, the plush-stuffed brown monkey Peter, at his side, "was good-looking; in fact, more handsome than some of his clients. He was more than an agent. He had a heart. He helped his clients, especially if they were down on their luck. He was an easy touch.

"No one who had worked at the big studios wanted to work at Columbia. Harry Cohn was a sonovabitch. When I was there we used to square off at each other regularly, natch. Herman Mankiewicz had written some big pictures, but he liked his schnapps. He had a bad reputation because he hated anyone to put him on a leash."

Lang placed his monocle in his breast pocket and put on a pair of glasses. "Charlie finally got Mankie a writing job at Columbia. Harry was a tightwad. He was only willing to pay peanuts. But Charlie knew that if Mankie completed the assignment with no squawks, he could get him other work elsewhere at his old salary, but he had to pass the test.

"Charlie forbid him to go into the executive dining room. 'If you do, Harry will fry you, so don't go near the place.' Mankie was doing fine. He was off the booze. The script he was working on was okay. He was almost ready to check off the lot, when he couldn't resist joining his friends—who had been bugging him to lunch with them. In comes Harry, and he blows on and on about a picture he'd just screened. He said that when his hinder twitched, he knew it was a bad movie.

"Now Mankie had this kind of a voice that could be heard without him raising it, and he drawled, 'Imagine, the whole world wired to Harry Cohn's ass!' " Lang chuckled. "Of course, he got fired."

Feldman's first official screen credit as a producer was during World War II, with the all-star *Follow the Boys*, but his name was actually connected with many other films before that time. The idea for *Boys* actually sprang out of war work that he was doing. He had left the agency for the duration to organize camp shows, and he utilized the performers in the film, which was just a parade of "turns" by famous performers playing themselves, entertaining the troops: Sophie Tucker, Gertrude Niessen, Orson Welles, Marlene Dietrich, George Raft and others, pasted together with a thin story line. It served the double purpose of showing the folks at home that their boys were not being neglected, besides showing a seldom-seen side of the stars. Orson Welles, for instance, displayed his famous magic act—cutting Marlene Dietrich in half. She also played the musical saw.

Feldman was born Charles Gould in 1904 , and orphaned as a child. His adopted parents sent him to the University of Michigan and then to the University of California. Becoming a lawyer in 1928, he was astonished by the monied contracts for film players that crossed his desk. Hollywood was making the transition from silent to sound pictures, and agents were springing up everywhere. Their commissions on clients' salaries were phenomenal compared to what a young attorney made. In 1932 he joined Famous Artists. His first clients were Irene Dunne and Claudette Colbert, who had not had a formal agent.

He realized that the one big weakness in a studio-run town was that each company had an array of talent under contract, to fit its particular needs. Although the studios turned out films in all categories, each specialized in certain types of films. MGM was noted for love stories, costume epics, heart-warming comedies, and all-star musicals; Warner Brothers picked their stories from news-paper headlines, specialized in gangster movies, and the kaleido-scope musicals of Busby Berkeley; Paramount did romances, light comedies, and the sex farces of Mae West; Samuel Goldwyn made "high class" products, bringing novels and Broadway plays to the screen; Universal was famous for its horror films and "B" pictures that filled the lower half of double bills; RKO-Pathe made prestige pictures with good casts, and escapist films like King Kong; and Columbia did hard-hitting exploitation pictures, along with a few well-produced Frank Capra films.

But the studios all had one thing in common: they had to use the stars and creative personnel under contract—their own "stock company." Borrowing players for particular properties was always a last resort, not only costly but also usually involving the trade of one or more important stars for another star. It went deeply against the grain to publicize another studio's star for a single film, only to have that player return to his own lot—sometimes with an Academy Award nomination.

Bette Davis, for instance, was loaned out only twice during her eighteen-year tenure at Warner Brothers—first (at her insistence) to RKO for her penultimate film of the period, *Of Human Bondage* (1934), and then again to Goldwyn for *The Little Foxes* (1941), which earned her a fifth Oscar nomination. Warners profited far more from these outside ventures than did either RKO or Goldwyn. The *Foxes* deal involved a trade for Gary Cooper to do *Sergeant York*, which won him an Academy Award the same year.

It was possible to go into a theater in the middle of a film, without knowing which picture was playing, and within two minutes know which studio had produced the picture simply from observing who was appearing on the screen.

As the 1930s wore on with the Great Depression, it occurred to Feldman—thinking always in legal terms, and being party to all that was involved in making a picture—that it would be easier for one person to purchase a property, assign a writer from his own stable for the screenplay, cast the leading and subsidiary roles from among his clients, line up his own producer and director, and then present the entire "package" for X amount of dollars to a studio. He would be paid for his work, and the studio in question would be given an infusion of new blood.

There were other advantages to the scheme besides money. If a star had appeared in several flops due to bad scripts, or was reaching an age when suitable material was difficult to come by, a famous novel or Broadway play that appeared made-to-order for the star could be purchased and packaged. Careers could be saved this way. When Universal did not have a follow-up film for Marlene Dietrich after *The Spoilers* (1942), Feldman provided *Pittsburgh* to finish out her contract. After war-work, performing overseas, she resumed her career at 43, wearing almost nothing and covered in gold greasepaint in *Kismet* (1944), at Paramount. She would make only ten more films during this phase of her career.

She returned to pictures just once to sing the title song in *Just a Gigolo* (1978). Dressed in a black gown and a huge black picture hat with a veil, she stood beside a piano and sang to David Bowie. She then retired to her Paris apartment. In 1983, Maximilian Schell

Director Fritz Lang played himself (here with Brigitte Bardot) in the 1963 Jean Luc Godard film, *Contempt*. *(Courtesy of Fritz Lang)*

Adolph Menjou and Edward Brophy discuss a musical career for William Holden in *Golden Boy*. *(A. L. Schafer/Paramount Pictures)*

George Raft, with Louis Jordan's quintet, caught in a downpour at an anti-aircraft station in *Follow the Boys*, cries to the troops, "If you guys can take it, I can too!" and goes right on dancing. The film was produced by agent Charles K. Feldman. *(Whitney Stine collection)*

made an *avant garde* award-winning documentary of her career in which he utilized tape-recorded voice interviews, but Dietrich at 82 declined to be photographed. Perhaps her most telling comment over the years: "I have a child, and I have made a few people happy. That is all."

Another Paramount alumnus with later career problems was Bill Beedle, who died tragically in 1981. After Paramount talent scout Milton Lewis discovered twenty-year-old Beedle playing in *Manya* at the Pasadena Playbox Theater, the studio gave him a contract at $50 a week, changing his name to William Holden (having first received an okay from another Bill Holden, an associate editor of the *Los Angeles Times*).

Producers were wondering what to do with the new kid on the lot. Holden was used as an extra in *Prison Farm* and had one line in *Million Dollar Legs*. With nothing further to do, he offered to perform in screen tests with actresses being considered for certain roles. A test that he had made with Margaret Young was shown to producer William Perlberg and director Rouben Mamoulian at Columbia, who were searching for an actress to play the girlfriend of Joe Bonaparte, violinist/boxer in *Golden Boy*. The men were intrigued by the actor who played the scene with Miss Young. Columbia bought out half of Holden's contract—25 dollars a week—and he was given the role opposite Barbara Stanwyck that put him on the map in Hollywood.

During the shooting of the film Mamoulian, who knew star quality when he saw it, advised Holden: "You must have representation. Charlie Feldman used to be a lawyer, and he is a fine gentleman as well as an agent."

Feldman signed Holden, and a long association resulted. Two years and six pictures later, Charlie managed to increase Holden's salary to $125 a week, even though he was stuck with the original contract. However, this was still not enough money for the young man to marry actress Brenda Marshall, *nee* Ardis Anderson. Set for a Columbia picture, *Texas*, Holden went on suspension, but to no avail. Even Charlie Feldman could not get him a raise. So the actor went back to work. When his salary reached $175 a week in 1941 he married Ardis, and they subsequently had two sons.

In 1942 Holden enlisted in the service, becoming a First Lieutenant and returning after the war to make such films as *A Stolen*

Life (1946) with Bette Davis at Warner Brothers, and *Rachel and the Stranger* (1948) at RKO with Loretta Young and Robert Mitchum. By this time Charlie had gone into producing films, and he assigned top Famous Artists agent Jack Gordean to handle Holden. He was able to get him raises in salary over the years and favorable clauses, such as a provision not to film after six in the evening. With an Academy Award behind him for *Stalag 17* (1953) Gordean renegotiated the contract with Paramount, obtaining $250,000 for twelve weeks' work a year. He received one-third interest in *The Moon is Blue* (1954), which earned him $600,000.

The big money years were ahead. Bob Thomas wrote in his biography of Holden:[2] "Released in December of 1957, *The Bridge on the River Kwai* proved to be an immense success and won seven Academy Awards, including best picture, best direction, writing, photography, editing, score, and acting—by Alec Guinness.

" 'I feel terrible,' Guinness remarked later to Holden. 'I received the award, while you were the star.'

" 'You deserved it, Alec, you were great in the picture,' said Bill, adding with a grin, 'You keep the Oscar; I'll keep ten percent of the gross.' "

The film made $30 million in its first release, and Columbia made a fortune out of the interest on the Holden fund alone. But Holden was able to keep only $9,000, after taxes and agent's commissions. Thomas continued:

"By 1979, Columbia was holding more than $3 million of Holden's earnings from *The Bridge on the River Kwai*. With income still mounting, more than sixty years would be required to repay him and his heirs under the existing contract. Deane Johnson negotiated a settlement. Terms of the settlement were secret, but the amount was reportedly $600,000, of which Ardis received half. Thereafter, Holden would receive his ten percent of the gross earnings from *Kwai* without the $50,000 limitation. He willed the income to the industry charity, The Motion Picture and Television Fund."

More money was forthcoming. *The Horse Soldiers* (1959) earned him and John Wayne each $750,000, plus twenty percent of the gross, but the picture did not make money.

When Feldman picked up his career after the war, he put together several packages. The most interesting (other than those already mentioned) were: for Warner Brothers *To Have and Have*

Not (1944) and *The Big Sleep* (1946) with Humphrey Bogart and Lauren Bacall; two Tennessee Williams plays, *The Glass Menagerie* (1950) with Jane Wyman, Gertrude Lawrence, and Kirk Douglas, and *A Streetcar Named Desire* (1951), with Vivien Leigh, Marlon Brando, and Karl Malden; for United Artists, *Red River* (1948) with John Wayne; for Twentieth Century-Fox, *The Seven Year Itch* (1955), with Marilyn Monroe and Tom Ewell, and *What's New, Pussycat?* (1965), with Peter Sellers and Peter O'Toole.

Feldman had also produced *A Walk on the Wild Side* and *The Lion* (1962), with William Holden and his discovery, Capucine. Two last projects that he managed to put together before he died in 1967 were: for Columbia, *Casino Royale* with William Holden, Ursula Andress, and an all-star cast; and for Twentieth Century-Fox *The Honey Pot*, with Rex Harrison, Susan Hayward, Cliff Robertson, Capucine, Edie Adams and Maggie Smith. For *Casino Royale* Holden agreed to do his cameo role for $40,000, feeling he owed it to his former agent, still a close friend.

The man who would eventually take over Famous Artists from Feldman was the son of a tailor, Ted Ashley. He was born Theodore Assofsky, August 5, 1922, in a poor section of Brooklyn. "When Ted was fourteen," Karl Fleming reported in an article,[3] "his mother called on her brothers, Nat and Julius Lefkowitz, for advice. What were her boys going to do? Like Ted's father, Nat and Julius were Russian Jews, but they had good jobs. Nat was general manager of the William Morris Agency in the R.K.O. building, and Julius had his own little accounting office right across the hall. Nat and Julius advised that her boys be enrolled in typing and shorthand at the Franklin K. Lane High School, where they went to school. 'It was sissyish, but you did what was required for survival,' Ashley says. He skipped two grades, and on the spring day he graduated, in 1937, he kept on the itchy tweed suit—the one suit he owned—and crossed the bridge into Manhattan for the first time to report for work at $14 a week with Uncle Julius . . . ."

He enrolled in the evening session of the City College of New York School of Business Administration in September 1937. After two years of working days and studying nights, he made the first major decision of his life—he dropped accounting for show business, because "I already knew this was for me." His instinct proved prophetic. He was a soft-spoken, quiet sort of man, five-feet-five inches tall, weighing 118 pounds.

By the time he was twenty, he was a fully-fledged agent for William Morris in what was then the radio and phonograph field, and he remained with the organization for nine years.

His first big coup came when he sold former Under Secretary of State Sumner Welles on doing a fifteen-minute radio show, *Time for Decision*, sponsored by Waltham Watches, on the Mutual Broadcasting System. Ashley was 21 years old.

Ashley told Fleming: "I had a radar system which permitted me to read and understand people. It still is one of the most important faculties I have. You have to be able to sense the other person and know what he's thinking. Number Two, you have to have the knowledge of your profession. If you try to sell something and don't understand all the nuances of the business, you're likely to make the wrong argument and not be persuasive—by virtue of that alone. Third, negotiating and selling, particularly in our business, requires that there be great credibility on the part of the salesman.

"If I say to NBC, as I did once say, 'Gentlemen, Danny Kaye's now ready, after a year of discussion, to go on television, and $135,000 is the fee I want for his program,' and they say, as one of them did, 'That's not possible. Nobody would pay that,' and then you say, 'I have half of the program sold to Old Gold and I have an order letter from them in my pocket,' and the fella says, 'Can I see it?' and I say, 'I told you I've got it,' then it is nice to hear one fella, who is now president of NBC, say, 'If Ted says he's got it, he's got it.'

"But this fella said, 'I'd like to see it,' so I said, 'I'll show it to you after I close the deal somewhere else.' And I did close the deal somewhere else—at CBS, for precisely the amount of money I asked for, which was the highest price anyone had ever paid for a program at that time, and I sent the fella at NBC a copy of the order letter, just as I had described it . . . ."

In 1946, Ted Ashley—much to the consternation of Uncle Nat Lefkowitz—left the William Morris Agency to put together his own company, Ashley Personal Management, becoming the "personal manager" of Morris clients Gertrude Berg, Bill and Cora Baird, Alan Funt, Tex McCrary and Jinx Falkenburg, and Henny Youngman, thereby earning ten percent of their salaries while they were still paying Morris ten percent for getting them jobs!

This money allowed Ashley to breathe easily for the first time. However, he had his sights set ahead: he loved show business and was bound and determined to be more than a personal manager. He was to succeed brilliantly. Soon he was hiring other managers with client lists, and his company became Ted Ashley and Associates.

In 1964 he bought Famous Artists, changing the name to Ashley Famous Agency. He quietly began to hire other agents with client lists, and soon his stable of stars included Yul Brynner, Ingrid Bergman, Rex Harrison, Robert Mitchum, and Vanessa Redgrave. He acquired writers Arthur Miller and Tennessee Williams, singers Perry Como and Trini Lopez, and rock and roll groups The Doors and Iron Butterfly. The agency was responsible for packaging and selling for telecast *Candid Camera, The Carol Burnett Show, The Doris Day Show, The Defenders, Dr. Kildare, Mission: Impossible, Star Trek, Tarzan,* and *The Twilight Zone*, among dozens of others.

Like many other agents, Ashley sought to maintain his privacy, and succeeded. He did not give interviews, and very little has been published about him. He communicated extremely well on a corporate level, and never raised his voice. In December 1967 Kinney National Service, Inc., which owned—among other concerns—mortuaries and a chain of shoe stores, purchased Ashley Famous for $12,750,000 in stock, of which Ashley reportedly owned sixty percent. One of the jokes around Hollywood and New York was that telephone operators answered the phones with, "Ashley Famous. We book you and we bury you!"

BLACKOUT: 1932

Agent

You'll be thirty years old, next month. It's time you got married.

Male Star

I don't want to get married, and even if I did, who would have me?

Agent

Just any female in America and Europe! Seriously, the studio's been after me. They're afraid if you wait much longer, the public is going to think something's wrong with you.

Male Star

So?

Agent

Don't get cheeky with me! Where would you be if I hadn't found you cooking hamburgers in that diner?

Male Star

Looking up at the ceiling in a male whorehouse!

Agent

Very funny! Pick some little broad, go to Las Vegas, tie the knot. After a year or so, get a quiet divorce. You'll have proved the point that you're a big he-man, and that'll be the end of it.

Male Star

Look, there are some things you can't fake!

Agent

All right, already! My wife has a cousin who's very pretty but doesn't like men. Marrying her might be convenient for you both.

Male Star

That's not my idea of a good time.

Agent

Hers either! Okay, but the studio won't renew unless you get hitched. This time, I can't help you.

Male Star

What did you say her name was?

Rock Hudson, formerly Roy Fitzgerald, was a Willson discovery
who later became a superstar in
films, but who also appeared on
stage and television. *(Courtesy of
J. Neyland collection)*

Art Gelien wanted to be an ice skater when he was discovered
by agent Henry Willson, who changed his name to Tab Hunter.
(Courtesy of Henry Willson collection)

12

HENRY WILLSON & TAB, ROCK, RORY, CHAD, TROY, RHONDA, ETC.

Producer Hal Wallis
I want Joe E. Brown for Midsummer Night's Dream. *I'm prepared to offer him a Cadillac.*

Agent Ivan Kahn
What do I get for my commission—a bicycle?

Selznick's Talent Department was headed by a smallish, chubby leprechaun of a man named Henry Willson, who in his heyday was a hard-driving, hard-drinking, ambitious dynamo, with a sharp, penetrating, icy gaze that could soften around beautiful people.

The offspring of a man who had once headed Columbia Records, Willson had been reared with a platinum spoon in his mouth in Forest Hills, New York. Early in his youth, in the era of tea dances, he had been thought a dilettante. He came to California to write a movie column for *New Movie*, and did occasional pieces for *Modern Screen*. In due course he met Zeppo (Herbert) Marx, who had gone into the agency business with brother Gummo (Milton). The men liked each other, and Willson came to work at the agency. He did so well that he was offered a vice-presidency at Selznick's Vanguard Productions.

When Vanguard folded he opened his own talent agency on Carol Drive in Hollywood, and in the 1950s he became one of the biggest and most powerful independent agents in Hollywood. Although he certainly made money and lived like a king, the investment in his clientele was expensive and he foolishly never salted his money away.

After his agency closed, Willson gradually faded from sight.

The house on Stone Canyon Road, a few blocks from the Bel Air Hotel where skittish neighbors often complained about the famous Sunday afternoon pool parties, was long gone, as well as the expensive foreign cars and the coterie of young hopefuls, who assumed that, with their attractive bodies and ingratiating manners, Willson could at the very least arrange a screen test.

With money gone and health in decline, Willson disappeared from the Hollywood scene. Marguerite Chapman mentioned that he was living at the Motion Picture Country Home—the first agent ever in residence.[1]

Over a glass of white wine "straight up," in a restaurant bar across from the facility, Willson fooled with the collar of his Sy Devore sport shirt. He was embarrassed to be found living in the Home, and extracted a promise that the interview would not state his whereabouts. He would not talk into a tape recorder, only a notebook was permitted. He also demanded to read and okay the written material. Then he smiled impishly and waved his hand. "Of course, if I should die before I wake, use all the material—even the stuff I've said is 'off-the-record.' "

He lounged comfortably in the banquette as if a two-hundred pound weight had been lifted from his chest, and began to speak in an ever-accelerating voice, as if he were continuing a conversation started some years before. Cheerful and beautifully mannered, he recalled the old Hollywood when producers, directors, those older than himself, and *all* stars were called Miss or Mister.

"You want to hear about Tab Hunter? His name was Art Gelien in those days, and he worked as a soda jerk at Wil Wright's Ice Cream Parlor on Sunset Strip. He wanted to be an ice skating champion, you know. In fact, I had met him in 1949 backstage at the Ice Capades when I went back to see Bobby Speck, one of the stars in the show. Bobby introduced us, and Art kept saying how he'd like to enter the Olympics. I looked at this blond kid with the open, friendly face, and I could see him in closeup on the screen. I can always tell within ten minutes if the person has *it* or not, and with this inner sense of mine, I knew he had picture potential."

Willson brightened, and his face took on a rosy glow, more from remembrance than the wine, "I don't know how I acquired this faculty, but when I was growing up, I attended a lot of Broadway shows, and like almost everyone I was always disappointed if the stage manager announced that an understudy was taking over a leading role for that performance. But, strangely enough, I began to enjoy these performances the most, and after a while I'd seek out productions where the star was on vacation or ill. I suppose it was the thrill of seeing a player being given that 'big chance' that we're always hearing about, and it does happen. Shirley MacLaine went on for Carol Haney one night in *Pajama Game*, and producer Hal Wallis was in the audience.

"All during those New York years, I was preparing myself, although I certainly didn't realize it at the time, for what was to come much later." He grew pensive. "Certain areas of my life have been disappointing to me, but the one thing that has sustained me over the years, is the knowledge that when dealing with actors, I have this inner feeling about what will come over on camera and what won't.

"But Art Gelien taught me something that day after the Ice Capades Show, when we ended up at the old Mocambo nightclub— owned by Charlie Morrison, once a Selznick talent scout. Art wasn't even supposed to be in the place, since he was only eighteen. He ordered a Bloody Mary." Willson laughed, "Can you believe that I had never heard of a Bloody Mary?

"I went over several names and finally came up with Tab Hunter for Art Gelien. I always chose simple names, given names with one syllable, and surnames with two syllables—or vice versa. I finally managed to get Tab a small part over at Paramount in *The Lawless*, produced by Pine-Thomas. On the strength of his muscular frame and that open face, I was able to get him the lead opposite Linda Darnell in United Artists' *Saturday Island*, which, because of the torrid love scenes, became *Island of Desire*.

"The critics were merciless, but we tried a Western next, *Gun Belt*, also at U.A. By this time, the fan magazines had discovered him, and the big feature articles began. With this type of publicity, I was able to get him a seven-year contract at Warner Brothers. They were looking for bright newcomers. But of all his pictures at the Bur- bank lot, my favorite Tab Hunter picture was the musical *Damn Yankees*. He was perfectly cast as the young Joe Hardy, the rein- carnation of his middle-aged self, who goes on to win the Yankee pennant. His vulnerability was very touching, and he played beautifully against Gwen Verdon, who had created the role of the beguiling Lola, 'the ugliest woman in Providence, Rhode Island,' who had sold herself to the Devil (played with such glee by Ray Walston), for eternal life and a beautiful body."

Willson finished his white wine and ordered another. "I got along very well with David Selznick, but the hours were horrendous—going into the night. The 'dailies' never arrived from the laboratory for viewing until late in the afternoon; then there would be a conference over dinner, and usually a preview or some other industry affair at night, and this brought about our only clash. After very late hours, I began to start my day at ten in the morning. He stopped me one morning, and growled, 'Bankers hours, eh?'

" 'No, Mr. Selznick,' I replied as quietly as I could, 'bankers go home at three o'clock.' That was the end of the discussion. It was never brought up again." Willson's eyes twinkled.

"But like his agent brother, Myron, Mr. Selznick was a wheeler-dealer. In some ways, he did more with his contract list and made more money than Myron, who was a plucky little drunk with a circular office building in Beverly Hills that was so elaborate it was written up in the architectural magazines. David's argument was that he had built their careers by loaning them out for important pictures that could only help their box office. He saw that they got versatile parts. He truly wanted to make more pictures after the successes of *Gone With the Wind, Intermezzo,* and *Rebecca,* but he didn't get around to it because he was so conscious of his reputation. I think he knew that he couldn't duplicate his earlier successes, although he tried very hard with *Duel in the Sun.*

"When he formed Selznick-Vanguard Productions, his dream was to make less-expensive pictures that still bore his stamp, but which wouldn't be considered a Selznick production in the same vein that *Wind* was." He paused. "When I think about his tremendous energy, I still get goosebumps. He'd work sixteen hours a day full-tilt, then write memos into the night. Everyone connected with him received these communications. He even sent one to the cashier at Schwabs Drugstore once, thanking her for saving some magazines for him!"

Henry Willson took a long breath and a short sip of wine. "I saved some of those memos, but I only have a couple left." He dug into his breast pocket and brought out a yellowed piece of paper. "I brought this along because it tells something of Mr. Selznick's philosophy concerning his contract list."

He read: "We must recognize the fact that we are able to launch certain players with success, but we are able to do little or nothing with another type of player. Betty Grable would not have gotten very far with us. On the other hand, Bergman and Fontaine and Leigh and Jones and McGuire and Cotten could have very likely become stars no place else, certainly not the great stars into which we made them."

Willson took another sip of white wine, "Mr. Selznick was a star-maker, perhaps the last of that breed. Agents like Jules Stein made stars, of course, but they didn't really discover them. MCA would take a piece of talent, build a package around them, which they'd sell to the highest bidder. Or, when they bought Universal, they'd star their own clients. But in Mr. Selznick's day it was totally different."

He picked up the memo again and continued: "Even if I knew we had another Grable, I would be very hesitant to sign her; first, because I don't think we could give or find her the right opportunities, and second, because we are known, and should be known for players of a certain quality (without discounting the qualities which other studios exploit, or in any way running them down); we have a pride in this type of player, we know what to do with them, and I don't want to change what we stand for simply in the remote hope that somehow or in some way that isn't apparent, we could put over a Betty Grable... Let's continue to look at these young people, by all means, but let's sign them with more discretion..."

Willson chuckled. "There was a famous story about Betty, who, it was said, left MCA to be represented by Nat Goldstone, because his wife, Bernice, owned a racehorse named Solidarity. Betty and her husband, Harry James, spent most of their time at the track in those days, and they also owned racehorses, and Betty felt they had more in common with their own ilk! But that memo, if I remember correctly, had to do with Roy Fitzgerald, whom Mr. Selznick had just turned down. It is typical of Hollywood that, ten years later, he would pay a fortune to that same young man, whom I named Rock Hudson, to star top-billed above Jennifer Jones, Mr. Selznick's wife, in the remake of *A Farewell to Arms*." Willson grinned, "But that's part of the business. He could have had him under contract all those years!

"I recently watched Rock being interviewed on a TV talk show, and when the host asked if he could not have become a star under his own name, without a moment's hesitation he replied: 'Certainly.' At his age, and with dozens of pictures behind him, he is entitled to believe this, but I wonder ... When I gave him his name, Hollywood was overrun with Fitzgeralds. There was Barry and Walter and Geraldine, and the name always ends up F-Z-G-L-D on the marquee—something that you always have to think about. What's it going to look like up there? I also thought the name 'Roy' was commonplace. I picked Rock because of the Rock of Gibraltar— big and rugged. Also, there was only one other Hudson in pictures—Rochelle—and she worked infrequently. The name sounded right, because he was six-foot-four and handsome, but awkward and rather shy."

Willson frowned, and his face did not look as pixyish as before. "Living expenses are always a problem for a young player who hasn't earned any money yet in pictures. Obviously, the agent cannot take on the financial responsibilities for every hopeful signed. Rock was earning about sixty dollars a week driving a truck when I went to Raoul Walsh, a brilliant, crusty, one-eyed director, and asked him to form a partnership with me. If he'd pay Rock's salary of $125 a week while I was trying to land a contract, I'd split my commission with him.

"Raoul believed in the boy, who he cast in a tiny role in *Fighter Squadron* at Warner Brothers, produced in 1948. Jack Warner liked Rock's one good scene, which had taken a great many retakes, but he wouldn't offer a long-term deal, which was what I wanted. Twentieth Century-Fox also turned me down. All of this took time, and when I interested Universal-International in the boy, Raoul had paid out about nine-thousand dollars in salary, for which he was reimbursed by casting head, Rufus LeMaire, when the contract was signed.

"Rufus wanted to change the spelling of 'Rock' to 'Roc'—after the big, mythical bird. I went to Ed Muhl, Universal's head of production, about *that*!" Willson's coal-black eyes flashed. "So, Walsh and I owned Rock Hudson for seven years.

"But new talent needs grooming, and Rock was no exception. He didn't have anything in his background to assist him. I saw to it that he had the best possible help—acting classes, diction lessons, voice exercises—and of course he had to learn how to ride a horse.

"Today, there are very few good voice or diction teachers to whom young actors can turn. Estelle Harmon, who I helped start in the business, is one; Stella Adler is another. While at Selznick-Vanguard, I hired three coaches: Lester Luther, Florence Cunningham, and Helen Sorrell—each a specialist. They not only tutored new talent, but helped our contract stars with dialects and accents.

"Early in his career, Rock came down with a bad case of laryngitis and phoned his coach to beg-off on an appointment, but was told to come right over and was given a long, strenuous lesson. When he recovered, his voice was lower—a baritone—more in keeping with his rugged appearance.

"At Universal, he studied with Sophie Rosenstein, who had married Gig Young when they were both at Warners. She helped Rock overcome his shyness, taught him good posture, made him stand up straight. To give him confidence, she also had him appear before live audiences at the studio talent school.

"Meanwhile, I was helping in other areas. I took him to see his first stage play, *Annie Get Your Gun*, with Ethel Merman. I noticed that he squinted at the stage all evening. After I got him a pair of hornrimmed glasses, he became a regular theatergoer. Although he had no ambitions then about appearing in legit theater, he became quite adept on the stage many years later. In 1976, when he appeared with Carol Burnett in *I Do, I Do*, at the Huntington Hartford Theater in Hollywood, he was poised and relaxed in front of the tough, hometown audience. I went backstage to congratulate him on a marvelous performance. And, as we shook hands, we suddenly both realized how far he had come in the last thirty years! He and Carol broke house records. Now he has done it all—features, radio, stage, and then television with *McMillan and Wife*.

"But with Rock, it wasn't only grooming and learning the social amenities," Willson continued in his rapid-fire style. "He worked like a Trojan. After *Fighter Squadron*, there was a series of small parts that no one remembers now: *Undertow, I Was a Shoplifter*, and *One-Way Street*, where he played, wouldn't you know, a truck driver!

"He was a prizefighter, detective, fighter pilot, football player, soldier, soda jerk, sea captain, cowboy, Indian, cavalryman, swashbuckler, fur trapper. He even danced the Charleston with

Piper Laurie in *Has Anybody Seen My Gal*.

"It wasn't until *Magnificent Obsession*, with Jane Wyman in 1954, that he hit his stride at the box office. Ross Hunter, who had been a juvenile actor, then a producer at Universal, cast him as the doctor who fell in love with a patient whom he has accidentally blinded. Pure soap opera, but the role opened up the way for more mature kinds of romantic roles. The picture made millions, and Rock's fan mail jumped to two-thousand and seven-hundred letters a week. His popularity increased enormously.

"Then came a big step forward with *Giant*, starring with Elizabeth Taylor and James Dean. He aged thirty years in the movie, and acted with his whole body. You felt he was actually growing old, and during the big fight scene he delivered the punches of a middle-aged man. The picture was barely finished when Jimmy was killed in an automobile accident, and both he and Rock were nominated for Academy Awards in the Best Actor category.

"The competition that year was very tough." Willson frowned. "Yul Brynner, *The King and I*; Kirk Douglas, *Lust for Life*; and Sir Laurence Olivier, *Richard III*—each actually deserving an Oscar. Brynner, of course, won the award. But, as often happens when two stars from the same film are nominated, the vote is split, and often a dark horse will come up winner. If the Academy had given Dean a posthumous award—taking him out of competition—I think Rock would have received the Oscar instead of Yul.

"Years later, when Rock made *A Farewell to Arms*, with Jennifer Jones, which Mr. Selznick was producing for Twentieth Century-Fox, he felt he wasn't getting a fair shake. He called me from Italy, and I took the next plane for Rome. There was a lot of trouble on the picture—mostly from Selznick's perfectionism—which was being shot at Cinecita Studios and in the Dolomite Mountains. There had been a change of director and cinematographer, dissension among cast and crew and, of course, tons of those damn Selznick memos!

"But I'd always had a good relationship with Mr. Selznick, and I must say that Rock was given more consideration after I arrived. I don't think that it was his idea to snub Rock, but he was trying to come up with another *Gone With the Wind* for Jennifer. With active representation around, Rock was invited to various social affairs at the Selznick villa, and was generally given better treatment.

"The picture was not a great critical success, but eventually made a little money. One good thing, however, that came out of the picture: Rock came up with a good title for a film—*Pillow Talk*— which was later used on a Ross Hunter production with Rock, won an Oscar nomination for Doris Day, and was a hit song. That was the picture that started all of Rock's light sex comedies like *Come September* and *Lover Come Back*, but I'm getting ahead of myself, as I'm inclined to do . . . ."

Willson indicated that it was after *Magnificent Obsession* that Lew Wasserman of MCA stepped in and, with Rock's permission, renegotiated his contract with Universal, with the result that Willson was given commission on the original contract that he had negotiated, and Wasserman received commission on the monies obtained over the initial amount.

Willson sighed gently. "This sort of maneuvering very often happened in those days, and I suppose it still does." He paused, and frowned. "I hadn't seen Lew in some time, and he looked weary and wrinkled. The fast-paced life of an agent can age one faster than any other profession—outside of wrestling. There is no time for a private life. Even heads of studios like Jack Warner, Louis B. Mayer, and Sam Goldwyn had an easier time of it, because they were kingpins of a group of contract players and technicians and, having huge working plants, knew how to delegate authority. A Lew Wasserman has to be in there pitching every moment, setting deals, knowing what star's contract is up with what agent and when to step in with a better offer, keeping track of pictures in production, holding hands with stars who are having professional or private problems, and supervising sub-agents. It can be killing. I know from experience.

"An agent often becomes a sort of father after discovering and grooming a personality. I've paid to get teeth fixed, ears pinned back, and contact lenses fitted. I've shown which fork to use and which wines to order, and taught all the amenities. After educating them in every way possible, and eventually wrangling a long-term deal at one of the major studios, then when it appears that the box office years are in the making, another agent comes along and takes over!

"If the first agent is protected by a contract, the commission checks keep flowing in: the Guild has a rule that if an agent gets a client fifteen days' work out of ninety, they can't up and leave. Sometimes though, you're left with egg on your face, while the other agent gets the bacon!

"The Screen Actors Guild, by the way, was really started at a Hollywood Cricket Club Dance at the Roosevelt Hotel in 1933. If I remember correctly there were such people as Lucille and Jimmy Gleason, Ralph Morgan, Claude King, Alan Mowbray, Boris Karloff, Noel Madison, Kenny Thompson, Richard Tucker, and a few more who said, 'Let's get together and fight the studios for rights that other professions get automatically . . . .' "

Willson grew pensive. "After a while, with all of these manipulations, Hollywood forgets who discovered and nurtured the star in the first place. With me, it was different, because everyone knew that I had named them. I'm not bitter about the stars who left me— that's just part of the agency business. When Jane Oliver died, some of the obits mentioned that she had discovered and groomed Dustin Hoffman, who had left her after his success in *The Graduate*, and this is just one of many cases.

"Success does strange things. It's usually so temporary, but the stars can't see that—even surrounded as they often are with has-beens. Monte Blue comes to mind. He was a big, big star in the 1920s, but the parts just got less and less until he was doing bits. His only consolation, I suppose, was that he did keep working in an industry that he obviously loved.

"It usually goes like this: first the agent is given the gate, then the husband or wife who has seen them through the lean years, then the old friends who 'don't fit in' anymore. After that, it never stops. When the star gets up there, it can be awfully lonely. I've known top stars who sit home by themselves, night after night. They've long ago cut off all the people who could have meant something to them. It's no wonder that they drink too much or start the drug scene. More so now, I would imagine, with all of the million-dollar-per-picture deals."

Willson laughed ruefully. "We thought that we got good money in the old days. A studio paid a star a few thousand dollars a week for *years*, and a top star might make $275,000 or $300,000 but no more. Selznick stars made considerably less. Ingrid Bergman, during all her big box-office years, could only have brought home about

$750,000, while Mr. Selznick, who constantly loaned her out to other studios, made a mint.

"He loaned her to Warners for *Casablanca* for $110,000, and she and the other cast members were very upset because it was written as they went along—on the back of envelopes as they say—which may account for that peculiar, edgy suspense that's all the way through it. They also paid him another hundred-thou for her for *Saratoga Trunk*, which he didn't want her to do, because he didn't like her as a 'woman with a past.' From Paramount, he got $150,000 for her Maria in *For Whom the Bell Tolls.* For *The Bells of St. Mary's,* for instance, he got $175,000 and lots of extras, and I think she got about $35,000!

"Selznick stars were like slaves in a way. In 1947, I made a deal for Universal to borrow Louis Jourdan from us for a Joan Fontaine picture, *Letters From An Unknown Woman.* We were paid $125,000 for his services, and he received one-fifth of that amount.

"I had met Fontaine years before when she was known as Joan Burfield, and was introduced to her by a Mrs. Thompson who owned the Ivar House restaurant in Hollywood. At that time, her sister Olivia De Havilland was the star, and Joan was sort of acting as her chauffeur and maid, and quite unhappy doing little more than bits. Later, Jesse L. Lasky at Paramount put her under a contract which he sold right away to RKO, where she made little money.

"Later she got very big for us, but she banked only $250 a week during *Rebecca* and *Suspicion,* for which she received an Academy Award! Her salary eventually rose to $17,000 a year, and she was big box office! After *The Emperor Waltz* in 1948, she went on suspension and ended her contract. But hers was a typical case. With great parts on loan-out, talent stayed with Selznick until they couldn't take it anymore financially.

"Gregory Peck got only $60,000 from us for *Only the Valiant* on loan-out to Warners; we pocketed $150,000! Dorothy McGuire never did a picture for us, but was loaned constantly. Selznick's personal productions made money: *Since You Went Away* returned four-millions profit; *Spellbound* grossed eight millions, but *The Paradine Case* lost four-millions, which was a big blow to Selznick's ego.

"But Selznick was most careful about the pictures in which his stars appeared. He was very story-conscious, and the parts had to be substantial. He never loaned his stars just for the sake of loaning them. And even his new people received good grooming."

Willson laughed roguishly, and his black eyes gleamed. "The story once made the Bel Air circuit that Joseph Cotten and Ingrid Bergman once dressed themselves as a butler and maid, and showed up at the back door of the Selznick mansion to serve at a party in place of two servants employed from an agency. Being actors, they were able to pull off the impersonation for a half-hour or so—who ever really looks at servants or tradespeople?

"Supposedly Mr. Selznick was not amused and, quite abashed, asked why they had pulled this trick, and they replied that since they were treated like slaves, they might as well act as slaves!" Now, I hasten to add that I do not know whether this event ever happened or not, but years later I asked Joe Cotten about it at a party, and he only smiled and walked away. But it's a marvelous story and could well have happened.

"But Mr. Selznick always needed money after 1949. He always lived in the most extravagant manner, and his gambling debts were high. He spent most of his time on the phone arranging deals for his contract people, and he became an unofficial flesh peddler.

"In 1946, I found a boy called Francis Durgin, whom I renamed Rory Calhoun. I got him a good part in an Edward G. Robinson picture, *The Red House*, with Julie London at United Artists, which Charlie Feldman was executive-producing. I'm going to digress a moment and talk about Charlie. He started out to be a lawyer, then became president of Famous Artists, a famous talent agency." He chuckled over the play upon words, and then went on seriously, "Charlie was brilliant, and a born wheeler-dealer. He was the first of the agents to break into the producing end of the business and, had he not died in 1968, he would probably have become head of a studio like others of our ilk—Freddie Fields, Ted Ashley, Ray Stark, and David Begelman. Incidentally, it was Darryl F. Zanuck who always said that one day agents would end up owning the business! And during his lifetime he's seen it happen.

"As I was saying before I interrupted myself, we loaned Rory here and there. One day, I heard that Julian Lesser and Frank Melford were producing a Western, *Massacre River*, and I telephoned about him.

Marilyn Lewis became Rhonda Fleming under Willson's aegis. Here she is doing the "starlet bit"for a fan magazine layout. *(Courtesy of Henry Willson collection)*

Henry Willson, with Mary Lou Gray and one of his 50s discoveries, Tom Irish, at the Mocambo. *Courtesy of Tom Irish, and Marvin Paige's Motion Picture and TV Research Service)*

"A few days later they called back, wanting to meet him. 'I'm sorry,' I replied, 'but he's out horseback-riding, but I'll go out to the ranch and get him.'

"I called Rory, who was home sleeping, and told him to put on his jeans and meet me at the studio. He came in, smiling sheepishly, and said, 'Sorry I'm late, but as you can see, I didn't even go home to change.' The producers took one look at him and he got the part—without a screen test!

"Next, Rory co-starred with Richard Basehart and Colleen Gray in *Sand* for Twentieth Century-Fox, which was slated to open at Grauman's Chinese Theater. On my way to the office, I looked up at the marquee and bristled. The billing read:

RICHARD BASEHART & COLLEEN GRAY in *SAND*

"I introduced myself to the theater manager, 'You know that Rory Calhoun is co-starring in this picture, don't you?' He said, 'Yeah, but there's no room for his name, and besides, it costs a hundred dollars to put up those marquee letters.' I gave him a long look. 'Then,' I replied, 'it will only cost a hundred dollars to take them down again. I've counted the letters and there is plenty of room if you do it this way.' I handed him a slip of paper, which read:

R. BASEHART—C. GRAY—R. CALHOUN in *SAND*

"I tell this story only to show that we gave personal service in those days, beyond the call of duty. Every personality required different handling, personally and professionally. I changed Merle Johnson Jr's name to Troy Donahue in 1957; Marilyn Lewis to Rhonda Fleming in 1943, and Robert Van Orden to John Smith in 1954. Hollywood thought that I had run out of names with that one, but the truth of the matter was that there were too many Vans at that time—Van Johnson, Bobby Van, Dickie Van Patton, Lee Van Cleef, Mamie Van Doren, Jo Van Fleet, Peter Van Eyck, Edward Van Sloan, Phillip Van Zandt ... I told the boy: 'You will be *the* John Smith! But I've been given credit for the name of one star whom I did not discover. I would never have picked a name like Rip Torn!

"Twenty-year-old Marilyn Lewis had appeared in bit parts in *In Old Oklahoma* for Republic in 1943 and *When Strangers Marry* at Monogram, which would be released the next year, and Fox had done nothing with her when I brought her to Mr. Selznick's attention. He was taken with her spectacular coloring—penny-colored hair and green eyes—and we gave her a bit in *Since You Went Away*, but I felt that she had more than just beauty to be used as window dressing, and came up with what I thought was an exotic name—Rhonda Fleming.

"A few months later, we cast her as the beautiful schizophrenic Miss Carmichael in *Spellbound*. I think she had two or three scenes, but what a sensation she caused! She turned from a sweet, loving girl into a clawing, vicious creature in a split-second. She was a big hit, and we loaned her to RKO with Dorothy McGuire for *The Spiral Staircase*. And three years later, she was being photographed in Technicolor, co-starring with Bing Crosby, in *A Connecticut Yankee in King Arthur's Court* at Paramount. Over the years, she has never failed to mention my name in interviews: she always gives me full credit for discovering her.

"Robert Mosely's first and only Selznick role was as the appealing young sailor in *Since You Went Away*. He filmed his three scenes while on shore-leave from the Coast Guard. How I found him makes an interesting point about my job. While it's true that I often went to theaters to scout casts, I first laid eyes on this 22-year-old coast guardsman in the audience! I could not avoid noticing him, because he was sitting in front of me in my direct line of vision.

"I had to keep peering around him to see Janet Gaynor, who had come out of retirement to recreate her role in the Lux Radio Theater adaptation of *A Star is Born*. Since I was 'on duty' I had gone backstage earlier to wish her well, and let her know that Mr. Selznick was tied up at home, working on the script of *Since You Went Away*.

"When I got up to leave, I noticed several young girls in the audience couldn't take their eyes off the tall, blondish coast guardsman. My mind flew back to a story conference Mr. Selznick had held that very morning concerning *Since You Went Away*. He wanted an appealing unknown for the small part of a lonesome sailor with whom Jennifer and Robert Walker spend an evening. He had said, 'Henry, I want the personification of the sort of guy that most girls would most like to meet. Because he represents a universal figure, I've named him Smith—Harold E. Smith.'

"Thinking this young man might be worthy of a screen test, I gave him my card—he recognized the Selznick name—and invited him to come to the studio the next day for an interview. He replied that he had to be back on duty in the morning. The more he talked, the more I was convinced that he was right for the part.

"I asked him to come with me to the telephone while I called Mr. Selznick who, since time was of the essence, told me to bring him up to the house, where he questioned him briefly. He was taken with Mosely's self-effacing boyishness, and signed him for the part. One thing about Mr. Selznick, when he felt strongly about something he never dawdled. It was only when he was uncertain that he drove people wild!

"Mosely's scenes went well, and Mr. Selznick told me to sign him to a contract, starting at $100 a week as soon as he got out of the Coast Guard. His name, of course, was impossible on a marquee, and I thought of how Mr. Selznick had first described the character to me, and I suggested Guy. A Dolly Madison pastry wagon gave me the idea for his last name.

"As it turned out, Guy Madison never appeared in another Selznick picture. And after the war we made a little money loaning him to RKO for *Till the End of Time* with Dorothy McGuire, and *Honeymoon* with Shirley Temple, and he stayed under contract until 1949. But, early on, the fan magazines went to town over him, and he was very popular among the bobbysoxers. Ten years later, he became a big hit all over again as Wild Bill Hickok on television. Every time I hear Glen Campbell sing 'Wichita Lineman,' I think of Guy, who worked outdoors for the telephone company before he went into the service.

"*Portrait of Jennie*, starring Jennifer Jones, Joseph Cotten and Ethel Barrymore, was a major disappointment. The problem, outside of a slight plot, was that it was over-produced. Robert Nathan had written a haunting story about a painter who falls in love with a girl who is actually a ghost, having lived a generation before, and who comes back to inspire a down-on-his-luck artist. In the first place, there's an old saying in Hollywood that 'fantasy doesn't sell.' But Mr. Selznick, an incurable romantic, never paid attention to axioms."

Willson laughed. "He was, as usual, before his time, and he created an ending to end all endings! He was much taken with Shirley Temple's *The Little Colonel*, a black-and-white film that featured a Technicolor fadeout. The climax of Jennie took place in a hurricane, on a rocky coast with a lighthouse. Mr. Selznick not only filmed the big storm that brought Jennifer and Joe together in green, with a wide screen and stereophonic sound, but the ending shot of the actual portrait was in Technicolor! I'll never forget the opening of the film at the Carthy Circle Theater, which had been especially equipped.

"The premiere crowd was quite unprepared when the masking on the screen was pulled back to reveal an enormous expanse of stormy green coast, assaulted on all sides by the frantic sounds of wind and rain. All of this spectacle simply drew attention to the fragile story. The box office was not good, and Mr. Selznick finally abandoned plans to equip all theaters showing the film with wide screen and surround speakers.

"I left Selznick in 1949, when he disbanded production after *Jennie* flopped. For a while I worked at Famous Artists. Those were good years, a very satisfying time of my life. Eventually, I opened my own agency on Carol Drive.

"Troy Donahue had big blue eyes and blond hair, and a natural body that looked great in trunks. His physique came in handy later when he starred in the TV series *Surfside Six*. He had had some experience playing in stock when I discovered him in 1956, when he was twenty, and got him a contract at Universal, but he didn't hit it really big until he went to Warners and did features as well as TV.

"Most of the talent that I discovered came into TV as a natural progression of their careers. A series can set up an actor for life, and when popularity fades they still have a bundle. Some stars like Alain Delon, whom I found in 1958 when he was 23 years old, are more suitable for motion pictures. He has made it big in both American and European films, but he prefers to work over there.

"Chad Everett, whose real name was Raymond Cramton, born in 1936, came along in 1960 after going to Wayne State University. I got him a part in *Claudelle Inglish* at Warners, and he was on his way. His *The Dakotas* and *Medical Center* TV series ran from 1969 to 1975."

Willson paused, "Oh, there were so many others, like busty, intelligent Marie Wilson, whom I found at the Bliss-Hayden Theater Workshop, who made so many 'dumb blonde' movies and worked for seven years in *Ken Murray's Blackouts* at the El Capitan theater, or sexy Race Gentry . . . .

"In April of 1967, I closed my office and joined Freddie Fields at Creative Management Associates, Ltd. I left the company after a year and started managing a few people, then I retired. I think that my timing was right. I'd had a long and fruitful career. I'd really seen it all."

Willson paused thoughtfully. "Now and then I'm asked why I chose such unusual names for my clients. I have a standard answer: 'If, in those days, a South African film buff picked up a fan magazine with a banner headline that read:

READ ALL ABOUT: ROCK, TAB, GUY,
RORY, TROY, and RHONDA,

that fan would know immediately to whom the article referred. But if that banner read:

READ ALL ABOUT ROY, ART, ROBERT,
FRANCIS, MERLE, and MARILYN,

who in the hell would know who they were?"

Henry Willson died in the hospital at the Motion Picture Country Home on June, 14, 1978. The chapel of Pierce Brothers Mortuary on Santa Monica Boulevard in Hollywood was packed with friends, old-time associates, and the "little people." Among his discoveries attending were Francis Durgin and Raymond Cramton.

But where were Roy Fitzgerald, Art Gelien, Marilyn Lewis, Robert Mosely, Robert Van Orden, and Merle Johnson?

BLACKOUT: 1947

Agent

This is a matter for an attorney rather than an agent. I'm afraid it will boil down to a "damned if you do, damned if you don't" situation. With the Un-American Affairs Committee gone public over television, the scare is on. There will be "friendlies" and "unfriendlies." If you testify in Washington, it will be worse than walking on eggshells. You can't help but appear defensive. Even an off-hand remark, taken out of context, can be damaging. You're going to require top legal advice.

Female Star

I wouldn't feel obligated to go at all, if it weren't for that film I made during the war. It was called "patriotic" then, remember? Today, it's obviously propaganda, which I realized when I screened the picture last night. I went to only one group meeting, taken there by a friend after dinner one night. It was so boring. God, it was deadly. I really didn't understand what was going on, and I certainly didn't sign anything.

Agent

Could anyone testify that you were there?

Female Star

If they remembered that I was at that one meeting.

Agent

I'm afraid, my dear, in the last analysis, the decision of whether to go or not to go will be between you and God.

Female Star

. . . and my legal beagle!

Sammy Davis, Jr., as Sportin' Life, Dorothy Dandridge as Bess, and Sidney Poitier as Porgy, in Samuel Goldwyn's production of *Porgy and Bess*. *(Courtesy of Columbia Pictures)*

Otto Preminger on the set of *The Cardinal*. *(Courtesy of Columbia Pictures)*

13

FROM PROMOTION TO PRODUCTION

W. C. Fields
I hate Catholics and agents.

It was not too long after films began to be cranked out of a primitive projector onto a white sheet on the back wall of a nickelodeon that it became apparent that, in order to get bodies into those rows of seats, some promotion was necessary. Garishly illustrated posters tacked outside the theater brought in a stream of the non-English speaking immigrants, but something more was needed. Newspapers were utilized for ads. Men wearing "sandwich boards" came next, then billboard advertisements.

When the "movie magazines" came into being in the 1910s and writers were employed to conduct interviews, promotion departments at the motion picture production offices were created. But by the 1930s, the working press was so jaded that more and more effort had to be expended by the studios to give them "new angles" to write about. Finally, one man thought up a new concept of promotion that has had a lasting effect on the film industry.

His name was Sigmund Charles Einfeld, and he created the "press junket." He was born October 25, 1901. Known as S. Charles Einfeld, he started out as an office boy and gag man at Vitagraph Studios, then became house manager for the Plaza Theater on 59th Street in Manhattan. He joined Warner Brothers in 1928, where he was to create audacious publicity campaigns that would be the talk of the town.

To promote *42nd Street*, the studio christened a train "The 42nd Street Special," and every Warner lovely and hunk that could be crowded on it were ordered to go on the junket by the studio—even players who were not in the film. On the train were Joe E. Brown,

Leo Carillo, Bette Davis, Ruby Keeler, Eleanor Holm, Glenda Farrell, Preston Foster, Ginger Rogers, Laura LaPlante, Dick Powell, Lyle Talbot, Toby Wing, Tom Mix and his trusty steed Tony, among others.

In her memoirs[1] Bette Davis described the event: "They had just completed an expensive musical, *Forty-Second Street*, with production numbers that could only have been staged on the steppes of Russia. Lavish, revolutionary and quite wonderful for its time, the investment had been tremendous; and while the public in its misery was looking for escape, the country was in a panic and money was scarce. The new President, Franklin Roosevelt, had just been elected and was about to be inaugurated. In order to entice the audience into theatres, Warners arranged a tie-up with General Electric in a stunt that was to cost sixty thousand dollars, most of it absorbed by GE. A special gold-leafed Pullman train, on its way to the Inauguration with an itinerary that included San Francisco, Salt Lake City, Cheyenne, Denver, Kansas City, St. Louis, Chicago, Cleveland, Pittsburgh, Baltimore, Washington, Philadelphia, Boston and New York, was scheduled to coincide with the picture's premiere in each city. It cut through the heart of the country like a golden scimitar. Factories were closed, millions jobless, and we really should have been publicizing the musical *Let 'Em Eat Cake*. Not only did we blind the poor with our glitter, we even had one whole car fitted out with sand, water and suntan lamps that transformed the Pullman into a mobile Malibu Beach . . . .

" 'A bevy of eleven chorus girls eleven—count them'—straight from the film included Lois January and Shirley Ross, who were always popping into opera hose and tremendous white polkadot halters and white coats. The poor girls had one costume apiece. They were not the most attractive sight at the end of the tour. White on a train for sixteen days! The whole affair was fabulous— traveling in such luxury during a depression. We were afraid we might incite a revolution; but unlike the eighteenth-century Frenchman, Americans love their royalty and we were welcomed everywhere with open arms, although a few did stick their tongues out at us . . . ."

The publicity stunt was very successful, and *42nd Street* started a new trend of musical pictures at Warner Brothers, offering a stage background, "show must go on" approach.

In 1939, Einfeld arranged to bring members of the press from all over the country to Dodge City, Kansas, the home of the famous Boot Hill—where outlaws and a few "soiled doves" were buried—for the glittering premiere of *Dodge City*, with Errol Flynn, Olivia De Havilland, and Ann Sheridan.

In 1940 he was able to arrange for the tiny island separating Seventh Avenue at 47th Street and Broadway in New York to be named "Duffy Square," to commemorate Father Francis Duffy, the famous World War I chaplain of the fighting 69th (Rainbow Division) as promotion for *The Fighting 69th*, with James Cagney, Pat O'Brien, and George Brent.

In 1941, he arranged with congressional friends to issue a memorial stamp in honor of Alvin York, coinciding with the release of *Sergeant York*, starring Gary Cooper. The same year Bette Davis wanted to raise money for the Littleton Hospital at Littleton, New Hampshire, near where she maintained a home, so Einfeld staged the premiere of her latest film, *The Great Lie*, with proceeds to go to the hospital, at the local theater on her thirty-third birthday, April 5, 1941. The press coverage included an NBC coast-to-coast "Your Happy Birthday" salute, and Luce correspondents did a "*Life* Goes to a Party" feature.

In 1942, Einfeld persuaded Billy Bishop—who had won the Victoria Cross in 1918—to lead a contingent of Canadian soldiers down Broadway in New York to promote *Captains of the Clouds*, with James Cagney and Dennis Morgan.

In 1943, he utilized the premiere of the patriotic *Yankee Doodle Dandy* (the story of George M. Cohan, starring James Cagney), to promote the sales of U.S. War Bonds as admission to theaters where the picture was playing.

In 1945, Einfeld left Warner Brothers to form Enterprise Productions with David L. Loew and produce films to be released by United Artists. It was his desire to use top box-office stars in well-produced films based on intriguing subject matter. However, he only had one minor hit, *The Other Love*, with Barbara Stanwyck, and one smash, *Body and Soul*, with John Garfield, both released in 1947. His monumental flop was the expensive *Arch of Triumph*, from the novel by Erich Maria Remarque, with Ingrid Bergman and Charles Boyer, for which he pulled out all of the publicity stops—including a press junket to Paris, and a visit to the Arch itself. But the public did not care to see the 33-year-old Bergman as a quasi-temptress with a 49-year-old leading man.

Edith Head,[2] costume designer for Bergman's *Arch of Triumph*, sipped coffee in the restaurant at Dulles International Airport in 1976, her flight to Los Angeles having been delayed. "Naturally, I've worked with many publicists in Hollywood, but I never really knew any of them well. Charlie Einfeld, although he was at Warners and I was at Paramount, was probably the most imaginative. The stars hated to go on those junkets, but the press loved them because it got them out of their cramped offices, and everything was gratis, including everyone's favorite liquor. Charlie knew what everyone in Hollywood drank, I think. If you were a Red Label man—that's what was delivered to your door.

"When I began to free lance, I worked with several publicists that I'd heard terrible things about, and not in one instance did I find any difficulty: they had a job to do and so did I, and if I had to accompany a star to a photo session or work some of the gowns I had designed for a star into a fashion show, I did it.

"Charlie Feldman was just as meticulous about his work when he went into production as he had been as a publicist. The clothes for Ingrid Bergman in *Arch of Triumph* were dark, and made of satins and heavy materials. She was playing against type, a sultry role, and she was very conscious of trying to do something different. I made many sketches for clothes that were not used. During wardrobe tests, we found the jewelry was not right. I found some pieces in my own collection. Then the matter of hats came up, and we finally settled mostly on berets."

Einfeld's other films fared almost no better, and Enterprise folded. A fortune gone, Einfeld returned to Hollywood and a vice-presidency at Twentieth Century-Fox, where he remained for fourteen years. He died at the age of 73 in Ascona, Switzerland, where he had lived in retirement the last few years. But when old publicists get together, they reminisce over all the food and booze placed next to their typewriters on all those free-wheeling press junkets.

Independent producers like Samuel Goldwyn, formerly Goldfish, depended upon mostly the written word for their products. He was 67 years old in 1959, when he produced his last picture, the George and Ira Gershwin folk opera *Porgy and Bess*, utilizing an all-black cast that included Sidney Poitier, Dorothy Dandridge, and Pearl Bailey.

Goldwyn, even at his age, had not lost his shrewdness. Being of the old school, he hated percentage deals. He had never minded hiring the best talent, both before and behind the camera (and paying high prices), but it irked him that anyone would share in the profits from his pictures.

Brilliant Rouben Mamoulian had directed the original play *Porgy* by DuBose and Dorothy Heyward for the Theatre Guild in New York, in 1927. He was again at the helm when the Gershwins turned the play into *Porgy and Bess*, seven years later on Broadway. So it was natural progression that he would also do the film. But he clashed with Goldwyn and was replaced by Otto Preminger (who had also replaced him as the director of *Laura*, with Gene Tierney, Dana Andrews, and Clifton Webb at Twentieth Century-Fox in 1944).

Poitier had been handled since 1954 by Martin Baum, of the Baum-Newborn Agency in New York. Their friendship had started when Baum had contacted him about a part in *The Phoenix City Story* in 1955, which he had turned down—much to Baum's amazement. Poitier was in the restaurant business at the time. He had started out as a dishwasher at the age of sixteen, in 1940, fresh from the Bahamas. He had made a U.S. Army documentary film in the service, then appeared on the New York stage and made four pictures. He revealed in his autobiography:[3]

"But months later I got another call from Martin Baum, saying, 'Come in and see me.' Now, Baum was a very dapper, elegant, sharp, and imaginative agent, always wheeling and dealing, always moving and tumbling, always in search of the creative element in every deal. There he was in his hand-sewn tailored suit, his silk tie and Gucci loafers, sitting behind a desk in his office that was itself magnificently decked out as befits a new-breed agency on the come. He was shaking his head and sighing in mock exasperation as if we were picking up exactly where we'd left off months before. 'You know something—I don't understand myself.' 'What's the matter, Mr. Baum?' 'Here I am—I've got a pretty good business going for myself. Some solid stable clients, some of whom are as hot as firecrackers. I have a partner, we're making money, we're doing very well, yet—for the last three months I can't get you out of my mind. What the hell is this?' 'I don't know, Mr. Baum. What is it?' 'I called you down here because—I don't have a job for you—I mean I called you down here to tell you to your face that anybody as crazy as you are, I want to represent them. I know you don't have a job and you haven't worked for some time. Now, do you want to be represented?' 'I'd love for you to represent me.' 'Good. I want to represent you. I don't know where I'm going to get the jobs, but I'm going to find something for you.' With a handshake we ended that discussion and began a remarkable association that was to thread its way through the succeeding twenty-five years . . . ."

Otto Preminger's contract was handled by his brother Ingo, who at that time headed a talent agency. Although it rankled, Goldwyn was willing to go along with a ten percent profit participation, but Ingo said it was not enough, whereupon Otto countered with the proposal that he would leave the amount up to Goldwyn after the film was completed.

Sammy Davis, Jr., had been shooting *Anna Lucasta* on the Goldwyn lot, which had been leased for the production, and he knew that he was right for the difficult-to-cast Sportin' Life. He meant to get the role. He noted in one of his autobiographies:[4] "I don't mind admitting I got all the pals I could muster—Sinatra, Jack Benny, George Burns, and guys like that—to root for me with Goldwyn. I nagged the William Morris agency to make it a top priority. I think Goldwyn must have finally got sick of the sound of my name because he appeared at the door of my dressing room at the Moulin Rouge nightclub one night and said, 'Mr. Davis, you are Sportin' Life. The part is yours. Now will you get all these guys off my back?' "

Davis acted, danced, and sang (the memorable "It Ain't Necessarily So") to perfection, finishing the picture without realizing that Sportin' Life was a drug dealer and that his "happy dust" was cocaine!

Davis continued, "When we finished shooting, there was a big fuss over my billing. Goldwyn thought I had a good chance of getting an Academy Award nomination. The William Morris agency had insisted, when I got the part, on the studio's giving me star billing, and at first I had been enthusiastic about that. But when it came to the crunch, we knew I would never get the nomination for Best Actor because I was by no means the leading player, so Goldwyn wanted to downgrade me to 'supporting' actor because he felt that the nomination would be in the can. He was eager because Sportin' Life had got the only significant world reviews. They had raved about the part in both America and Europe. In the end it was the lawyers who decided. They said we couldn't start changing the billing after the film had been released. So the only possibility I ever had of meeting Oscar was plucked away."

Preminger was certain, now that the picture was finished and the reviews were laudatory, that his percentage would far exceed ten percent. Goldwyn shook his head, and reminded him that the profit participation had been left to him. Preminger was left holding the bag.

The brothers Preminger were multi-faceted. While directing features during World War II, Otto had been a credible actor in beefy Nazi roles, and in 1967 Ingo Preminger grew tired of the agency business and was determined to switch roles and get into active production. Aligning himself with Jack Smight—who had formed Solitaire Productions, he completed pre-production work on *Running Scared*, but it was not until 1970 that he was involved with a blockbuster film.

"Ingo Preminger combined blood and laughs in his 20th-Century-Fox production of *MASH*," noted *Daily Variety* on December 10, 1970, "and, as a result, he terms himself a producer 'with a serious tax problem—I hope.' This kind of problem should happen to everybody, for the reason that Preminger's production unit at 20th should walk away with a profit of $5,000,000 . . . .

"Quondam agent Preminger, free-wheeling and uninhibited in conversation, says Jack Valenti is not to his liking and he characterizes the MPAA's rating system as 'we're stabbing ourselves in the back' by way of imposing self-inflicted censorship which just is not needed . . . ."

Preminger went on to say that he did not care to produce another picture on the order of *M*A*S*H*, and that he might do a film with the family values of a Disney Studio picture. He felt that to pay Norman Jewison $1,000,000 for *Fiddler on the Roof* was bad, and he elaborated that he would pay Paul Newman $200,000 for a film but not $750,000. He stated that he believed the industry was in great shape, but cautioned that rip-offs of *Easy Rider* or *M*A*S*H* would not make money. He could not foretell that not only would *M*A*S*H* (brought in for something like $3,000,000) make several fortunes, but that its spin-off as a television series, and *its* spin-off *After M*A*S*H*, would continue on the tube well into the 1980s.

While the brothers Preminger worked both sides of Sunset Boulevard, the brothers Cagney were more active in the San Fernando Valley, where Warner Brothers studio was located.

James Cagney was not discovered by a talent agent, but by Al Jolson, when he and Joan Blondell were appearing in *Penny Arcade* on Broadway in 1929. Jolson took an option on the play. Under contract to Warner Brothers at the time, he suggested the studio also option the "two kids." Cagney went to Hollywood for $500 a week for six weeks, and stayed under long-term contract for $400 a week.

Cagney made 25 pictures in five years, during which time his brother Bill visited Hollywood, was screen-tested, and performed in three pictures for RKO. However, Bill preferred the business side of the industry, and became his brother's manager.

In 1931, after *Blonde Crazy*, Cagney demanded more money, finally settling for $1,000 a week, and later $1,250. However, the next year he walked out in protest. Other stars on the lot were making $4,000 to $6,000 per week and were not bringing in the money. He told a reporter: "My stand is based on the fact that my pictures, for the time being, are big money-makers—and that there are only so many successful pictures in a personality. And don't forget that when you are washed up in pictures you are really through. You can't even get a bit, let alone a decent part .... I don't care if I never act again. If I never had to do another scene, it would be all right with me. I have no trace of that ham-like theatrical yen to act all the time no matter what. I shan't miss trouping."

Warner Brothers reluctantly gave him $3,000 a week, and while all of his four 1933 films did well, the exhilarating musical *Footlight Parade* took in $1,750,000. Two years later, when he made the list of top-ten box-office stars for the first time, he had five pictures in release—including his portrayal of Bottom in *A Midsummer Night's Dream*—instead of the four that his contract stipulated.

Since the paycheck was low for what Cagney's films were grossing, brother Bill found a point on which a suit could be filed. Cagney's contract called for him to be billed first over the title of his films: by chance, the Warner Theater on Hollywood Boulevard had billed Pat O'Brien over Cagney. A photograph of the marquee was submitted with the court evidence.

Waiting for the case to be resolved, Cagney made two pictures in

1937 for Grand National, *Great Guy*, and *Something to Sing About*. Then, with the financial affairs worked out, he returned to the studio grind.

During the next years, Bill Cagney became an associate producer at Warner Brothers and was largely responsible for obtaining the rights from George M. Cohan to do his life story, *Yankee Doodle Dandy*, in 1942—which would bring his brother an Academy Award.

"Many people think I learned to dance for *Yankee Doodle Dandy*," James Cagney said in his autobiography,[5] "the prevailing impression being that when a fella gets up and does a dance routine, he learned it the day before yesterday. Not so. A song-and-dance man, which is what I am basically, becomes one over many years of unrelenting work. I'm amazed by reading reports of actors who say, 'I'm studying voice and dance now, and I'm going to do a musical comedy next season.' Unfailingly, it never happens. To become a dancer, initially you've got to be a little bit off your chump in order to put up with the pain—the sprained ankles, torn tendons, and bumped knees. A person dedicating himself to that kind of hardship needs a particular attitude. I think dancing is a primal urge coming to life at the first moment we need to express joy. Among pre-language aboriginals possessing no music and the most primitive rhythm, I suspect dancing became their first expression of excitement. And an extension of that idea is embedded in my belief, quite applicable to myself, that once a song-and-dance man, always a song-and-dance man . . . ."

Aside from those musicals of the 1930s, the public today thinks of Cagney only for his gangster roles, and perhaps for the bad impressionists who hike up their trousers, throw their heads back, and rasp, "You dirty rat!"—a line that he never uttered.

But even with the prestige of the Oscar for *Yankee Doodle Dandy*, the studio was unwilling to spring for more money. Weary of fighting, the Cagneys bravely formed a company—William Cagney Productions—with pictures to be released through United Artists.

The decision for Cagney to go on his own was courageous and daring. Few stars since the 1920s felt they could buck the major studios. The big exodus for the independents was ten years away. The Cagneys were very concerned about subject matter, as well as good production values—bored with all of the gangster pictures with fifteen to eighteen-day shooting schedules, miscast actors, and inept scripts. The four films that they produced were artfully turned out, but did not bring the expected returns.

Johnny Come Lately (1943), with the elderly Grace George as the head of a newspaper who hires Cagney, received a lukewarm reception from the public. Somewhat more successful was *Blood on the Sun* (1945), with Cagney as a 1920s reporter who discovers a Japanese conspiracy, opposite Sylvia Sydney as the beautiful Eurasian *femme fatale*. While brother Bill was lining up the next property, Twentieth Century-Fox wanted Cagney for *13 Rue Madeleine*. The money was right. The film made money.

William Saroyan's *The Time of Your Life*, the next William Cagney production, was faithfully adapted, but lost $500,000. To make up the exchequer, Cagney went back to Warner Brothers for one of his most successful pictures, *White Heat*, then returned to the production company for *Kiss Tomorrow Goodbye*.

During the next eleven years he made sixteen pictures, including the enormously successful *Love Me or Leave Me* (1955), where he portrayed the "Gimp," the gangster boyfriend of Doris Day's Ruth Etting. The same year, he played the Captain in *Mr. Roberts*, then portrayed silent film star Lon Chaney in *Man of a Thousand Faces* (1957). But it was during the production of *One, Two, Three* (1961) in Germany that Cagney decided to retire.

After 31 years, he had his fill of making films in dark, cavernous sound stages. He loved the outdoors. Cagney and his wife Willie had always lived simply, compared to others in the movie business. He owned a ranch in the desert, a place on Martha's Vineyard, and Verney Farm, in upstate New York.

Twenty years later—to Hollywood's surprise, since he had always sworn that he would never act again—Cagney, at 83, came out of retirement to star in the film version of *Ragtime*, E. L. Doctorow's best seller, which was produced mostly in England. Cagney noted that his doctor had recommended that he go back to work. *Ragtime* was not a blockbuster, but Cagney was praised for his role as the police commissioner.

Two years later, he was back before the cameras in a television movie, *Terrible Joe Moran*, which was shot in a luxurious townhouse in New York on a month's schedule.

Wrote Rod Townley:[6] "Producer Robert Halmi was worried. There was $3 million tied up in this TV movie and here was his star, a sick, 84-year old man in a wheelchair, his head drooping toward his chest. In recent years the old actor had been hit with diabetes, a stroke, spurs on his spine, sciatica, bursitis. The script called for him to be in nearly every scene . . . ."

The film was scheduled to air March 27, 1984. Friends and family again wondered why, in his deteriorated physical condition, he would want to act again. *Life* magazine was also intrigued, and assigned Anthony Cook to investigate. The comprehensive, extremely well-researched article, "Yankee Doodle's Curious Comeback" was printed in the March 1984 issue, explosively suggesting that Cagney was under the influence of a "mysterious" woman.

"The mysterious woman in question is about 60," Cook wrote. "Young enough to be his daughter, she has been mistaken for Cagney's wife, his physiotherapist, his nurse. In *Ragtime*, she was billed as his assistant. In *Terrible Joe*, her credit will likely be associate producer. She pays his bills, gives him his medication, manages his farm, arranges his schedule and makes his deals. She is agent, business manager, majordomo and occasional chauffeur. Her name is Marguerite Zimmermann. She calls Cagney Jamesie. Everyone knows her as Marge . . . ."

Zimmermann and her husband, Don, had first met the Cagneys when they came into her restaurant in Millbrook, New York, located near Verney Farm. The two couples became friendly. The restaurant ran into financial problems and finally was closed. Gradually, Zimmermann moved into the Cagneys' lives, eventually becoming indispensable to them. Friends began to report that they could not reach Cagney. Even his children and brother Bill had difficulty getting through to him. His sister, Jeanne, was removed as executrix of his estate.

Encouraged by Zimmermann and a local doctor, Cagney came out of retirement again for *Terrible Joe Moran*, first commissioned by producer Robert Halmi for Katharine Hepburn and called *Terrible Tess*. It was intended that Hepburn would portray a retired tennis player (probably using footage for the necessary younger flashbacks from one of her earlier films). She turned the property down.

"Halmi," the *Life* article continued, "sent the script to Milos

Forman's agent, who knew that Marge was scouting for properties. It was a long shot. Obviously there weren't many roles Cagney could play at this point. Marge had considered a revival of *The Man Who Came to Dinner* because the leading role could be performed in a wheelchair. But that hadn't worked out—she was still looking. She read *Terrible Tess* eagerly and found it so touching she said she wept. Here was the perfect role for Jamesie. There was the small matter of changing the sex of the star, but never mind. Within ten days, the scriptwriter had transformed *Terrible Tess* into *Terrible Joe* . . . ."

About *Life* magazine's assertions regarding Zimmermann, producer Halmi was quoted in *TV Guide*: "Cagney is the toughest S.O.B. around. You can't boss him around." Then he spoke of Zimmermann: "Sure, she can create enemies faster than anyone else. She yells. Then, after you yell back, you smile and everything's O.K. . . . ."

"Terrible Joe Moran made its air date March 27, 1984, to curiously mixed reviews. Some critics said Cagney had not lost his old sparkle, others regretted that he had made the appearance. But the ratings were excellent: the film took fourteenth place among the week's top twenty shows. Whether Cagney had again retired remained to be seen. Apparently the film had given him confidence that he could work again, despite his infirmities.

Early in 1984, he was reportedly out of his wheelchair, making use of a walker. On July 2, 1984, the *Boothbay Register*, a Maine newspaper, reported that Cagney had checked out of the Fisherman's Wharf Inn and Motel to return to Verney Farm. He had been released on June 30 from St. Andrews Hospital, where he had been admitted on June 16 after a heart attack. With him in the limousine was Willy, a paramedic attendant, and his agent, Marge Zimmermann.

BLACKOUT: 1943

Agent

It's really nice to see you again, Max.

Studio Head

Last time was the Racquet Club in Palm Springs. Eh?

Agent

You've got a photographic memory, Max. (Pause, a beat) Your wife is well? The children?

Studio Head

Fine. All fine. (Pause, two beats) I know Jimmy, who you've handled for thirty years, gets 8 G's a picture. How about Stebbens?

Agent

Since he got an Oscar last year for writing *Jordan*, he's expensive. (A beat) Look Max, let me give give you the whole magilla—the entire package for $200,000—star, story, writer.

Studio Head

You sold the same people to Warners for $165,000.

Agent

Yes, but Jimmy went for less, because he got 10 percent of the gross after the picture went black. You want such a deal?

Studio Head

I don't share profits. $165,000 is as high as I go.

Agent

I honestly can't ask my people to go for less, Max.

Studio Head

You still got the guy who shot *Cherokee*?

Agent

Herbie Mack? Yes. Fantastic cinematographer.

Studio Head

Throw him in and you've got the $200,000.

Agent

Up it $40,000, Max, and Herbie's in the package.

Studio Head

$230,000 is all I can scrape up, and that's taking oatmeal out of my kids' mouths.

Marilyn Monroe as she appeared in *The Asphalt Jungle* at MGM, a part that agent Johnny Hyde arranged for her. *(Whitney Stine collection)*

M. C. Levee with client Warren William and friends. *(Courtesy of The New York Public Library, Astor, Lenox & Tilden Foundations)*

14

GOING INDEPENDENT

Lee Marvin.
He was my friend always and then my agent. I have never discussed any of my work with anybody—my family, the elevator operator, nobody. I discuss it with Meyer [Mishkin]. Including my personal problems. If there's a fee involved, I'm not concerned about it. I like Meyer.

Whodunit author Raymond Chandler, once handled by Ray Stark, possessed a dry sense of humor that approached the lethal. He created the character of private eye Philip Marlowe, his alter ego, who stalked through such films as *Farewell My Lovely* (1945 and 1973) and *Lady in the Lake* (1947), and Chandler himself collaborated on the memorable *Double Indemnity* (1944) and *The Blue Dahlia* (1946). In 1952, at the age of 65, he composed a vitriolic piece on Hollywood agents:[1]

"Here is a guy who really makes with the personality," he wrote. "He dresses well and drives a Cadillac—or someone drives it for him. He has an estate in Beverly Hills or Bel Air. He has been known to own a yacht, and by yacht I don't mean a cabin cruiser. On the surface he has a good deal of charm, because he needs it in his business. Underneath he has a heart as big as an olive pit . . . .

"The law allowed him to incorporate, which, in my opinion, was a fatal mistake. It destroyed all semblance of the professional attitude and the professional responsibility to the individual client. It permitted a variety of subtle maneuvers whereby the agent could make a great deal more money after taxes, and it allowed him to slide, almost unobserved, into businesses which had nothing to do with the agency. He could create packaging corporations which delivered complete shows to the networks or the advertising agencies, and he loaded them with talent which, sometimes under another corporate name, he represented as an agent. He took his commissions for getting you a job, and then he sold the job itself for an additional profit. Sometimes you knew about this, sometimes you didn't. In any case the essential point was that this operator was no longer an agent except in name."

Chandler continued, "His clients and their work became the raw material of a speculative business. He wasn't working for you, you were working for him. Sometimes he even became your employer and paid you a salary which he called an advance on future commissions. The agency part of his operations was still the basic ingredient, since without control of talent, he had no bricks to build his wall, but the individual meant nothing to him. The individual was just merchandise, and the 'representing' of the individual was little more than a department of an entertainment trust—a congeries of powerful organizations which existed solely to exploit the commercial value of talent in every possible direction and with the utmost possible disregard for artistic or intellectual values.

"Such trusts, and it is fair to call them that regardless of whether they meet an exact legal definition, cover the whole field of entertainment. Their clients include actors, singers, dancers, mouth organ players, trainers of chimpanzees and performing dogs, people who ride horses over cliffs or jump out of burning buildings, motion picture directors and producers, musical composers, and writers, in every medium including those quaint old fashioned productions known as books.... Of course you don't have to become their client, but the inducements are glittering. And if they reduce you to a robot, as eventually they will, they will usually be very pleasant about it, because they can afford to employ well-dressed young men who smile and smile."

One of these typical well-dressed young men who smiled and smiled, and came from a large agency, telephoned a well-known comedy-writer/producer who had created one of the most innovative and hilarious television series of all time, had been involved as a producer-writer on several other hit shows, had written monologues for talk show hosts, and had some standing in the creative community.

The agent waxed enthusiastically about a famous screen team

finally considering going into television. "The thinking is," he went on excitedly, "that you would be perfect to develop this project. Meet me on the corner of Doheny and Sunset at three p.m. and I'll take you to up to their house in Bel Air."

The writer swallowed hard. "Just give me the address and I'll meet you there," he replied quietly. "I have some errands to do in the area."

"No. No." The agent continued hurriedly, "It's best that you meet me."

The writer was losing patience, but kept his temper. "If I get there before you do, I'll wait in my car. What's the address?"

"I can't give it to you," the agent replied at last.

"In the first place," the insulted writer/producer exploded, "I don't wait on street-corners, and in the second place, oh, what the hell—just go fuck off!" And he slammed down the telephone. The series was never made.

This is a typical encounter in the present-day suspicious climate of Hollywood, and indeed illustrates why some projects never get off the ground. All those in power guard their flanks so carefully and play the political games so adroitly that they not only do disservice to the client but often maneuver themselves out of a fat commission.

Thirty or forty years ago, agents also covered their flanks—with clients under contract to the studios—but since the agents knew everyone in town on a more-or-less speaking basis, suspicion and mistrust was not encouraged. Some agents had risen from the ranks and knew the score better than others, as in the case of M. C. Levee, producer-cum-agent, who was born in Baltimore, Maryland, on January 18, 1891.

Levee started out in the film industry as a property man for William Fox in 1917. He showed such a flair for the business that he founded Brunton Studios (with Robert Brunton and Joseph Schenck in 1920), which was later sold to Paramount Pictures. He then produced *White Moth* (1924) and *Sweet Daddies* (1926) for First National in Burbank.

By the time Levee made *Isle of Lost Ships* (1929), he was vice-president and business manager of First National, having supervised the building of several giant sound stages for the company. However, First National—caught in the crossfire of the talkie revolution—sold out to Warner Brothers for $10,000,000 cash.

Levee was a powerful force in the movie industry. He was first Treasurer of the Academy of Motion Picture Arts and Sciences, a position that he held for twelve years, and he also served as its third president.

After the sale of First National to Warners, Levee went to work as executive manager of Paramount, but left the studio in 1932 to form The Screen Guild, a cooperative producing organization, founded on the belief that stars, writers, directors, and producers could turn out their own products and share the proceeds. His great supporter was Bank of America's "Doc" Giannini. Although the creative community gave the idea lip service, and many stars expressed interest in taking less salary in return for profits, the studios wanted nothing to do with the concept, and The Screen Guild was disbanded. M. C. Levee's plan was ten years before its time.

It was at this time that he became an agent, and would handle stars Joe E. Brown, Joan Crawford, Bette Davis, Leslie Howard, Merle Oberon, Jeanette MacDonald, Paul Muni, Mary Pickford, Dick Powell, Claude Rains, Franchot Tone, and Ethel Waters; directors Lloyd Bacon, Frank Borzage, Cecil B. De Mille, William Dieterle, Alfred E. Green, and Mervyn LeRoy; writer Ben Hecht, and opera star Madame Ernestine Schumann-Heink.

Jerome Lawrence noted in his biography of Paul Muni:[2] "Mimi Levee, the wife of Muni's agent, remembers the day Muni took her to lunch at the Players Restaurant on the Sunset Strip and asked her wistfully, 'Tell me. How did you manage a family in this town?'

"Beyond his growing sons, M. C. Levee had established a family atmosphere representing actors, directors, and songwriting teams. Instead of a sterile office building, his agency was headquartered in a rambling house at the corner of Crescent Heights Boulevard and Fountain Avenue. He conducted business on a sunny patio, over lunch he prepared himself with flair and style. Levee, a gourmet cook, took delight in serving his clients *quiche Lorraine*, fish soup, and marinated steaks while studio contracts were being marinated simultaneously . . . ."

Levee remained a force in the industry, even after some of his major stars left to be handled by Music Corporation of America, the William Morris Agency, and smaller outfits. He headed the Artists Managers Guild from July 1937 until April 1940. The years were kind to him, and he retired in 1956.

Ten years later on his seventy-fifth birthday, Levee took out a full page announcement in the Hollywood trade magazines, which listed his past accomplishments and noted that he was now president of Royal Hawaiian Estates (located at the corner of South Palm Canyon Drive and Twin Palms Drive in Palm Springs), and had "2 beautiful furnished units for sale, with the land." And he added: "Howz about cummin out n' see em sum time."

When he died May 26, 1980, he was the same wise, interesting man that he had been at the height of his career as an agent.

Another agent of Levee's era was Morris Stoller who joined William Morris in New York in 1937, and moved to the West Coast ten years later. On December 10, 1980, he became chairman of the board; newly elected members were Norman Brokaw, Roger Davis, Tony Fantozzi, Stan Kamen, Lee Stevens, Don Weiss, and Walter Zifkin. Stoller, who had been responsible for forming the Morris International Division in the early 1950s, said on the latter occasion: "The entertainment industry keeps growing by leaps and bounds. All forms of entertainment affect us favorably. We represent the people—as their industry grows—we grow."

Still another agent who had grown up in the business was George Wood, whose father Joe was a producer for the Keith and Orpheum circuits. *Variety* noted in Wood's obituary on November 13, 1963: "It was natural that he turn to the theatre. He opened an office during the Prohibition era with a seeming knack for finding the right talent for the various cafes. The operators sought out his counsel and the associations made at that time, many of them reputed underworld figures, refused to let Wood go when the Prohibition era was over. He had extensive contacts in spots that were said to have been controlled by the mob and held the confidences of key underworld figures . . . ."

Wood, who handled such stars as Harry Richmond and Ed Wynn in the beginning, brought his contract list with him when he joined the Morris Agency in 1941. Partially responsible for the opening of the Club Riobamba, he booked Jane Froman for the first attraction and later brought in Frank Sinatra fresh from the Tommy Dorsey band, who made a great hit, following him with Dean Martin.

The *Variety* obit continued: "In a measure, he was thus partially responsible for the emergence of Sinatra. He later was assigned the singer when Sinatra was floundering. He had been 'fired' by MCA and the swooner's career seemed a dead issue. Together with agency head Abe Lastfogel, they set about to revitalize Sinatra. Lastfogel handled the Hollywood end, and Wood took care of him in the East. The venture was successful. However, Sinatra some years later elected to go *sans* agency, and resigned from the Morris office."

Other clients George Wood handled were Tallulah Bankhead, Jimmy Durante, and Rita Hayworth. Wood had an intuitive feel for the business . At the time of his demise, he was responsible for the agency taking on the marketing rights to Scopitone, a jukebox equipped with a back-projection screen to show color musical shorts of leading artists performing their hits. He was twenty years before his time: Scopitone—the precursor of mid-1980s' jukebox videos—had only a brief surge of popularity.

But perhaps the most colorful agent of the 1940s was diminutive, dapper, dynamic Johnny Hyde, a senior partner in the William Morris Agency. He handled several blond stars, including Lana Turner. He loved many pretty girls, but he was almost fifty when he met the one girl that would change his life—and vice versa. Her name was Marilyn Monroe, and she was half his age. He talked her up all over town, but everyone thought he was pushing her career only because they were lovers. (To pump up his ego when they were in bed, she used to whisper, "Oh, Johnny, you're hurting me!")

Hyde read the screenplay of *The Asphalt Jungle*, which John Huston had written from the book by W. R. Burnett, planning to direct and produce for MGM. Hyde talked Huston into making a screen test of Monroe for the role of Louis Calhern's mistress. Huston liked the test very much and cast her in the picture.

Hollywood columnist James Bacon wrote:[3] "As soon as she had busted out in those brief scenes in *The Asphalt Jungle*, the whole town was talking about her. It was not a blockbuster picture but it was a classic movie of its day, a favorite on the Bel-Air circuit. That's the private projection rooms of the directors and producers. Marilyn's emergence was all the more noteworthy because she had shone in scenes with Calhern, one of the finest actors of stage or screen. I had seen Calhern, with his back to the camera, steal scenes—like a Jack Oakie or Victor McLaglen. But in *The Asphalt Jungle*, he was the victim this time.

"A year or two later, he and I were talking about it at lunch in the

MGM commissary. Louie said: 'Jack Barrymore always used to say, "Never do a scene with a kid or a dog." After *Asphalt Jungle*, I amend that to include beautiful tits . . . .' "

"It wouldn't have happened, any of it, if not for Johnny," Marilyn told Garson Kanin, who remembered the incident in his book, *Hollywood*.[4] "When I did *The Asphalt Jungle*, it was like that was some kind of a discovery. But Jesus, I'd been knocking around, and I mean knocking around, for about six years before that, modeling and everything . . . . Look, I had plenty of friends and acquaintances—you know what I mean, acquaintances? And, sure, I played the game the way everyone else was playing it. But not one of them, not one of those big shots, ever did a damn thing for me, not one, except Johnny. Because he believed in me . . . .

"You know what a creep town this is and, naturally, when I was living with Johnny, it was like I was doing it because he could do me some good. He was the first kind man I ever met in my whole life. I've known a few since, but he was the first. And smart. Remember how fast he used to talk and how high?" She smiled in fond recollection. "Once he got an idea or some kind of a strategy, he would just stay on it, and he wouldn't stop. He would pace around, or walk up and down, for hours, sometimes till two or three in the morning, figuring out all the angles. He was certainly a wonderful man. When he died like that, all of a sudden, I really thought maybe my whole life was over, too. But just before he died, he got me this contract with Twentieth, a second one. And without him around to promote me—it's something I don't know how to do. I mean, I know how to put my body over, but I don't know how to put *myself* over . . . ."

Before Johnny collapsed and died of a heart attack, he had appealed to Joseph L. Mankiewicz, whom William Morris also handled, to give her the small but telling part of Miss Caswell, the girlfriend of George Sanders in *All About Eve*. Mankiewicz was willing, but after the head of the talent department, Lou Schreiber, turned her down, Johnny went to Darryl F. Zanuck, head of the studio, who gave the go-ahead. The part of Miss Casswell was a preview of the sorts of roles that Marilyn could perform brilliantly. It was the formal start of her career.

Other agents had fallen briefly in love with clients, whom they touted all over town, usually to no avail, except for getting them a few walk-ons. "Look," a Hollywood columnist has said, "you know the person will be dropped as soon as the hot-pants cool off, so you play along with a few plugs, a couple of directors give them a scene with a line or two, and that's it. It's far more difficult now to use the 'playthings' in pictures, because most films are shot independently and on location. In the old days, a studio contract at $150 a week was not all that difficult to promote, and options were usually dropped after six months. The town is full of people who thought the way to the top was between the sheets; they are secretaries and limo drivers or waitresses or parking lot attendants. But Johnny knew that Marilyn was different—an absolute original at the time. I think he fell in love with her because of her delicious giggle."

Over the years, there has been much speculation in Hollywood about what would have happened had Hyde lived, married Monroe, and taken over her career. Under his guidance, she might not have turned into the high-strung, neurotic girl that she became, nor ended her life with pills.

When Marilyn Monroe died, John Bradford, (who took over Mike Connolly's column when he was on vacation, and later after he died) wrote: "There is no one to replace her. Marilyn, with her built-in vulnerable quality that made Hollywood history. Saturday she was swimming, playing with her dog, 'Maf,' and setting up appointments with J. Lee Thompson, the Mirisches and Gene Kelly! Her *Esquire* cover and 10-page spread was set for Sept. 12 in New York . . . . Fox looked at *Something's Got to Give* rushes and were making plans to go ahead in Dec. with Dino after he finishes *Toys in the Attic* . . . . Will anyone forget Marilyn, the eclipsed little Gemini, in *Prince and the Showgirl*, who took the brunt of her last assignment's schedule problems. Very few know or realize *Something* was shut down for only two days—shooting around Marilyn for Steve Allen to get his TV show started, Phil Silvers to begin *Mad World*, and Wally Cox for *Spencer's Mountain* . . . ."

Another William Morris client was director Frank Capra. In 1961, when he decided to remake his 1933 movie *Lady for a Day* as *Pocketful of Miracles*, he had to deal with the "new Hollywood" of packages. He first offered the role of Dave the Dude to Frank Sinatra, who turned it down, then to Dean Martin, who did likewise. He met Glenn Ford while having lunch at the Naples Restaurant on Gower Street, north of his old stomping ground, Columbia Pictures.

Ford said he would like to play Dave the Dude, and the deal was made.

Capra wrote in his autobiography:[5] "Abe Lastfogel was the agent representing all four clients in the Capra-Ford deal: producer-director Frank Capra (a hired man), Frank Capra Productions (a hiring corporation), actor-star Glenn Ford (a hired man), Ford's Newton Productions (a hiring corporation). Mr Lastfogel's William Morris Agency (and all other talent agencies that put together package deals) negotiated for both employers and employees and collected 10 percent of their respective salaries and profits. Cozy. You wouldn't think there was any additional way in which an agency would have it made. But there was . . . .

"On paper, I was the producer-director for the co-venture. That was on paper. Legally, all partners in a co-venture have an equal vote regardless of whether individual partners own one percent or 99 percent of the venture. That meant that, technically and lawfully, Glenn Ford had a voice equal to mine in all film production decisions. What happened if we disagreed? The co- venturers had to give the tie-breaking vote to a disinterested third party. And who was the agreed-upon 'disinterested' third party in our deal? Correct. Abe Lastfogel. With his power to vote either with Ford or with Capra, Lastfogel was, in fact, the *executive-producer* of the film."

Lastfogel put together the package deal for the co-venture, called Franton. United Artists, the releasing company, was down for twenty percent of the profits for financing, and the Ford and Capra companies would go fifty-fifty on eighty percent. Ford's salary was set for $350,000 for ten week's work; Capra would receive for his 65-week involvement as producer-director-writer-editor about $1,500 a week.

But the problems were only beginning. Capra discovered that before Ford would sign, he wanted the co-venture to hire his own makeup man, wardrobe man, secretary, chauffeur, publicity man, and still photographer. In addition, his clothing—as Dave the Dude—had to be tailor-made and become his property after filming. He wanted first choice on special props or furniture bought for the picture. Lastfogel appealed to Capra to "make the boy happy." Capra had already received a commitment from Helen Hayes, represented by Lucy Kroll, to play the co-starring role of Apple Annie.

Capra wanted Shirley Jones, who had just made a hit as the prostitute in *Elmer Gantry*, for the third part of the brassy gun moll "Queenie" Martin. Ford agreed. Jones had already accepted the role through her William Morris agent, Lennie Hirshan, for a salary of $75,000 for eight weeks, when Lastfogel informed Capra that Ford wished Hope Lange, his best friend, to play Queenie.

In his book, Capra reported Lastfogel as saying: " 'He laid it on the line, Frank. If I don't vote with him on Hope Lange, he won't sign the United Artists contract.'

" 'But did you tell Glenn that he committed himself to Shirley Jones? That we owe her seventy-five thousand whether she plays the part or not?'

" 'He says that's William Morris's headache, not his. He gave me till midnight. It's Hope Lange or he's out.'

" 'Well, I'll be a sonofabitch.' I jumped up to keep from blowing up. 'Abe, look at me! Are you going to let some punk actor run your business? Fuck Glenn Ford! Let's replace him.'

" 'With whom?' he asked with a tired sigh.

" 'With anybody. There must be a thousand actors in Holl—'

" 'Name one. That UA will lend money on. The fun's gone out of picture-making, Frank. Let's face it. If I vote with you against using Hope Lange, Ford pulls out. And UA cancels the picture unless you replace Glenn with another star. Which you're not going to do this year or next. And if you do, you'll just start all over again with a new co-venture. And the new star will tell you how to cast your film. Fun, huh?'

" 'Meanwhile, your Frank Capra company is stuck with a quarter of a million in story costs, and maybe another hundred G's for Helen Hayes if she's committed. Now, Frank. You tell me. As the third party, who do I vote for—you or Glenn? Every damn decision is a four-foot putt these days.' "

Capra reluctantly acquiesced. At the age of 64, some of the fight had gone out of him. But the problems were far from over. When the schedule on the picture was delayed for three months while the part of Queenie was re-written to fit the softer Lange, Helen Hayes had to withdraw because of a State Department tour, and Bette Davis, through her agent at MCA, was finally signed for Apple Annie for a straight salary.

Capra began suffering from a series of devastating "cluster" headaches that lasted, intermittently, throughout the troubled film. The reviews were excellent, but the picture made no money. Over the years, however, it has become a Christmastime classic on television, but it was Frank Capra's last motion picture.

The business had changed so much over the years that old-timers like Capra who had proven their worth in Academy Awards and box-office successes were thrown for a loop.

Barry J. Weitz, a graduate of New York University in 1962, who had joined William Morris in 1963 (where he was employed in the public appearance department until 1968, when he went over to the motion picture department) contributed a chapter, "The Talent Agent," in a book entitled *The Movie Business,*[6] in which he discussed some of these changes. He wrote: "In the triangle of buyer, seller and agent, the agent obviously performs two important functions. First, he sets up a very clear delineation between the buyer and the seller, and second, he gives the buyer a professional person to deal with on a constant basis and in a business atmosphere. Thus a freedom from emotion is established, allowing the parties to cut to the core of the negotiation and agree upon what each party considers essential. The presence of an agent is certainly a great aid to the buyer, since he does not have to become too closely involved with the artist during the negotiations. The buyer can deal with the artist on a creative level, and with the agent on a purely business and career level. For these reasons, the talent agency is a very real part of the entertainment business. Indeed, it is essential to it . . . ."

He explained that the Morris agency has separate departments for Motion Pictures, Literary, Stage and Personal Appearances, Television, Television Packaging, and Commercials.

"Although," Weitz continued, "there is size and stature to the William Morris Agency, we tend to keep the agent-to-client ratio very low. In the motion picture area there are 13 agents in Beverly Hills—the base of our operations—six agents in New York, and agents in London, Paris, Madrid, Rome, and Munich. Here in California, we hold staff meetings two days each week in which we review either current casting of films or general activities in the business. The meetings help us determine what we can do to effect changes in our client's careers, and serve as a clearing house for communications, helping each agent to be more knowledgeable about what is going on in everyone else's respective area, and in the industry as a whole . . . ."

But the independent agent has no such assistance. According to a top independent agent,[7] "What differentiates me from an agent employed by a large concern is that I have no 'clearing house' of information available. I have to constantly hustle. I must be highly visible in industry circles and, thank God, I've got a beautiful wife to add window dressing wherever I go.

"We must devote a lot of time to party-going, attend screenings and film premieres, take clients to luncheons and dinners at the 'in' places of the moment. I have many on-the-lot contacts who pass the word about important properties that are in the works that might have roles for my clients, whom I must diligently visit on sets when they are working. I drink only burgundy—and not very much of that—and my wife doesn't drink at all. I know agents in this town who are boozers and drug addicts, others who snort cocaine between appointments, and still others who drive the most expensive foreign cars obtainable. That's their life-style, and it's fine—for them. But I don't want that kind of image. I would rather be thought of as square, because I have a reputation for giving square deals, and I haven't lost a client in years.

"I must be well but conservatively dressed without being 'designer conscious,' and never wear faddish clothes. I don't even own a pair of Gucci loafers, and while my wife has a mink coat and an ermine wrap, she dresses down. We can't outshine clients. My Cadillac is black and small—my wife has a blue Rabbit. I would love to drive a Mercedes, which I can afford, but it's a car that's 'in' at the moment and three-quarters of my clients drive one, so that's out.

"I'm a Phi Beta Kappa, but I never wear my key; my wife is a graduate of the Sorbonne in Paris, but we are careful not to throw our intelligence around—especially when we are out with clients who haven't finished high school. Our work is a twenty-four-hour job, which we never take lightly.

"The agent with a large organization must be equally 'on top' of what is going on in the industry, yet the pressures are less because he has the prestige of his agency behind him, and older hands to plumb for advice and counsel. There is always someone to step in if he goofs. I can't afford to goof.

"When I was a kid just starting out, Cecil B. DeMille cautioned: 'You can't go wrong, if you always remember that you're in a service business.' It was good advice, which many agents today well might heed. The youthful Hollywood, with the big splashy, cigar-smoking agents who knew everyone, is over. The town was small then, and incestuous. Today, Hollywood has regained its youth as far as executives go—dozens are in their twenties, only the players are older . . . . It's difficult to believe that the reigning queen television-sexpot is Joan Collins, who is in her 50s. Ann-Margret is in her early 40s. We don't think of age as much anymore. Clint Eastwood is 53. When Loretta Young, Irene Dunne, and Joan Crawford reached 40 it was a catastrophe! But old agents never die—just no one picks up their option."

One of the biggest problems to confront agents, after the demise of the major studio contract lists in the late 1940s, was how to acquire copies of scripts slated for production. It was essential to find out what parts were going to become available for newly-out-of-work clients, who were accustomed to scripts being delivered to their doors. In 1971, a young man named Gary Marsh conceived of a way to make enough money to send himself to college. He formed a company called Breakdown Services Ltd, which provided a unique benefit for the motion picture industry: descriptions of individual characters in up-coming productions were compiled and sent out with scripts to agents and managers. Ultimately, 10 major studios, 3 TV networks and some 100 independent casting directors were contacted each day for material.

"It's invaluable for an agent to be able to look at the breakdown to see all the different parts for actors and all the stories," Scott Zimmerman, a casting agent for William Morris, told Heidi Evans for her piece[8] on Breakdown Services Ltd., "It's also the best way for those [smaller agents] who don't have access to studio heads to know what's happening."

Evans reported: "Billing itself as 'the communications network for the entertainment industry,' Breakdown Services charges each agent $28 a week for summarizing the scripts, identifying the roles and dispatching the breakdowns within 24 hours . . . ."

"Before, all the agents would run around to all the studios to pick up scripts," Marsh told Evans. "The favored few were given copies or invited into a casting director's office to read them. Everyone else would frantically run around town trying to get their hands on the same information . . . ."

Marsh and co-owner Peter Weiss employ a staff of 39 in Los Angeles, London, and New York, and each of the company's five drivers deliver approximately 70 breakdowns every morning.

Marsh was a former actor who found a lucrative new field, just as producers, directors, actors, agents and managers are also changing hats. With agents moving over to the production end of the motion picture business, personal artists' managers are doing likewise. Perhaps the most successful is multi-millionaire film-and-Broadway-play-producer Alan Carr, a chubby, witty, stylish, bespectacled leprechaun of a man, who has more homes than Irving Lazar—and at least as much chutzpah.

The son of a Highland Park, Illinois, furniture dealer, he came to Hollywood in the late 1960s. Famed as a party-giver and goer, he made his fortune transforming a low-budget Mexican feature *The Survivors of the Andes* (about a soccer team struggling to live after a plane crash, through cannibalism) into a hit, by vigorously re-editing and dubbing. The resulting exploitation film, *Survival*, grossed $6,975,000.

Carr used his money-sense wisely and well, purchasing the rights to film the hit stage-play, *Grease*, casting John Travolta and Olivia Newton-John in the principal roles, and buying a French play, *La Cages aux Folles*, which he turned into the stunning Broadway musical with Gene Barry and George Hearn.

He was also the power behind the success of Universal's five-Oscar winning film, *The Deer Hunter*, which he launched with a brilliant promotional campaign. "I've never told anyone about this before," he revealed to Richard Hack,[9] "but after the Oscar ceremony I drove home in a limo with Christopher Walken, who had just won his award as best supporting actor. And as he walked me up to my front door, he said, 'I want you to keep this Oscar for six months out of every year, 'cause you earned half of it.' I still cry when I remember that moment . . . ."

But managers and agents who have turned film and stage producers, and film and stage producers who have turned agents, and the heads of studios who have come up in the ranks from ten percenters, and with all of the other switcheroos occurring in the business, lists have to be kept on who is who and who is where at any given moment.

According to *California* magazine,[10] which printed a long list of those who had "Power in Hollywood," the ten top agents are: Mike Ovitz, Stan Kamen, Sam Cohn, Jeff Berg, Jim Wiatt, Nick Nicita, Ron Meyer, The Gersch Brothers, John Gaines, and Lee Rosenberg. An editorial explained that the list had begun to form on or about July 4, 1984, under the auspices of a talented director's wife by the name of Liberty, who worked closely with the magazine's research department, and whose husband was, naturally, included in the list. But events progressed so rapidly that even he did not make the final cut!

Aljean Harmetz, in an article accompanying the list, noted:[11] "Today, power in Hollywood is fragmented. Michael Ovitz, who is at the top of everyone's list of star agents, can supply Robert Redford, Dustin Hoffman, and Sidney Pollack to a studio in need of an actor or director. He can, even more impressively, gift wrap the three of them as one package. But his power is only that of his clients. If they were to leave him tomorrow, he would be replaced at the top of the list by Sam Cohn (Meryl Streep, Bob Fosse, Mike Nichols) or Stan Kamen (Barbra Streisand, Goldie Hawn, Diane Keaton) . . . ."

Can't Help Singing (1944) was illustrative of the "fairytale" characters that Deanna Durbin portrayed as a young adult.

BLACKOUT: 1960

Male Star

You've been looking over those accounts all day.

Wife

That old buzzard has been stealing you blind!

Male Star

We go back a long way. That "old buzzard" is the most brilliant of them all. He's my manager, but he also choreographs my act.

Wife

I say fire him.

Male Star

I know what I'm doing. He knows my limitations and makes me look good with those four gals in back of me. Sure, I may have trundled out on the stage at the age of four, and I've been dancing ever since, but I'm not as nimble as I used to be. I need him.

Wife

I say fire him.

Male Star

So he steals seven hundred and fifty grand! I'll make ten million on the European tour alone. When I get back, we'll send him to the slammer. We won't need him then. I'll have made enough to retire.

Jay North, age 7, star of *Dennis the Menace*, lines up a shot with Bill Russell on the set in 1960. *(Courtesy of CBS)*

Doris Day and her husband Martin Melcher were a famous team. He produced 16 of her 39 films, made millions, and at his death left her in debt to the tune of $450,000. *(Globe Photos, Inc.)*

15

FAMILY AFFAIRS

Army Clerk
Your allotment check goes to your wife, right?
Drafted Star
Yeah, but ten percent goes to the Morris Office!

"Apart from his values as a salesman, business guardian, and confidant, the next most substantial asset a Hollywood agent can provide his client is information," wrote William Fadiman.[1] "All agencies have 'leg men' who haunt studios, restaurants, race tracks, theatre opening nights, dinner parties, film premieres, any and all places where film folk assemble and fraternize. The leg man's sole purpose is to pick up information. What picture is being considered? Is the property available for sale? Can the agent secure its representation or does a rival agent already control it? Does the projected film need a writer, a director, a cameraman, a composer, a designer? Is a certain player or writer 'unhappy' with his current agent? Facts, rumors, whispers, confidences, intimations, all carefully recorded in a little black book and all presented meticulously at agency staff meetings—ordinarily twice a week at eight in the morning .... It is only by such checking and questioning that the agent can serve his client well, for the client cannot find out on his own all the various maneuvers going on in Hollywood on any single day, which pieced together may mean a job or sale for him ...."

Although in the 1980s movie children have agents, their parents or guardians still reign supreme. The California Child Actor's Bill to protect the rights of child performers—known in the industry as The Coogan Act—was enacted after the famous Coogan trial of the 1930s, which forced parents or guardians to bank a percentage of earnings, to be released after the performer was 21. But Shirley Temple's parents, for instance, invested her money so cleverly that she became a multi-millionaire when barely out of her teens. She distinguished herself as an actress, a mother, and in 1968 was appointed U.S. representative to the United Nations by President Nixon. She was the U.S. Ambassador to Ghana from 1974 to 1976, when she became the U.S. Chief of Protocol.

Other movie children were not so fortunate.

Baby Peggy Montgomery, born in 1917, the daughter of a screen extra and a stuntman, made her debut at age three in a two-reeler, followed by several other shorts and several feature films, including *Peggy Behave* (1922) and *Speed Demon* (1924).

In her poignant memoirs,[2] which dealt with the exploitation of child stars, she wrote: "A child star's contract was a very sobering legal instrument that most movie mothers, to whom a week's work for their child constituted a career, would have paled to read . My own gilt-edged agreement with Sol Lesser, for example, left small room for error and was shot through with ominous references to suspension 'due to illness or injury of said Peggy.' A still more chilling passage touched upon her possible 'refusal to work,' spelling out the swift and lethal reprisals for such sabotage. Small wonder that parents' palms grew damp as they read these documents, and their already obsessive preoccupation with the health and good will of their child rose to even higher levels of anxiety . . . .

"In an industry built on contradiction," she continued, "the child star was Hollywood's ultimate paradox. Certainly Jackie Coogan and I were, for although we were both cheerful, tireless, and co-operative on the set, our parents, producers, and most other adults were careful to talk down to us, as though we were appealing but mindless pets. They instinctively turned away our most innocent questions about what we were doing, why, and sometimes for how much with fatuous replies, as though they feared candid answers would give us a sense of self-importance, power, and perhaps even trigger a mutinous refusal to comply . . . . Repeatedly, too, total strangers took it upon themselves to advise me that I had the most generous, self-sacrificing parents they had ever met, adopting a threatening 'and don't you ever forget it' tone that implied I was a spoiled ingrate on the brink of rebelling and casting my poor family penniless into the street."

By the time Peggy had reached the awkward age and could no longer find roles, her parents had spent all of her money, and were reduced to poverty level. Fortunately, she was able to go on several extended vaudeville tours, and the money was rolling in again—$200,000 in three and a half years. Her father purchased a ranch at Laramie, Wyoming, but when the stock market crashed and the mortgage payments could not be met, a friendly banker advanced three-hundred dollars to get the family back to Los Angeles for another try at films which were "talking." But this time her career did not recover, and by the middle 1930s Baby Peggy found that she was a "has been"—along with many other children of her era.

Dennis the Menace, starring Jay North, debuted October 4, 1959, and went off the air September 22, 1963, with 146 filmed black-and-white episodes. Jay North began the series at age seven.

"I was never a stage mother," Jay North's mother, Dorothy,[3] emphasized with raised eyebrows, as she fed a cat poolside at her home in Studio City. A pretty, petite blond woman, she was friendly and outgoing. "All the years that Jay worked on *Dennis*, I also was employed, and his aunt took him to the studio and was present on the set.

"Jay was handled by agent Hazel McMillan, and when she passed away he went with Michael North—no relation! I didn't know very much about The Coogan Law, because I put everything away for Jay. I hoped that he would keep on working after his series folded, but in the event that he didn't work regularly, I wanted him to have all that money that he earned as a child. I did travel with him when he filmed *Maya* in India, because the series was shot on various locations, but Jay's been on his own for many years. He's been married and divorced, and is thankful that his money was well-invested. He appears now in dinner theater productions like *Butter-flies Are Free* and *Norman, Is That You?*, makes an occasional picture, and appears in television series like *General Hospital*. He's 32, and adult roles are opening up for him."

Eddie Cantor, who got his start in vaudeville, told this story about a grown-up child star:[4] "A Christmas story I'll never forget concerns one of Hollywood's former stars. Tough breaks had left him penniless so in desperation he applied for a job at a Beverly Hills store. The personnel manager recognized him and was shocked.

'But you can't be serious,' he said. The actor replied, 'Not only serious, but hungry. Just let me play Santa Claus in your toy department and I'll give the best performance you ever saw!'

"It turned out to be an almost perfect performance. A cute little boy was rattling off the presents he wanted. The jovial Santa Claus promised 'You'll have them all! Where's your mommy?' A woman in a mink coat stepped from behind the huge Christmas tree. Santa's laughter stopped. It was his ex-wife. He couldn't tell if she saw through his disguise. Her entire attention seemed to be taken up by her son's breathless tale of Santa's promises and his plea that she give Santa their address just to make sure.

"She laughed, and sat down at a nearby counter to write on a slip which she slipped into an envelope. Joyously the little boy handed it to Santa. When they were gone, he opened the envelope and read, 'You're still a great actor. Merry Christmas.' With the note was a check."

Most ex-wives are not that generous, and if there are several wives—Mickey Rooney has had eight—the alimony payments can be back-breaking. When Mickey Rooney filed for bankruptcy in 1962, nothing remained of the $12,000,000 that he had earned in his forty-year career. He was—and is—the consummate performer. Rooney was born in 1920, and his dad, Joe Yule, incorporated him into the act when he was fifteen months old. At the age of five, he was touring with Sid Gold's dance act. He was an outrageous mugger, could sing on key and dance, and his "want to please" personality came over in a big way.

His first film appearance, as Joe Yule, Jr., was as a midget in *Not to be Trusted* (1926). He changed his name to the character he was to play in a long series of Mickey McGuire shorts, then became Mickey Rooney for his first Universal picture, *My Pal the King* (1932), with cowboy star Tom Mix. His career was booming, and MGM placed him under contract in 1934.

Even when he tried Shakespeare—Puck in *A Midsummer Night's Dream* (1935), for Warner Brothers—he got all the reviews. He had the inside track on the foibles of youth, with his Andy Hardy series, but sandwiched many other characterizations in between: comedies, dramas, musicals. It seemed he could play anything— except tall, dark, romantic leads.

According to a poll conducted by *Motion Picture Herald*, he was the most popular star in America in 1939 (nudging out Shirley Temple), 1940, and 1941. When he and Bette Davis were crowned King and Queen of the Movies by columnist Ed Sullivan in 1940, being somewhat shorter than Davis, who was five-feet two-and-a-half, he declined to pose wearing the ermine-trimmed crown, which was so huge it overpowered him.

When he returned from service in World War II, although he was as extroverted as ever, his career gradually lost momentum, but he hung on, making fewer pictures and appearing on television.

In 1938, the Academy of Motion Picture Arts and Sciences awarded Deanna Durbin and Rooney a special award for "significant contribution in bringing to the screen the spirit and personification of youth, and as a juvenile player setting a high standard of ability and achievement."

When he received an honorary Oscar in 1981, he told how difficult it was to maintain a career when he had been forgotten by Hollywood. His heartfelt speech touched many, but he was having a career resurgence with the musical *Sugar Babies*, with Ann Miller, which debuted on Broadway in 1979 (following a lengthy pre-Broadway tour), and which he was still playing on the road in 1985. In the emotion of accepting his Oscar, he did not forget to graciously thank his agent, Ruth Webb.

On May 2, 1938, while Jackie Coogan was in one courtroom, a different sort of suit, involving seventeen-year-old singing star Deanna Durbin, was taking place next door: Rita Stanwood Warner, the wife of veteran film actor H. B. Warner, versus agents Jack Sherrill and Frederick Falkin.

Mrs. Warner charged that she had introduced Durbin to the agents and was to receive one-fourth of the ten percent they were to receive from her salaries. Judge Joseph Vickers awarded Mrs. Warner $4,139.88 of the $16,500 cut that Sherrill and Falkin had received from the $165,000 Durbin had earned thus far.

Blue-eyed, dark-haired Edna Mae Durbin was born on December 4, 1921, in Winnepeg, Canada, and emigrated to Los Angeles with her family two years later. She was attending Bret Harte Junior High School, when Mrs. Warner introduced her to Sherrill, who took her to MGM where *Gram*—a picture based on the life of Madame Ernestine Schumann-Heink—was being prepared. A girl with a voice was needed to play her as a teenager.

MGM signed her to a contract with the usual six months option, and she began to study music with famed opera coach, Andres de Segruola. She made a two-reel musical short in 1935, *Every Sunday*, with Judy Garland at MGM, and a feature, *One Rainy Afternoon*. However, when Madame Schumann-Heink died, so did *Gram*.

Louis B. Mayer, weighing the star possibilities of the two young girls, chose Judy Garland. Supposedly, this was the result of a mixup: he is reported to have said "Drop the fat one," and they let the wrong girl go. (Both girls were rather plump.) Sherrill took Durbin to Universal, where she made such an impact during the first few days of filming *Three Smart Girls* that her part was enlarged, and the budget was upped from "B" to "A" status. During the shooting of the picture, Sherrill introduced her to Eddie Cantor, who was impressed with her beautiful soprano voice and gave her a spot on his radio show, which she held for some years. She enjoyed a spectacular money-making decade, during which time—like Mae West at Paramount—her films saved the studio from bankruptcy.

After she made Universal solvent, the studio could scarcely deny her raises in salary, which escalated from $1,500 per week to $3,000 and a bonus of $10,000 for each picture. By 1940, she was making $400,000 per picture. In both 1945 and 1947, she was the highest-paid woman in the United States.

Deanna Durbin married Charles-Henri David, her third husband, on December 21, 1950, a director who had guided her through *Lady on a Train* (1945) and her last film, *For the Love of Mary* (1948). They retired to the small village of Neauphle-le-Chateau in France, where they lead a quiet, secluded life. Her parents saved her money, and she left Hollywood an extremely wealthy woman.

Referring to her Hollywood self as a "fairytale character," she granted a rare interview to David Ragan.[5] Amusingly, she said, "When we married, we made a deal .... My husband would protect me from spiders, mosquitos and reporters whilst it was my job to protect him from lions, tigers and dinosaurs. For years I have not had to give an interview, or pose for pictures, whilst it's ages since a dinosaur has breathed down my husband's neck." Ragan continues: "In 1972, in Seal Beach, Calif., where they lived in comfortable retirement on an annuity established for them by their

daughter, Deanna Durbin's aged parents, James and Ada, celebrated their 64th wedding anniversary . . . ."

Another songbird who toiled at Universal twenty years after
Durbin was Doris Day, born Doris Kappelhof in Cincinnati on
April 3, 1924. She made her "debut" singing in a Chinese restaurant
when she was fifteen years old, then a year later became the vocalist
for Barney Rapp and his New Englander band. She changed her
name to Day, after the song "Day by Day," although she never
cared much for it and would have preferred another name.

Day was a marvelous singer, but in private life naive and trusting. Like so many people in the entertainment world, she did not
have a business sense. In her autobiography, *Doris Day, Her Own
Story*, she recalled that when she worked for Rapp, the band
manager had set her salary at twenty-five dollars per week, which
was not enough to meet her expenses. Some time later, she learned
that her actual salary was fifty dollars a week and the manager had
been taking half for himself!

But Day believed in people, and for the most part, her warm personality attracted true friends over the years, but also lured certain
people who took advantage of her friendship. She was not unique:
very few star performers have a talent for business, nor do they have
time to keep books, write checks, and take care of household matters. Therefore, they are often preyed upon by those whom they
employ to look after their affairs.

Day became a big band singer with Bob Crosby and his Bobcats
at the age of sixteen, and a short time later in 1940, went over to the
Les Brown and His Band of Renown orchestra, opening at Mike
Todd's Theatre Cafe, where Gypsy Rose Lee was the headliner. She
had a bad marriage to a musician, by whom she had a son, Terrence,
went into radio, and had a couple of hit recordings—"Sentimental
Journey" and "My Dreams Are Getting Better All the Time." After
that, she married another musician, moved to California and
worked for scale as a vocalist in 1945 on a local CBS radio
station.

Doris Day was acquainted with agent Al Levy, who introduced
her to Dick Dorso and Marty Melcher, his partners at Century
Artists Agency. Working in the mailroom was a young man named
David Susskind, who was later to work for Warner Brothers as a

press agent and MCA as a talent agent, before heading his own agency, Talent Associates, and then going on to produce television shows, Broadway plays, Hollywood films, and head his own TV talk show. Century Artists handled such stars as Gordon MacRae, the Andrews Sisters, and Jack Smith.

But no jobs appeared on the horizon for Day until Monte Proser booked her into The Little Club in New York. Then, Day's second marriage on the rocks, Al Levy took her to a party at composer Jule Styne's house in Beverly Hills, where the guests customarily performed. On this occasion, lyricist Sammy Cahn played the piano, while Doris Day sang "Embraceable You."

By the end of the evening, she had an audition at Warner Brothers for the role of the nightclub singer in the Styne/Cahn musical, *Romance on the High Seas*, starring Jack Carson. The part had been written for Judy Garland, who had bowed out, and then cast with Betty Hutton, who had become pregnant.

Hungarian director Michael Curtiz liked Day's audition and personally shot her screen test. Day was undeniably photogenic; there was a vitality that came over in the camera. She won the role, and it led to a seven-year contract that would encompass seventeen films and make her a box-office queen. At this time, her former husband introduced her to Christian Science, which gave her a new spiritual outlook on life.

When Al Levy began to show more than a fatherly concern, Day threatened to leave Century Artists, but when he was transferred to head the New York branch, Marty Melcher began representing her interests. Melcher, a tall, dark-haired, pleasant-looking man, born August 1, 1915, in North Adams, Massachusetts, had packaged shows for network radio, before becoming general manager of Exclusive Music, a publishing company.

When he met Doris Day he was married to Patti Andrews, of the Andrews Sisters, for whom he had acted as road manager and agent. Many people in the industry felt that he had been attracted to his wife because of her money, and that when Day came along he set his sights on marrying her because her career potential was very great. There is no doubt that his life was ruled by dreams of amassing a great fortune; money to him was God, and he apparently thought of himself as a wheeler-dealer among wheeler-dealers. He could be charming and delightful, and he was born (as with most people in the talent agency field) with a genuine gift of gab: he could be very persuasive. He was not much liked among Hollywood people, who thought he was an opportunist, and he could be very petty and venal. Les Brown called him "Farty Belcher."

By the time he obtained a divorce from Andrews and married Day (on her 27th birthday) in 1951, he had renegotiated her contract upwards to $2,000 a week. Hit film followed hit film, in an endless chain. Her position was secure in the Hollywood firmament. He sold Century Artists to MCA Artists Corporation, and formed Adwin Artists Music and Arwin Records.

In 1954, their company Arwin Productions produced *Young at Heart*, with Frank Sinatra. After Day left Warner Brothers, she went to MGM for *Love Me or Leave Me* (1955) with James Cagney, the compelling story of singer Ruth Etting and the adverse psychological hold that Marty "the Gimp" Snyder had on her career. There were those in town who felt that the relationship between Etting and Snyder paralleled that of Day and Melcher. Sixteen out of her total of 39 films were either produced or co-produced by Melcher, who was also her business manager. He received $50,000 for his screen credit, although performing no appreciable work on her films after *Julie*. She had been handled by agent Arthur Park, Lew Wasserman at MCA, and quite a bit later by Ted Ashley.

But *Pillow Talk*, (1959) with Rock Hudson at Universal, started the romantic, "professional virgin" films that lasted until 1968.

An interview with Peter Bart[6] began, "Martin Melcher sat slumped in an easy chair, supping a soft drink and holding forth on a subject on which he was undeniably an expert—the life and times of Doris Day. As her husband, producer, agent and publicist, Melcher had evolved some plans to enhance the Doris Day legend.

" 'It's a natural progression,' he explained. 'In her first series of movies Doris played the nice clean girl next door who was always being duped by boys and whose virtue was being challenged. Like in *Pillow Talk*. Then she became the married woman like in *Please Don't Eat the Daisies* with the problems of a wayward husband and children. The picture she's making now, *Do Not Disturb*, marks the end of this cycle. So the next thing that will happen is for Doris to play the widow and the divorcee—roles that fit her maturity. It's a natural progression . . . .' "

Later, during the interview, Day came into the room and listened to some of Melcher's philosophy about her career, and when asked her opinion replied that she guessed it was fine, but that she left those things to Marty. Later she averred, "I am not the career businesswoman type. I never even particularly wanted to make movies but here I am. Before that, I never wanted to sing with bands but I had a little boy to support and I had to do it. I really never had a drive for a career . . . ."

Four years later, Day made her last film, *With Six You Get Egg Roll* (1968), with Brian Keith at Warner-Pathe. She was 44.

By the time of the shooting of *Julie* (1956), Melcher was working with a lawyer named Jerome Rosenthal on tax shelters. Day found herself with money invested in oil wells, cattle ranches, and luxury hotels. Rosenthal had many Hollywood clients, including Dorothy Dandridge, Frank DeVol, Kirk Douglas, Irene Dunne, Billy Eckstine, Zsa Zsa Gabor, Gogi Grant, Norman Granz, George Hamilton, Ross Hunter, Van Johnson, Stanley Kubrick, Art Laboe, Gordon MacRae, Harold Mirisch, and others.

For five years, Day headed the top ten in box-office polls, and her career soared with light, witty, romantic comedies opposite leading men like Rock Hudson, Cary Grant, James Garner, Rod Taylor, and Richard Harris.

Her relationship with Melcher had deteriorated. When she desired a divorce, she discovered that their investments were so tied into one another that if they split, she would end up with almost nothing, after making millions. Melcher had invested every penny of Day's earnings in Rosenthal's schemes. She reconciled with Melcher, and although they lived in the same house for five years, they did not share intimacy.

When Melcher died April 20, 1968, after a short illness, a report turned up that he had ordered from the famous accounting firm of Price-Waterhouse, which recommended he pull out of the Rosenthal Melcher-Day investment program. The report had gone unheeded. Furthermore, to her puzzlement, Day discovered two shooting scripts for a Doris Day television show. Her subsequent investigation revealed that Melcher had made a firm commitment for the show without obtaining her permission!

But it was only after Terry Melcher was named executor of the estate that the full force of the mismanagement of funds came to light. He found that not only was his mother broke, but all the millions were gone; in fact, she had debts of some $450,000!

In her memoirs,[7] Day wrote, "Marty was certainly a fool, to have been duped to this degree by a man who had mismanaged my life's earnings, twenty million or so, to the point of wipe-out. I could try to understand Marty's being a fool. He was a fool to tie up with Rosenthal, a fool not to see through him. But was he devious? Was he in league with Rosenthal? Did he knowingly plunder and siphon off and manipulate what I had placed in his care with trust? Did Marty know there was no oil . . . . in those many wells? That the hotels were a disaster? That the cattle ranches had no cattle? Was he duped by Rosenthal's fake reports or was Marty a part of Rosenthal's operation, taking advantage of my trust in him with lies and connivances? Who was this man I had lived with all of those years—fool or thief or both? The answer would have to come from those who knew him and saw him with some perspective . . . ."

She continued, "The more I thought about it, the more it seemed to me that Marty had suffered a peculiar death—death by resignation—which could have been caused by guilt over what he discovered had been done to me, or anguish when he knew that what he had been doing was about to be found out . . . ."

She soon realized the television show to which she had been committed contained elements that she did not like. After the first season she turned the show around, and it became a success, remaining on for the next four years. Meanwhile, the case against Rosenthal was building, and on March 4, 1974, came to trial in the Superior Court of California. The trial lasted one-hundred days.

Although Rosenthal was supposedly broke, there was a possibility of being awarded money, because there were six malpractice insurance companies involved.

Judge Lester E. Olson gave an oral decision in the case: his scathing words went on for many pages. He said, in summary: ". . . . nearly twenty lawsuits and petitions were commenced by Rosenthal using confidential information he had obtained from his former client, all the while refusing to supply Doris Day with the same information.

"It is true that Doris Day granted to her husband, Martin Melcher, a general power of attorney and he used the power of attorney over a long period of time to sign documents on her behalf. It is also true that she had knowledge of this fact.

"The defense has urged that this fact precludes Doris Day from now complaining as to the documents signed by Martin Melcher but the court does not agree. In fact, the extensive use of this power of attorney and Rosenthal's knowledge of the relationship between Doris Day and her husband heightened rather than lessened the need for independent legal advice to be given to her. This she did not receive.

"Rosenthal took advantage of the confidential relationship which existed between himself and Martin Melcher.

"He grossly failed to meet his obligations as an attorney for Doris Day and Martin Melcher.

"He misled them with false, misleading, and inaccurate financial statements.

"When Martin died he misused his position of trust and engaged in loan transactions involving over $100,000 with Terrence Melcher to his own benefit without disclosing all the facts.

"When discharged as attorney for the Melchers he failed to meet his obligations of trust and fidelity in turning over his clients' records . . . ."

On and on, each statement further built up the case against Rosenthal. After specifying individual damages, the total damages awarded Doris Day was $22,835,646!

It was the largest amount of money ever awarded in a California civil suit.

BLACKOUT: 1951

Male Star

I told you I don't give a tinker's damn about how much they offer. I won't perform in a place where I can't have a suite. I refuse to work in a room where I have to enter and exit through the kitchen, and can't even play a little craps in the Casino! To say nothing of my kids not being allowed in the pool. Then, after working my butt off in the Main Room, I've got to go back to the black ghetto to sleep. If those bastards can applaud a black cat in the show room, they sure as hell can put up with seeing me in the lobby or the elevator.

Agent

Now look, baby, I agree. But the country's not quite ready yet. It takes time, meanwhile you've got to make a living, support the band and your personal people. Do it again this year. Maybe next year will be different. How do you think I feel when I set up a deal and they say, "We're restricted but . . . ."

Male Star

You can tell them to fuck off!

Lennie Hayton and his wife Lena Horne were seldom photographed together. She spent almost all of her years under contract to MGM, posed before a pillar singing torch songs in musicals—a scene that could be cut out in the South. *(Globe Photos, Inc.)*

16

STARS OF A DIFFERENT STRIPE

Sidney Poitier
*My agent and I have been together from the days when I was wash-
ing dishes for $3 a week—that includes 29 years, 38 motion pic-
tures, two plays, one Academy Award . . . . In scripts where there
were no black actors, Marty Baum created them for me.*

There have always been prejudices in Hollywood. There was a
time when it was considered anathema for a young leading man to
be married, because the consensus of opinion was that his fans
desired him to be single, and therefore "available." Later, it was
thought that a leading man should be married by the time he was
thirty, otherwise, his fans might think he was not interested in
women. Time was when it was thought that a leading lady should
not have children because it lowered her sex appeal; at other times, it
was not considered chic to be blond, bi-sexual, yellow, brown, black,
or Jewish.

A retired agent living at Rancho Bernardo, who at one time was
blond and who is gentile, remarked:[1] "An agent has far more responsibilities than appears on the surface. It takes money to run an
office and maintain a client list, when all you get is 10 percent of
earnings that may or may not come in. If you're head of a big
agency with big stars that pull in a lot of money, that's a different
proposition, but if you're a fairly little guy, like I was, it's impossible
to gauge your quarterly payments to the I.R.S., because you don't
have any idea of what's coming in!

"When the studios had the contract system going—which
everyone always bitched about—your clients knew what their
salaries were and we knew what our commissions were. I retired at
exactly the right time ten years ago. With everyone freelancing now,

clients don't work all that much. You're lucky to get them a picture a year, and with the featured players, you try like hell to get them at least enough work so that they can draw their unemployment checks. In the old days it was the joke of the town that if tourists wanted to see movie people, all they had to do was hang around the Unemployment Office! Now, of course, the checks are mailed out.

"It's getting so now that big stars make television movies or appear in either a series or a mini-series, so an agent with a decent client list can usually get them jobs. In my day, stars were either in features or in TV. They either got a lot of money for a film or they didn't work. And the studios finally wised up that TV stars couldn't make the grade in features. Milton Berle, the most famous comic on television, couldn't make the transition with *Always Leave Them Laughing* or Liberace with *Sincerely Yours*. The commercial field is a good bet too, for over-the-hill stars, those millionaire stars that have 'greed' for a middle name, or those cute little old ladies spouting out about Hamburgers 'n Hondas. But one or two guys in partnership can't handle the traffic anymore. There's too many parts in TV being cast, and you can run your butt off.

"If you dig into your bankroll and buy out a star's contract, you're taking a big chance: they may fall on their face, and you're left holding the bag. There was an agent who bought Victor Schertzinger from another agent. Vic was a talented composer and a hell of a director. He did some of the *Road* pictures with Crosby and Hope at Paramount. Anyway, he up and died and left the new agent, who had paid a lot of money for him, holding the bag. These are things that no one can prevent.

"Agents have the reputation of tooling around in big cars and lunching everyday in expensive restaurants and giving big parties, and some of them do, but not the little guys. If you get a featured player $750 for two days work, that means you only get $150 which is luncheon for four at Scandia. You've got to have an awful lot of good people and keep them working all the time to pay your own bills. It's not the profession it's cracked up to be . . . . I was one of the few gentiles in the business, but I never had a chip on my shoulder." He laughed, "There was a famous story that made the rounds for many years. It was supposed to have some basis in fact and concerned a big star. The way I heard it, it was Gary Cooper. Any big name will do, but let's use his name. He was a nice guy, and I don't think he would mind in that big rock quarry in the sky.

"Gary Cooper walks into an agent's office that's so small and cramped there's only room for a tiny desk and one chair. The telephones had long been taken out, and a pay telephone installed, and on the wall around the instrument are scrawled a lot of numbers of past clients who'd left the little guy and gone on to better things. 'I understand,' Cooper says in that quiet, unassuming way of his, 'that you still have the ideals of the old days, that you're scrupulously honest and never blow a deal, that you can write the sharpest contract in town without losing any integrity . . . .'

"Now this agent can scarcely believe his ears, and he keeps saying to himself, 'Gary Cooper is in my office, Gary Cooper is in my office . . . .' As the great star continues on and on in a like vein, the little guy, who's expecting an eviction notice to be pasted on his door any minute, is so flabbergasted he bows and nods, and he's almost down on the floor licking Cooper's boots.

" 'Very well, then,' Cooper says finally, 'It's all settled. We'll meet for lunch at Scandia tomorrow at high noon, and sign representation contracts.'

" 'Yes! yes!' The little agent cries, almost in tears. In his mind's eye, he's already seeing his new plush office in Beverly Hills with a gorgeous bosomy secretary taking his calls, and a cream-colored Mercedes parked in the lot, 'Yes, yes, anything you say, anything you say,' he says, his heart almost bursting with gratitude, 'I'll be there at high noon.'

"Cooper pumps his hand enthusiastically, and he's at the door before he turns back. 'By the way,' he asks seriously, 'you aren't Jewish are you?'

" '. . . not necessarily . . . .' replies the little man!"

The retired agent raised his eyebrows, "I tell this story because in the agenting business sometimes it helps being Jewish and sometimes it doesn't. With me it worked both ways. I'm sure I gained a few clients because I wasn't Jewish, and I lost a few because I wasn't. But through the years, I don't really think it mattered all that much. The minority that really had problems were the black actors. I never handled any, not because I was prejudiced, but because they didn't come to me and I didn't go to them."

Being black in the 1980s is certainly a different proposition than in the 1940s. MCA's first black clients were Eddie "Rochester" Anderson, Jack Benny's memorable sidekick, and Hattie Mc-Daniel, the first black woman to win an Academy Award. Rival agents tried to use these stars against Stein, muttering to their own clients, "Surely you don't want to be handled by an agency that has niggers under contract!" However, the country was "growing up," and increasing numbers of white clients had no objection to being represented by agents and managers who also had black clients.

Among the most successful black performers is Lena Horne. A scene that was created again and again in many MGM musicals of the 1940s era: the beautiful, copper-skinned actress leaned against the tall, white pillar and sang the slow, dreamy ballad, caressing the lyrics of the song the same way that a woman would smooth the fur of a cat. She was mesmerizing. But this scene, complete in itself, could be snipped from the musical in question in any of the southern states that objected to black performers being presented as a "class act."

Lena Horne was born June 30, 1917, in the Bedford-Stuyvesant section of Brooklyn, New York. Her childhood was spent scurrying between several different homes, where she was often beaten; her mother Edna was a member of the well-known stock company, the Lafayette Players of Harlem, which occasionally toured.

Her grandmother was active in the Urban League, the National Association for the Advancement of Colored People, and other negro causes. By the time Horne was fourteen, Edna had divorced her husband, who was an educated man, and while touring in Cuba, married a white native, Miguel Rodriguez, but he was not accepted by her circle of friends in either Brooklyn or Harlem.

Horne dropped out of school at sixteen. Edna wrangled an audition for her at the famous Cotton Club in Harlem, which catered to white people who came to applaud the most famous black artists of the day. A transcontinental radio show was beamed from the club's stage. Horne became a dancer in the chorus, performing in three shows a night, seven nights a week, for $25. Yet, in the terrible Depression year of 1933, with millions upon millions of people out of work and laborers earning 75 cents a day, she was told that this was good pay. Cab Calloway and his band were appearing on the program. Edna was a tireless chaperone, accompanying her to the club, waiting for the shows to finish, then escorting her back home.

Then the venerable plot of *42nd Street* was once again played out: this time the star—in this case, the girl in a featured spot—quit, and was replaced by Horne, who sang and danced the Harold Arlen-Ted Koehler number "As Long As I Live." She was a success, and there was sufficient word-of-mouth for her to be cast in a role in the Broadway musical production, *Dance With Your Gods*, which opened October 8, 1934. But, during the short run, she returned to the Cotton Club for two shows a night.

When the musical folded, Horne became the female singer for Noble Sissle and his orchestra, taking along her mother and step-father as chaperones. The band was accustomed to seeking out black neighborhoods in which to find lodgings, and picking up food from the rear doors of restaurants in white sections of the cities, but the white Miguel sometimes posed problems.

Sissle, Lena, and the orchestra were the first negro performers to play at Boston's ritzy Ritz-Carlton Hotel, where they were obliged to enter and exit from the rear entrance, staying at a black hotel. Later, they were the first black band to be booked into the Moonlight Gardens in Cincinnati. But as fate would have it, Sissle, who was traveling in a private car, was involved in an accident. He called Horne from the hospital, asking her to "lead" the band until he could rejoin them on the road. Billed as Helena Horne, she fronted the men with her baton, while the musicians actually followed the first trumpeter.

Two men came into her life at this time, who were to change her outlook on life. Number one was Louis Jones, who was almost ten years older, and with whom she fell in love. He was smooth, educated, and charming. They married in January, 1937, and became parents of a baby girl, Gail. Number two was white agent Harold Gumm, who managed to get her a role in an all-black film musical, starring Duke Ellington—*Duke Is Tops*—filmed in Hollywood.

Horne then appeared on Broadway in *Lew Leslie's Blackbirds of 1939*, which opened February 13 of that year, but lasted only eight performances. A few months later, a son, Edwin—"Teddy"— was born, after which she decided to separate from Jones.

Next, Charlie Barnet asked her to replace his band singer who was ill, and a long road tour of the northern states ensued. But the problems of obtaining accommodations were even more difficult for a white band with a negro singer, with the result that hotels had to be located that would make exceptions.

Another inconvenience was that, at the clubs, Horne was not permitted to sit on the stage between songs; she had to either sit in the powder room or in the band bus parked at the rear of the building. Even with the difficulties encountered, new territories were being expanded for future black performers.

After Horne appeared with acclaim at Greenwich Village's Cafe Society Downtown (at $75 a week), Harold Gumm found her a spot with Katherine Dunham's revue at the Little Trocadero in Hollywood. She was an immediate success. However Gumm was not licensed to work on movie contracts, so he introduced her to agent Al Melnick, partner of Louis Shurr. She made a test at Universal studios, but Roger Edens—who worked in the Arthur Freed unit at MGM—was impressed with her work and thought she might do well at his studio.

Lena Horne confided to Richard Schickel:[2] "A few days later I went back to Freed, this time with my father along, as well as my agents. My father was great in that meeting. His basic mistrust of white men is so deep he was able to be very cool with the studio people. Flattery and empty promises get you absolutely nowhere with my father. I know those MGM executives had had to deal with parents of child stars at the start of their careers, but I'm sure this was the first time that a grown Negro woman ever arrived with a handsome, articulate, and unimpressed father who proceeded to show them the many disadvantages, spiritually and emotionally, that his daughter might suffer should she be foolish enough to sign with them. It was marvelous for me to watch them listening to him . . . .

" 'I don't want my daughter to work, I want to take care of her myself,' my father said. 'Now many people are telling her how wonderful it is to be a movie star. But the only colored movie stars I've seen so far have been waiting on some white star in the picture. I can pay for someone to wait on my daughter if she wants that . . . .' "

When Horne was placed under a seven-year contract, starting at $200 per week (eventually going up to $40,000 a year in 1945), there was a proviso that she would not perform in the traditional roles given to many negro actors: maids, and other underlings. She was only the second black player ever to win a long-term contract. The first was Madame Sul-Te-Wan in 1915, whom D.W. Griffith admired as an actress, and who had more recently worked at Twentieth Century-Fox (1938 to 1940).

Daniel J. Leab has stated:[3] "At MGM Lena Horne encountered many of the same difficulties that even the most notable black performers had to face until well after the end of the war. The studio first tested the light-skinned, beautiful singer for a maid's role opposite Eddie Anderson in a comedy melodrama. To make her skin color as dark as Anderson's, she recalled, she was smeared with so much makeup that she looked like 'some white person trying to do a part in blackface.' Ultimately the makeup department worked out a shade dubbed 'Light Egyptian.' Horne did not 'feel too good or too proud' for such roles but felt it 'essential . . . . to try to establish a different kind of image for Negro women.'

"She did not plead for special privileges. 'All we ask,' she said in 1943, 'is that the Negro be portrayed as a normal person . . . .' "

Probably the reason that MGM acquiesced to Horne's unusual contractual demands was that the studio was preparing an all-negro musical, based on the 1940 Broadway hit, *Cabin in the Sky*, and realized that she was perfect casting for the role of sexpot Georgia Brown. Ethel Waters would portray Petunia, the patient and lovable wife of Joe Jackson (Dooley Wilson). Before this film was shot, Horne was cast as a singer in *Panama Hattie* (1942) with Ann Sothern and Red Skelton, but it was Hedy Lamarr (in Light Egyptian makeup) who played the beautiful Tondelayo in the drama *White Cargo*—a role that would have temperamentally suited Horne.

According to James Haskins,[4] a group of veteran black actors served as bosses in the black acting community, and had formed a kind of unofficial union of black performers. "Although," Haskins stated, "the 'members' of this union paid no dues and carried no union cards, they relied on the good graces of the 'union bosses' to get them work. Under the very strict, but informal, system, studios that needed black actresses and actors for films would get in touch with the bosses, who in turn would suggest the names of favored friends. So efficient was this system in a town where roles for blacks were few, that the major studios didn't have to sign black actors to term contracts; they could use the established, and far less costly, route. Since most parts for blacks in Hollywood were those of extras, the bosses could always be relied on to provide a few actors for a few days, at day wages, rendering unnecessary the sort of contract that Lena had signed, which called for her to be paid a maintenance salary even when she wasn't working. But the bosses did not understand how they, and the black actors and actresses in their 'stable,' were being used, or if they did, they saw no alternative to it. When Lena took her independent and principled stand they were upset by the potential destruction she could cause to their tiny sphere of influence. They called her an 'East Coast upstart' and a 'tool of the NAACP'; and it was made known to Lena that in their view, she was not a pioneer but a traitor . . . ."

After *Cabin in the Sky*, Horne was loaned to Twentieth Century-Fox for another all-negro musical, *Stormy Weather*, where she movingly sang the title song, which for many years was to be her trademark song. In 1943, besides appearing in *Sky* and *Weather*, she also made the all-star *As Thousands Cheer* and the Red Skelton comedy, *I Dood It*. She was on her way to the top.

Horne saw a great deal of Joe Louis, whom she had dated in New York, but while she had occasionally encountered Lennie Hayton, ex-bandleader and now music arranger at the studio, they did not become friendly until they had a conversation in the commissary. They started to date, and he fell in love with her. Louis Jones had wanted to become her agent and manage her career, but the obstacles had been overwhelming. By the time she divorced him, she had grown to depend more and more upon Hayton.

Horne entertained at the Hollywood Canteen, but when she went on various USO tours she found that black and white troops were segregated, just as blacks and whites were still segregated in the South.

Since the studio did not often cast her in pictures and she had a great deal of free time on her hands, she hungered for paying outside engagements. Booked into the negro Howard Theater in Washington, D.C., she was greeted with a meager house on opening night. She was alarmed that she had lost her audience. Upon further investigation, she pinned the low turnout to high admission prices.

After speaking with her agents in California a press conference was called, and she explained that she had not known that ticket prices were so high, announcing an immediate reduction. Now that the ordinary black community could afford to see her, the Howard did excellent business.

Horne and Hayton finally became man and wife in December of 1947, but did not announce the marriage: the black/white situation was still paramount and they did not wish to harm her career. In 1948, before Horne made *Words and Music* for MGM, *Ebony* magazine mentioned the film, and noted: "She will be featured in a single production number, probably will not talk to any whites because the South won't like it. Someone at MGM slipped in her last picture, *Till the Clouds Roll By*, and as Julie the quadroon in a scene from *Showboat*, she spoke to Magnolia as a friend or sister. 'But I didn't say Mam or Missy, so naturally some higher-up cut all my speaking part. I guess it isn't telling any secrets to admit that MGM kept me in drydock for a long time because I wouldn't play a gambler's floozy in *St. Louis Woman* on Broadway.'

"Lena feels that she has yet to realize her ambitions in Hollywood to be a first-rate actress. 'I'm in Hollywood but not of Hollywood because I'm negro,' she says. 'I'd like to do a good, serious role in a mixed cast movie instead of being confined to cafe singer parts.' "

When MGM decided to film the venerable *Showboat* in 1950, to Horne's shock and disappointment they did not cast her as Julie, the character who is driven off the boat because she is a light-colored negro who passes for white. Ava Gardner, wearing the Light Egyptian makeup, played the part. It was a stunning blow.

She was not to get her wish of playing in an otherwise white film until 21 years later, when she played the role of a Madame in *Death of a Gunfighter* (1969).

Horne did not work for some time after refusing *St. Louis Woman*, and the bosses at MGM ignored her. When Joan Crawford advised her to make a change, she signed with Music Corporation of America, which purchased her contract from Shurr. Her new agents broke the ice at the studio, which permitted her to perform club dates. While she was a star with a glowing reputation and a large following, and more money was coming in, she still often had to endure the indignity of being relegated to dingy rooms in white hotels and having to enter and exit through the service entrance. In 1948, Horne bought out her contract with MCA and chose a road manager.

Meanwhile, fewer and fewer blacks were cast in important film roles. Horne would have been ideal for the part of a light-skinned black girl who passes for white in *Pinky* (1949), with the two Ethels—Waters and Barrymore. Jeanne Crain, in Light Egyptian makeup, played the title role.

On November 29, 1980, the Harlem Cultural Council screened several of Horne's films, including *Stormy Weather* and *Cabin in the Sky*. Explaining why she had appeared in so few films, Horne told Mel Watkins in an interview,[5] "Also I was a friend of Paul Robeson's—my family had known him since I was a child—and I think that association influenced some people's estimate of my politics. I never even considered breaking that relationship. To me he was just a marvelous friend. But I was listed in Red Channels, and for six or seven years, during the late 40s and 50s, I couldn't get any work in films or on radio. They even tried to cut off my nightclub engagements . . . .

"The singer, actor, athlete, and activist Paul Robeson was under a cloud in the United States during the cold war years for being a political dissenter and an outspoken admirer of the Soviet Union. Red Channels was a small newsletter of that era purporting to list Communists and Communist sympathizers. It was influential far beyond its size in Hollywood and broadcasting, where it became a blacklist."

A great contingent of black people resented Horne, until one night, after she had finished her show at the Cocoanut Grove in Los Angeles, when she and Hayton dropped by the Luau restaurant for a drink. She was sitting at the bar alone, while he used the telephone. When a drunk approached and called her a "nigger," she "just went blind." All the years of built-up frustration came out in a flash, and she punched the man in the face. Soon the police arrived and the incident made the newspapers. Mail from blacks began to pour in, saying that, thank God, she really cared . . . .

In her one-woman show, *Lena Horne : The Lady and Her Music*—which debuted on Broadway in 1981 and has enjoyed a long, lucrative, and extremely successful tour—she sang and spoke of her life. According to a Rex Reed article,[6] she said: "Last night some people came back to see me after the show who remembered me from the old Cotton Club days. They were remnants of what we used to call cafe society. They said they were glad to see I could still fit into tight dresses and sing sexy, but one of them said, 'You're so different, you're not the same Lena!' I don't know what people expect. They must think I'm living in a flashback. But I have changed. I hate nostalgia. And it wasn't all that great anyway, you know? So I kid the different Lenas people used to see in the show. I kid the Harlem days, I kid the MGM days, I kid the big-band days, and I give them me. It took me a long time to figure out who I am, and I'm not going to cop out now. I used to be so confused that I'd withdraw from the audience. I avoided eye contact. Now I want to get so close that sometimes I almost fall off the stage . . . ."

"Yes," Reed stated, "she sings 'Stormy Weather'—not only once but twice. First, the way she used to sing it, cool and remote and bluesy; later, near the end of the show, the way she feels it now, building to a passionate crescendo, letting the pain and the anguish hang out. 'Honey, I never knew what that song was all about until now. I was 16 years old when I heard Ethel Waters sing it and it scared me so much I never wanted to go near it again. I only sang it in the movie because MGM loaned me out cheap to Fox. It was always Ethel's song, and it formed a big psychological block for me all my life. Now I feel differently. It's my song, too, because I've had stormy weather all my life and if anybody can sing about the trouble they've seen, it's this old broad . . . .' "

But Lena Horne has survived an impoverished childhood; divorce; racial prejudice; motion pictures in which her scenes had been eliminated; the blacklist; the death of Lennie Hayton, her son Teddy, and her mother, all in 1972; an expensive flop musical, *The Wiz*, 1980, to achieve the greatest success of her career—her one-woman show, *Lena Horne: the Lady and Her Music*.

The Wiz was to have extraordinary repercussions. Harry Belafonte, who had turned to producing films, told Richard Natale in an interview:[7] "There's no question that *The Wiz* was used as a barometer for the visibility of black films . . . . It starred the biggest black female singer, Diana Ross, Richard Pryor and Michael Jackson, and it was still not a box office success. Unfortunately, it was judged as a black film and not on the merits of the film itself."

Of Belafonte's new production of *Beat Street*, Natale stated: "It is only because of his personal power as a performer and his partnership with David Picker on the production of *Beat Street* that enabled the film to be considered and eventually accepted, especially in light of its unproven subject matter (the hip-hop culture of the South Bronx) and the lack of star names. 'I give Orion Pictures a lot of credit for the faith they put in us,' says Belafonte of the company which financed the $10 million film . . . . But his future as a producer with the ability to finance and create black oriented projects hinges on the fate of *Beat Street*. 'If it's very successful I will be able to get people to at least listen to a lot of ideas that I've had for a long time. Success has a way of doing that. If it fails, they'll say there's another black film that didn't make it. And it will be another inaccurate signal as to the viability of black-themed movies. But that's the reality we have to live with . . . .' "

As popular in his own way as Belafonte is thirteen-year-old, Emmanuel Lewis, whose Burger King television commercials caught the eye of Lewis Erlicht, president of ABC Entertainment. Enchanted with the youngster, he signed him to a contract.

A conference was set with Emmanuel that included his mother, who had quit her job as a computer programmer to handle his career, former footballer Alex Karras, his wife, Susan Clark, ten people from the network, seven from the William Morris Agency (which handled Emmanuel), four from Paramount Pictures, writer Stu Silver, and co-executive producer Bill D'Angelo.

According to Kenneth Turan,[8] "Silver, D'Angelo, and the actors worked out the *Webster* concept of a newly married ex-football player who 'inherits' the child when the boy's parents die. 'They wanted him to look like a stranger in a strange land, a fish out of water,' says Stu Silver. 'That was the hook.' Though obviously, the show will be compared to Gary Coleman's sitcom, the people behind *Webster* believe they have carved out a niche that is unique unto itself. Says D'Angelo, 'The show is conceptionized as a trio. We're allowed to watch a family become a family, which is rare in a sitcom . . . .' "

But Emmanuel is talented in his own right. On *The People's Choice* Awards show, as determined by a special Gallup poll, March 15, 1984, Ben Vereen started to sing "Chicago Is" when, to the delight of the audience, the forty-inch star joined him in the number. Although he looked seven, Emmanuel's singing and dancing ability, his self-possession and smartz were that of a twelve-year-old. He stole the show, to Vereen's obvious delight. Their number harked back to the memorable solos of Bojangles Robinson and Shirley Temple of the 1930s, where the dancing ability of one star depended upon the proficiency of the other.

Aside from films written, directed, or produced by black actors, another minority was making headway *behind* the camera in the 1980s. More and more frequently, females were becoming useful in production. There was also a new breed of actress going into the business end of the industry. Women were displaying brains as well as bodies. Melissa Gilbert of TV's *Little House on the Prairie* formed Half Pint Productions to produce films for television, Barbra Streisand produced, directed, and acted in *Yentl* (1983), and Jessica Lange acted and co-produced her box-office hit, *Country* (1984).

But a few years ago, women were also a minority in the talent agent field. Lillian Schary started out as a band singer with Abe Lyman and his orchestra, then hosted a show on WMCA in New York, before marrying talent agent Paul Small. She was content to settle down as a housewife, bearing two children, and being active in community affairs. She was famous for intimate dinner parties, where she entertained her husband's clients. She was knowledgeable in industry matters, partly because her brother, Dore Schary, had been a publicist for Admiral Richard E. Byrd, had dabbled in acting—supporting Spencer Tracy in *The Last Mile* on Broadway—before he began to write and produce pictures, first at MGM, then at RKO, and finally returning to MGM as chief of production.

In 1953, Paul Small—who was ailing—asked his wife, then in her fifties, to come into the business with him. She had barely moved into the office when he died. Philip K. Scheuer, in an interview,[9] reported: "Friends, including Agnes Moorehead, Roy Rowland, Sammy Cahn and the late Louis Calhern, persuaded the grief-stricken Lillian to carry on the agency. 'My first reaction, emotion, was to perpetuate Paul's business, to keep Paul's name alive. But soon it became a chance, an opportunity, to prove something I believed in—that an agent could be successful by treating talented people as human beings. I really felt the business needed a little more heart and understanding, things I might be able, at my age, to impart to people along the way.

" 'Paul had handled just stars, stars exclusively in motion pictures. The growing popularity of TV was one reason he wanted me to come in. Also, he wished to represent writers. After his death, and when I was not sure I could continue, I sold a great many of our contracts, but friends stopped me.' "

With her son Edgar in the business with her, the agency became successful and moved from a tiny office on Olympic Boulevard to a ground-floor suite on North Canon Drive in Beverly Hills, staffed by nine people. Small even worked every day while recuperating from a broken hip. Her clients included Keefe Brasselle, Nanette Fabray, Eva LeGallienne, Kevin McCarthy, Sidney Poitier, Gena Rowlands, Richard Todd, Walter Slezak, and Inger Stevens, whose eyes "grabbed her" on a television show.

Before Lillian Schary Small handled rotund, character actor, Walter Slezak, he had come to Hollywood under contract to a New York agent named Mayers, who had representation in Los Angeles with Edington & Vincent (they once handled Garbo). However, Edington & Vincent were unhappy to be sharing their percentages with Mayers. Slezak called the office one day to inquire if there was any work for him and was told by the switchboard operator that he was no longer with the firm, that his contract had been sold to the Swinburn Agency.

In his autobiography[10] he wrote: "Now I was really baffled. Why would anybody buy my contract? I was certainly not a hot property. But Mr. Swinburn was honest and told me. It seemed that he and Mr. Edington were indulging in the great California pastime of golf and got bored playing for money. So they began betting their unimportant clients on each hole. I was lost on a putt on the seventh green.

"It is Lillian's great hope," Scheuer continued in his interview, "that the business will eventually free itself of the 'flesh peddlers' and that producers will learn to honor the word of an agent when it comes to talent—'rather than wait for the talent to express itself.... or die.' "

She mentioned Jason Robards, Jr., in *Long Day's Journey Into Night*, and Anne Bancroft in *Two for the Seesaw*, as examples of newly-emerged talent on Broadway, when two years before they "couldn't be sold for love or money."

Agents with stage clients—whose careers were in the doldrums—were often urged to come west to appear in films. Screen clients with the same problems were urged to go east to perform in plays. But in the case of European screen or stage stars, traveling to New York or Hollywood was a major career move, especially if they were not well-known to American audiences. It was essential that these performers be handled by someone with an understanding of their backgrounds and who could present them to the ever-decreasing circle of important producers. Such an agent was Paul Kohner.

Bohemian-born Paul Kohner was brought to the United States in 1921 by Carl Laemmle, whom he had met when the Universal studio chief was taking the cure in Karlsbad. Settling in New York, Kohner was employed as a shipping clerk at $108 a week (his confederate in the department was future director, William Wyler).

But soon he was in charge of foreign publicity at $25 a week. He was transferred to Hollywood and worked his way up at Universal, becoming casting director. Then, in November 1926, he was promoted to a unit supervisor on future Edward Sloman productions. "Kohner is credited with having first brought Rudolph Schildkraut to the screen," announced a Universal press release, "and having been instrumental in launching the screen careers of George Lewis, Barbara Kent, Dorothy Gulliver, and other promising young players developed in the past year. He will work under Henry Henigson, Universal general manager."

Kohner became a producer in the days before producers received screen credit. The years passed, and finally he got screen credit on *Next Time We Love* (1936), which starred James Stewart and Margaret Sullavan. In the mid-1930s, Universal was having financial problems. There were rumors the studio might be sold. Kohner was working on a $500 week-to-week basis and when Laemmle refused to come through with a promised contract, Kohner smashed an ashtray on the desk and left in a fit of anger. Agent Frank Orsatti, who had an "in" at MGM, arranged an interview for Kohner with L. B. Mayer.

Orsatti advised Kohner to tell Mayer he was making $750 a week, and against his better judgment he complied. Mayer promised that he would continue the same arrangement for the first year at MGM, and Kohner would receive $1,000 a week for the second year. When Eddie Mannix, business manager of the studio, heard about the deal, he was furious because he knew that Kohner had only received $500 a week at Universal. Mannix told him that he would be paid that same amount for the entire two-year contract at MGM, and that he would see to it that he never got a production assignment.

After his tenure at MGM, Kohner went to Columbia. However, after a confrontation there he left, and Orsatti offered him a job at his agency. But Paul Kohner decided to go into business himself, renting a small office on Sunset Boulevard and hoping, with his knowledge of all phases of European production, that he could interest some of the foreign contingent in Hollywood to be his clients. "On his first day," wrote Charles Champlin,[11] "he went out to Universal for lunch with old friends, learned that Joe Pasternak was looking for a new story for Deanna Durbin, ran into a writer he knew named Konrad Bercovici and found that Bercovici had a story which might do fine, went back to Pasternak and sold the story for $25,000 plus another $25,000 for the screenplay (Bercovici had hoped to get $5,000). Kohner, as they say, has never looked back."

Later in the article he noted, "Kohner also takes a fierce and paternal pride in the career of Charles Bronson, whom he has represented for more than ten years, since Bronson was a character actor not well-known on any continent. A French producer came to Kohner looking for an actor in the Widmark tradition. Kohner urged Bronson on him and the film (*Goodbye, Friend*, never seen in the U.S.) was a hit. Bronson subsequently did *Rider on the Rain* for Rene Clement, probably still his finest and warmest performance, and commenced the rise to worldwide fame that is at last touching his home country as well.

" 'He once said he never expected or hoped to be anything but an acceptable character actor,' Kohner says, 'I told him he would one day get a million dollars for a picture. He said when he did, he would give me a Rolls-Royce. Finally, I got it for him and he told me to go over to the Rolls place and pick one out. I confess I went and looked at one. Then I realized that if it cost $35,000 it was going to mean $70,000, with the taxes he pays for Charlie to give it to me. I turned it down. I said, "Charlie, one day you'll get mad as hell at me over something, and you'll say, 'To think that I even gave that s.o.b. a Rolls-Royce.' Better you just plain get mad at me.' "

Among the stars that Kohner discovered were Jeanne Crain, whom he found in Laguna, and Peggy Middleton, whom he introduced to Walter Wanger in 1945 as Yvonne de Carlo, for *Salome, Where She Danced*. Kohner is probably the only agent in Hollywood whose daughter, Susan, has been successful in the acting profession.

Paul Kohner, whose brother Walter is an associate in the agency, has handled such stars as Geraldine Chaplin, Dolores del Rio, Mia Farrow, Henry Fonda, Greta Garbo, Walter Huston, Mick Jagger, Rita Hayworth, Myrna Loy, Jeanne Moreau, Malcolm McDowell, Peter O'Toole, Pola Negri, David Niven, Luise Rainer, Charlotte Rampling, Vanessa Redgrave, Martin Sheen, Maria Schneider, Eric von Stroheim, Max von Sydow, Robert Taylor, Liv Ullmann, and many more.

Lana Turner recalled in her autobiography[12] that after the Johnny Stompanato/Cheryl Crane scandal had caused headlines all over the country, and about six weeks after her last film, *Another Time, Another Place* (May 1958), began to show poor receipts after its initial showings: "My agent Paul Kohner never lost faith in me.... He called me to do a picture. It was the remake of *Imitation of Life*, the Fannie Hurst story, and Ross Hunter, the producer, wanted to meet me.

" 'See him, Lana,' Paul urged. 'This is just what you need to come back. It's a proven story.'

"But I was scared. What if the picture flopped? And maybe it was too soon. Maybe I was still too notorious and people wouldn't come to see me. If the movie bombed I knew what could happen—I probably would never work again ...."

She met Hunter, and Kohner worked out a percentage deal for her. She continued in her book: "*Imitation of Life* grossed more than any Universal film ever had. And, thanks to Ross, it was my financial salvation.... I don't know exactly how much I made—my managers took care of that—but it was more than the highly publicized million dollars that Elizabeth Taylor got for *Cleopatra* some years later ...."

Kohner's brother Frederick (of *Gidget* fame) wrote an entertaining book about the family, with emphasis on Paul, called *The Magician of Sunset Boulevard*.[13] Kohner's associate in New York is the urbane, continental, good-humored Robert "Robbie" Lantz, friend of many stars, who never betrays a confidence.

The 50th Anniversary of Lupita and Paul Kohner at the Bel Air Hotel, was hosted by son Pancho Kohner and daughter Susan Kohner Weitz. Director John Huston had flown up from his home in Puerto Vallarta for the event. He exclaimed, according to *Daily Variety* columnist Army Archerd, " 'I'm Paul's oldest client—I've been with him for fifty years—just like his wife. Forty years ago, my father sang a song at their 10th anniversary party. I'd now like to ask Andy Williams to sing it for you.' Williams sang (beautifully) "September Song" and there wasn't a dry eye in the house . . . ."

One of the few offsprings of agents to enjoy a successful acting career is the reigning queen of night-time television, sexpot of *Dynasty*, Joan Collins. At fifty-two, she has been connected with show business since birth. Her father, Joe Collins, was partner in a theatrical agency, with Lew Grade.

In her candid autobiography,[14] Collins wrote: "My father was second-generation show business. He was born in Port Elizabeth, South Africa, in 1902, to a successful theatrical agent, Will Collins, and a saucy soubrette and dancer, Henrietta Collins. Hetty must have been an early emancipated woman since she continued dancing with her sister act, 'The Three Cape Girls' until a month or so before Joe's birth. Considering it was still the Victorian Age, this showed a remarkable lack of concern for convention, something I obviously inherited from her . . . ."

Henrietta's two daughters entered show business, Pauline becoming a theatrical agent, and Lalla, a dancer. Collins made her film debut in *Lady Godiva Rides Again* (1951) in England. For the next 25 years, she appeared in pictures with quaint titles that almost tell a story: *The Virgin Queen* and *The Girl in the Red Velvet Swing* (1955), *Can Hiermonymus Merkin Ever Forget Mercy Humppe and Find True Happiness?* (1969), *Inn of Frightened People or Terror From Under the House* (1971), *The Devil Within Her* (1975), *Empire of the Ants* (1976), *The Stud* (1978), *The Bitch* (1979), *The Wild Women of Chastity Gulch* (1982), and *My Life as a Man* (1984). But it was as Alexis Carrington Colby on *Dynasty* that brought her the most fame. In December 1983, she appeared nude in *Playboy* magazine, photographed by Hurrell.

Another British actress who also did a *Playboy* session is June Wilkinson, currently handled by Ben Pearson. Her first agent in England was also Lew Grade. Now divorced from footballer Dan Pastorini, she had just returned from a three-month engagement at the Union Plaza Hotel in Las Vegas in the comedy, *The Owl and The Pussycat*. She lounged[15] in the art deco living room of her luxurious condominium in Encino, California, and ran long fingers through her creamy silver-blond hair. She wore no makeup other than a pale lipstick and mascara that highlighted her perfect complexion.

Known for her incredible body proportions, she sighed, "Early in my career, I had to play up my body because I had little else to offer. For instance, I did that *Playboy* layout when I was sixteen, and yet I still run into that picture tacked up on someone's back wall. I've worked like hell since then, in all the media—stage, pictures, television. I'm ready for other things."

She turned to her mother, Lily. "Remember when I was a little girl, how awkward and ugly I was? Even then I knew I was going to be an actress. I didn't know how, I just *knew*."

"That's true," the attractive Lily conceded. "Even then, you never let any flies light on you. You knew what you wanted."

"When I was fourteen," Wilkinson commented, "I looked down one day and bang, bang, they were there—my bosoms, I mean. I don't remember them growing—suddenly they were there. I saw myself in the mirror and I was pretty. My first job came along shortly afterward at the Windmill Theater in London, which was a sort of British Ziegfeld Follies. Next, I played at the Embassy Club on Bond Street, and although I was a lead dancer, my big opportunity came a little later in the evening when I posed behind a plate-glass window and the customers shot little rubber-tipped darts at me. Wherever the dart landed, I removed that article of clothing.

"Actually, my life has always been governed by events outside my control," Wilkinson continued in her slightly clipped accent, "freaky, spooky things. For instance, the man who had discovered Anita Ekberg, Jimmy McCullough, came into the Embassy one night. The next thing I knew, I was in New York appearing on the old *Dave Garroway Show*, and dating fashion designer Oleg Cassini, who later did all those neat clothes for Jackie Kennedy."

Since those days, Wilkinson has practically made a career out of playing in *Pajama Tops*, but has done a number of interesting plays—*Any Wednesday, Ninety Day Mistress*—on the road and in dinner theaters, where she always plays before sold-out houses.

These packaged dinner theater shows also revived the careers of stars such as Lana Turner, who switched from being represented by Paul Kohner to Stan Kamen, and toured in such plays as *The Pleasure of His Company* and *Bell, Book, and Candle*.

Meanwhile, television sitcoms resurrected the careers of other stars who would have been regarded as "middle-aged" in the 1940s. With the support of a powerful agency, veteran stars could make spectacular comebacks on the tube. This incident made all the rounds:

The story idea had been difficult to peddle, but finally the big New York talent agency had sold the TV package to a big network. The storyline had a middle-aged, rather lovable former physicist (portrayed by an old vaudeville star) giving up his pressured career for a new beginning among a bevy of colorful characters on a Midwest chicken farm.

The newly-completed pilot was finally being screened at the big agency. The vice-president who had sold the property was a few minutes late, having been caught in cross-town traffic. He slid into the back row of the projection room just after the opening credits. At the first appearance of the comic, he laughed derisively. "Boy!" he exclaimed, "what a lousy actor! We were lucky to unload this no-talent! Couldn't even sell him Off-Broadway in a two-bit play, and here he is with his own series!"

Later, as the plot unfolded, the agent clapped his hands. "This is just a piece of shit! Wheels who would buy this chicken farm concept are total idiots!"

The lights came up to full in the projection room. The vice-president found himself the object of a dozen pairs of glaring, fire-filled eyes. The agent prayed that the sewers of Manhattan would open up and suck him down into the depths. The entire contingent of network brass had assembled for the screening!

BLACKOUT: 1955

Male Star

I've had it! I want you to get me out of the contract at the end of this season. After five years, the scripts are really bad. I'm sick to death of this damn cowboy image. I started out in Shakespeare!

Agent

I understand the situation perfectly. But the series is still in the top ten. You have only three more segments to shoot, then a long hiatus. After three months away, you'll be your old self again. I'll see to it that you get some good scripts next season. The network's projection is that the show is good for at least two more years—maybe more.

Male Star

In two years I'll be forty! I want some of those starring parts in features that every schlock actor in Hollywood has been getting while I'm working my ass off . . . .

Agent

You've been around long enough to know that when you're on a hit series with all that exposure every week, every studio in town wants you. It's because you're unavailable. My advice is to stay with the series.

Male Star

So you can keep collecting your thirty-five-hundred a week commission with no sweat?

Agent

That's not fair and you know it! I just don't want you to give up a sure thing. You've got plenty of time. Syndication rights are right around the corner.

Male Star

Money doesn't mean that much. I just want a nice romantic role, while the face is still pretty good.

Agent

I'm also thinking about Martha and the kids, and the annuities for college educations . . . .

Male Star

Cut the horseshit. I told you I want out of the series and I mean it. It's time people in the business realize I am a serious actor.

Abe Lastfogel's career at the William Morris agency spanned 72 years. He started with the agency in 1912 at the age of 14 and continued to serve until his death in 1984. *(Courtesy of Marvin Paige's Motion Picture and TV Research Service)*

For James Stewart, in *Winchester '73*, Lew Wasserman of MCA demanded fifty percent of the profits for his star and made Stewart $600,000. *(Courtesy of Universal Pictures)*

17

MOGULS, MERGERS, & MAYHEM

Maurine Oliver

*Agents are the last people with any courage or any vision about peo-
ple. We take a chance. It isn't easy, but it's very exciting.*

Major changes in the motion picture industry came about between Pearl Harbor and V-J Day. Box-office receipts skyrocketed:
90 million people flocked to the movies each week. Because many of
Hollywood's leading men were away in the war, 4F actors were
much in demand. With the studios turning out approximately one
film a week, and contracts for talent constantly being written and re-
written, the agency business prospered.

MCA had attracted young men in their late twenties or early
thirties. Lew Wasserman was head of the Hollywood office, and
Sonny Werblin was head of New York branch, while the theatrical
department was headed by Johnny Dugan. Hal Hackett handled
radio; Harry Moss, one-nighters; Earl Bailey, locations. Irving
Lazar was an MCA lawyer in New York. Later, Freddie Fields and
David Begelman would become New York and Hollywood agents
for MCA.

Because the usual breed of Hollywood ten percenters dressed
flamboyantly, Wasserman established a dress code. His men wore
black suits, white shirts, and black ties. Legend has it that when he
once wore a red tie, it was noted in *The New York Times*!

Jules Stein waited for four years before he decided that the move
to Los Angeles was going to be permanent, and in 1940 (the same
year that he gave about forty percent of MCA to the executives who
had help build the company), he made one of his most profitable personal investments. Famed director Fred Niblo, who had made a for-

tune in silent pictures but had not made a major film in years, placed his sprawling, semi-circular Tudor showplace on the market. Designed by renowned architect Wallace Neff, and built on eight acres in the hills at 1330 Angelo Drive, the mansion had cost $285,000 in 1928. In 1940, since real estate in the area was moving very slowly, the asking price was $50,000.

Stein offered $40,000, which Niblo refused. Finally, the owner traded the mansion to someone else for a piece of business property. As luck would have it, the new owner had second thoughts, and accepted Stein's offer of $35,000. This gives some idea of the bargaining talent of Jules Stein. In 1981, the property was worth seven-million.

MCA's drive for talent escalated during the war years. Stein purchased Betty Grable's contract from Vic Orsatti for $2,500. Under his tutelage, she became a high-priced performer in Twentieth Century-Fox musicals. Many people assume that Grable met Harry James, her husband-to-be, through MCA connections, since they were both under contract there. They did not actually meet until both were donating time at The Hollywood Canteen, in 1942.

Grable's erstwhile agents, the Brothers Orsatti, were probably the only talent agents to come from the sports world. Victor and Frank Orsatti set up their talent agency in 1933. The Orsatti family had one other distinction; in 1902, their father, Morris, was responsible in a back-handed sort of way for bringing six-year-old Frank Capra and his family to Los Angeles. (After a series of wild adventures, an uneducated runaway Capra brother had come to Los Angeles from Sicily, met Morris, a steamship ticket agent, who wrote a letter to the Capra family, inviting them to come to America.)

In 1935, Frank Orsatti was involved with the Warner Brothers picture, *The Irish in US*. At one time or another, the agency handled—besides Grable—Alice Faye, Judy Garland, Margaret O'Brien, and Edward G. Robinson, as well as directors Frank Capra, William Seiter, George Stevens, and Preston Sturges.

Victor Orsatti was born in Los Angeles, November 25, 1905, and was a graduate of Manual Arts High School, where he starred in football and baseball. In 1923, he was honored as the best all-around athlete in Los Angeles. He received his B.A. at University of

Southern California in 1928, where he played quarterback, and was a test pilot at Lockheed during World War II. Victor was responsible for luring figure-skater Sonja Henie to Hollywood after her championship performance in the 1936 Winter Olympics, and they subsequently became engaged. However they did not marry. Victor was married several times—to actresses June Lang and Marie McDonald, and to model Dolores Donlon, whom he wed in Las Vegas in 1949. When Donlon sued him for divorce in 1958, she asked for $1,700 a month support pending the trial, estimating her husband's income at between $40,000 and $50,000 a year. His fourth wife was Arla Turner.

Victor kept the agency going after Frank Orsatti died,[1] and then turned producer in 1956, when he formed Sabre Productions, making *Flight to Hong Kong*, with Rory Calhoun and Dolores Donlon. Orsatti himself turned actor and played the "heavy" in their next picture, *The Hired Gun*. Unlike Charles K. Feldman, MCA, or other large agencies, he followed through on picture deals from beginning to end—somewhat like Leland Hayward, but on a smaller scale.

About Rorvic Incorporated, formed with Calhoun, Victor said in an interview with Philip K. Scheuer:[2] "We are an independent organization brought in by a studio. We come in with story and star and use its facilities, which are charged against us. We could do it outside cheaper, but we need the facilities of the lot—and its prestige . . . .

"We make a picture for around $300,000—no preparation cost except for the script. If we're in doubt about a sequence we don't shoot it. The general plan is to do location pictures (*Hired Gun* at Lone Pine) at a price we can live with. On location we have atmosphere and real crowds. We use two cameras and shoot rain or shine—in about 10 days. We get every dollar up there on the screen—instead of writing it off somewhere . . . . When I played that heavy, it was the right type-casting to my clients!" He grinned, "Actually, as an agent I always tried to make a deal that was liberal on both sides . . . .

"As an agent I know how to make this type deal." Vic added, "it takes training. I also know the actual mechanics of making pictures. Years ago, I was an assistant director here at MGM. It seems funny to be coming back as a producer."

In May 1940, an incident occurred that pointed directly to the future of the talent agency business, although it was not apparent at the time. Both CBS and NBC radio went forward with plans to sell their "artists' bureaus"—departments that represented the bulk of talent heard on the major national networks. The Federal Communications Commission criticized both companies in an anti-monopoly report.

While CBS announced its withdrawal from the field of talent management and the sale of its Columbia Artists, Inc., to MCA, NBC announced that it was negotiating with the William Morris Agency for the sale of its bureau.

The New York Times reported:[3] "The FCC report had charged that the artists' bureaus were acting in a dual capacity in that on the one hand they were representing an employer's interests and on the other hand an employee's. The anti-monopoly division of the Department of Justice also has been reported to have had agents investigating the bureaus, partly in connection with its inquiry into the activities of the American Federation of Musicians, headed by James C. Petrillo . . . .

"In its formal statement, however, Columbia said it was 'certain that there has never been an instance in which such a criticism was justified,' but that 'it nonetheless recognizes that those not familiar with all of the circumstances of network broadcasting might be led to believe otherwise.

"Columbia said that its two subsidiaries were originally founded to insure 'an adequate supply of talent,' but that they were no longer needed 'because artists of all kinds are now readily available to it and other broadcasters.

"Present executives of Columbia Artists, Inc., of which Herbert Rosenthal is executive vice-president, will continue their functions under the ownership of Music Corporation of America, it was said . . . ."

When CBS and NBC divested themselves of their talent agencies, no one thought that Music Corporation of America would be forced to make the same kind of move 23 years later.

During World War I, few American stage personalities entertained troops. Several vaudeville stars, like Elsie Janis, went into the trenches sponsored by the Y.M.C.A., and Sarah Bernhardt, along with many English stars, performed in France. After Pearl Harbor, however, when it became evident that American troops would be stationed over much of the world, an effort was made to form an organization for putting together shows to entertain servicemen.

Wrote E. J. Kahn, Jr., in a profile of Abe Lastfogel:[4] "The idea that led to the formation of U.S.O-Camp shows came from Thomas J. Watson, the International Business Machinist, who knew the commanding general of the 27th Infantry Division, a New York National Guard outfit that was called up for active duty as early as the fall of 1940. At the general's request, Watson and a few philanthropic cronies banded together informally as the Friends of the 27th Division and sent packages to its personnel. Soon Watson's group was calling itself the Friends of New York State Soldiers and Sailors and was sending more packages to men of more units.

"By January, 1941, it had given up its regional view of the emergency, had renamed itself the Citizens' Committee for the Army and Navy, and was distributing books, phonograph records, and other recreational paraphernalia to men from all the states. In the meantime, the U.S.O. had been set up as a clearing house for the operations of the Y.M.C.A. and other welfare groups, and there was also a Joint Army and Navy Committee on Welfare and Recreation, an advisory body headed by Frederick H. Osborn, a New York businessman. Osborn was subsequently commissioned a brigadier general and put in charge of the Army's Morale Branch, which later became known as Special Services. By May of 1941, the Citizens' Committee was presenting shows, in seven trunks that served as mobile stages, in Army camps east of the Rockies. On the other side of the mountains, several other committees were corraling movie actors and leading them to camps. Lastfogel, who was then in California, was involved in this activity . . . ."

Lastfogel was named president of U.S.O. Camp Shows, and began to run the organization just as he had co-run (with William Morris, Jr.) the Morris Office: with imagination, diligence, and attention to detail. Camp shows, which took about ten weeks to put together, were just another phase of the business to Lastfogel, whose agency regularly handled about a thousand performers— their total income was about $23,000,000 a year. His first edict after being named president of U.S.O. Camp Shows and moving into an office on East 40th Street, was that the Morris Agency would not except commissions on the earnings of clients who performed for the servicemen. Other talent agencies followed suit.

The drab office on East 40th Street was a far cry from the plush premises at Rockefeller Center that Lastfogel had left, its hallways hung with photographs of stars going as far back as 1898, the "Gold Book" (displayed on the pedestal that singing star Nora Bayes once used as a bar in her dressing room) filled with the autographs of the greats who had visited the office, and the 45 identical photographs of William Morris, Sr., that graced various offices and corridors.

On the wall in dapper William Morris, Jr.'s office, was an eighteenth-century French map of the world, which had been referred to by his father as the "blueprint of their business." He told Kahn: "Father used to say that when you booked acts into these spots marked *terra incognita*, you'd be close to real peace in the world." Lastfogel had booked acts that entertained troops in many of those areas.

There was far more work at the new office than Lastfogel could handle, and now and then he was aided by five associates from the Rockefeller Center office who were paid by the agency, rather than by the U.S.O. Most of the entertainment units consisted of a vocalist, a comedian, a dancer, a novelty act, and an accordionist or piano player.

The War Department usually restricted the number of performers in a show to five, because of the problem of transportation. In the fall of 1944, however, regulations were eased and more acts could be added to the roster. By 1945, Lastfogel was able to send larger bills overseas, and some ninety legitimate stage plays and musical comedies were touring, with casts numbering as high as sixty. Some three-hundred movie stars made the trip overseas, and there were literally thousands of lesser-known personalities and variety acts playing for the troops.

Lastfogel himself made two trips abroad, one during the conflict and the other immediately after V-J Day. On the latter journey he met General Eisenhower, who complimented him on the work being done for the servicemen. It was a proud moment for Lastfogel, who knew that his job was not finished with the war's end, but that shows would be necessary for occupation forces.

In 1942, on a trip to New York City, John Garfield dropped by The Stage Door Canteen, which was supervised by Jane Cowl, and where show business entertainers performed for servicemen. He returned to Warner Brothers determined to open such a facility in Hollywood—which was overrun with military personnel who had nothing to do while on leave.

Garfield presented his idea to Bette Davis whom he encountered in the Green Room restaurant at Warner Brothers, after she had returned from a hugely-successful bond-selling tour. (She had been named Princess Laughing Eyes by an Indian chief in Oklahoma.) She was enthusiastic, and plans were formed that would involve the membership of fourteen unions and guilds to donate time for converting a former livery stable and nightclub, the Old Barn on Cahuenga Boulevard, into The Hollywood Canteen.

"I knew the finances on such an undertaking would be enormous," Davis recalled,[5] lighting the fire in the huge, black onyx fireplace in the living room of her West Hollywood condominium, "and I appealed to Jules Stein. I was somewhat apprehensive at doing so, because Jules was a very private person. He kept an exceedingly low profile, had never been interviewed, and had even refused to have his biography appear in *Who's Who in America*. Although everyone in Hollywood knew his name, few outside his clients and the heads of studios had ever met him personally.

"But Jules was an extremely patriotic man, and he would be dealing with segments of the industry in which he had some influence. He became head of our financial committee, and even if he gave up his privacy, I think he enjoyed himself. His wife Doris agreed to head the committee that provided hostesses to dance with the servicemen. Jules ran the financial affairs of the canteen, which opened on October 3, 1942, as brilliantly as he ran MCA, and after V-J day there was still a half a million dollars left in the canteen account. These monies Jules continued to invest, so that every year since November 22, 1945, when the canteen closed, funds have been distributed to veterans' organizations. This is one part of my life that I'm very proud about."

At the same time that Jules Stein was managing the finances for The Hollywood Canteen, Frank Sinatra—who was to come into his own during the war—had been having career problems. MCA's quest to acquire his contract was quite complicated. A client of General Amusement, he was handled by vice-president Michael Nidorf, who had gone into the armed services. Sinatra felt neglected. He had obligated an unbelievable 53⅓ percent of his earnings.

Tommy Dorsey, for whom Sinatra worked as a singer, received 33⅓ percent; 10 percent went to agents, and 10 percent to his personal manager. Also, Axel Stordahl—who wrote his arrangements—was not cheap, and there were other expenses such as a press agent and writers.

The upshot of the deal was that General Amusement shared agents' commission fees with MCA until their contract with Sinatra ran out, November 30, 1948. The deal also stipulated that, if he signed with MCA after that date, they were to give General Amusement one quarter of their commissions.

MCA during this period was growing very large and fat. But with all of the new agents Stein hired there was an unwritten rule: no nepotism. Stein told columnist Joyce Haber, "I've always said 'No Relatives': for every good relative you have, you get 10 bums. So when Lew Wasserman's daughter Lynn married [MCA agent] Ronnie Lief, he had to quit."

This feeling of family members being involved in business was emphasized again years later in Stein's will, which noted: "I take special pride in the founding of MCA and building it with the assistance of my able and loyal associates into an immensely successful public corporation . . . . I adopted certain principles. One of these principles is avoidance of nepotism. I trust that this principle will be followed after my death; in particular, I would hope and expect that none of my issue or my wife's issue or their spouses or any other of my wife's relatives by blood or marriage shall be acquainted, retained, or elected as officers, employees or directors of MCA . . . ."

In 1943, near his fortieth birthday, Billy Goodheart announced, as he had so often before, that he was going to retire. He had earned his million dollars. What sort of a deal he made with Stein has never been recorded, but after he left Music Corporation of America his name slowly dimmed in company annals and, as time went on, the fact that he had founded the company with Stein was played down, or if his name came up in conversation his role was minimized. Newcomers assumed that the few people who occasionally mentioned a "Bill" from the old days were referring to Jules' brother, Bill Stein.

Goodheart operated a ranch in Eaton, Ohio, from 1943 to 1951, when he became president of Official Films in New York. He also served as a vice-president of National Broadcasting Company, after leaving Official. He moved to Phoenix, Arizona, where he was executive vice-president of a real estate firm until his death at 58 in 1960.

In 1959, aside from MCA and the William Morris Agency, there was one other agency that dealt in a wide range of talent—the Hayward-Deverich Agency, headquartered in New York. Leland Hayward, having been in the talent business since the late 1920s, was 43 years old and tired of piloting his own plane back and forth from New York to Los Angeles three times a month, endeavoring to keep the three-hundred stars, directors, and writers working and happy. He had reached the point where he either had to expand or sell.

What Hayward really wanted was to produce stage plays on Broadway. When he made the deal with Stein to buy him out, it was with the provision that he would assume a vice-presidency, and stay with the agency only long enough to make the transition as painless as possible. Stein was flabbergasted by the prestigious list of clients—with everyone from Garbo to Hemingway. This acquisition made MCA the largest talent agency in the world.

With MCA's purchase of Hayward-Deverich, the William Morris Agency looked around frantically to augment its own clientele, and the next year a merger was arranged with the Berg-Allenberg Agency, whose clients included performers Linda Darnell, Clark Gable, Peter Lawford, Charles Laughton, Robert Mitchum, Joel McCrea, Edward G. Robinson, Loretta Young; and directors Frank Capra, John Farrow, Stuart Heisler, Henry Koster, Joseph L. Mankiewicz, Charles Vidor, William Wellman; and numerous other performers, directors, producers, and writers.

Indeed, the problem clients experienced when "sold" to a large agency like MCA was that they were in danger of being overlooked in such a large array of talent.

An amusing story making the rounds at this time—and dealing with this problem—involved agent Phil Berg. According to Alva Johnston, Berg was having a rare night-out-on-the-town at the Trocadero when he was introduced to screenwriter Thomas Monroe. The band was very loud and Monroe did not catch Berg's name. Passing the time of night, the agent solicitously asked how Monroe was doing.

"So-so," was the answer. "I have a lot of ideas, but I'm having difficulty getting them before the right people."

Berg commiserated with him. "Who's your agent?" he asked.

"I haven't been able to talk to him."

"That's terrible. What's his name?"

"Phil Berg."

The major agencies faced many problems with over-extended talent lists. When male stars began to be mustered out of service after the war, it was often difficult to get them lined-up for picture work; many performers never regained their pre-war following.

A case in point was bachelor James Stewart, who returned to Hollywood in 1945 as a Lieutenant Colonel after serving overseas in the Air Force. He had received the Distinguished Flying Cross with Oak Leaf Cluster, having flown twenty missions over Germany. He was to become the highest-ranking show business personality in the military, retiring as a brigadier general in 1968. In 1945, he was 38 years old. A client of MCA, courtesy of Leland Hayward, he had fought with Louis B. Mayer at MGM. Mayer had told Stewart bluntly that his two years of military service would be added to his contract. Olivia De Havilland's court case against Warner Brothers was still pending—she had sued because suspension time had been added to her contract by the studio. She felt the contract had ended at the specified time. She could not work in films until the decision came down. A year later she won, and her gain was a triumph for all actors and actresses. The court decreed that contracts could not be elongated beyond the ending date, whatever the reason—and of course this ruling also applied to military service.

However, Stewart was given relief from his MGM contract in a more convoluted manner: MCA reportedly told Louis B. Mayer that none of their agency talent would ever be booked into MGM's huge theater chain unless he did some soul searching. Mayer was furious, but released Stewart. MCA then arranged several free-lance deals for their star, including *It's a Wonderful Life* (1946) and *Magic Town* (1947) at RKO. He returned to MGM for *The Stratton Story* (1949), and *Malaya* (1950). Then came a turning point for Stewart, as well as for the motion picture industry itself.

Universal Studios had fared well with its class B "sex 'n sand," horror, and adventure movies during the war years, but its contract list had dwindled. Big stars were needed in big productions. Studio head Bill Goetz had the script of a Western entitled *Winchester '73*, which called for a middle-aged man with enormous charisma, and he approached MCA. Lew Wasserman, one of the few talent heads who actually *read* scripts and did not depend upon subordinates to "tell" the story or give him a synopsis, realized the story was perfect for Stewart, who coincidentally had told him "get me a Western."

Goetz, who was Louis B. Mayer's son-in-law, was pleased that Stewart was available: having him in a Universal picture would be a coup. Wasserman was anxious to revive the star percentage deals that had been popular in the 1920s, but he had been apprehensive about talking such terms to the major studios. Now he knew that the time was ripe—Goetz was desperate. "You can have Stewart," he said, "but only on a percentage deal. We won't hold you up for much cash up front, but we want 50 percent of the profits."

Goetz knew that he could cast the picture with low-salaried Universal stock players, like Rock Hudson and Shelley Winters, give the picture a class "A" production, and still come out on top, but he wanted Stewart, so he accepted the deal. The picture was a tremendous box office success, and made Stewart some $600,000.

The heads of the other studios gnashed what was left of their teeth; the stampede was on, and the star participation deals became a hated part of the business, making way for multi-million-dollar deals, commonplace in the 1970s and 1980s. But in defense of the stars, it is important to note that few of the 1930s crop were millionaires. They had grown into prominence under the "star system," with salaries escalating over a seven-year period. When a top star had finally reached a weekly peak of five or six thousand by the early 1940s, Uncle Sam took ninety percent of the earnings. Unless they had invested in real estate like Mae West, Alan Ladd, Bob Hope, Marion Davies, or Francis Lederer, many stars were not extremely well-off.

In 1946, Jules Stein resigned as president of Music Corporation of America, becoming chairman of the board and appointing Lew Wasserman to succeed him. "In that same year, 1946," noted *Current Biography*, May, 1967, "the name most often hurled at MCA by its critics, 'octopus,' was first applied, by a federal district court judge in Los Angeles in a suit against MCA by Larry Finley, the operator of an amusement park and ballroom in Mission Beach, California. Finley charged that MCA could and did control some of the best talent in show business 'in restraint of trade.' He said that he had refused to sign an exclusive contract with MCA and that, in consequence, he was unable to obtain any entertainment represented by MCA. Whenever he asked for an act, he said, a rival named Wayne Daillard, who did have an exclusive contract with the agency, got the act instead. Found guilty of violating the Sherman Anti-Trust Act, MCA was ordered to pay damages to Finley . . . ."

Stein and Wasserman, in a position to assess the state of the industry from an overall viewpoint, were far more incisive than the protected heads of studios. They realized that the men who had returned from battle had changed—weary, jaded ex-servicemen had other things on their minds than attending glossy movies filmed on the back lots. With men home again, women had homes to maintain and children to bear. Families became interested in all types of recreation.

For the first time in many years, theaters had real competition. Change—similar to the revolution of talking pictures twenty years before—was imminent in the form of the "box" in the living room. Cocktail bars that featured television sets were crowded to the rafters, and families were saving money to purchase their own audio and video equipment.

Television first caught the public's fancy in 1947, with the televised opening of Congress on January 2. Suddenly, the glowing tube in the darkened living room had impact. Later in that year, President Truman was seen in the White House, the World Series was telecast, children watched *Howdy Doody*, and adults viewed dramas on *Kraft Theatre*, and variety-vaudeville hours were popular.

The year 1948 saw Morey Amsterdam, Milton Berle, Jack Benny, Eddie Cantor, Perry Como, Arthur Godfrey, Bob Hope, Faye Emerson, Ed Murrow, Ed Sullivan, Dinah Shore, Frank Sinatra, and Gloria Swanson appearing on 600,000 television sets (escalating to 51,000,000 in the next ten years.)

Charles Laughton, one of Hollywood's biggest stars, having difficulty finding good film roles, and playing in such trifles as *Abbott and Costello Meet Captain Kid* (1952) for Warner Brothers, had turned to public readings. He made a smash appearance on the live

Ed Sullivan Show, reading *The Fiery Furnace*. MCA agent, Paul Gregory, who worked in the Concert Department and handled bookings for Spike Jones, happened to be watching the show in a bar, located near the Ed Sullivan Theater in New York. Suddenly overcome with a brainstorm, Gregory immediately rushed to the stage entrance of the theater, introduced himself to the actor, and explained that he would like to book him for a series of concert readings all over America.

In her splendid autobiography,[6] Laughton's wife Elsa Lanchester wrote: ". . . . the whole thing took form in seven or eight days. Soon Paul Gregory arrived in Hollywood with the MCA concert booking files tucked underneath his arm. I remember the tall, dark figure I met at the front door. He hadn't even changed his MCA charcoal suit to a 'civilian' outfit. I figured that he must have just walked out on MCA. Rather proudly, in his own way (whether it was actually true or not), he said that he had stolen the card index of all the college auditoriums and women's clubs that MCA had collected over many years. I supposed that he somehow already had a copy, because he felt he might one day be on his own and was just waiting for his chance. When it came, he would be ready to go—card index and all . . . ."

The many Laughton tours were phenomenally successful, and Gregory was the driving force behind the launch of the first of the one-man/one-woman shows that later became a staple of the American stage tour—a concept which had actually found its roots in television.

Yet there were many Hollywood producers who did not own a TV set. Stein and Wasserman, who did have sets because they had clients appearing all over the tube, saw the handwriting on the wall. Realizing that Hollywood was in a depression that showed no signs of abating, they went to the major studios with a proposal that was essentially: "Television is here to stay, make use of those empty stages and facilities and film shows especially for home viewing."

Abuse was heaped upon their heads; MCA—in 1949, the name of Music Corporation of America was changed to MCA, which is what everyone had called the company since the beginning—was accused, mildly, of biting the hand that fed it, and a good deal more. To the studio moguls, television was competition, and they would have no part of it: no executive would listen to reason. With

Hollywood making only a fraction of the films turned out during the fabulous box-office years of World War II, it was apparent to Stein and Wasserman exactly how dire the situation was in the motion picture industry. It was at this point that they knew there was only one course open to them—find a studio.

They were to set Hollywood aflame.

BLACKOUT: 1969

Agent

This part is something else. Now, you really must cooperate with everyone—and that includes the press. This picture has a twelve-mill-eight budget and you could get a nomination out of it—but you've got to have the media behind you all the way.

Female Star

Set up a press conference.

Agent

If I may venture an opinion, that's condescending. The First Lady of the United States can set up a press conference, but if you do, it will smack of "pulling the big star bit," which you can't afford to do. You've got to show that all the gossips are wrong, that you aren't difficult and can be the wonderful, charming woman I know you to be. This is a chance to do a class "A" feature in a part that's tailor-made for you!

Female Star

Why should I give individual interviews? I've been crucified by those bastards? I can field questions for an hour with everyone, and you know I'm quick with a comeback. I'll get twice as much coverage.

Agent

It's not a wise move. If you like we can limit the interviews to eight or nine. You'll have to do *Newsday* and *The New York Times*, and something for the "People" section in *Time* magazine, because everyone reads that first. If we can't work that out, then we'll go to *Newsweek*. *The Chicago Tribune* will take care of the Midwest, and *The Denver Post* will do likewise for the Rocky Mountain area. On the West Coast, there will be the *Los Angeles Times*—the "Calendar" section if I can arrange it. Then Bob Thomas with the Associated Press—he likes you—and Vernon Scott . . . . It will be nostalgia time.

Female Star

Nostalgia time? No, thanks. I either give one press conference or none at all!

Agent

Then I'm afraid, my dear, the producer says it will be none at all.

Universal Studios vice-president and former talent agent Jennings Lang chats with George Kennedy on location in Switzerland for *The Eiger Sanction*. *(Courtesy of Universal Pictures)*

In happy days, producer Walter Wanger, wife Joan Bennett, and baby at their house on Mapleton Drive. *(Fritz Lang collection)*

18

MCA & MONOPOLY

I wouldn't trust that P.R. guy as far as I could throw Mama Cass!
Young wives' tale.

In the fifth decade of this century, MCA rented the old Republic lot on Ventura Boulevard in Studio City, where Gene Autry and Roy Rogers had filmed so many interiors for their Western movies. They then purchased old television shows for reruns and bought old movies, which they released through syndication to sponsors and local stations.

MCA was now in business in more ways than one. Executives went after stars they had wanted to represent for some time. Rita Hayworth was acquired as a client in 1950, when Jules Stein reportedly loaned her $125,000 to purchase a house in Paris. Since she had given up her career in 1949—and $250,000 a year under a Columbia Studios contract—to marry Prince Aly Khan, MCA must have been given some indication that she would make more films. She had been handled by Johnny Hyde of William Morris (who apparently would not lend her the money).

In 1950, Jennings Lang—a husky six-footer and an influential agent with the Jaffe Agency—joined MCA, where his expertise was put to work in the development and supervision of such television shows as *Bachelor Father*, *McHale's Navy*, and *Wagon Train*.

The son of a prosperous German immigrant/merchant, he was born in 1915 in New York City, graduated from St. John's University, took a law degree, and started a practice. A talent agent friend offered him fifty percent of the amount that he could collect from an orchestra leader living in Los Angeles, who owed him money. Lang paid his own way to Hollywood, couldn't collect a dime from the recalcitrant musician, but did meet comic Hugh Herbert at a party. Herbert, who had recently fired his agent, was impressed with Lang's urbanity and intellect, and asked if he would be interested in representing him.

"I had only the foggiest notion of what's expected of an agent," Lang said in an interview,[1] "but the next day I called a movie producer and offered my client's services at $5,000 a week. The producer protested that Hugh's previous agent had asked only $1,500 a week. I was stumped for a couple of seconds, then blurted out, 'That's why he changed agents.' "

Surprisingly, he got his asking price.

Lang, 37, had been with Music Corporation of America barely two years when he was involved in a far-reaching scandal that shook Hollywood. On December 13, 1951, having had a business luncheon with client Joan Bennett, age 42, he was dropping her off in the MCA parking lot in Beverly Hills when her husband of twelve years, producer Walter Wanger, age 58, accosted him with a gun and shot him in the groin. Since the police station was located across the street, it only took a moment for officers to arrive.

"I've just shot the sonofabitch who tried to break up my home," Wanger told the policemen, before being lead off to jail.

After Wanger had directed the unsuccessful *Joan of Arc*, with Ingrid Bergman, produced by Enterprise Productions, which was headed by former agent Charles Einfeld, he owed so much money to the Bank of America that he almost lost his house on Mapleton Drive, and had barely avoided bankruptcy. Bennett had been accepting any jobs available to improve the family exchequer, but the marriage had been rocky from the beginning.

In her autobiography,[2] Bennett wrote: "About that time I was stricken with a sudden illness. Walter was out of town and it was Jennings Lang, my agent of several years, who helped me make some of the necessary arrangements for medical attention in Walter's absence. Suddenly I was offered the sympathy and gentleness I found lacking at home, and I turned to Jennings more often after that with feelings that went beyond our business relationship . . . ."

After the accident, the parking lot attendant helped Bennett get Lang to a doctor's office and then to Midway Hospital, where an emergency operation was performed. Bennett then called friend Jane Wyman, at whose house Lang and his wife, Pamela, were scheduled to attend dinner, asking Wyman to inform Pamela Lang about the accident. Then Bennett called publicist Maggie Ettinger (who, ironically, had accompanied her and Wanger to Arizona for their marriage, January 12, 1940) to come to the hospital. Ettinger, one of the smartest flacks in the business, went with Bennett and two detectives—sent by chief C.H. Anderson—to the police station. Bennett was detained as a material witness, and endured a period of questioning.

Bennett recalled, "I was 'grilled,' and the examination was rude and rough. Anderson dismissed Maggie, and midway through our conversation, he said, 'You're pretty cool about all this, aren't you?' I don't know where he got that idea. I may have given the impression of coolness, but I felt as if I were sitting in the middle of a blast furnace. I told him, however, that if he thought I was going to break into hysterics for his benefit, he was very much mistaken. I was barbecued on both sides for what seemed an interminable period and then was informed that Assistant District Attorney Ernest Rolls wanted to see me before I was free to leave."

Bennett was shocked to discover that, instead of Anderson arranging a meeting with Rolls in an office, he led her into a barrage of reporters and photographers. Photographs subsequently appeared in the newspapers, showing Anderson standing beside Bennett, "looking," as she said, "stern, official and properly important . . . ."

Bennett's lawyer, Grant Cooper, told her that a press statement was necessary. With newspapermen gathered at her home, she said: "I hope that Walter will not be blamed too much. He has been very unhappy and upset for months because of money worries and because of his present bankruptcy proceedings which threaten to wipe out every penny he ever made during his long and successful career as a producer.

"We have lived together in my Holmby Hills home for some eleven years, with our children who love Walter dearly. Jennings Lang has been my agent and close friend for a long time. Walter and I have been close friends of Jennings and his wife, Pam, and I saw them often.

"I feel confident that Walter would never have given voice to the suspicions expressed by him in the newspapers were it not for the fact that he has been so mentally upset with the complexities of the financial burden he has been carrying for such a long time.

Leland Hayward, seen here in 1960, shortly after selling the Hayward-Deverich Agency to MCA to concentrate on his theatrical productions. *(Whitney Stine collection)*

"Knowing Hollywood as I do, knowing how good, wholesome and sincere by far and away a majority of motion picture people are, I want to express my deep regret that this incident will add to the opinions entertained by so many."

Lang, a few days later, made the following statement: "I'm bewildered by the unfortunate and unprovoked event that has occurred. I've represented Miss Bennett for many years as her agent and can only state that Walter Wanger misconstrued what was solely a business relationship. Since there are families and children concerned, I hope this whole regrettable incident can be forgotten as quickly as possible."

On January 7, Wanger pleaded "not guilty by reasons of temporary insanity," but famed criminal lawyer, Jerry Giesler, waived the trial on a reduced charge—"assault with a deadly weapon"—and on June 4, Wanger was transported to the Wayside Honor Farm near Los Angeles to serve a four-month sentence, working in the library. Afterwards, he returned to his wife on a "separate quarters" basis; although they did not live together, he did not grant her a divorce until 1965.

Having studied penology first-hand, Wanger made *Riot in Cell*

Block 11 (1954), *Invasion of the Body Snatchers* (1956), and *I Want to Live!* (1958), the story of Barbara Graham, which won Susan Hayward an Academy Award.

Bennett wrote, "Without question, the shooting scandal and resulting publicity destroyed my career in the motion picture industry. Within a short time, it was painfully clear that I was a professional outcast in Hollywood, one of the 'untouchables.' I was excommunicated, and evidence lies in the fact that before December 13, 1951, I'd made sixty-five films in twenty-three years, while in the decade that followed I made five . . . ."

Over the next few years, Bennett concentrated on stage and television work, and then she became a hit all over again in the TV serial, *Dark Shadows*, which ran from 1966 to 1970. A feature film based on the material, *House of Dark Shadows*, was released in 1970, followed by several television movies.

But tragedy for Lang was not over: on October 22, 1952, Pamela (who had been a soloist with Benny Goodman's orchestra before marriage) died of an acute coronary thrombosis. It was an extremely difficult period for Lang, who buried himself in work at the studio.

In later years, Lang would produce or executive produce a number of films for Universal. Among them, *Winning* (1969), *Slaughterhouse Five* (1972), *Airport* (1975), *Earthquake* (1974), and *Little Miss Marker* (1979).

Since MCA was a talent agency only, Stein and Wasserman asked permission of the Screen Actors Guild—where old client Ronald Reagan was president—to go full speed ahead into television program production. The guild had given other agencies the okay to produce shows on a one-time basis, or for specific segments of a television series, or for a specific number of pictures. However, the industry was filled with unemployed actors. Few feature films were being made—with a television set in almost every living room, movie houses were being closed because of poor attendance.

The guild drew up a blanket-waiver letter to Revue Productions, Inc., on July 3, 1952, that said in part: "At the present time you are engaged in the motion picture and television film agency business, and the television film production business; you expect to continue in both. You have explained to us your reasons for so doing. We agree that for a period commencing with the date hereof and expiring October 31, 1959, if any contract, rule or regulation made by us prevents your engaging in both businesses, we hereby give you a waiver thereof for such period . . . ."

Revue began active production, offering acting opportunities in half-hour dramas for performers who had not recently made pictures. While it is true that television created its own stars, famous film luminaries such as Loretta Young, Jane Wyman, and June Allyson hosted—and sometimes appeared in—their own series. Unemployed actors and technicians went back to work, not at the snail's-pace rate that feature films were made, but in a factory that turned out shows in a few days.

Bill Davidson, a writer who had once been handled by MCA, quoted an ex-MCA agent in a critical two-part essay on the organization:[3] " 'We were supposed to be battling for commissions with the William Morris Agency, the General Artists Corporation, and the other talent agencies who were our competitors, but I found that my most ruthless enemy was the man in the next office at MCA. I'd go to an advertising executive and sell him a TV show, and then a fellow MCA man would go to him and say, "Why do you want to buy that piece of junk? The show I represent would be much better for you." We were pitted against each other by the nature of the agency, and it was like living in a snarling, cannibalistic, primitive society where your survival depended on your brutality and your guile.

" 'We got comparatively small salaries plus a big Christmas bonus which we received at the end of the year. The bonus was based on what you had sold during the year to contribute to the profits of the company, and it could amount to as much as fifteen or twenty thousand dollars. Thus we were all out scrambling for the bonus, and if you had to assassinate one of your colleagues to up your bonus, you assassinated him. Spying, memo-stealing, eavesdropping were all common practice. Once I was talking to an executive at Metro-Goldwyn-Mayer about a deal. Two minutes later, I got a call from my superior at MCA, berating me about what I had said to the Metro man. He had the conversation almost verbatim. Later, I learned that my colleague in the next office had flattened himself against the wall outside my door and had listened to every word of my conversation with the M-G-M executive. Then he had reported it to my boss . . . .' "

In early February of 1958, needing even more product, MCA acquired all movies made by Paramount prior to 1948, paying $10,000,000 down, with $40,000,000 to be paid from earnings. By the next year, Revue was providing a major portion of the evening programming on NBC.

In late February 1958, it was revealed that the Anti-trust Division of the Department of Justice had opened an inquiry into the operations of the Music Corporation of America and the William Morris Agency. The power wielded by these large agencies was enormous. They were estimated to control about 40 percent of night-time television programming. The star system, which had floundered when the major studios allowed their star contracts to run out in the late 1940s and early 1950s, was firmly entrenched in television.

The public clamored for familiar star faces on the tube, and the agencies cheerfully supplied the talent. There was something cozy and intimate about entertaining a famous name in your living room, while that famous name was also entertaining you! More and more middle-aged film players turned to television, either heading their own series or appearing in the many popular anthology programs.

In 1959, while the investigation was proceeding, MCA purchased Universal International Studios, with its 40 acres, for $11,200,000 in cash, the largest transaction of its kind since Warner Brothers had bought First National Studios—within walking distance of Universal—for $10,000,000 in 1929. The deal was that Universal would lease some of the facilities back, since MCA would require only about two-thirds of the property.

In the 1959-1960 season, Revue supplied sixteen hours of film for television. In two years it would produce forty shows per week, using an enormous number of stars, directors, producers, and writers from its own stable of talent. Shows in the works or planned were *The Adventures of Ozzie and Harriet, Checkmate, Bob Cummings Show, G.E. Theatre, The Jack Benny Show, Frontier Circus, Alfred Hitchcock Presents, Leave it to Beaver, My Three Sons, Tales of Wells Fargo*, and *Wagon Train*.

With the expansion of MCA, there were interested parties other than the Justice Department. On October 24, 1961, it was announced that the Screen Actors Guild had reached an agreement whereby MCA promised to withdraw, either as a producer of films for television or as a talent agency. What it all boiled down to was that the guild was terminating the waiver issued to MCA in 1952, permitting the organization to produce television films while still maintaining a talent agency.

In a membership letter, the guild reminded actors that it had granted the waiver in the first place to "encourage the growth of a TV film industry and the employment opportunities of motion picture actors. At that time, in spite of the enormous economic impact of television on the theatrical box office, a large segment of the industry was determined to resist the new medium. Under the terms of the waiver, TV production increased substantially and our purpose was fully achieved . . . ."

The guild said that it would seek termination of the waiver because it "recognized that renewal of the waiver under present circumstances could open the doors to any and all applicants to play the dual role of employer and agent simultaneously."

Davidson wrote in the March 1962 issue of *Show* magazine: "Martin Jurow, president of a large agency called Famous Artists, told me that he had repeatedly requested an MCA-type blanket waiver from the Screen Actors Guild so Famous Artists could merge with Seven Arts Productions and compete with MCA on equal terms. Also, Herbert Siegel, board chairman of another sizable agency, General Artists Corporation, insisted that he had asked for the blanket waiver in order to go into production through the purchase of Desilu studios, but General Artists, too, had been turned down by the Guild. Siegel, in fact, told me he was so incensed that his company was prepared to spend millions to break the MCA-Screen Actors Guild 'monopolistic arrangement' through filing private antitrust suits. He said, 'I've never run across anything like this in all my years in the business. MCA and we are playing in the same ball game, but there's one set of rules for them and a different set of rules for everyone else. Our batters can't even get up to the plate. Their batters can swing all afternoon and the umpire doesn't even call any strikes on them . . . .'"

On November 20, 1961, a Federal Grand Jury was impaneled in Los Angeles, and on the 24th the contents of a letter from the Attorney General's office made the Hollywood rounds: "The Department of Justice is informed that violations of the Federal Antitrust laws may have occurred and may still be occurring in connection with the activities and conduct of certain persons, firms, corporations, associations, organizations and others engaged in the sale of talent to the entertainment industry in the United States and in the production and sale of television programming. The Department has reason to believe that an indictable offense may have been committed and accordingly, investigation and consultation by a Grand Jury seems appropriate."

Murray Schumach noted in *The New York Times* on December 17, 1961: "The movie industry, which prefers its plots complex but its characters simple, has never been able to cope with the sort of Dostoevski creature who is both good and bad. It likes to separate its villains from its heroes. Perhaps that is why Hollywood is having so much trouble these days trying to find the right niche for the Music Corporation of America.

"For years, it was easy. MCA, the most powerful talent agency in the world, was the villain known as 'the Octopus.' Producers and executives groaned to one another about the arrogant power of an organization that had, as clients, so many of the most important stars and directors . . . .

"There was much quiet glee among movie executives as Federal investigators began to circulate in Hollywood, asking questions about MCA. Here, it was said, was a situation clearly ripe for investigation. A talent agency selling talent to itself . . . ."

Reputedly, on June 11, 1962, MCA sent to each client an amendment to its agency agreement for signature, stipulating that contracts could be assigned to another organization, as long as a specified agent now in the employ of MCA was employed by that other organization. The intent was to prevent loss of talent after MCA relinquished its talent agency.

"When the government sued us for being a monopoly it was the major surprise of my life," Wasserman told J.A. Trachtenberg in a rare interview.[5] "It was a useless, unwarranted act."

Unwarranted or not, in September of 1962, MCA withdrew from the talent agency business, and Revue Productions merged with Universal International Pictures and became the umbrella firm, Universal Pictures Co., Inc.

So ended the story of the most famous talent agency of all time.

It was not, however, the end of Jules Stein.

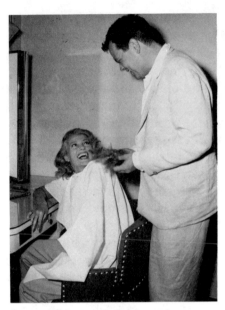

Million dollar haircut: extensive press coverage was engendered when Rita Hayworth's hair was cut for the title role in *The Lady from Shanghai*, in which her husband Orson Welles not only co-starred but also produced and directed. *(Courtesy of Columbia Pictures)*

Inventive publicity for the start of *Son of Paleface*: Trigger dines with friends Bob Hope, Jane Russell, and Roy Rogers in the Paramount commissary. *(Courtesy of Paramount Pictures)*

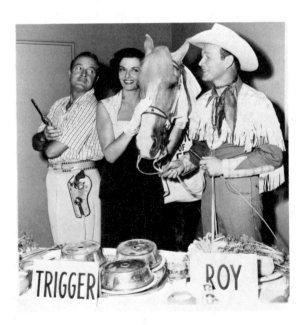

BLACKOUT: 1949

Female Star

I'll be very honest with you. I'm shopping around for a press agent. This is new territory for me, because, of course, my publicity was always handled by the studio, but if I'm going to free-lance I'll need someone to arrange everything. I think I would be happier with a male. My lawyer says you know what you're doing.

Press Agent

He's a fine man. (pause) I was distressed to hear about the flareup at the studio. It's the pits. That director has really been coming down on you.

Female Star

You heard about that?

Press Agent

You know the town. Word travels fast.

Female Star

I hate to leave Paramount after twenty years, but the scripts they have lined up for me are terrible. They cast me in this thing that's unplayable at my age. I've got one more week on the picture, I'm telling that bastard tomorrow that if he wants it finished—and the budget is a million-two—the studio has to give me my release.

Press Agent

The media must be handled very carefully. I know just how to do it . . . we'll call a press conference, and state your case openly . . . appeal to their sense of right and wrong, after all you're a big star, and no one gives more to charity . . . .

Female Star

You don't understand. I want you to keep my name *out* of the papers!

Hedda Hopper, posed here in a gag recreation of The Mona Lisa, co-ruled, with Louella Parsons, the Hollywood gossip columns. *(Courtesy of Henry Willson collection)*

Louella Parsons, seen here with writer Dewitt Bodeen and her daughter Harriet, was Hollywood's first gossip columnist. *(Courtesy of Henry Willson collection)*

19

FLACKS & FLIM FLAM

Alva Johnson
A press agent who worries about taste is as badly miscast as a soldier who faints at the sight of blood.

Tom Selleck, fresh in from Hawaii locations for *Magnum P.I.*, stood at the podium on the stage of the huge International Ballroom of the Beverly Hilton Hotel at the April 6, 1984, Publicists Guild luncheon to present the Les Mason outstanding achievement award to Esmee Chandler.

Miss Chandler, unknown to the general public, was a beloved figure to the overflowing crowd of publicists, agents, Hollywood "big" and "little" people, and Selleck graciously stood out of the limelight when she made her acceptance speech. She recalled the "golden days" when she had worked for Howard Strickling at MGM. "These are golden days of another nature," she concluded wistfully.

When the omnipresent studios had controlled Hollywood— from approximately 1916 to about 1952—very little was printed that was not a direct handout in one form or another from their publicity people. These departments were headed by tough, experienced, strong-willed, hard-working men and women who knew more about life among the moguls, love in the dressing rooms, the pursuit of happiness (in the form of the dream contract) than did agony columnist Dorthea Dix. They protected their stars more jealously than a mother protects her cubs—and were sometimes "clawed" in the process.

Probably the best portrait of a flack ever given on screen was the abrasive press agent, Libby, in *A Star is Born*. Both Miles Stander, in the 1937 version, and Jack Carson, in the 1954 version, knew exactly how to play him. (The character was a combination of hoopla and human understanding.) He never let dislike for the people he was representing affect his job.

Conversely, probably the best-written part of an "old time" agent was the character of Gus, portrayed by Sammy White in *The Bad and the Beautiful* (1952). He was a loyal little guy who burst into tears when a producer gave a starring role to his prize female client, whom everyone in Hollywood had written-off as a tramp and a drunk.

Newspaper editors had learned to be suspicious of any story planted by a press agent that reeked of that highly developed art of "fantastic coincidence." Lost in antiquity is the first, elaborately-conceived "plant" that turned out to be an embarrassing phony. Part of the folklore is the one still told in the business:

Flack Harry Reichenback was justly famous for both a lack of guile, and a rich imagination. Late in January of 1919, while working for Universal Pictures, he hired several New Yorkers and had them costumed in Turkish robes. The men settled into the posh Navarre hotel, letting it be known that they had come to this country looking for runaway virgins who had escaped from their harems. Police dragged a lake in Central Park.

The exotic story made the papers, and it was only when editors were checking over ad copy for a new Universal film did they realize they had been had—again. The picture, starring Priscilla Dean, was appropriately called *The Virgin of Stamboul*, which was to be released in February 1919.

Consequently, the State of New York passed a law that forbade giving false information to the newspapers. Reichenback fought back by threatening to prosecute legislators for broken campaign promises! Reichenback is credited with being the first outside flack paid to publicize a film, *The Squaw Man* (1913) (in which interiors were shot in a barn at the corner of Selma Avenue and Vine Street, the barn now across the street from the Hollywood Bowl).

Sometimes, an originator of a scheme was not at fault when a legitimate stunt backfired. Famous in the annals of tub-thumpery is the promotional gimmick that Bill Thomas and Bill Pine, heads of advertising and exploitation at Paramount Studios, devised for the Mae West starrer, *It Ain't No Sin* (1934).

They acquired fifty African parrots known for their linguistic ability. For weeks, the birds were housed and fed while a recording of the line "It ain't no sin," was played over and over again. "The disc became worn," Thomas said later, "and had to be replaced several times, so the parrots wouldn't sound like a scratched recording. Every care was lavished on those damn birds and they almost drove everyone nuts, but finally they were letter perfect."

Colorful cages were fashioned, and everyone in the publicity department could imagine the look of surprise and delight—and the reams of publicity that powerful columnists like Walter Winchell would manufacture when the birds, screeching, "It ain't no sin, it ain't no sin!" reached their desks.

Full-page advertisements were prepared for the movie magazines, and lobby posters were devised featuring a stunning shot of West wearing a white, form-fitting, spangled, off-the-shoulder gown, with a huge white feathered hat on her head, and carrying a large matching fan.

In 1934, the novelty of sound was wearing off—with the country in a staggering economic depression, the grosses of many films were down. To bring the public into theaters, movies with sex and violence were made rapidly and released. When the number of gamey films increased, there were outcries from women's clubs and church groups.

Richard Griffith[1] wrote about this situation: "The harbinger, or *agent provocateur*, was, of all people, Mae West. Miss West was not one of the 'new shady dames' of the screen, a heroine who lost her virtue in a fit of absentmindedness and atoned for her sins, and her penthouse and mink, by the shedding of copious tears which glittered as brightly in the camera's eye as the diamonds around her neck. Mae was Diamond Lil herself, and diamonds, she said, were her career. It was that openness, termed brazenness by the righteous, which made Mae her enormous hit and also brought about her downfall . . . .

"Sin, the righteous agreed, was a fact of life, but it was no laughing matter, and the Mae West films rocked the whole nation with laughter. Between Miss West's first starring vehicle, *She Done Him Wrong*, and her second, *I'm No Angel*, the Legion of Decency had been formed, the Production Code Administration set up, and producers put on notice that sin was no longer 'in.' By the time her third picture, *It Ain't No Sin*, was ready for release, the title had to be changed to *Belle of the Nineties*, though advertising under the original name had already been printed . . . ."

New posters were rushed out. With no time to prepare elaborate artwork, the new ads displayed only the full-length silhouette of West's familiar hourglass figure, with the legend: *Coming events cast their shadow before . . . .*

What happened to all those trained birds? Some said they were loosed in the jungles of South America, but it has not been recorded whether generation after generation of birds are still parroting a cry that echos through the steamy rain forests: "It ain't no sin! It ain't no sin!"

A "bird" of a different sort, famous in his "jungle" was Russell Birdwell, perhaps the most colorful press agent of the 1930s and 1940s. He was a master of inventing such ingenious stories that sometimes editors printed the squibs, just because they were so well-conceived. Birdwell, a wiry Texan with a pencil-thin mustache, given to wearing pinstriped suits and dark felt hats, was well-liked because he probably upheld more confidences than anyone in Hollywood—besides Howard Strickling, head of publicity at MGM—and never ratted on anyone. Sometimes, he was accused of promoting himself, but only among Hollywoodites.

He had a checkered career even before he took on flack work in Hollywood in 1928. Still in his teens he had been a newspaperman in Houston, and a manager of a jazz band in Mexico City. While working for the *Los Angeles Times*, he was assigned to cover the Jack Pickford and Marilyn Miller wedding on July 30, 1922, which took place at Pickfair, the Mary Pickford-Douglas Fairbanks mansion.

He was dictating a fabulous account of the affair on the kitchen telephone to the rewrite man downtown, when Fairbanks walked by and overheard the conversation. He knew a jewel when he found one, and hired Birdwell to become the "ghost" of Mary Pickford, writing feature articles under her byline.

Later, he switched over to the *Los Angeles Examiner*—a job he would leave for greener pastures, only to return again and again. Longing to become more actively engaged in the production end of motion pictures, he turned director for two films, *Street Corners* (1929) and *Flying Devils* (1933) for RKO. Much later, he also directed *The Come On* (1956) for Allied Artists, and *The Girl in the Kremlin* (1957) for Universal.

In the middle 1930s Birdwell went to work for David O. Selznick, a man whom he admired, and he performed admirable P.R. work on such films as *Young in Heart*, a delightful comedy with Janet Gaynor, Douglas Fairbanks, Jr., Paulette Goddard, Minnie Dupree, Roland Young, and Billie Burke; and *Nothing Sacred*, a hilarious screwball romp, with Carole Lombard and Frederic March.

Said Alva Johnson in a three-part profile[2] of Birdwell: "Birdwell's ideas of propriety are strictly geographical—bad taste in the West, good taste in the East. Instead of a white body on a white horse, swallow-tailed statesmanship marked the opening of *Nothing Sacred* in the East. The premiere was an exclusive party in Washington, thrown by the late William Gibbs McAdoo and attended by platoons of senators. *Little Lord Fauntleroy* opened in the West with the two-mile sign and other barbarities; on this side of the continent, it opened with a quiet premiere for children under treatment in Warm Springs. In the West, Birdwell would, as the saying goes, vulgarize the Day of Judgement; in the East, he is as refined as an undertaker's helper . . . ."

Birdwell's office in Radio City was austere and antique-ridden, while his Beverly Hills office was sleek and modernistic. Somehow he was able to combine both lifestyles without becoming schizoid. He was the first bi-coastal press agent—while Leland Hayward was the first bi-coastal talent agent. During the time that Carole Lombard was one of the highest-paid women in the United States, she became so angry listening to a foreign-born director complain about income taxes that, after he left the set, she lashed out in her colorful, profane way, defending the bite that Uncle Sam was taking out of her salary—which happened to be a great deal more than that of the director. "What does that lousy son-of-a-bitch know?" she yelled. Birdwell knew the making of a story when he heard one. Johnson commented in his *New Yorker* profile: "Within a couple of hours an interview was clicking out over the telegraph wires to hundreds of newspapers: Carole Lombard loved to pay her income tax. The interview told her life story and what the country had done for her and how happy she was to fork over a hundred thousand a year or so for the privilege of being an American. This was a natural, or a 'unique,' from the news standpoint. Reproaching the tax gatherer is one of the oldest recreations of the wealthy, and Miss Lombard was said to be the first plutocrat in history to cheer the soak-the-rich

The original advertisement for Mae West's *It Ain't No Sin* was flossy, glossy, and gorgeous, and appeared in all the fan magazines.

Coming events cast
their shadows before

You will soon be seeing MAE WEST in her new picture, "BELLE OF THE NINETIES," with ROGER PRYOR, John Mack Brown, John Miljan, Katherine DeMille and Duke Ellington's Orchestra. Directed by Leo McCarey. A Paramount Picture.

When the new Production Code nixed the suggestive title, Paramount hurriedly released another advertisement with the new title, *Belle of the Nineties*.

policy. Probably no other news item ever did so much to increase the popularity of a star . . . ."

In 1939, when Birdwell left Selznick and opened his own offices, he sent out invitations to many people in the literary world to come to a certain address to meet Irene Doorbeltz. The startled literati were confronted with a window stacked with copies of a satiric book that he had written called, *I Ring Doorbells*.

During World War II, he wrote a thoughtful book, *Women in Battle Dress*, but it was not until ten years later that he turned serious again, and wrote the original story upon which Warner Brothers based their film, *Jim Thorpe—All American*, starring Burt Lancaster.

In business for himself, Birdwell announced that he was charging each client a flat fee of $25,000 a year. Six stars signed up immediately. Howard Hughes promptly employed him to start tub-thumping *The Outlaw*. When the well-endowed, nineteen-year-old Jane Russell was signed for the picture, he started a campaign that would make her famous overnight. Soon, her revealing Hurrell photographs were on the cover of magazines on every newsstand. One of his ideas that paid off: she became the official pinup girl of the British corvette flotillas in the North Atlantic, and her provocative poses were glued to the inside lids of countless footlockers of servicemen all over the world.

One of his schemes to publicize *The Outlaw* backfired, however. Emulating Charles Einfeld's famous press junkets, Birdwell invited fifty important columnists and press correspondents to San Francisco for the premiere of the picture in February of 1943. Invited guests guzzled champagne and sampled caviar in Birdwell's five-room suite at the Mark Hopkins hotel. The critics loved Birdwell, hated the picture.

Occasionally, a legitimate story contained all of the familiar time-worn, patently-phony earmarks of a publicist's dream factory—(1) outrageous coincidence, (2) star performing some newsworthy deed, and (3) prominent utilization of star's current endeavor. Columnists would toss the press release aside, with the usual comment: "This time he (or she) has gone too far!" Such was an incident that truly happened to Gene Autry.

In the late 1930s, Autry was scheduled to appear at a theater in Columbia, Tennessee, when his press agent, George Goodale, discovered a bug in the theater sound system. Time was of the essence, and the only person in town who knew anything about speakers and microphones worked as a telegrapher for Western Union. He was willing to repair the equipment, but had no backup to take over his shift.

The upshot was that the most famous cowboy in the United States "sat in on the wire," while the man fixed the sound system! Autry had actually been a telegrapher in Chelsea, Oklahoma, ten years before. The payoff was that no newspaper editor would use the plant! Finally, three years later, Gene convinced Chicago columnist Irv Kupcinet that the incident was true, and the story finally saw the light of day.

The powerful fan magazines, *Photoplay, Motion Picture, Modern Screen, Screen Book, Silver Screen*, and the others, were the funnel by which most stories reached print. They were also controlled in the main by the studios, via their advertising clout and planted content. Interviewers even worked within well-established studio guidelines.

Most of these writers, famous for purple prose, had been in Hollywood for many years and knew their way around a cocktail glass. They also knew who was sleeping with whom; who was drinking or mainlining drugs; who the wife beaters were; which married stars were having affairs with other married stars; how much was lost at gambling; who was bi-sexual; which females liked girls and which males liked boys. They just did not write about any of these personal items.

Typical *Photoplay* articles, not noted for their depth, were EXPLODING THE GARBO MYTH (April 1931), GINGER ROGERS' RULES FOR SLAYING THE STAG LINE (May 1936), and BEHAVIOR BY BOGART (September 1938).

Independent publicists also kept up good public relations with the fan magazine community. They stroked egos by seeing that clients were photographed with starstruck columnists, virtually assuring that the shots showing them elbow-rubbing with the Hollywood elite would appear in the magazines. Displayed for many years on top of one Hollywood columnist's grand piano was a silver-framed photograph of Clark Gable standing beside the smiling columnist, but waving to someone off-camera!

Free-lance fan-book feature writers were notoriously underpaid: neophytes received $50 per story, but a trusted news-hen or news-hawk might get $300 or more, depending on how "hot" the subject of the moment might be. Most of these people were married, and their spouses had to work to make ends meet. In return for observance of the "rules," fan-book writers were usually treated with courtesy; they were never expected to pay for meals, because interviews were most frequently conducted during luncheon in the studio commissary. Booze and other appropriate gifts were frequently distributed to the faithful.

Well-paid columnists like Louella O. Parsons, who had been a newspaperwoman since 1900, and Hedda Hopper, who also had a radio show, were treated with great deference. Christmas presents were especially lavish. A famous story concerns Parsons, whose driver annually picked up her bounty at the studios. When the gifts were stolen one year, strategically-placed phone calls were dispensed from her office, notifying all concerned that her limousine would make a return trip to pick up identical merchandise. She also kept lists of who gave what, and meted out favorable or unfavorable stories accordingly. It was a symbiotic "you scratch my back, I'll scratch your back" relationship. Columnists needed publicists, and vice versa.

One of Parsons' assistants was George (Jerry) Hoffman, who had been editor of New York City's *Dramatic Mirror* and *Billboard* magazine in the early 1920s. After leaving her employment, he became associate motion picture editor at the *Los Angeles Examiner*. In 1938, he joined Twentieth Century-Fox and was associate producer on *Speed To Burn* and *Winner Take All*. Later, he headed the West Coast division of Screen Gems, and in 1960 partnered the Hoffman/Pelligrino Agency. He died at the age of 83, on June 10, 1984.

Dorothy Manners, who went to schools in Los Angeles, New York, and Washington, D.C., had been an actress (leading lady to Western star Buck Jones) and worked for Parsons for thirty years, before taking over her column on December 1, 1966, after Parsons, aged 85, had broken a hip and a shoulder and was moved to a convalescent home.

Hedda Hopper, *nee* Elda Furry, born in 1885, began her syndicated newspaper column in 1937 at the age of 53. She had made her Broadway acting debut in *The Pied Piper* (1908); her first film appearance was in *The Battle of Hearts* (1916). She appeared in some eighty-odd pictures, her last being *The Oscar*, released in 1966, the year of her death.

About Hopper's several jobs in 1934, George Ells wrote:[3] "In looking for new ways of earning money, Hedda lasted one day with Major Zanft's talent agency. She hated being crowded into an office with two secretaries, and although she swore like a longshoreman, she claimed his language offended her. But she was not too proud, after joining the Rebecca and Silton Agency, to meet the incoming train when a client, the famed singer Helen Morgan, arrived to begin rehearsals for a new play . . . ."

But it was not the acting profession in which Hopper was to shine, nor any of the other jobs that she took solely to earn money. She was a natural-born gossip, and it was this quality that enlivened her column. It is difficult to imagine the Hollywood of the 1930s to 1960s without Parsons and Hopper; their scoops, feuds, and quarrels turned the town on its ears. Most communities are ruled by one royal personage, but in Hollywood *two* queens shared a shaky throne.

Sheilah Graham, born "about 1908," started her column "Hollywood Today" in 1935 and became prominent. "Miss Rona" Barrett would also become powerful in the 1960s and 1970s, with a group of magazines that bore her name, and her appearances on segments of various television shows.

Brainy Joyce Haber, born "about 1931," went to Barnard College, was a researcher for *Time* magazine from 1953 to 1966, and made her reputation as a columnist reporting about "A" and "B" parties, and making frequent references to "X," "Y," and "Zee" instead of using actual participants' names. Her wit could be cutting—her description of Julie Andrews: "There's a kind of flowering dullness about her, a boredom in rowdy bloom." (Retorted Andrews: "She needs open-heart surgery, and they should go in through her feet.")

When the stars' major studio contracts were not renewed in the late 1940s and early 1950s, belt-tightening closed down the "in house" publicity mills that had so relentlessly, and so successfully, ground out tons of eulogizing copy. Strong contacts with magazines like *Life, Time*, and *Newsweek* deteriorated, and expensive press junkets for the premieres of regional pictures became a thing of the past. Gossip columnists were losing their power, and Hollywood "stringers," employed by the big newspapers in the large cities across the country, were suddenly out of work. Newspapers depended upon Associated Press, United Press, or other wire services for the bulk of Hollywood coverage.

Also eliminated were the huge portrait galleries where famed glamor photographers had made use of huge 8 by 10 cameras, with careful composition, elaborate lighting, and painstaking retouching, to further their art and glorify their subjects. The glamor years were gone.

Free-lance photographers, using 35mm cameras, specialized in catching stars off-guard and supplying candid shots to the media. Consequently, the public was exposed for the first time to pictures of their idols attired in jeans—and possibly minus a hairpiece. The hazy, mesmerizing veil that had always existed between star and public was yanked up like a fire curtain in a theater—ruthlessly exposing freckles, pockmarks, crooked teeth, and dyed hair. So-called realism had hit Hollywood like a sledgehammer.

Taking the lead from *Confidential* magazine, which pioneered the so-called "inside" stories obtained by hired detectives and disgruntled Hollywood fringe-types, the fan magazines, no longer supplied with material from the studios, began to sensationalize stories. The editors went outside the entertainment industry and started the notorious "Jackie" Kennedy pieces, then moving on to other international celebrities—from that point on falling into disgrace.

Out of these unsavory journalistic practices evolved the current "gutter" press, with the various tabloids available at supermarket checkstands.

Prior to the 1960s, if a magazine moved out of line or alluded to forbidden subjects, the writers were banned from the studio lots. This blacklisting policy even extended to the trade magazines—*The Hollywood Reporter* and *Daily Variety*—which the studios could not prevent from publishing items, but could—and did—refuse to have displayed on the lot until penance was enforced. These "trades," while not enjoying huge subscription lists, were—and are—read by everyone in the business. First, readers always turn to the gossip columns, the "Rambling Reporter," and "Just for Variety."

The practice of *The Hollywood Reporter*'s Mike Connolly was to arrive at his office about noon and read the mail, which had already been opened and arranged on his desk, along with a list of phoned-in items. He then selected the stories for that day's column, starting out with the most important plant for the lead squib, typed the material, and finished his office day early in the afternoon.

Constantly interrupted by the telephone, he might change the lead several times. His evenings were spent going to important parties, attending premieres, and pursuing an insatiable thirst for reading everything from James Joyce to all major columnists in the country (to avoid being double-planted.) He seldom had a night free.

One advantage of working at the *Reporter* was that the print shop was located in the basement of the building, allowing last-minute changes in the column. One night, Connolly attended a party given by agent Kurt Frings. Louella Parsons was in one room and Hedda Hopper in another. Connolly, having arrived at about nine o'clock, was dancing with a very pretty woman who introduced herself as his hostess, Ketti Frings. She casually mentioned that her husband was going to announce that Elizabeth Taylor had just signed for the title role in *Cleopatra*. Connolly immediately excused himself, rushed to the telephone and, under the envious eyes of Parsons, called the composing room at the *Reporter* to change his lead to the up-coming announcement—thereby scooping both Louella and Hedda.

Occasionally, retractions would be necessary. They were handled in various ways. When Jack Bradford took over the "Rambling Reporter" column upon Connolly's death, he printed that Richard Harris had suffered a slight heart seizure. When this was denied, Bradford opened the next column with a telegram he had received from the star: "I did not have a heart seizure but a priapism and I can assure you it was not slight. P.S. I have had 19 film offers since 'Camelot.' Happily, R. H."

The town was in an uproar: never were so many dictionaries riffled, never were so many secretaries requested to look up the term, never did the public libraries get so many telephone calls—but the offices of psychiatrists received even more inquiries. Everyone wanted to know, what was a "priapism?" And when they found out, the roof on every house from Hollywood to Beverly Hills raised seven-and-a-half inches with hilarity. Websters definition: "priapic, pri-ap′ik, a. Phallic; class, mythol. relating to Priapus, god of male procreative power." (Mr. Harris was referring to an erection!)

Two dynamic women important to the press relations field from the 1920s to the 1960s were Maggie Ettinger and Helen Ferguson. Both used different approaches, though adhering to the same axiom: "clients come first."

Maggie Ettinger (Oettinger) was a "double cousin" of Louella O. Parsons. Both had been born in Freeport, Illinois, and their respective mothers and fathers were sisters and brothers. She was employed by the *New York Evening Telegraph*, which sent her to Hollywood in 1922 to write a daily column. In 1924, she went to work for MGM, and two years later formed the Ettinger Company. Later there was some resentment from her peers, who thought that Parsons gave her inside information about stars who might be potential clients.

Ettinger's first account was the Technicolor Corporation, which was still with her at her death at 70, on January 12, 1967. She represented the Brown Derby for years, and gave "half-price cards" to the press people who would publicize the restaurants. The publicist for Schick razors, she was also the West Coast representative for the New York based N. W. Ayer Advertising Agency, which represented DeBeers diamonds.

Among clients were Joan Bennett, Edgar Bergen, Irene Dunne, Betty Hutton, George Montgomery, Dorothy Lamour, Norma Shearer, and Edward G. Robinson. Carol Channing once said that she modeled Dolly Levi in *Hello, Dolly* after Ettinger, " .... because of her great vitality."

Helen Ferguson (64 inches tall, 99 pounds) came into public relations through the front door, having been a star of silent films. At age thirteen, she made her first film for Essanay in 1914, and then starred in such films as *Miss Lulu Bett* (1922), *The Unknown Purple* (1924), *Jaws of Steel* (1927), and *Scarlet Pages* (1930).

Ferguson's voice did not record well. She was on the verge of retiring when her friends complained that the studio publicists were so busy with stories on the talkie phenomenon that they were neglecting their bread-and-butter stars, whereupon she decided to go into public relations.

Her first client was Johnny Mack Brown. A former All-American halfback at the University of Alabama, Brown had played in the Rose Bowl game in 1926, signing with MGM a year later. He appeared with Greta Garbo in *The Divine Woman*, with Joan Crawford in *Dancing Daughters* (1928), with Mary Pickford in *Coquette* (1929), then starred in *Billy the Kid* (1930)—a role that made use of his soft, distinctive southern accent, and started him on a long series of Western films.

In those days, Ferguson's fees ran from $300 to $400 a month.

Other clients were Jeanette MacDonald, Henry Fonda, and Pat O'Brien (for 27 years), Barbara Stanwyck (for 22 years), Loretta Young (for 19 years), as well as Constance Bennett, Joan Blondell, Ed Byrnes, Eva and Zsa Zsa Gabor, Miriam Hopkins, Dina Merrill, and Joel McCrea. Robert Taylor was also a client, and she once said of him to a photographic retoucher: "He has his own plane and those are flyer's lines in his face, not really wrinkles!"

Ferguson fretted and clucked over her clients like a den mother—going over every word of an interview, passing on all photographs, often supervising their makeup before a public appearance, and helping select their wardrobes. Her assistant, Jewel Smith, who was with her for 27 years, was just as meticulous. Ferguson once told a reporter, "We don't deal in fiction, but we certainly present the facts as dramatically as possible."

Ferguson retired in 1961 to care for her ailing, ninety-year-old mother, Nana, moving from her big house in Beverly Hills to Park La Brea Towers, where she had a wall opened between two large apartments. She suffered a stroke, and both she and Nana ended up in wheelchairs with 24-hour nurses.

"People may think I am lonely," Ferguson said one evening, after Nana had gone to bed,[4] "and I suppose in a way I am. But after being around crowds all those years—both when I was in films and then later, when I began to handle stars—it is kind of nice to not have the phone ringing off the hook all the time. Talking now is like having a big, high-calorie dinner. I enjoy talking now." She paused, and took a sip of coffee. "For years, everyone said that I should write a book about my life. What they meant was I should write a book about my clients—and that I would never do! Much of my work was confidential, and I have no intention of talking about Joan Bennett or Barbara Stanwyck or Jeanette MacDonald and Gene Raymond—those were my favorites. I deplore those tell-all books by a cook or a butler or a valet writing about their employers. I think it's dreadful. My life was built around famous people. I was their confidante, their friend, and I have my memories which I won't share with anyone." She laughed, "Besides, it's all old-hat, anyway. I've had a good life and I've enjoyed every moment of it, and there is a time to close the gate."

After her mother died, she moved to Palm Desert and then Clearwater, Florida, where she died on March 14, 1977. When Mike Connolly received calls from her in later years, he would wave associates aside until the conversation, which would be slow because of her frailty, was finished. "She was one of the first," he always said, "and when she calls, out of respect, I listen."

There were only six people at Ferguson's funeral at Forest Lawn. Attending were glamor photographer, George Hurrell, fanbook writer Dora Albert, the widow of Johnny Mack Brown, an elderly makeup woman who had worked for Perc Westmore, and a hairdresser at MGM.

Gene Raymond gave the informal eulogy. "To show you the kind of deeply-caring woman that Helen was, I'll give an example. When I proposed to Jeanette [MacDonald], we agreed that the wedding was to be private, with no press or public display. Even our respective studios would not be informed. I had wanted to purchase a new home, but knew that I could not buy it myself or the real estate agents would let everyone know I was moving, and the press would put two and two together. Helen came to our rescue, and not only bought the house in her name but, knowing Jeanette's taste, decorated it herself. Coming back from the wedding, I drove up to the house and gave Jeanette the keys! Helen did not consider the time and effort and heart that she put into this lengthy project extraordinary at all. She was thrilled to be of service."

Hollywood funerals are notoriously badly attended. Sometimes stars even forget to send flowers—it is a reminder of their own mortality. There is an amusing story about a famed actor who, after his young Hollywood career was finished, moved to another metropolitan city, where he proceeded—by his reputation as a screen lover—to romance many ladies of the town, almost all of whom had husbands. When he died, his former amours dared not be seen at the funeral. But, fondly remembering his phenomenal ability as a Lothario, they sent tons of flowers as well as their maids, butlers, and chauffeurs, so that at least he would have a decent turnout!

Senior publicist Maidie Lyons, a spry 92, who once tub-thumped for Ziegfeld, sat in a wheelchair at a table in the Palm Court of the Plaza Hotel in New York, toying with a slice of three-layer chocolate cake.[5]

"It's true that females are better-suited to the publicity field, rather than agenting," she said to her nurse, and then managed a self-deprecatory smile. "We're natural-born gossips, and picking up the phone and planting a story is duck soup."

She had just returned from the hairdresser's, and her white hair was drawn severely back from her face and curled into a chignon at the nape of her neck. She had a Mae West white-and-pink complexion, and her mouth was a slash of red. "No one wears their hair like this anymore," blue eyes aglitter. "In the old days, it was just Helena Rubenstein and myself. Now, about this agent business, I almost became one in 1916, but I chose the flack route instead—I think it was Abel Green at *Variety* who first called us 'flacks.' Then I had sense enough to quit, and get married and have a family before I was forty.

"Mr. Ziegfeld—no one called him Flo, except maybe his lady friends. And of course, Miss Burke—you didn't call her Billie, either! I've got a wonderful story about her. She was doing a live talk show in Los Angeles in the early fifties, and her usual makeup man was ill, and a substitute was taking over. I should preface this by saying that she was in her middle-sixties, and used those facial lifts to draw back the skin and make her face and neck smooth. Well, about three o'clock in the afternoon she came into Makeup, and sat down in the chair. The young substitute looked at this decrepit old woman, and said, 'I'm sorry, I can't take you. I have a three-o'clock with Miss Burke.' She gave him a withering glance and piped: 'But, I am Miss Burke!' "

She laughed. "Now, getting back to Mr. Ziegfeld: he said agenting wasn't an honorable profession, and he was right—then. You used to be able to walk down Broadway, near 47th Street, and pick out the agents by their clothing and their cheap cologne. They used 'dems' and 'dose,' and few of them had even a high school education."

She bit into a piece of chocolate layer-cake and took a sip of tea. "It began to change in the 1930s, when the ones who knew what they were doing stopped dressing like racetrack touts, and stopped smoking those terrible Havanas they got from their gangster friends. Show business was looser then. A lot of the vaudeville theater-owners had just come over on the boat, and out in Hollywood book-learning was kind of a scourge: picture people thought that something was wrong with you if you had a degree. But gradually everything began to change, and if you went to Harvard or Princeton for a couple of years, it didn't hurt a bit. Agents even began to go to tailors and have tuxedos in their closets, and their wives began to have dressy frocks and know the difference between daytime clothes and things to wear after five.

"Now, the better education you have, the better you can deal with high finance—and that's where it is today. You must deal with lawyers and corporate people—old school tie—and you better have something upstairs. Shrewdness is considered crass today. Back then, it was an asset to have a wheeler-dealer as an agent.

"I think why so few women are drawn to the talent agency field is they don't have enough time to be women! It's difficult enough for female stars, who at least can have some privacy in the evenings and weekends, and today there's usually a break between pictures. With television, there's always the hiatus interval to recharge batteries and play with the kids. While I don't get out much anymore, I do take the trade papers and try to keep up, and friends do call once in a while and tell me what's going on. I mostly shudder at their tales.

"I wouldn't know how to handle Paul Newman, for instance, and I think it's more than the generation gap. My stars were cooperative: Gloria Swanson would break her neck to publicize something she was interested in—even if it didn't pay off. She was a health-food nut for thirty years, and I often told her she should bring out her own line of foods with no preservatives. Stars choose a profession that's all public, and behaving in public and being cooperative with the press is a good part of it. I'm not taken at all with what I call the 'Designer Jeans Generation.' Hell, they don't know what it's all about!

"Now, it seems as if the stars are doing their publicists a favor showing up for one or two interviews. The women get on television and giggle and tell about their sex lives, and sometimes, if the interviewer doesn't bring it up, they forget that they're there to plug a picture or a TV series!

"The men are just as bad. They talk about their boats and their racing cars, and how the gutter press is doing them in by publishing untrue stories of who they're sleeping with! They draw attention to the fact that they're not really all that masculine. Even in the fifties, a writer or publicist gave them a few good quotes so that they wouldn't make fools of themselves. Look at little Marilyn Monroe, scared of her own shadow, but she was always prepared with a few one liners that stopped everyone dead.

"Once in a while you run into something that smacks of an old-time flack. I was in Las Vegas at the Sands Hotel in 1966, and for one entire day the telephone operators paged a 'Miss Daisy Clover.'" She laughed, "Finally, I suppose, someone wised them up that they were giving free publicity to a Natalie Wood picture called *Inside Daisy Clover*!"

Maidie Lyons was growing tired, and her nurse moved behind her wheelchair. "One thing about the female flacks today," she said in parting, "is that they sure as hell get to travel all over the world with their clients. I spent years in a nine-by-twelve office, pecking out 'exclusive in your area' press releases on a Woodstock with one hand, and answering the phone with the other. I didn't even have time to go to the bathroom!"

As the nurse swung the wheelchair around, Maidie Lyons' face lighted up. She could not resist a parting quip: "Did you hear about the press agent who was so furious at her ex-partner she added a codicil to her will, forbidding her former friend from even attending her funeral?"

But when old-time flacks gather and recount famous old stories, one incident always re-surfaces—an episode that Howard Strickling was fond of telling on himself. After Garbo had finished *Susan Lennox, Her Fall and Rise* (1931), Pete Smith, head of publicity, "Strick," and the staff at MGM had a brainstorming session, trying to come up with a more provocative title for the picture.

Garbo had appeared in *Love* (1927); *The Divine Woman* and *The Mysterious Lady* (1928); *A Woman of Affairs, Wild Orchids, The Single Standard*, and *The Kiss* (1929); *Anna Christie* and *Romance* (1930), and *Inspiration* (1931).

"Obviously," Strickling expounded slowly, "one-word titles look better on the marquee and are easier for people to remember. Let's try to think of a name that's descriptive of the hot love-scenes...." Suddenly, he hit his knee. "I've got it!" he cried. "Look at it on a billboard one-sheet!" He waved his arms enthusiastically and, in the excitement of the moment, his stutter came back: "G-G-Greta G-G-Garbo in *H-H-HEAT!*"

The picture was released as *Susan Lennox, Her Fall and Rise.*

BLACKOUT: 1982

Female Star

For old time's sake, get me a part—any part. I'm hurting.

Agent

Do you have any recent film on yourself?

Female Star

You know I retired when I married Jeff.

Agent

I've forgotten. When was that?

Female Star

1961. But now that he's gone I've got to get back to work.

Agent

But I thought he left you well-fixed?

Female Star

Well-fixed! He sure as hell did! The bastard even cashed in our insurance policies. I've sold all the property to pay off the debts. I'm living in that little house I bought mother on Wilton Place in 1938. It was the only thing in my own name.

Agent

How old are you? I want the truth.

Female Star

I'll be fifty-two in March, but I can play a young forty.

Agent

Hummmm. I don't have anything in features. But there is a television commercial coming up in your age range. They're looking for a recognizable face from the 1950s.

Female Star

I . . . hadn't thought about . . . commercials. What would I wear? How would I have my hair done? Oh, I suppose I should ask what the product is. Perfume?

Agent

The thrust is this: the son comes home with filthy jeans, and his mom throws them in the washer along with a half-cup of Puritee Detergent. . . .

Female Star

I won't play a *mother!*

Robert Osborne of the *Hollywood Reporter* is representative of a new breed of columnist. *(Courtesy of the* Hollywood Reporter*)*

Historic photograph of members of the press, honored by the Los Angeles Variety Club, Tent 25: *Left to right seated*: Dick Strout, KCOP-Chris Craft Stations; Army Archerd, *Daily Variety*; Vernon Scott, United Press International; Joyce Haber, *Los Angeles Times* News Syndicate; Raoul Gripenwaldt, United Western Newspapers; Hank Grant, *Hollywood Reporter*. *Left to right standing*: Gary Owens, TV-Radio personality; Sherrill C. Corwin, international president of Variety Clubs; Dorothy Manners, King Features-Hearst Headline Service; Syd Cassyd, *Boxoffice*; Bill Kennedy, Mr. L. A. of Los Angeles *Herald-Examiner*; and Spero L. Kontos, chief barker of Tent 25. *(Whitney Stine collection)*

20

FLACKS ACQUIRE CLASS

I kicked my press agent in the heart and broke my big toe.
—old Hollywood saying.

After the studios went independent, hiring stars for one or two pictures and buying outside packages, the careers of press agents flourished. Celebrities were forced to hire people to manage the media. Today, it is a thriving business.

Perhaps the largest and most successful P.R. firm is Rogers and Cowan—the granddaddy of them all—with offices in Beverly Hills, New York, Washington, D.C., and London, and with a staff of about 130. Rogers and Cowan's clientele is worldwide, embracing sports and big business, as well as television and films. Among the firm's many clients are James Caan, Doris Day, Dudley Moore, Sylvester Stallone, and Joanne Woodward.

Henry Rogers first opened a small, one-man office in 1935, after having served a year as an office boy (at five dollars a week) for casting agent Grace Moller. His first clients were Kirby and DeGage, a dance team. Later, when he handled Rita Hayworth—whom he was able to place on the cover of *Look* magazine—his reputation increased, and he was able to sign other clients.

In 1945, he hired Warren Cowan, who had been referred to him by *Hollywood Reporter* columnist Edith Gwenn. At the start, Cowan was paid $85 a week, but within five years he was a full partner. "Both have developed well-deserved reputations for exceptional on-the-job creativity...," Kelly Garret noted in an interview.[1] "They're also known for going to great lengths to land a client, flying all over the world and sometimes, in a manner of speaking, out of it. Henry Rogers once promised Mike Love of the Beach Boys that he would take up transcendental meditation if his group would sign on with Rogers & Cowan. The Beach Boys became clients, and Henry Rogers practiced meditation for two years . . . ."

Cowan recalled that, when the office was still small, he and Rogers would have dinner once a week to discuss clients. One night, Rogers asked Cowan if he had a lawyer. When he replied that he did not and asked if he had need for one, the answer was in the affirmative. An attorney was required because he was making him partner, and they had to sign some important papers.

Rogers recalled the incident differently: "Now, I will tell *my* version, because I don't remember that at all. Kirk Douglas was a very good friend of ours. And we had an agent friend at the time named Kurt Frings, who represented Audrey Hepburn and Elizabeth Taylor, among many others. Kirk and Kurt were very fond of Warren. Well, Kirk Douglas and Kurt Frings came to my office one day, put me up against the wall one at a time, and said, 'unless you make Warren a partner, we're going to put him in business and we'll steal all your clients away from you. So you better do it, or else . . . .' Then they put the papers in front of me. That's my version. Somewhere in-between, there might be the truth of the matter."

Among their many clients was Joan Crawford, who hired them after she had left MGM and was badly in need of good media coverage, because her latest pictures had not been successful. She went to Warner Brothers to appear in *Mildred Pierce*. "Through a great number of circumstances," Cowan recalled, "we helped create and focus attention on her performance to reach Academy members. She won, and for many years we developed programs focused at impressing Academy members. What is now called an 'Academy Award campaign,' began with a lady named Joan Crawford in 1945."

Rogers & Cowan also handled Olivia De Havilland, who won the Oscar a year later with *To Each His Own*—coincidentally after she had left Warner Brothers to sign with Paramount. Jane Wyman was a client, and won the award for *Johnny Belinda* in 1948; Claire Trevor, also signed by the firm, won the supporting Oscar in 1947 for *Key Largo*. But client Rosalind Russell did not win for Eugene O'Neill's *Mourning Becomes Electra*. Her performance was skillful, but the film itself was heavy-handed.

Rogers continued, "That was a shocker. We were already celebrating; the champagne was flowing. Henry and Warren had done it again! That really was—forgive the expression—the first kick-in-the-ass that we ever had in this business. And it taught us a good lesson: that you can't get the public or the industry to buy something they don't want."

Many of the later press agents in Hollywood got their start with Rogers & Cowan, including Dick Guttman and Jim Mahoney. Three ended up running studios—Tom Wilhite at Walt Disney Productions, Guy McElwaine at Columbia, and John Foreman at MGM.

All was not a bed of roses for Rogers & Cowan, however. The firm once lost Elizabeth Taylor and Frank Sinatra, both within an hour! They always counted this as the high point of their careers, because they were able to stay in business! A lesser firm, losing two big accounts, would have had to cut personnel, and might have missed a couple of payrolls.

They have also brought a dignity and a trust to the profession that had been lacking in the 1920s and 1930s, when press agentry consisted mostly of wild and sometimes improbable schemes to attract public attention.

One advantage of owning a prosperous firm like Rogers & Cowan—both partners agree—are the doors that automatically open to them, doors that would be closed if they were not the successful businessmen that they have turned out to be. Another advantage is the opportunity to meet celebrities outside of show business—presidents, prime ministers, and royalty such as Prince Phillip and Prince Charles.

One of their clients at one time had been talent agent Jennings Lang, co-partner in the Jaffe Agency, before he joined Music Corporation of America.

In recent years, Kathie Berlin has been the head of Rogers & Cowan in New York, handling Ali MacGraw, Paul Newman, and Marlo Thomas, among others. As Helen Dudar reported,[2] ".... the prize talent to have is a gift for nurturing. Kathie Berlin will gently tell an actress that her makeup is wrong and her dress adds pounds to her hips. She has coaxed reluctant actors into believing that a week spent hyping a picture can be fun. 'God,' Robert Mitchum once said to her, 'if they had sent you twenty-five years ago instead of that short, bald guy with the cigar, I probably would have had a completely different career.' "

Most press agents agree that, if they are to be hired as publicists on a film, their assignment should come before the film is begun, so that they can develop a campaign tailored to that film, its stars, its director, its producers—as well as to the property itself—especially if its author is famous or the subject is controversial.

The consensus is that if a flack comes in after principal photography is over, it takes too much time to become familiar with the project and agree on how it should be sold. The vaults of the studios are filled with films that seem to have been shot in secrecy and released in a vacuum.

"But just as important as plenty of publicity on a picture," one New York publicist has said, "can be the danger of overkill. Too much attention can be as harmful as too little, and there's often a fine line between the two. It's our job to make the public aware of the picture, without becoming tired of hearing about it. Over-exposure—no pun intended—can be deadly for film, and adversely reflect on the P.R. firm in charge.

"A menopausal lady I know was so distraught over strategy that backfired that she retired, and to my knowledge is still in Ireland. She was going through a messy personal crisis at the time (she had a teenage lover, who left her for a man) and had, in her confusion, promised exclusive cover interviews with her star—who was a hot property—to both *Life* and *Newsweek*. Lord knows this was enough to blacken her name on both coasts, but then the star, a son-of-a-bitch, however beautiful, decided not to give any interviews at all—even to the very sympathetic *Women's Wear Daily*!

"I believe that the ideal 1985 publicist should be female, between the ages of thirty and forty, attractive—but not too attractive —because she must handle, but not fondle, beautiful clients, and there is a difference! She should be single; not too tall, because she must not tower over shorter male clients; drink only minuscule amounts of white wine; be born with a good sense of humor; harbor some feeling for business—having been a secretary for a lawyer helps. Absolutely necessary is a fair amount of intuition; she should be genuinely enamored with 'children,' because ninety percent of her clients are child-like; the possessor of a one-track mind; and above all, a sense of humor—both overt and about herself—is *de rigueur*. She does not need to know how to cook, and a reputation for being exquisite in the hayloft is a hindrance, not an asset."

According to Dudar, the press agent's fees begin at $1,500 a month, with the price escalating according to the agency's size and the client's stature. Rogers & Cowan's fees run about $3,000 a month, and rise to $4,500 for personalities requiring special attention, or on rare occasions—the effort to turn singer Julio Iglesias into a household word in the United States—can hit $5,000 a month.

"Bigger money," Dudar reported, "and greater interest, lie in having a movie as an account. An important star or a strong producer can insist on having an outside agency supplement the studio publicity staff at fees that go from $40,000 to $200,000 a picture. Publicists love the work and, if a project is particularly promising, will actively solicit the account. For one thing, a movie has a beginning, a middle, and, above all, an end. Moreover, a movie will never wake a publicist at 3:00 a.m. to announce it has slashed its wrists."

John Springer, a big man with penetrating eyes that sparkle with a great understanding of the business, started out as a studio publicist in the mid 1940s. About twenty years ago, he established his own firm.

"John is the soul of discretion," admits a rival. "He's genial and warm and affectionate, and has the closest mouth in our field! His clients are the superstars: Bette Davis, Elizabeth Taylor, Marlene Dietrich, and the late Henry Fonda, Judy Garland, Marilyn Monroe. You name them, John has maneuvered their publicity. When the American Film Institute presented Davis with its Achievement Award in 1978, it was Ray Stricklyn, actor and Springer representative on the West Coast who did the seating arrangements at the Beverly Wilshire Hotel. Every detail is important to John. Whenever there is great controversy surrounding a star, and the press quotes a 'spokesman,' he's usually that person. Anyone starting out in the business today should take pointers from the way he conducts himself."

Springer is also a knowledgeable film historian, and has had several books published, including *They Had Faces Then* and *All Talking! All Singing! All Dancing!*

He also produced a series of "Legendary Ladies of the Movies" programs (Bette Davis, Joan Crawford, Rosalind Russell, Lana Turner, and Sylvia Sydney) which began with 45 minutes of film clips carefully chosen by Springer, after which he introduced the star, who then answered questions from the audience. The first program with Bette Davis, at Town Hall in New York, February 11, 1973, was the most successful, and a tour was undertaken that debuted in Denver, March 11, 1974, ending in Hartford, Connecticut, April 6. Davis later took the show to England and Australia, and to the West Coast.

Another popular male flack is Bobby Zarem, who has handled such films as *Scarface, The Cotton Club*, and *The Four Seasons*. He is famous for his opening night parties.

Lois Smith is a pleasant, round-faced blonde, known as Earth Mother by other female publicists. Her partner is Peggy Siegal, a dark-haired, attractive young woman. Their clients include William Hurt, Nastassia Kinski, and Kevin Kline.

Dudar discussed Smith:[2] "She speaks nervously, at a rate approaching the speed of sound, and has a rare capacity for self-mockery. 'I'm known as "The Hounder," ' she reports, confirming a reputation for tenacity—the quality that helped her get a modest comedy like last fall's *The Big Chill* splashed across almost every major magazine . . . .

"For some years, Siegal was a foot soldier and Smith a dominant figure at Pickwick Public Relations, an enterprise known as 'The Pickwick Ladies,' staunch advocates if not originators of the thesis that less is more, or when in doubt, don't do it. 'Actors who didn't want to deal with the press came to Pickwick,' Siegal recalls. 'Pickwick would say no before it would say yes, or "We'll let you know next week," or "we'll see." ' (In press circles, 'We'll see' is translated into a vulgarism describing sex without a partner.)"

Pickwick Public Relations merged with another agency to become the tongue-twister, Pickwick/Maslansky/Koenigsberg, after Smith went to work for a short time in film production. Another New York publicist is stocky, dark-haired Marion Billings, who likes to handle directors such as Robert Benton, Paul Mazursky, and Martin Scorsese.

In the spring of 1984, when confronted with recalcitrant performers Sean Penn, Elizabeth McGovern, and Nicolas Cage (who believed that they had fulfilled their obligation to a film the moment they left the set), Marion Billings was forced to build publicity on *Racing With the Moon* around Sherry Lansing, the co-producer with Stanley Jaffe.

Commented writer, Michael London:[3] ". . . .there'll be no interviews with McGovern in this week's *People* magazine or with Penn this evening on *Entertainment Tonight*. Instead, promotion will come from producer Sherry Lansing . . . Sherry Lansing . . . Sherry Lansing.

"Penn, McGovern and Cage are all notoriously publicity-shy. While reclusive stars are an old story, no recent film has confronted a studio with three such performers—and no other cast members to carry the ball."

Lansing noted that she was eternally grateful for the performances delivered by her stars, and for creating something that she cared about so passionately, "But it's terribly frustrating and it puts me in a very uncomfortable position as far as creating an awareness of the film . . . . Let's face it, Stanley Jaffe and Sherry Lansing are not Elizabeth McGovern or Sean Penn."

The dark-haired, beautiful, articulate Lansing, who looks like a movie star herself (and before her stellar executive career appeared in a few films), agreed to appear on the CBS *Morning News, Good Morning America, The Today Show*, and others. She and Jaffe together taped *The Merv Griffin Show*. She was photographed by *Vogue* magazine and spoke with the *Wall Street Journal*. Elizabeth McGovern did agree to a *New York Times* interview—if it would be slanted partially to promoting an Off-Broadway play in which she was appearing.

"Efforts were made," London recalled, "to lure the performers out. *People* magazine agreed to put Penn and McGovern on the cover of this week's issue if granted a ten-minute phone interview with the performers, according to sources on the production. But Penn objected, concerned that the questions would focus on the pair's impending marriage rather than the movie."

Star publicity, crucial during the opening week of a film, can affect the box-office returns as much as 30 percent, but Paramount Pictures, who released the picture, hoped that the positive reviews and a gradual release plan would build good word-of-mouth for what the critics had noted was a fresh and emotionally satisfying film.

"When it comes down to selling the movie," Lansing commented to London about her stars, "I respect their integrity, but I disagree with their position. I honestly believe that your job doesn't end until the movie's on the last screen in the smallest city."

Racing With the Moon grossed $4,815,858 in its first two weeks of release, but was down 38 percent from its first weekend gross. Would there have been a more sustained popularity had the stars publicized the picture? There is no way of knowing, of course, but insiders say that the gross might not have dipped so severely if the stars had made the public appearances.

Noted columnist Robert Osborne:[4] " 'Any star knows, or should know, the importance of publicity.' (Are you listening, Sean Penn, Elizabeth McGovern and Nicolas Cage?) Carole Lombard wrote that statement in an exclusive 10/24/38 *Hollywood Reporter* article after she'd spent six days working in the David O. Selznick publicity mill to see what made the wheels go round; according to Lombard, she found 'Publicity is journalism, plus salesmanship. It has always been a prideful point with me that I have taken a personal and necessary interest in publicity.' (How times have changed in those past 45 years! Or have they? The big and enduring stars still seem to know the value of promotion.)"

An article[5] in *The Hollywood Reporter* by Maurice Segal, continued the Lansing debate:

"From the day the first ancient Greek impresario had lunch with the town crier to solicit his aid in informing the citizenry of an upcoming production of *Oedipus Rex*, in a little theatre off the Parthenon, publicity has played a major role in the entertainment world.

"It was not unexpected, therefore, that more than a few eyebrows were raised in this capital of hyperbole when producer Sherry Lansing publicly bemoaned the fact that none of the principals of *Racing With the Moon* was of a mind to participate in the publicity campaign for the picture . . . ."

He then reiterated Lansing's remarks, and called some key people at the studios for their reaction. Barry Lorie, Disney's marketing vice-president, gave the opinion that stars should be obligated to play a role in publicizing their films, and that the studio should be obligated to make certain that the stars in question give pertinent interviews. "A newspaper story about an actor's marital problems, certainly isn't helpful to the picture."

Lorie went on to say that it was sometimes better not to have actors participate. He recalled that, on the gambling picture *California Split*, when neither Elliott Gould nor George Segal were available because of other work, he arranged a tour for the film's technical advisor on poker, ending up with more media space than he could have hoped for if the stars had participated.

Elizabeth Landon, vice-president of publicity for Twentieth Century-Fox, felt that stars should help sell their pictures because of the fierce competition for today's entertainment dollars, and went on to say that since some performers are not articulate, they can do more harm than good if forced to participate in a campaign. She noted that on a five-city junket for *Romancing the Stone*, Michael Douglas, Kathleen Turner, and Danny DeVito's participation contributed meaningfully to the gross of the film.

Rob Friedman, vice-president and executive assistant of advertising-publicity for Warner Brothers concurred with Lansing, while Kathy Orloff, senior vice-president of publicity and promotion for Columbia Pictures, could not recall a performer who flatly refused to do publicity. Much of the success of *The Big Chill*, she maintained, was due to the unstinting publicity effort on the part of all the stars and the director. Priscilla McDonald, publicity director of Cannon Films, praised the stars who worked hard to publicize *That Championship Season*.

Lloyd Leipzig, senior vice-president for publicity and promotion at Orion Pictures, was adamant in his belief that actors who earn large sums of money should have a responsibility to help publicize their pictures. He called attention to Burt Reynolds, Nick Nolte, and Dudley Moore, who take public appearances as a matter of course. Leipzig told Segal: "I urge our production and casting people not to hire performers who won't cooperate in selling a picture." That view was also supported by Patricia McDonald, while Bob Crutchfield, publicity vice-president at Lorimar Productions, felt publicity was more valuable than advertising. Ed Russell, publicity and promotion vice-president at Embassy Films, was of the opinion that performers' involvement in publicity was extremely important, and that an actor did not need to be a star to generate good returns.

"We had great success with *Spinal Tap*," he related, "using Harry Scherer, Christopher Guest and Michael McKean, none of whom as yet is exactly a household name."

The flap, however, was not over. On April 10, *The Hollywood Reporter* published a letter from Ilene Feldman of Herb Tobias & Associates, who gave the opinion that it was extremely unfair for filmmakers to knock artists for not promoting films, and that actors would be far more inclined to do publicity if it was pertinent to the film, rather than exploitation. She elaborated to say that she agreed with Barry Lorie, and as an agent she had said several times that clients would do publicity if the interview was limited to the making of the film. She said that she had yet to receive a guarantee of that type and probably never would, so the blame should not be placed on the actor, but on the few publicists who preferred to exploit the stars' personal lives rather than the actors' experiences in making films.

Yet another letter in reply to the article was printed on April 16: Julian Myers, vice-president of worldwide motion picture and TV publicity and marketing for Hanson & Schwam Public Relations, maintained that film producers who wished to increase grosses should automatically hire stars who were willing to help sell tickets by being interviewed. He indicated that actors who avoided the media made many appearances at the unemployment office.

But the difficulties of promoting domestic films are small in comparison with overseas products. Pleasingly-stout Renee Furst specializes in handling foreign films, which many publicists will not touch, due usually to translation involved in interviews with stars or directors (who also might not be well-known to American audiences). Therefore, more time is required to come up with an "angle" on how to sell films from other countries. Furst seems to thrive on the challenge.

Publicists have also become a very important part of book publishing, operating in a manner similar to motion picture press agents. The publicity departments of book publishers plan campaigns for important books and famous authors. This can be an unsettling part of the business, because many authors—accustomed to working in solitude—often can't deliver a decent interview.

"Capable of composing the most glorious prose," says one weary publicist,[6] who is as beautiful as a movie star, "some authors can't come up with an intelligent answer to the simplest question asked by interviewers, and often 'freeze' on camera. If they have had some public-speaking experience and aren't frightened of crowds or the camera, we assist them in other ways. I think that the worst-dressed people in the book business are authors. We work with them on wardrobe and hair, and such things as manicures or, in desperate cases, pay for acrylic nails. I don't know why so many female authors have such bad hands and nails. If male authors have a heavy stubble, we teach them how to apply pancake makeup on tours where they appear on TV (national shows have their own makeup department), so that they won't look like a bum who has been out on the town all night. We also supply them with ankle socks, so that if they cross their legs, the audience won't see a mile-long stretch of white leg where their socks end and their trousers begin!

"We drill them on questions that will probably be asked, groom them, take them by the hand to the studio, and never ever give them a drink before they go on. Reputations have been sullied by authors with feverish eyes and sarcastic tongues. Many interviewers have had such problems with authors that they tape their segments, so that if it is really awful they can discard the whole thing.

"If you're tub-thumping a movie star who's just written an autobiography, there are other things to worry about. Limousines to get them to the program on time and back to their suite at the hotel, flowers and scotch (to be drunk afterwards) in the dressing room, sometimes a special makeup person (if they require wigs and facial lifts). If they're to appear at a banquet at a hotel or other public facility, and if the star is very famous, old, or fragile, and there is a danger of being mobbed, I get up very early that day and 'walk' the entire route myself—from the time the limo discharges them at the door, through the back lobbies and service elevators to the room where they're to appear. This is time-consuming and tiring, but necessary, and a procedure that other publicists who deal with stars every day take as a matter of course.

"The consummate author—who actually became famous in his own right as a ranconteur—was Alexander King, an elderly, white-haired gentleman, who used to appear regularly on the *Jack Paar Show*. I remember watching him when I was a little girl, and being mesmerized by his gift of gab. Unfortunately, I've never worked with an Alexander King—I always seem to get the duds."

Another press agent, a waspish, middle-aged male who had worked on both coasts, raised heavy eyebrows, lifted delicate hands, and exploded:[7] "The flack ladies in this business are okay, up to a point, but... hero worship! These broads with their palpitating, undersized bosoms are inclined to wet their pants in the presence of a Great Hunk Star—who hasn't even written his autobiography, but hired a hack ghost who's put together a cut-'n-paste job.

"One reason Springer does so well is because, with his diplomacy, if he hadn't become a press agent, he could have represented the United States in the Court of St. James!

"But you get a star who's been around since the War of the Roses, and they devour those kids. Superstars have conducted thousands of interviews, and know their way around a press conference. If you want to see a pro in action, watch Ronnie Reagan field questions! These old stars have worked with press people who invented the term, and who broke them in when they were young and impressionable on how to conduct themselves properly. But these stars can be so wonderful and yet so humble, and leave you in the clouds just to be in their presence, but they can also be self-indulgent and nasty. One must always realize that no matter how 'regular' they appear to be, they're still the most self-centered people on God's green earth—but that's one reason they have staying power. A great career takes great concentration, right?

"The big stars know that they have to let it all hang out. That's the real secret behind an interview, no matter what section of the media they're dealing with. And they also come prepared with an 'angle'—a 'hook'—for the interviewer to hang his magazine or newspaper article upon."

He examined his manicure. "Show me a star who stays in an ivory tower—aloof from the press—and I'll show you an insecure performer who has so many hangups they're scared to death to give an opinion about anything. Many can barely dress themselves in the morning, let alone give a penetrating, in-depth interview. Now, this attitude is okay. Better not to disgrace themselves, right? But then they give you all this horseshit about being a 'private person' and 'caring for their art' . . . . .

"On the other side of the business, I won't touch rock stars—with their insane groupies! That's another piece of pizza. I won't bill people for crashed hotel rooms, fifty bodyguards, nor supply booze, drugs, call-girls or boys! Many of their hangers-on are stoned all the time. I won't operate in that atmosphere.

"Some of the relative newcomers to star-heaven are uncouth, too." He shook a forefinger. "There's the famous story of a Screen

King, not noted for P.R. cooperation, who really had to appear on a certain television special because of the occasion. Backstage was one of the really great Screen Queens, who very innocently asked what he was going to do on the show, and he dryly replied, 'I'm going to go out there and take down my pants.'

"Now, it's understandable when a great lady like Katharine Hepburn won't do publicity. It's certainly not that she can't. When she gives a rare interview, like she did to *Life* magazine after Tracy died, it was wonderfully revealing. Her two appearances with Dick Cavett on television were penetrating and amusing, and captured her personality exactly, but after seventy-four years and three Oscars she's paid her dues and has her rights. When Hepburn did appear once on the Academy Awards show to present an award to John Houseman, she had nothing to wear, and showed up in what looked like an old pair of black pajamas, and talked on and on . . . ."

Few publicists have reputations for philanthropic work, mostly because the big-money years barely get them over the bad-money years, and many P.R. people end up living on social security. But, among flackeries, the name of David Epstein is always remembered with affection, because he truly cared about his friends and associates. A father figure to his clients, he had a tiny office with one secretary. He kept a cigar box filled with cash in his desk—to bail-out favorite clients in the wee hours who might have swigged a touch of the grape and ended up in the slammer.

Epstein started his career after World War I on the *St. Louis Times*, worked as court reporter for a while at Los Angeles Superior Court, then joined the scenario department of Universal Pictures in 1924. He graduated to producing serials and Westerns, starring Art Acord, Harry Carey, and Hoot Gibson, then directed *Of Men and Music* in 1951 for Twentieth Century-Fox.

Two weeks before he died September 8, 1970, Epstein was taking up contributions for Milton Stein, a contemporary publicist, who was in a sanitarium in West Covina.

On Friday, June 21, 1984, a whoop and cry could be heard echoing in publicity offices in Los Angeles and Manhattan: a former female flack was appointed president of the television division of a major studio! The woman was Barbara Corday, and the organization was Columbia Pictures Television, Inc. Herman Rush, who had formerly held the position, had been moved up to a newly-created post: president of Columbia Pictures Television Group.

Corday had been a writer, producer, and former ABC network executive, and had worked with Barbara Avedon on several series, including *Cagney & Lacey* (which they began to develop in script form in 1975). In 1982, Corday returned to the writer/producer ranks, but decided that she missed the environment of being part of a team, and being able to work on a variety of projects at once.

"It's a tremendous challenge," she told Lee Margulies of the *Los Angeles Times*, in a telephone interview. "Also, it's not easy for women to get these kinds of positions. I think it's real good for the whole community for somebody to do this for a while."

In noting that Columbia's current roster of prime-time network series contained no women in leading roles, she said, "That's the first thing I'm going to change."

But another bright lady, not a publicist but an expert in merchandising by the name of Dawn Steel (*a.k.a.* Spielberg), was waiting in the Hollywood wings. She had made a name for herself by acquiring the right to print *The Book of Lists* on bathroom tissue. Having joined Paramount Pictures in 1978 as director of merchandising, she enticed McDonald's and Coca Cola into the advertising campaign for *Star Trek: The Motion Picture*, which was so successful that she was soon promoted to vice-president of the department. She was both attractive and tough.

When the Hollywood studios' shakeup started in 1984, with Michael Eisner, Paramount president, and Jeffrey Katzenberg head of production, resigning to cast their lots with Walt Disney Productions, Steel was in line for the president's role—which she assumed on April 16, 1985. Reportedly one of the bosses told her: "If you can market toilet paper you can market motion pictures."

BLACKOUT: 1984

Female Star

But I haven't appeared on Broadway since 1938! And then I was only supporting Katharine. I don't know if I could take the strain of appearing every night.

Agent

What's there to be afraid of ? Stage acting is like typing or screwing, you never forget how to do it!

Female Star

But learning all those lines! A hundred pages of dialogue. I'm used to learning three, and then promptly forgetting them. And big crowds scare me shitless.

Agent

But audiences are different. And we'll insist on footlights—then you won't be able to see anyone. You'll be able to build a character from start to finish. Besides, you act before all of those technicians on the set.

Female Star

But they're my friends!

Agent

You'll be making new friends. We'll open in Omaha and work out the rough spots. Then Detroit, Washington, Philadelphia, Boston, then Broadway!

Female Star

I'm not sure that I . . . .

Agent

After the run, Hollywood will open up and every producer in town will want you again.

Female Star

And . . . if I flop ?

Agent

Well, there's always Europe. You're still very big in England . . . .

Michael Jackson, seen here with Donna Summer, was expected to make an estimated $1,000,000,000 from his *Thriller* album, the Jackson's Victory Tour, and various merchandising. *(Jack Gillespey collection)*

Brooke Shields and her mother Teri, who received producer credit on *Sahara*. *(Whitney Stine collection)*

21

FAMILY AFFAIRS EIGHTIES STYLE

First Comic
What do a secret service man and a business manager have in common?

Second Comic
I dunno, what does a business manager have in common with a secret service man?

First Comic
Both have important positions—but nobody knows 'em!

When Michael Jackson was 25 years old, he won eight Grammy Awards and made the cover of *Time* magazine (March 19, 1984). His album, *Thriller*, sold more than twenty-million copies, and he became probably the most recognizable young face in America. He was the talk of the nation.

No Michael-come-lately, he had paid his dues. At age 13, along with his four brothers—Marlon, Jackie, Jermaine, and Tito, who made up the Jackson Five—and their parents, Joseph and Katherine, he had appeared on the cover of *Life* magazine.

Motown's first Jackson Five release, the single "I Want You Back," with eleven-year-old Michael, had taken only twelve weeks to reach number one in the charts. As the Jacksons, their albums *Destiny* and *Triumph* had been platinum best-sellers. But Michael was destined to bridge the adolescent age-gap to become a remarkable adult performer. *Off the Wall*, Michael's solo for Epic Records, was a smash hit, and started his new solo career.

Mark Bego wrote:[1] "Since Michael's career so totally eclipses his brothers' successes how do they feel about his incredible superstardom? 'The family enjoys what I do,' Michael explains, 'each person in the group has a thing that he does. I sing and dance and the other brothers sing and dance, but I sing lead. A lot of inter-viewers and fans ask the brothers if they ever get jealous because Michael does this or he's out front all the time and they all scream for him a little more. It's a silly question, but it's interesting. When they ask me I just answer that they know what I do. I've been doing this since I was five-years-old onstage and I feel it's something that God gave me to do. I'm the one who sings lead. They can sing lead but I've been chosen to sing lead on the songs and I'm thankful to be chosen. They kind of understand it, and they accept it because that's what I do . . . .' "

A Jehovah's Witness, Michael Jackson's spirituality seems to not only guide his life but his work as well. He is a vegetarian, and keeps a simple lifestyle in the opulent surroundings of the family estate in Encino, California. Joseph Jackson has played a major part in the career of the boys, and prior to June of 1983 (with Ron Weisener and Fred DeMann) helped to manage Michael.

"Jackson and his five brothers are scheduled to hit the concert trail in June," a *Time* cover-story related, "in what is billed as the biggest music tour in history. Pepsi is sponsoring the tour and has already given the Jacksons $5 million. Co-promoter Don King has kicked in an additional $3 million. The Jacksons will receive 85% of the net receipts; King and their parents, Katherine and Joseph Jack-son, the remaining 15%. King, a congenially bombastic presence whose recent show-business experience has been limited to booking prizefights, estimates that 'if the boys decide to exploit every avenue of merchandising and marketing available to them—T-shirts, pay-per-view TV concerts, clothing lines, perfume lines, product iden-tification—the four could gross $100 million.' "

The tour turned out to be an incredible success—both finan-cially and artistically. The last playdate was the huge coliseum in Los Angeles. There was only one question in Hollywood's collec-tive mind: how long would it be before Michael Jackson followed up his success with a starring role in a megabucks feature film?

In March 1984, Michael Jackson chose Frank M. Dileo, thirty-six, the Epic Records promotion vice-president who helped him turn *Thriller* into the best-selling album, as his personal manager. For the time being, he will be the only client of the newly-formed Frank M. Dileo Artists Management Company. "Michael is very interested in his record career," Dileo stated, "and from working with each other on the records, one day he just said, 'Gee, would you like to manage me?' "

When Mark Bego asked Jackson about his writing, he answered, "I wake up from dreams and go, 'Wow!' Put this down on paper! The whole thing is strange. You hear the words, everything is right there in front of your face. And you say to yourself, 'I'm sorry, I just didn't write this. It's there already.' That's why I hate to take credit for the songs I've written. I feel that somewhere, someplace, it's been done, and I'm just a courier bringing it into the world. I really believe that. I love what I do. I'm happy at what I do. It's escapism . . . ."

Steve Pond in an interview[2] stated: "Marlon Jackson is a friendly, garrulous, outspoken talker. But on a recent afternoon at a Silver Lake recording studio, he and his more reticent brother, Tito, had a tricky and unenviable job.

"The task: to talk about the new Jacksons' album, 'Victory,' and that group's summer tour, which may well be the biggest pop tour ever.

"The problem: Marlon and Tito were doing the talking because younger brother Michael, 25, doesn't do interviews. Period. And Michael, whose 'Thriller' album has made him the world's biggest pop star, is unquestionably the reason why the tour will be the year's hottest ticket . . . ."

Later in the piece, Marlon was quoted. "Put yourself in my situation: I've been doing this since I was 6," he said. "We've toured our whole lives, and it comes to the point where we said, 'This is is getting old. Let's try something new.'

"But by us not touring very often, it doesn't mean that we've broken up. People read that we were broken up, that Michael came back to do one tour and then he's going to leave the group. That's *not* the way it is. Jermaine hasn't toured with us for nine years, but Michael has always been a part of the group.

"You read articles that say Michael doesn't want to tour, Michael's only touring for the brothers. If Michael Jackson doesn't want to tour, he doesn't have to tour. He knows that . . . ."

In the interview, Marlon spoke of Joseph Jackson: "My father had a five-year contract with us, which we renewed for seven years. The contract just expired, and we decided not to renew it. It's not that he's done anything wrong. It's just that we needed breathing room.

"Being in business with your parents is a touchy thing. To disagree with your father...touchy. So the way we got out of it was not to renew his contract . . . ."

Doing business with a parent is somewhat different from dealing with one's husband. Ann-Margret's money affairs are overseen by her husband, Roger Smith.

Ann-Margret (Olsson) was born in Valsjobyn, Sweden, on April 28, 1941. "Ann-Margret's father, Gustav Olsson, had already lived in the United States for five years when he sent for his wife and their six-year-old daughter to join him in 1949," noted Christopher P. Anderson.[3] "When Gustav became an invalid, the only way for the family to survive was for Mom to work as a receptionist in a funeral parlor, where they were given boarding privileges. For three years her parents slept on a Murphy bed in the dining room while Ann-Margret slept beside a casket in the mourning room . . . ."

Ann-Margret, who had appeared on the Ted Mack Amateur Hour on television in 1957, came to Las Vegas a year later singing with the Sutteltones—a pianist, drummer, and bass player—a group formed at Northwestern University where she had been a student for one year. She joined George Burns' act at the Sahara Hotel in 1958, and played in Frank Capra's *Pocketful of Miracles* at Paramount in 1964.

While drawn by talent to the acting profession, like many stars she was repelled by the inner workings of show business. She understood almost nothing about agents, how deals were put together, about packaging properties or handling money affairs.

In 1964, she met actor Roger Smith—the memorable, grown-up Patrick to Rosalind Russell's *Auntie Mame* (1958), who had three children from a previous marriage. In an interview[4] conducted by Jane Ardmore, Smith commented: " 'She had no training in the business world. It wasn't long from the time she came to Los Angeles that she was making a lot of money and working a lot; but by the time we met and fell in love, I was aware that her career was being mismanaged and going down the drain.

" 'When Annie found that out and retreated, she became almost a recluse. For two years I kept out of it. After two years she asked me for help . . . . My wife is my responsibility,' he always said. 'If a man doesn't feel that way, he can't have a very good marriage, which is why I've become so involved in her career. I have had little time for my own. I want her to achieve the feeling of knowing that she's a superstar, a rich, full human being who's realized her potential . . . .' "

Smith weathered bad comments from some quarters when he allowed his wife to return to stage work ten weeks after her serious accident in Lake Tahoe, in which she fell 22 feet from a platform moments before her scheduled entrance on stage. But he knew it was essential for her to work, to prove to herself that she could perform as well as she had before. Her jaw had been smashed, requiring extensive reconstructive plastic surgery, including having her mouth wired closed until the bones healed. She had also broken an arm, and suffered a cut in her kneecap. Her later comeback was brilliantly handled.

Kenneth Turan, in an article[5] that explored the difficulties of the star's role of Blanche DuBois in the television film version of Tennessee Williams' *A Streetcar Named Desire*, wrote of the relationship between Ann-Margret and Smith: "There, too, a lot of public carping of the Svengali-Trilby variety has taken place over the years, a situation that Ann-Margret admits has been 'painful. If I said no, it wasn't, I'd be lying. But I'm still here, he's still here, everything's hunky-dory. I've been with Roger for 20 years and I'm very proud of that . . . .'

"The two were married in 1967, and Smith and impresario Allan Carr began re-shaping her career. Though the actress in question likes to say, 'Every time I turn around the corner, there's another Ann-Margret,' this restructuring, centering around TV specials, Las Vegas work and a shrewder selection of roles, resulted in increased respect as well as Oscar nominations for her work in both *Carnal Knowledge* and *Tommy* . . . ."

With all of Ann-Margret's success, 1980 proved to be the most crucial in her private life, when it was discovered that Smith was suffering from the same affliction that Aristotle Onassis had contracted—a rare, incurable neuromuscular disease called myasthenia gravis, a physical condition that is extremely debilitating. "Some days he feels well," Ann-Margret has said, "other days he is so weak he must stay in bed. We must live each day as it happens. We live with the hope of a cure, but now we are going to devote less time to my career, and more time to being together."

At the 1983 Emmy Awards show, after Barbara Stanwyck

received the statuette for her role as the grasping, white-haired matriarch in *The Thorn Birds*, she complimented fellow nominee Ann-Margret upon her "superb" performance in the television film, *Who Will Love My Children?* Not only was it the gracious gesture of a veteran actress who might never make another film, but an unexpected accolade for Ann-Margret, who was seated in the audience with Roger Smith. Both Stanwyck and Ann-Margret are clients of the William Morris Agency.

Another wife and husband team, Suzanne Somers and Alan Hamel, have fought the tides of television—and won.

Suzanne Somers was born Suzanne Mahoney, October 16, 1945, in San Bruno, California. In 1963, when she was seventeen, she married Bruce Somers and soon had a baby, Bruce, Jr. After their divorce, she financed an acting career by working as a cocktail waitress in San Francisco, appearing in bits in *Bullit* and *Magnum Force*, filmed on location in the Bay city. In 1969, when she was in financial straits, she was photographed in the nude for *Playboy* magazine (which finally published the shots eleven years later, after she had acquired an enormous television following). Her big break came when she played the elusive blond beauty in *American Graffiti* (1973), after which she moved to Southern California. She met Alan Hamel, host of a Canadian talk show, in 1968. He employed Somers to open refrigerator doors on "The Anniversary Game," a show for which he was master of ceremonies. They married ten years later.

Her television comedy series, *Three's Company*, starring John Ritter, was based on a British series, *Man About the House*, and was first aired March 15, 1977. Her character, Chrissy Snow, a zany typist, lives with florist Janet Wood (Joyce DeWitt); to make ends meet, they invite Jack Tripper (John Ritter), studying to be a chef, to share their apartment. They tell their landlords (Norman Fell and Audra Lindley) that Jack is gay.

Aljean Harmetz authored a Sunday article[6] for *The New York Times* dealing with the financial affairs of Somers and her husband. "Commenting on the financial and emotional position of actresses in Hollywood, Kim Novak once described herself as a 'piece of meat.' Twenty years later, Suzanne Somers would be more likely to refer to herself as a personal corporation."

Harmetz spoke of Somers receiving $30,000 per segment for

Three's Company; the MGM Grand Hotel in Las Vegas contract that will pay her $700,000 over the next two years; the percentage of the distributor's gross of a movie, *Nothing Personal*, in which she starred with Donald Sutherland; fees and residuals on commercials for Life Savers and Ace Hardware, and other monies. Harmetz continued: "However much as times may change, the Internal Revenue Service does not. The I.R.S. would like to collect $117,514 of the first $215,400 she earns and 70 percent of the rest. How can Miss Somers legally make sure that it does nothing of the sort? . . . ."

Alan Hamel, long-time spokesman for the Alpha Beta super-market chain in hundreds of television commercials, became Sommers' business manager.

"Many major stars make $2 million or $3 million and just write half of each check to Uncle Sam," Hamel told Harmetz. "They don't trust anyone to make investments. Or their business manager buys Treasury bills or municipal bonds, something that won't go wrong. When you get a tax-free 5 percent and inflation is 15 percent, your money is eroding. The preservation of capital income is as important as the deal itself."

He proceeded to explain that money is eroded by $300 upon receipt of $1,000 of deferred income, suggesting that the ideal way to save money is by investing in a pension program. Jay Troulman of Creative Business Management set up the Hamel-Somers pension plan, one of the first to use as an actual assumption two new factors—early retirement and continued inflation after retirement, which legally entitled the Hamels to shelter a very large portion of their earnings. All fees paid to the Hamels go into Hamel-Somers Entertainment, a personal corporation, where Hamel is listed as treasurer and Somers as president. She has an exclusive employment agreement with the corporation, paying her a salary that is taxed as ordinary income.

Later in the interview, Hamel told Harmetz: "As trustees of the pension funds, we can use the money to make prudent investments. We have loaned money for venture capital which is collateralized by mortgages on real estate. We have loaned money and attached the right to have a piece of any conversion of an apartment house to condominiums. Even if there is a recession, the market for good property has never collapsed in history . . . ."

"You can make a king's ransom if you score with a movie," Hamel said, "but we're not taking away the safety net of *Three's Company*. Being wildly successful in one medium doesn't mean you can transfer the success to another medium."

Although the series was extremely successful, the relationship between Somers and the producers has not been one of the most idyllic in Hollywood. Indeed, there have been numerous disagreements. An article[7] by Tony Schwartz examined the dispute: "Somers and her manager-husband, Alan Hamel, say her $30,000-a-week salary is below that of comparable stars on other successful television series and that her contribution to *Three's Company* should entitle her to a share of the profits in a series that is expected to earn its producers more than $100 million.

"The producers, Michael Ross, Bernie West and Ted Bergmann, contend that Somers' demands are excessive, that she began as an unknown, that she has received generous raises during the last four years and that they are under no obligation to share the show's profits with her. ABC has taken the side of the producers."

The Schwartz article quoted Somers as saying: "When you're talking about these sums of money, it's difficult to generate much sympathy. Even my own father, who worked as a gardener and made $60 a week, has a hard time understanding it.

"The point is that it's all relative to what is the norm. Thirty thousand a week in this industry is not a high salary. There is no pension plan for actors, no security in the cocktail hour of their lives. You have to build a nest egg while you can."

The nest egg needed building. In July 1979, the cast and crew of *Three's Company* were ready to begin taping for the new season, after the usual hiatus. Hamel needed Somers for an additional two weeks work on *Nothing Personal*, a movie that they had been shooting during the break. She came back and did the shows for the season.

Contract time came up in July 1980, and Ron Sunderland, ABC vice-president of business affairs and contracts, stated to Hamel and Stuart Ehrlich, who represented DeWitt, that henceforth the salaries of their clients would be $35,000 per episode, and there was no room for negotiation. Apparently Hamel planned to ask $50,000 a show and a percentage for Somers.

In October 1980, during the second week of taping, Somers

complained of a back injury, although she had just completed a long dancing and singing tour that had lasted several months. Rehearsals, on this first episode of the season, proceeded until late on October 18, but Somers called in sick the next day, saying she was unable to get out of bed because of a cracked rib. Later in the week, Hamel asked to reopen negotiations on Somers' contract. Reportedly the principals met, but did not discuss the matter seriously. As a result, Hamel became angry and asked for $150,000 per episode and a piece of the action.

With Somers still ill, one episode was discarded and another placed into rehearsal, which she taped. On October 30, 31, and November 1, the cast rehearsed a third show. However, Somers was excused on November 1, so that she could attend a hockey game in which Bruce Somers, Jr., participated. Just before the scheduled taping of the show on November 2, she called in sick. The episode was quickly rewritten, removing her character from the script, and the segment was taped. Producer Mickey Ross told Hamel before the November 2 taping that he had passed the point of no return.

"That was it; it ended there," co-producer Bernie West told reporter Peter H. Brown.[8] "After that, we had to fight for our own show."

" 'We knew by then,' says Ross, who created the show with partners West and the late Don Nicholl, 'that Alan Hamel was the villain of the piece. He reminded me of the line in *Hamlet*—'that he can smile, and smile and smile and still be the villain.' At that moment, Ross lost faith with his star of five years and began relegating her to 60 seconds a week."

" 'Those are blatant lies,' says Hamel. 'Here was a girl with a bad injury and they dumped all that venom out on us because we were trying to get the money she deserved. We had the X-rays. We offered to let the ABC doctor come out and evaluate her.' (ABC will neither confirm nor deny that offer.)

"There was verbal sparring about whether the injury was serious enough to keep Somers from working, and about the influence Hamel had on her career. 'It's become fashionable now for everybody to point to Alan, and all those evil things he's making me do,' said Somers, far from the furor on the set and relaxed in the seven-story beach condominium that they own in Venice. 'We became a true partnership and it makes a lot of other people jealous, but they're wrong when they think that I'm just being maneuvered. They think I'm Chrissy Snow, but I'm not. That's the problem. They want me to remain that same lovable but dumb character they created for TV . . . .' "

The way out of the dilemma was for Somers to report on the set at CBS Television City each week and tape a one-minute, audience-less telephone scene, to be placed in the regular taped show. A new cast member, Jenilee Harrison, was added to the cast.

There was much newsprint all over the country concerning the tenuous relationship between the star and the show, and Somers and Hamel appeared on the *Phil Donahue Show* to air their views. As a result, mail supporting her began to come in at the network. Somers reportedly wanted to come back to the show, and Hamel apparently had second thoughts about the negotiations, but the die was cast. In April 1981, Somers was officially dropped from the 1981-1982 season.

Somers had a three-year backup deal at CBS, where she would produce her own shows, and also star in an annual movie-of-the-week, with the money for each film to escalate from $50,000 to $100,000 by the end of the third year. And there was also a lucrative Las Vegas contract, and the Harrah's Reno contract, and . . . .

Time has worked well for Somers, and some of the old wounds have healed. The December 1984 issue of *Playboy* magazine featured Somers on the cover, and inside was a nude layout!

Ann-Margret and Roger Smith, Suzanne Somers and Alan Hamel, have weathered the storms of controversy to become prime examples of successful star-wife and manager-husband teams. Brooke Shields and her mother, Terri, also have had "press problems."

In a frank and amusing *Playboy* (May 1984) interview with Calvin Klein, journalist Glenn Plaskin asked the famous designer why he ran scared after several television stations banned, or placed restrictions on, some jeans commercials that had Brooke Shields say, "You know what comes between me and my Calvins? Nothing." Calvin Klein replied: "I have the *New York Daily News* to thank for the jeans controversy. ABC received perhaps 300 letters protesting two of our commercials with Brooke, and we were running about seven of them at the time. Then the *Daily News* ran a full front-page of Brooke in one of the shots from the ads and in the upper right corner printed, 'DOW JONES BREAKS 1000.' Its story caused CBS and NBC to drop some of the commercials, too, and provoked *Time, Newsweek, People* and every other publication, radio and TV station to call me. I was crazed.

"Actually, we were using Brooke as an actress; she was playing different roles: a liberated woman, a teenager, a vamp. The intention was to do something that was interesting and different. I worked very seriously with Dick Avedon on the graphics, and the commercials were very beautifully photographed. I didn't think I was doing anything different from what *Vogue* did when it used Brooke as a model for expensive *couture* fashion. *Vogue* put $3000 dresses on her, but it wasn't expecting to sell those dresses to 15-year-olds. It was using her as a model and I was using her as an actress . . . ."

People thought he was taking advantage of a fifteen-year-old. Klein denied this, stating that people read things into his commercials that were not there. "I love Brooke," he continued. "She's a very sweet girl, a very fine girl, and her mother and I talked all the time, because the press would knock Brooke and knock the commercials and we were all going crazy! It's the American way. Exploiting her was never my intention."

Brooke Shields was born May 31, 1965, in New York City. Her first modeling job came at the age of one year, so it can be said that she has been in the public eye almost all of her twenty years.

After playing a bit in *Alice Sweet Alice* (1977), she played the role of a child prostitute in Louis Malle's *Pretty Baby*, then went on to do *Tilt*, and *Just You and Me Kid* (1979). She was receiving a great deal of publicity, and the modeling jobs continued, climaxing with the Calvin Klein jeans flap.

"The indomitable force behind the Brooke Shields phenomenon," said Christopher P. Anderson in his book,[9] "is Brooke's divorced and hard-as-nails stage mother Teri Shields (Brooke was born four months after Teri's marriage to Helena Rubenstein vice-president Frank Shields, a marriage which lasted a matter of weeks). Brooke's father has grudgingly come to accept Brooke's career. Teri, who went on the wagon at Brooke's insistence, has a reputation for being a tough negotiator and has managed to inflate her daughter's per-film asking price from $27,500 for *Pretty Baby* to $300,000 for *Wanda Nevada* to $500,000 for *The Blue Lagoon* and an estimated $750,000 for *Endless Love* . . . ."

"Brooke's extraordinary," says a woman who has worked with

her, "and she can take direction very well, if the director has everything worked out in advance. If he's done his homework, scenes progress well. She has a model's discipline, and she moves well, and of course, her beauty is so spectacular that she always looks smashing. She's not much good at improvising, and she gets impatient if the director doesn't know what he wants. Her mother is something else. I've worked with stage mothers for years and can read them like a book, but Teri is demanding if things aren't going the way she expects, and she doesn't understand much about delays.

"I didn't work on *Sahara*, where Teri was executive producer. Usually nowadays, 'executive producer' can mean anything—and it can be a sop they throw at some relative, but I understand she directed some of the scenes. I know there was an awful lot of bad feeling during the shoot. It was a big flop, but that may have been that the story was weak and who wants to see sex 'n sand stuff again, no matter how you modernize the story. I'd say that Teri better look for good properties for her baby, and get an exciting, young, box-office co-star who can add some weight to the story, and give her someone to play against, instead of casting big people like Horst Buchholz, John Mills, and Steve Forest to support her. Her career needs direction as never before."

In a bylined piece in *Family Weekly*,[10] Brooke Shields wrote about the uncertainties of going away to college, comparing it with the first year in high school, when she had few friends, sat with the teachers, and called home every day at lunchtime, crying to her mother to take her away. Within a month, after students realized that she was just a normal teenager, she settled into the curricula.

She enjoyed her work, felt her early modeling days were fun, and was always interested in the feedback she received from cohorts. And she felt acting was terrific. "There have been a few unpleasant moments," she said, "but they make me appreciate the good times. After *Pretty Baby*, I said, 'Ma, I'm not doing any more movies.' I had gotten tired of working 12 and 14 hours a day, six days a week and I had no time for school. But that feeling didn't last long . . . ."

In *Sahara* (*Playboy* called it "Shameless camp"), she played the test-driver daughter of a car company owner, whose dream was to enter and win the Sahara World Rally. When the father dies, the daughter—who wants to perpetuate his name—disguises herself as a boy and enters the race. One of the factors that Shields liked about the movie was playing a boy, which she considered a challenge. The first time she came on the set dressed as a boy—with her little mustache—her leading man didn't recognize her.

She also learned to use real emotion in difficult sequences. One scene required that she be pulled by the hair and whipped. Although the whip was made of soft felt, while enacting the fight the three-hundred-pound villain accidentally hit her hand with the wooden butt of the whip. It hurt, and she started to cry, but instead of fluffing the scene, she continued, using the emotion. When the camera stopped turning—realizing this was the first time she had shown real emotion in front of people on the set—she stood with her hand in front of her face to regain her composure. She had found that she could make emotion work for her, and in another scene where she was required to whimper, she was able to draw forth the proper mood.

"As much as I've enjoyed the success that has come with acting and modeling," she emphasized in the article, "there have been some tough moments. One of the hardest aspects has been seeing the things written about me that just aren't true: the stories that I'm not happy, that I'm an exploited child who's pushed into everything and couldn't wait to get away to college . . . .

"And it's awful to see the lies that have been written about my mother. I wish sometimes that I could be the person who was not my mother's daughter, only so I could speak about how wonderful she is—because, of course, coming from her daughter, people don't believe it.

"When I was 12, I remember wanting to call Barbara Walters and ask her to interview me so I could tell the truth about myself. It's been hard hearing people say that I was a child sex object. I was almost in disbelief when I first read that. I liked the work I did, even when I was younger, and the thought that I was some kind of sex symbol just seemed ludicrous to me . . . .

"I think one reason I've been able to handle some of these problems is because my mom and I have had such a good relationship. We've talked about everything and she taught me what was right and wrong, and then I just started making my own decisions."

Shields concluded the article by saying: "But I try to keep things in perspective and not get caught up in what I have. I've been helped by my mother and my family and my religion. I try not to think too much about all the fanfare, and when I do have to, I realize how very fortunate I am . . . ."

She received $1,500,00 for *Sahara*, an enormous sum when the highest paid actor of the 1970s was Steve McQueen at $3,000,000 per film, but a few years later Burt Reynolds earned $4,000,000 for *Cannonball*, Sylvester Stallone supposedly made $7,000,000 for acting, writing, and directing *Rocky III*, and Dolly Parton made $4,000,000 for *Rhinestone*. In the 1980s, in the $3 to $4 million per film class are Alan Alda, Clint Eastwood, Jane Fonda, Paul Newman, Christopher Reeve, and Barbra Streisand.

Leading the television salaries is Johnny Carson with $5,000,000 and Merv Griffin at $3,000,000. According to *People* magazine, March 25, 1985, the highest paid TV actor is Tom Selleck at $220,000 per episode, or $4,800,000 a season; Jane Wyman earns $60,000 per episode, or $1,600,000 a year; Larry Hagman earns $3,000,000 a year for *Dallas*; both Joan Collins and Linda Evans receive $40,000 per episode, or $1,200,000 a year for *Dynasty*; Lee Majors gets $65,000 per episode for *The Fall Guy*, Gavin MacLeod $1,400,000 a season for *The Love Boat*, and James Brolin takes $1,100,000 from *Hotel*. It is interesting to note that Bette Davis and James Stewart earned $250,000 apiece for the HBO film, *Right of Way*, but Robert Mitchum took home $1,200,000 for the mini-series *The Winds of War*. Topping everyone is the $70,000,000 earned by Michael Jackson for the *Thriller* album, as well as merchandizing, which *People* pointed out might eventually bring in $1,000,0000,000!

But earning big money appears to be not as big a problem as keeping some of it. On February 23, 1984, Joe Landau, former business manager of Marty Engels and his wife Shirley Jones, was sentenced to five years in prison by Judge Ringer, for bilking them of $300,000 during the years 1981 and 1982. Landau took two other clients to the tune of $250,000. He had pleaded guilty to the three counts of grand theft. Engels remarked that he hoped that the decision would "deter other slickos from descending on Hollywood and the vulnerable actor."

But the classic story of a celebrity who unknowingly worked for years almost *gratis* was that of the late writer Anita (*Gentleman Prefer Blondes*) Loos. A trusting creature, she magnanimously shared screen credit on her hit movies with husband/manager, John Emerson—even though he never wrote a word. A sly character, he invested all of her earnings in his own name, and spent the last eighteen years of his life in a posh rest home, paid for by the annuities.

Suzanne Somers' career in Las Vegas came about because of her appearance in TV's *Three's Company.* *(Courtesy of J. Neyland collection)*

Ann-Margret became a superstar under the guidance of her husband, former actor Roger Smith. *(Courtesy of J. Neyland collection)*

BLACKOUT: 1985

Agent

I've just formed my own agency, and I'm going to buy out your contract. Bernie's okay, but he's done all he can for you . . . .

Male Star

But I feel . . . Well, we go back a long time.

Agent

The business is changing, and frankly his age is catching up with him. With so many accountants running things now, he's confused. Don't forget I was a CPA before I got into the business.

Male Star

Intellectually, I know you're right, but emotionally . . . I'm the godfather of his eldest son!

Agent

He'll understand that you didn't have any say in the matter. I'm just buying you.

Male Star

But he may not want to let me go!

Agent

You're the last in his stable that's worth megabucks. Besides, I've got him by the short and curly. He owes money.

Male Star

The bookies?

Agent

Uh huh.

Male Star

Well, I bailed him out once or twice. . . I've got weaknesses, everyone knows about the broads, but gambling is as bad as dope on your back.

Agent

You've known him a long time. Have a few drinks with him and . . . break it to him gently.

Male Star

I happen to like the way he operates. I can't stand CPAs. I'll pay off the bookies.

Paul Newman, seen here directing *Never Give an Inch*, took no salary, only deferred payments when he directed *Rachel, Rachel*, which won an Oscar nomination for his wife Joanne Woodward. *(Courtesy of J. Neyland collection)*

Former agent Freddie Fields on the set of *Victory*, which he produced for Paramount Pictures in 1980, talking to the director John Huston. *(Courtesy of Marvin Paige's Motion Picture and TV Research Service)*

22

CMA & ITS OFFSPRING

Jean Stapleton
Actors and agents have an alliance from the word go. They are inextricably connected.

Creative Management Associates had been organized by two ex-Music Corporation of America agents, David Begelman and Freddie Fields, in 1963. Begelman had started with MCA in New York in 1949, and had resigned as vice president of special projects in 1960. Fields had been a vice-president and board member of MCA-TV. He formed Freddie Fields and Associates in 1961, with only four clients: Polly Bergen (his wife at the time), Judy Garland, Phil Silvers, and Kirk Douglas. Some executive agents who joined CMA during the 1963 to 1965 era were John Foreman, Mike Grushkopf, M. C. Levee, Jr., Stephanie Phillips, Warren Bayless, Marty Ulfand, Shelly Wile, Mike Medavoy, Joe Wizen, Don Kopoloff, Mike Wyse, and soon Sue Mengers.

"CMA was extremely attentive to details," relates a man who worked in the New York office.[1] "Richard Shepherd, especially, was known for his detail work. John Foreman was effective in bringing clients together into packages for production. But all were motivated by the guidance of Fields and Begelman, who often acted as one entity.

"Freddie was an impressive man, with a marvelous kind of pure energy. He had that rare talent of instilling confidence, not only in his clients—after all that was part of the game—but in his employees as well. He made everyone feel important, and he was an expert at whipping-up confidence.

"I was invited to join CMA in 1964, just at the time when the agency was mushrooming and moving into its plush new offices on

Madison Avenue. Our individual tastes were catered to, and we could choose our own color schemes for our offices, select furnishings, with the advice of a decorator. Our furniture was expensive but comfortable, elegant and substantial, all accouterments of art quality: fabric-covered walls and handsome, woven carpets from Italy or France. David said that CMA wanted its people to be happy with their surroundings, since everyone would spend more time in the office than at home. He was right. We came in early, and David was always in his office no matter what the hour, and we left late most nights.

"'No talking in the elevators,' was the order, because competitor Ashley-Steiner was located on a higher floor, and one never knew who was in the elevators. Executives at A-S had not been so cautioned, and at CMA meetings one of the topics might be: 'elevator news'—quite a bit of information was picked up between the first and 24th floors!

"There was a blanket edict that agents always travel first class. 'After all,' Freddie was fond of saying, 'you never know who is going to be on the same plane.' In fact, one television series was actually sold on a flight between New York and Los Angeles. Fields happened to be seated next to Jim Aubrey, head of CBS, and casually mentioned a possible series based on some short stories that had appeared in *This Week* magazine. They concerned a fascinating fictional character named Selena Meade, daughter of a diplomat, educated in Europe, an out-of-house spy. Aubrey bought the CMA package—Polly Bergen to star, with a CMA writer and director."

A pilot was made, and everything was geared for a go-ahead when CBS fired Aubrey on Washington's Birthday weekend in 1966. His projects were cancelled, including *Selena Meade*. But Fields had protected CMA and Bergen's company, with a "pay or play" (or buyout) clause in the contract, and it was said that CBS paid through the nose—several hundred-thousand dollars—to drop the series under its new management.

"Now, at this point," the former CMA associate said, "Freddie was not a reader, *per se*. But his powers of concentration were so great that he absorbed a concept or a story-line the moment it was given to him. Then, amazingly, on the telephone five minutes or five days later, he could launch into discussions of the project with such knowledgeable enthusiasm and conviction, and with such creative embellishment, that you could swear on your mother's honor that he had read every word of the material!"

Fields' lifestyle was discussed in a 1966 interview:[2] "Fields himself lives in a style to which the new-style agent would like to become accustomed. He drives a white Bentley (equipped with a phone), is married to movie star, Polly Bergen, hobnobs with celebrities, weekends in Palm Springs and generally operates in a grand manner. His clients include Barbra Streisand, Paul Newman, Kirk Douglas and Peter Sellers. . . .

"C.M.A. still is dwarfed when compared with William Morris which has about 2,000 clients but Fields says that he likes it that way, explaining that he would rather handle a relatively small group of 'top talent' than try to shuffle hundreds of undistinguished clients. Fields says that this approach has forced him to turn down three times as many clients as he has accepted.

"Like most top agents, Fields says he gets most of his kicks from 'packaging' or 'pre-producing' as he prefers to call it. Some of Fields' clients say he is remarkably adroit at this delicate craft though they confess bewilderment as to his methods. A case in point is Fielder Cook, a producer-director who was having trouble getting his film, *A Big Hand for a Little Lady*, off the ground.

"After working for several months on preparing the film, Cook recalled, Warner Brothers suddenly took a second look at the budget and cancelled it. Cook phoned Fields and urgently solicited his help. 'For the next hour,' Cook said, 'I received a series of calls from Freddie over his car phone as he plied the freeway. I could hear the traffic supplying a background for his reassuring words.' In the space of an hour, Cook said Fields had phoned Warner Brothers and induced them to reverse their decision, phoned Henry Fonda in Spain and talked him into shifting his schedule to accept a role in the picture and also nailed Jason Robards for a key role . . . ."

A philosophy of both Fields and Begelman was that every client had all 36 CMA agents working for him. All agents met all clients, read each other's mail, and were apprised of all projects, current or pending. They kept up-to-date with everything. Agents also had certain freedoms, and were encouraged to give honest opinions about projects, scripts, suitability of roles for stars, etc. And although comments on various memos for internal use could be scathing, they were not openly criticized, nor were any opinions seemingly held against the employees.

An important man with the company was senior vice-president, Shep Fields, Freddie's older brother, who had been a well-known orchestra conductor, of Rippling Rhythm fame, and was responsible for booking many acts in Las Vegas. It seemed that Shep knew everyone in that part of the business. From New York, Dan Welkes also operated in the personal appearance field.

Everyone was always on the lookout for potential stars. When Faye Dunaway was appearing in *Hogan's Goat* Off-Broadway, David and Stephanie Phillips signed her, and she made her first screen appearance in *The Happening* in 1967. Then came *Bonnie and Clyde*, with Warren Beatty, which made her a star.

"Stephanie Phillips was quite extraordinary, highly professional to her toes," the ex-agent continued. "One evening, she had dinner with Robert Redford, then excused herself and went to the hospital to have her baby! Another time, she suffered a broken leg in a skiing accident, but never missed a day's work. She lugged around that heavy cast for weeks. It was her philosophy that one used anything that came along for the good of the clients, and if that cast drew attention—all the better!" It surprised nobody in the least that she is now important in the film business. She produced *The Best Little Whorehouse in Texas* on Broadway, and performed the same chore at Universal for the picture.

Even though the CMA office in Hollywood was very powerful, there was a great deal of decision-making in New York. Excellent communications kept both coasts apprised of all projects. Fields and Begelman, having been with MCA—where there was sometimes not only lack of communication but actual rivalry between departments—made certain that this same situation did not exist with CMA.

The astute Harvey Orkin, who headed CMA's office in London (followed later by Sandy Lieberson), was attentive to Patricia Neal when she suffered a series of strokes that left her in a state of semi-paralysis in 1966. When she was stricken at MGM several days into production on *Seven Women*, which the agency had packaged, to be replaced by Anne Bancroft and moved to her home in England, Orkin was very solicitous through her long period of rehabilitation. Two years later, back at MGM when she was sufficiently recovered to work, she garnered excellent reviews for *The Subject Was Roses*.

Orkin returned to the New York office about 1967, and operated effectively on several packages for TV and film projects.

CMA's man in Rome was Franco Reggiani, whose delightful Italian accent charmed American clients. He was very attentive to clients, and part of his job was arranging the professional and social life of American and English performers working in Italy. A great many films were being shot in Europe in the mid and late 1960s, and Franco often visited locations and sets of clients who were making pictures in other parts of the continent. He also set up films made for Italian consumption only—millions of lira for Italian stars with whom Americans were not acquainted.

Fields and Begelman kept tabs on what was happening by mentally filing reports about clients the agents took to lunch or dinner, including what was discussed. Several weeks might go by, and one of them would ask the reporting agent: "What happened with the lunch with Kirk Douglas at Sardi's?" or "What was Henry Fonda's comment about that script you sent him?" or "Did you get that manuscript from the agent you took to the theater?"

Fields and Begelman took the time to send personal thank-you notes to the agents when they had performed well—which, in many cases, meant more to them than bonuses, though they were also generous with bonuses. Agents were very well-paid. When the time came for an agent to leave, he was never fired. His resignation was requested, and suitable compensation was arranged.

CMA clients were encouraged in their private, special projects, even if there was no real money in it for CMA. John Foreman, who handled Paul Newman, helped him develop *Rachel, Rachel* for Joanne Woodward and daughter, Annie Potts. Newman did not take a salary; everything was deferred. It was obvious that the picture was going to be a "little film"—the kind that might get great reviews and win a few awards, but not take in a lot of money at the box office—but the agency went along with him all the way, attending screenings and supporting the projects. Newman obtained a distribution deal through Warner Brothers, and *Rachel, Rachel* earned Woodward an Academy Award nomination in 1968, established Newman as a talented director, and brought CMA a lot of attention.

Toward the end of the 1960s, great changes were being brought about in CMA's offices because of expansion necessary to the changing times. Sue Mengers came over from Korman Contemporary Artists, and absolutely flourished. Her early success appeared to be the result of sincere belief in her clients. She would ask an enormous price, and then back it up with the statement: "But they're worth it!" And, because she was totally convinced that they were worth the money, more often than not—to the amazement of other CMA agents—she would get everything she asked for, sometimes more. Totally loyal and supportive of her clients, she put together with David Begelman the film production of *Funny Girl*.

When MCA had to divest its talent agency, Fields and Begelman took over many of its stars, including Paul Newman, Joanne Woodward, Barbra Streisand, Henry Fonda, and many others whom they had known from their days with the company. Ted Ashley and Ira Steiner also took over a great many of MCA's clients.

Prior to becoming a part of the talent agency field, Steiner had a publicity office in the big band era of the 1930s, and represented such bands as Count Basie, Benny Goodman, Woody Herman, Harry James, and Vaughn Monroe, among others. He joined the William Morris Agency in 1940, where he remained for ten years. (Before his death—February 8, 1985, age 70—he had produced the feature film *Valdez Is Coming* and, in association with Ivan Goff and Ben Roberts, the TV verson of *Logan's Run*.)

In 1968, Creative Management Associates absorbed General Artists Corporation. Martin Baum, age 44, and the West Coast head of GAC, became a senior executive vice-president of CMA. The agency also took over Henry Willson, who brought his clients with him, and several smaller agencies were purchased. Sam Cohen was a large part of the GAC power in the merger.

On April 25, 1969, Kinney sold Ashley Famous to Marvin Josephson Associates, the parent company of International Creative Management, for $10,000,000 cash. Kinney was obliged to sell its talent agency in order to avoid conflict of interest, because it was buying W.B.-Seven Arts, the erstwhile Warner Brothers studio in Burbank. Ted Ashley became chairman of the board and chief executive officer of the studio. He was 48 years old: another agent was running a motion picture studio.

In March 1985, the former Ashley Famous Agency personnel gathered for a reunion at Chasen's restaurant. Ted Ashley, now vice-chairman of Warner Communications, flew in from New York to address the 70-odd alumni. He remarked: "Those were the days of the candid microphone, not candid camera. Instead of spending my first profit on an apartment or a suit, I put the money into hiring new and experienced agents, and we focused on the unexplored world of TV."

Josephson's acquisition of Ashley Famous, which had affiliates in Rome and Paris, also included London International, and he brought all of the firm together as International Famous Artists. "Marvin Josephson, 50, appears to be the antithesis of the popular image of an agent," *Time* magazine noted,[3] "but, unlike many of the modern breed who prefer euphemisms for their trade, he readily admits he is one . . . .

"Soft-voiced, genial, unhurried and conservatively dapper, he launched International Creative Management in 1955 with $100 capital and two clients, Robert Keeshan (Captain Kangaroo) and Newscaster Charles Collingswood. Since then, Josephson has built I.C.M. into a $30 million-a-year multinational company, embracing agents, a concert-booking bureau and a TV station. His 2,250 clients include actor Laurence Olivier, playwright Tennessee Williams, musician Isaac Stern and dancer Mikhail Baryshnikov. Josephson's empire has grown so vast that he now spends most of his time delegating and supervising . . . . 'His astuteness is with procedure, and he has an accounting machine in his head,' says producer Robert Evans . . . ."

In 1975, Josephson bought CMA from Fields for $6,650,000. The conglomerate already owned Chasin-Park-Citron and Robert J. Woolf Associates, a sports firm, under the umbrella name of International Creative Management, or simply ICM.

Fields achieved his dream: after producing several films, including *American Gigolo*, he moved over to MGM as head of production, where he stayed until 1984, when he became an independent producer.

Sue Mengers stood rather quietly between Barbra Streisand and Jon Peters, engaging in amusing chit-chat. To anyone who did not know that she was the highest-paid female talent agent in the world, she might be taken for a cousin, or perhaps even a secretary. Blond, plumpish, diminutive, bespectacled, she mixed easily with the beautiful people who had gathered to pay homage to 75-year-old director William Wyler. It was his birthday: June 25, 1977.

Many of the beautiful people belonged to another era of stardom. Merle Oberon, with her new husband Bob Wolders, was a

Wyler alumnus—*These Three* (1936) and *Wuthering Heights* (1939)—and almost seemed younger-looking than when she had appeared opposite Laurence Olivier in the latter film. The party was an expert mix of the old and the new, but when Paul Henreid (who had given up smoking) lighted two cigarettes—one for himself and one for Bette Davis, who had given three award-winning performances for Wyler—the 1940s loomed up nostalgically.

Streisand, who had performed for Wyler in *Funny Girl* (1968), was dressed spectacularly, wearing carnations in her hair. Mengers, while expensively gowned, was under-dressed. As Streisand's agent, she could not do otherwise. It was not good form to outdress a client; besides, she did not have a clothes-horse figure. Her taste ran to texturized woven materials and silk prints. As she moved gracefully into the stunningly decorated garden, poised and very sure of herself, a male guest snorted, "I see that Sue has cleaned up her act."

His companion raised her eyebrows. "Possibly. But she'll always be a secretary at heart."

Fresh out of high school, Mengers began her career in show business in the least-recognized job in an office; she was a receptionist at MCA in the 1950s. Her parents had emigrated from Germany in 1939, with their little tow-headed girl in tow, to settle in Utica, New York. Menial jobs were all that were available to them because of their poor English. After her father committed suicide in 1943, Mengers moved with her mother to the Bronx.

When she left MCA, she moved to the Baum-Newborn Agency, which was as different as possible from the sedate, antiseptic dark-suit-and-tie atmosphere that was required by Lew Wasserman. Agents at Baum-Newborn hustled in the same way that the old-time vaudeville agents hustled. Next came a secretarial job at William Morris, the oldest privately-owned talent agency in the world. Here she was exposed to protocol, much of which she tossed aside when Tom Korman, formerly of Baum-Newborn, asked her to become his partner in 1963. She joined CMA five years later.

Mengers told Marcia Borie in an interview[4] in 1975, "Seven years ago, when I gambled and came out here, there was more opportunity to become established. I don't know what the statistics were, but back then there was a lot of activity—double what there is today. There was a place for another hustling agent to get involved and make a reputation .... I was also very fortunate in getting clients just as they were on the crest. I started representing Hackman when he was making $35,000 a picture in *Hunting Party*. I represented Peter Bogdanovich before he did *The Last Picture Show*. He was just starting it. I signed Ryan O'Neal before *Love Story* opened. An agent's success is totally dependent upon his client's success. If people want Streisand, and feel that they have to come to me in order to communicate with her in the initial stages, because that's all an agent is, a conduit; I am important because of her. I don't make creative decisions for my clients. I can recommend; sometimes they listen, sometimes they don't. If tomorrow I lost five of my major clients, my importance would diminish overnight.... If I attribute my relationship to my clients to anything, it's that I am always available to them. I speak to my clients every day, or at the very least once a week. If I'm away, no matter what time of day or what, I always have a line open to my clients ....

"Because I am a woman, I was able to be aggressive without being offensive. And yet because I am a woman it took me a lot longer to get through to certain people. Now, thank God, I don't have that problem.... For instance, it took Barbra Streisand a long time before she referred to me as her agent. I was always her friend, Sue. She used to kid me and say, 'You're my girlfriend. You're this little blonde girl. You're not my agent.' In truth, I didn't sign Barbra to the agency. She was with them when I joined it. So, it was a gradual thing ...."

She told writer Louise Farr in an interview:[5] " 'Oh, fuck!' says Sue Mengers when asked about the importance of entertaining. 'Oh, my God, I'm so scared. Please be kind. The only reason I said yes to *Ms* was I thought they wouldn't go for that Cosmo bullshit. It's like the only reason I've made it is I'm some kind of a freak and I give parties, which is so stupid ....' "

But she does give smashing parties, and she does make deals so daring that Myron Selznick would have dropped his teeth. Her parties have become as famous as her reported $40,000 a year expense account. She has even been parodied in films. Dyan Cannon, a former client, probably based her agent characterization in *The Last of Sheila* (1973) on "early" Mengers, and author William Murray, in his book *The Dream Merchants*, used an actual interview with her to startling advantage.

In Mengers' future was a partnership contract, to be signed in 1978 for a reported $600,000 a year, as well as a time when she would lose four of her favorite clients: Barbra Streisand, Burt Reynolds, Diana Ross, and Ali MacGraw. Streisand left, said the gossips, because Mengers had persuaded her to take second billing to Gene Hackman in *All Night Long* (1981), a film directed by Mengers' husband Jean Claude Tramont, which none of the New York reviewers liked—except Pauline Kael, who was ecstatic.

"In certain circles, it's considered very chic to put down Sue," said one very funny lady in 1978,[6] who is married to an agent. "She's okay in my book, although frankly I'd never want to cross her. I rather admire her because she's ballsy on one hand, and star-struck on the other. I wouldn't at all be surprised if she still didn't occasionally say to herself with amazement, 'I'm having lunch with Liza Minnelli today!' But if you're a woman agent, other male agents automatically hate you. They can have friendly enemies in the business with whom they play golf once in a while at Hillcrest, or meet when one of the guys shows a porno movie, but if you have five or six of the up-and-coming stars on your list—as Sue does—and a talented foreign-type husband who has a name in his own right—as Sue has—someone who can support her if she ever decides to retire, and you're chic and funky too—as Sue is—then the male agents are going to give you the shaft.

"Also, producers and directors will attend your parties and drink your booze, and compare your great food to camel shit—as someone supposedly did; or someone else will say that your parties are catered by the Salvation Army, and you just can't escape such cheap shots. My husband is a gentleman in public and a drunk at home. A lot of agents are on booze pie these days. I put up with it because his ulcers get noisy when he closes a four-million-dollar deal. But we're the other generation—the one that goes back to Harlow. I don't think that any of the young agents have ulcers. I'm certain that Sue doesn't. But she does have days when I'm sure she'd rather be back typing at William Morris for $135 a week than cooped up in that office on Beverly Boulevard, answering forty-dozen phone calls."

At Christmastime 1983, the same funny lady, now ex-wife of the agent, grew pensive. "Sue has quieted down now; she's matured to the point where deals come more easily. She's been hurt, too, and she's reached a certain plateau. There's almost nothing published about her now—it's as if that's all behind her. When a star has a series of solid hits after a long dry period, and she's at last accepted by the industry and there's a certain dignity attached to her name, well, Sue's like that.

"She's not a kid anymore, four-oh is behind her and five-oh is coming up. Oh, she's still wild and funny and girlish, but there's a deepening, and when Streisand went over to the opposition it must have hurt like hell. Sue once thought she would like to be like Thalberg—heading a studio—but who needs that kind of pressure? I think she might go into independent production one day, if she could find the right spot, or Pay-TV. She can still out-talk and out-guess the big boys, and has succeeded in delivering a low profile. She's learned, I think, she can't wear her heart on her sleeve."

But agents like Sue Mengers do not double-talk. It is the new ten percenters, eager to protect their ignorance, still wearing their university colors under navy blue blazers, who accelerate in high gear—for a time.

This new-type agent has a counterpart: the rich, new producer, also determined not to show his naivete—although still brushing the desert sand from his shoes in his posh, transitory suite at Century City. This youthful little man received a magnificent script written by a two-time Academy Award winner. A meeting was arranged, and the distinguished writer appeared. The producer arose from behind his desk and held out his hand. It was obvious to the writer that this powerful producer had been born about the same time that he had won his first Oscar.

The amenities went on and on, weather was discussed, as well as the preview of a movie the night before, the whereabouts of various acquaintances and, finally, when the small talk was in danger of floundering, the writer swallowed his pride and asked, "And how did you like the script?"

The young man smiled, "Oh, I liked the sub-texture all right, but," and he frowned, "I didn't care for the cross-grain."

The famous writer took the script from the producer's desk and, without a word, left the building. He was no doubt reflecting on the mores of yet another changing Hollywood, and probably wishing that Jack Warner, Louis B. Mayer, or Darryl F. Zanuck were back on earth to scream out their blunt opinions.

But the new breed of Hollywood agent will have to deal with the new breed of Hollywood producer. They deserve each other.

The two men who held more power in their four hands than all of the present group of agents put together are gone: Jules Stein and

Abe Lastfogel. After his retirement from MCA, Stein surprisingly became social—he allowed his biography to appear in *Who's Who*, granted an occasional interview, gave and attended parties and charity events. In 1960, he founded and became first trustee chairman of Research to Prevent Blindness, a New York organization that raised millions of dollars for eye programs at medical schools. He donated more than $1,500,000 for the Jules Stein Eye Institute at UCLA, which was dedicated November 3, 1966. He died April 29, 1981, of heart failure, at UCLA Medical Center. He was 85 years old.

Doris Stein outlived her husband only three years. She died at the age of 82 on April 7, 1984, at UCLA Medical Center, very near to the Jules Stein Eye Clinic which she had urged him to build.

"Some years ago, I told Jules," she said before her death, "that he had made his point about accumulating wealth. I always said that I was his second love. He had already built his empire, now it was time to go back to medicine and accomplish something for his first love. He built that marvelous research facility. Actually, when he looked into it, he felt that ophthalmology had progressed—well, not as far as it should have since those early days when he had practiced. So Jules, I think, died a happy man."

With Jules Stein dead, Abe Lastfogel was the last of the industry giants of that early era. Chairman emeritus of the William Morris Agency, he still lived at the Beverly Wilshire Hotel, and although less active in recent years, he still made a pilgrimage to the office every day. He went into the Cedars-Sinai Medical Center early in August of 1984, complaining of chest pains. Complications from a gallbladder operation then set in, and on August 25th he passed away at the age of 86. On September 4, he was buried at Hillside Memorial Cemetery, where one of his first clients—Al Jolson— also rests.

Formerly, they were called: *Jackals, Leeches, Toadies, Stooges, Parasites, Wastrels, Squeezers, Tapeworms, Bootlickers, Flesh Peddlers, Ten percenters . . . .*

Now, they are simply called agents.

Talent Agents.

They handle the stars . . . .

ACKNOWLEDGMENTS

I am grateful to the many people who have been kind enough to give me information for this book over the last ten-year period. I am obliged to Mrs. Helga Greene and College Trustees, Ltd., for permission to quote from the Raymond Chandler article, "Ten Per Cent of Your Life," from the February, 1952 issue of the *Atlantic Monthly* magazine. I am especially appreciative of the Margaret Herrick Library of the Academy of Motion Picture Arts and Sciences; the New York Public Library; the staff of the Pomona Public Library; the Upland Public Library; and the Pasadena Public Library. I am indebted to my secretary for thirty years, Josephine Clay Forbes, who typed early drafts of the manuscript; my late manager for thirty years, Harold M. Madison; my C.P.A., Ida Green; my agent Albert Zuckerman of Writers House, Inc.; and my editor, James Neyland—the "midwife" on *Mother Goddam*—who gave me the impetus to complete *Stars & Star Handlers*.

CHAPTER NOTES

1: Vaudeville & America's First Agent

[1] *The Palace*, by Marian Spitzer. Atheneum, New York (1969).

[2] *Vaudeville*, by Joe Laurie, Jr. Henry Holt, New York (1953).

[3] *Show Biz from Vaude to Video*, by Abel Green & Joe Laurie, Jr. Henry Holt, New York (1951).

[4] *Vaudeville*, by Joe Laurie, Jr. Henry Holt, New York (1953). It is worth noting that Morris Sime Silverman, the founder of *Variety*, was born May 19, 1873, the same day as William Morris, making them non-biological twins. They formed a close friendship.

[5] *The Great White Way*, by Alan Churchill. E.P. Dutton, New York (1962).

[6] "The Quiet Guy in Lindy's," by E.J. Kahn, Jr., in the *New Yorker* magazine, June 20-27, 1944.

[7] *Mister Abbott*, by George Abbott. Random House, New York (1968).

2: Silents Weren't Golden

[1] *A Million and One Nights*, by Terry Ramsaye. Simon & Schuster, New York (1926).

[2] *The Movies, Mr. Griffith and Me*, by Lillian Gish, with Anne Pinchot. Prentice-Hall, Englewood Cliffs, NJ (1969).

[3] *One Reel a Week*, by Fred J. Balshofter & Arthur C. Miller. University of California, Berkeley & Los Angeles (1967).

[4] *Movie facts and feats*, by Patrick Robertson. Sterling, New York (1980).

3: Fathers & Big Daddies

[1] *A Life on Film*, by Mary Astor. Delacorte, New York (1971).

[2] *Swanson on Swanson*, by Gloria Swanson. Random House, New York (1980).

[3] *Harlow*, by Irving Shulman and Arthur Landau. Bernard Geis, New York (1964).

4: Movie Moppets

[1] *Charlie Chaplin*, by Theodore Huff. Abelard-Schuman, New York (1951).

[2] *Hollywood, The Pioneers*, by Kevin Brownlow. Alfred A. Knopf, New York (1979).

[3] *A Million and One Nights*, by Terry Ramsaye. Simon & Schuster, New York (1926).

[4] *Please Don't Shoot My Dog*, by Jackie Cooper, with Dick Kleiner. William Morrow, New York (1981).

5: MCA in Chicago, The Origins

[1] "What Made Jules Run?" by Michael Pye, in the London *Sunday Times*, Business News, June 17, 1973.

[2] *Jule*, by Theodore Taylor. Random House, New York (1979).

[3] "Hollywood's Music Mogul," by Murray Schumach, in *The New York Times*, July 21, 1963.

[4] "What Made Jules Run?" by Michael Pye, in the London *Sunday Times*, Business News, London, June 17, 1973.

[5] "Jules Stein: Eye Doctor, Movie Visionary," by Joyce Haber, in the *Los Angles Times*, May 16, 1974.

[6] *Auld Acquaintance*, by Guy Lombardo, with Jack Altshul. Doubleday, Garden City, NY (1975).

[7] *The Third Time Around*, by George Burns. Putnam, New York (1980).

[8] Author interview, July 24, 1979. Will Ahern died in 1983.

6: Agents Gain Power . . .

[1] *David O. Selznick's Hollywood*, by Ronald Haver. Alfred A. Knopf, New York (1980).

[2] *A Private View*, by Irene Mayer Selznick. Alfred A. Knopf, New York (1983).

[3] *The Movies, Mr. Griffith and Me*, by Lillian Gish and Ann Pinchot. Prentice Hall, Englewood Cliffs, N.J (1969).

[4] *The Lion's Share*, by Bosley Crowther, E.P. Dutton, New York (1975).

[5] "The Star-Spangled Octopus," by David G. Wittels, *The Saturday Evening Post*, July 10, 17, 24, 31, 1946.

[6] James Bacon column, the *Los Angeles Herald Examiner*, April 30, 1981.

[7] "Cultivating His Legend Is An Agent's Best Bet," by Wayne Warga, in the *Los Angeles Times*, Sept. 21, 1975.

[8] *Show People*, by Kenneth Tynan. Simon & Schuster, New York (1979).

[9] "Irving Lazar: The Artful Pitchman," by Enid Nemy, *The New York Times*, Nov. 2, 1980. In Mel Brooks' *The History of the World Part I*, one of the characters was an agent named "Swiftus Lazarus."

[10] *Off With Their Heads*, by Frances Marion. Macmillan, New York (1972).

[11] "Who Serves and Who Pays," in *The Screen Guild* magazine, Oct. 2, 1935.

[12] "Turnaround At Awards Fete: Actors Make Nice With Agents," by "Tush," in *Variety*, Feb. 22, 1984.

7: . . . And More Power

[1] *Child of the Century*, by Ben Hecht. Simon & Schuster, New York (1954).

[2] *The Wind at My Back*, by Pat O'Brien, with Stephen Longstreet. Doubleday, Garden City, NY (1964).

[3] *An Unfinished Woman*, by Lillian Hellman. Little Brown, Boston (1969).

[4] Author interview, Sept. 5, 1974.

[5] "Former business manager recalls her twenty-one years with actor Clark Gable," Associated Press, Feb. 23, 1985.

[6] *A Life in Comedy*, by William Robert Faith. Putnam, New York (1982).

[7] *Haywire*, by Brooke Hayward. Alfred A. Knopf, New York (1977).

[8] *Film, An Anthology*. Simon & Schuster, New York (1959).

[9] *Hollywood*, by Garson Kanin. Viking, New York (1974).

[10] *Katharine Hepburn*, by Gary Carey . St. Martin's, New York (1983).

[11] Author interview, Mar. 12, 1977.

[12] *The New York Times*, Mar. 19, 1971.

[13] *The Borscht Belt*, by Joey Adams and Frank Tobias. Bobbs-Merrill, New York (1966).

8: The Hundred Percenters

[1] "Hollywood's Ten Percenters," by Alva Johnson, in *The Saturday Evening Post*, Aug. 15-22, 1942.

[2] *Please Don't Shoot My Dog*, by Jackie Cooper, with Dick Kleiner. William Morrow, New York (1981).

[3] *Starmaker*, by Hal Wallis and Charles Higham. Macmillan, New York (1980).

[4] *Don't Say Yes Until I Finish Talking*, by Mel Gussow. Doubleday, Garden City, NY (1971).

[5] *The Film Finds it's Tongue*, by Fitzhugh Green. Putnam, New York (1929).

[6] *The Hollywood Reporter*, 45th Anniversary edition.

[7] *The Film Enclopedia*, by Ephraim Katz. A Perigee Book, New York (1979).

[8] *Booty and the Beasts*, by Laddie Marshack, in *TV Guide*, Mar. 4, 1984.

[9] *Back in the Saddle Again*, by Gene Autry, with Mickey Herskowitz. Doubleday, Garden City, NY (1978).

10 "This Shoe's Made to Last," by Kevin Brass in *American Way* magazine, Feb. 1984.

11 *The Studio*, by John Gregory Dunne. Farrar, Straus & Giroux, New York (1968, 1969).

12 Author interview.

9: MCA Goes to Hollywood

1 "Waiting for . . . Lew!" by Susan Deutsch in *California* magazine, Mar. 1985.

2 *King Cohn*, by Bob Thomas. Putnam, New York (1967).

3 *It Takes More than Talent*, by Mervyn LeRoy, as told to Alyce Canfield. Alfred A. Knopf, New York (1953).

4 When Darryl F. Zanuck left Warner Bros. to form Twentieth Century in 1933, among his investors was Louis B. Mayer to the tune of $100,000. Incomprehensible to persons outside the industry, such arrangements in Hollywood—rivals investing in competitive concerns—were commonplace. When David O. formed Selznick International in September, 1935, investors were Myron Selznick, John Hay Whitney, Joan Whitney Payson, Cornelius Vanderbilt Whitney, John Hertz, A. H. Giannini, Robert Lehman, Lloyd Wright, and Irving Thalberg, through wife Norma Shearer.

5 *Long Live The King*, by Lyn Tornabene. Putnam, New York (1976).

6 *The Hollywood Greats*, by Barry Norman. Franklin Watts, New York (1980).

7 *Ladd*, by Beverly Linet. Arbor House, New York (1979).

8 Ladd refused the role of Jett Rink in *Giant*; he wanted to play Bick Benedict. This was a major career error on Ladd and Sue Carol's part. Rock Hudson was cast as Bick, and James Dean played Rink.

9 *June Allyson*, with Francis Spatz Leighton. Putnam, New York (1982).

10 *Life is a Banquet*, by Rosalind Russell and Chris Chase. Random House, New York (1977).

10: Selznicks at the Top

1 *Confessions of an Actor*, by Laurence Olivier. Simon & Schuster, New York (1982).

2 *My Story*, by Ingid Bergman and Alan Burgess. Delacorte, New York (1980).

3 The Selznick-Joyce Agency, in concert with Leland Hayward in New York, at one time or another represented: Walter Abel, Adrienne Allen, Rosemary Ames, Richard Arlen, Fred Astaire, Mary Astor, Leslie Banks, Binnie Barnes, Richard Barthelmess, Elizabeth Bergner, Ben Bernie, Edna Best, Charles Bickford, Mary Boland, Clive Brook, Billie Burke, Mrs. Patrick Campbell, Tulio Carminati, Ruth Chatterton, Constance Collier, Peggy Conklin, Walter Connolly, Gary Cooper, Jackie Cooper, Ernest Cossart, Frances Dee, Dudley Digges, Ann Dvorak, Sally Eilers, Henry

Fonda, Kay Francis, Pierre Fresnay, Sir Cedric Hardwicke, Helen Hayes, O. P. Heggie, Katharine Hepburn, Miriam Hopkins, Benita Hume, Ian Hunter, Josephine Hutchinson, Boris Karloff, Roscoe Karns, Elsa Lanchester, Charles Laughton, Evelyn Laye, Frank Lawton, Carole Lombard, Myrna Loy, Ida Lupino, Victor McLaglen, Fredric March, Herbert Marshall, Raymond Massey, Thomas Meighan, Adolph Menjou, Thomas Mitchell, Owen Moore, Jean Muir, Merle Oberon, Pat O'Brien, Laurence Olivier, Maureen O'Sullivan, Eugene Pallette, Pat Patterson, ZaSu Pitts, Lily Pons, William Powell, George Raft, Stanley Ridges, Barbara Robbins, Ginger Rogers, Sir Guy Standing, Dorothy Stickney, Margaret Sullavan, Verree Teasdale, Genevieve Tobin, Lee Tracy, Lupe Velez, Helen Vinson, Hugh Williams, Robert Woolsey, Fay Wray, Loretta Young, and Roland Young.

[4] *No Bed of Roses*, by Joan Fontaine. William Morrow, New York (1978).

[5] *Selznick*, by Bob Thomas . Doubleday, Garden City, NY (1970).

[6] *Memo From David O. Selznick*, by Rudy Behlmer. Viking, New York (1972)

11: Packages and Percentages

[1] Author interview, Sept. 16, 1975.

[2] *Golden Boy*, by Bob Thomas. St. Martin's Press, New York (1983).

[3] "Who is Ted Ashley? Just the King of Hollywood, Baby," by Karl Fleming, in *New York* magazine, June 24, 1974.

12: Henry Willson & Tab, Rock, Rory, Chad, Troy, Rhonda, etc.

[1] Author Interview, series of four, August 1977.

13: From Promotion to Production

[1] *The Lonely Life*, by Bette Davis. Putnam, New York (1962).

[2] Author interview.

[3]This Life, by Sidney Poitier. Alfred A. Knopf, New York (1980).

[4] *Hollywood in a Suitcase*, by Sammy Davis, Jr. William Morrow, New York (1980).

[5] *Cagney by Cagney*, by James Cagney. Doubleday, Garden City, NY (1976).

[6] "Nobody Ever Said Cagney Wasn't a Fighter," by Rod Townley in *TV Guide*, Mar. 24-30, 1984.

14: Going Independent

[1] "Ten Per Cent of Your Life," by Raymond Chandler, in *Atlantic Monthly*, Feb. 1952.

[2] *Actor*, by Jerome Lawrence. Putnam, New York (1974).

[3] *Hollywood is a Four-Letter Town*, by James Bacon. Contemporary Books, New York (1976).

[4] *Hollywood*, by Garson Kanin. Viking, New York (1974).

[5] *The Name Above the Title*, by Frank Capra. Macmillan, New York (1971).

[6] "The Talent Agent," by Barry J. Weitz, in *The Movie Business*, Hastings House, New York (1972).

[7] Author interview, April 8, 1985.

[8] "Firm Finds a Script for Profit," by Heidi Evans, in the *Los Angeles Times*, Mar. 15, 1985.

[9] "Alan Carr: Caftans Courageous," by Richard Hack, in *The Hollywood Reporter*, 53rd Anniversary Edition.

[10] "Power in Hollywood: a *California* Beadroll," in *California* magazine, Mar. 1985. An editorial explained that the list changes very quickly.

[11] "Who Counts," by Aljean Harmetz, in *California* magazine, Mar. 1985.

15: Family Affairs

[1] *Hollywood Now*, by William Fadiman. Liveright, New York (1972).

[2] *Hollywood's Children*, by Peggy Montgomery. Houghton Mifflin, Boston (1978).

[3] Author interview, December 15, 1984.

[4] *Variety*, Diamond Jubilee Issue, Jan. 5, 1966.

[5] *Who's Who in Hollywood*, 1900 to 1976, by David Ragan. Arlington House, New York (1976).

[6] "All in a Day's Work For Mr. Melcher," by Peter Bart, in *The New York Times*, Feb. 14, 1965.

[7] *Doris Day, Her Own Story*, by A. E. Hotcher, William Morrow, New York (1976).

16: Stars of a Different Stripe

[1] Author interview, Oct. 9, 1983.

[2] "Lena," by Lena Horne and Richard Schickel, in *Black Films and Filmmakers*, edited by Lindsay Patterson, Dodd Mead, New York.

[3] *From Sambo to Superspade: The Black Experience in Motion Pictures*, by Daniel J. Leab. Houghton Mifflin, Boston (1975).

[4] *Lena*, by James Haskins, with Kathleen Benson. Stein and Day, New York (1984).

[5] "Lena Horne Films are Headline Acts in a Festival," by Mel Watkins, in *The New York Times*, Nov. 28, 1980.

[6] "A Life on Stage," by Rex Reed, in the *New York Daily News*, May 10, 1981.

[7] Richard Natale, in *The Hollywood Reporter*, June 5, 1984.

[8] "He's the Tallest 40 inches in Hollywood," by Kenneth Turan, *TV Guide*, Jan. 14-20, 1984.

[9] "Lillian Small Ranks High as Talent Agent and Lady," by Philip K. Scheuer, in the *Los Angeles Times*, Apr. 27, 1958.

[10] *What Time's the Next Swan?* by Walter Slezak. Doubleday, Garden City, NY (1964).

[11] "Paul Kohner: Agent Long at the Top," by Charles Champlin, in the *Los Angeles Times*, May 11, 1975.

[12] *Lana*, by Lana Turner. E.P. Dutton, New York (1982).

[13] *The Magician of Sunset Boulevard*, by Frederick Kohner, Morgan Press, Palos Verdes, CA (1977).

[14] *Past Imperfect*, by Joan Collins. Simon & Schuster, New York (1984).

[15] Author interview, Jan. 18, 1984.

17: Moguls, Mergers & Mayhem

[1] Victor Orsatti died June 9, 1984.

[2] "Agent Vic Orsatti Producer of Own," by Philip K. Scheuer, in the *Los Angeles Times*, June 30, 1957.

[3] "Networks to Sell Artists' Bureaus," in *The New York Times*, May 29, 1941.

[4] "The Quiet Guy at Lindy's," by E.J. Kahn, Jr., in *The New Yorker* magazine, Apr. 1944.

[5] Author interview, Mar. 8, 1983.

[6] *Elsa Lanchester, Herself*, by Elsa Lanchester, St. Martin's, New York (1983).

18: MCA & Monopoly

[1] *Home* magazine, in the *Los Angeles Times*, Feb. 19, 1978.

[2] *The Bennett Playbill*, by Joan Bennett and Lois Kibbee. Holt, Rinehart & Winston, New York (1970).

[3] *Show* magazine, Feb., Mar., 1962.

[4] *W.*, Oct. 8-17, 1982.

19: Flacks & Flim Flam

[1] "The Talkies, the Depression and 'Decency,'" by Richard Griffith, in *The Talkies*. New York (1971).

[2] "Profile," by Alva Johnson, in *The New Yorker* magazine, Aug. 2-8, 1944.

[3] *Hedda and Louella*, by George Ells. Putnam, New York (1972).

[4] Author interview, Apr. 8, 1975.

[5] Author interview, December 18, 1984.

20: Flacks Acquire Class

[1] "Rogers & Cowan: Polishing the Stars," by Kelly Garret, in *The Hollywood Reporter*, 53rd Anniversary edition.

[2] "All the Right Moves," by Helen Dudar, in the *American Film Magazine*, Mar. 1984.

[3] " 'Moon' is Lansing's Balloon," by Michael London, in the *Los Angeles Times*, Mar. 23, 1984.

[4] "Rambling Reporter" column, by Robert Osborne, in *The Hollywood Reporter*, Mar. 26, 1984

[5] "Concern Over Stars Shirking Publicity Tasks," by Maurice Segal, in *The Hollywood Reporter*, Apr. 6, 1984.

[6] Author interview, Feb. 26, 1983.

[7] Author interview, Feb. 27, 1983.

20: Family Affairs Eighties Style

[1] *Michael!* by Mark Bego. Pinnacle, New York (1984).

[2] "Michael, Jacksons Gear Up for a Team Victory," by Steve Pond, in the *Los Angeles Times*, Apr. 28, 1984.

[3] *The Book of People*, by Christopher P. Anderson. A Perigee Book, Putnam, New York (1981).

[4] "Ann Margret: There is Something I have to Do, to Give to the People," by Jane Ardmore, in *The Daily Report*, Upland, CA., Mar. 12, 1984.

[5] "It was Very Frightening," by Kenneth Turan, in *TV Guide*, Mar. 3-9, 1984.

[6] "One Family's Finances: Suzanne Somers," by Aljean Harmetz, in *The New York Times*, Mar. 23, 1980.

[7] "Behind Suzanne Somers' $150,000 Smile," by Tony Schwartz, in *Los Angeles Herald Examiner*, Mar. 10, 1981.

[8] " 'Rashoman' revisited: L'affaire Suzanne Somers," by Peter H. Brown, *Calendar* section, in *Los Angeles Times*, Apr. 5, 1981.

[9] *The Book of People*, by Christopher P. Anderson. A Perigee Book, Putnam, New York (1981).

[10] "Breaking Away," by Brooke Shields, in *Family Weekly* magazine, Dec. 4, 1983.

22: CMA and Its Offspring

[1] Author interview, August 22, 1983.

[2] "He's Where the Money Is," in *The New York Times*, May 15, 1966.

[3] "Sherpas of the Subclause," in *Time* magazine, June 13, 1971.

[4] Marcia Borie, in *The Hollywood Reporter*, 45th Anniversary Issue.

[5] "And Now From Hollywood: The Sweetening of Sue Mengers," by Louise Farr, in *Ms* magazine, June 1975.

[6] Author interview, August 4, 1982.

INDEX

[For the sake of brevity, titles of all films, books, radio and TV shows, and record albums have not been included in this index. Films discussed at length are listed in the table of contents.]

Abbott, George, 16
Abraham, F. Murray, 112
Acord, Art, 351
Adams, Edie, 196
Adams, Joey, 129
Adler, Stella, 207
Ahern, Gladys, 87-90
Ahern, Will, 11, 87-90
Albee, E. F., 5, 10, 12, 13, 14, 15
Albin, Charles, 39, 40
Alda, Alan, 1, 36
Allenberg, Bert, 2, 157, 160, 162, 167
Allen, Fred, 5
Allen, Steve, 242
Allied Artists Studios, 320
Allyson, June, 167, 168, 310
American Film Institute (AFI), 22
Amsterdam, Morey, 300
Anderson, Ardis (See Brenda Marshall)
Anderson, Gilbert M. ("Bronco Billy"), 143
Anderson, C. H., 307
Anderson, Christopher P., 365
Anderson, Eddie "Rochester," 270, 273
Anderson, Maxwell, 102
Andress, Ursula, 196
Andrews, Dana, 225
Andrews, Julie, 327
Andrews, Patti, 260, 261
Andrews Sisters, 260
Ann-Margret, 247, 358, 359 360, 364
Aranson, William, 35
Arbuckle, Roscoe ("Fatty"), 56
Arcaro, Eddie, 147
Archerd, Army, 283
Ardmore, Jane, 358
Arlen, Harold, 271

Armstrong, Louis, 153
Artists Managers Guild, 238
Arthur, Jean, 167, 173
Ashley, Elizabeth, 103, 168
Ashley-Famous Agency, 378
Ashley Personal Management, 197
Ashley, Lady Sylvia, 162
Ashley-Steiner Agency, 374
Ashley, Ted, 2, 196, 197, 261, 378,
Assofsky, Theodore (See Ted Ashley)
Asta (Dog), 141
Astaire. Adele, 124
Astaire. Fred, 123, 124
Astor, Mary, 39-42
Aubrey, Jim, 374
Autry, Gene, 143-146, 148 305, 324, 325
Avedon, Barbara, 352
Avedon, Dick, 365
Axelrod, George, 127
Azzie (Cat), 140

Babbin, Jacqueline, 140
Bacall, Lauren, 102, 188, 196
Bacon, James, 100, 240
Bacon, Lloyd, 238
Bailey, Earl, 289, 305
Bailey, Pearl, 224
Baird, Bill, 197
Baird, Cora, 197
Baker, Carroll, 168
Balshofer, Fred J., 35
Bancroft, Anne, 121, 280
Bankhead, Tallulah, 173
Barnet, Charlie, 271
Barnold, Charles, 134
Barrett, Rona, 327
Barry, Clara, 89
Barry & Whiteledge, 87

Barry, Gene, 248
Barrymore, Diana, 173
Barrymore, Ethel, 216
Barrymore, John, 41, 96, 161, 241
Barrymore, Lionel, 125, 159
Barthelmess, Richard, 31
Bart, Peter, 261
Baruch, Bernard, 36
Baryshnikov, Mikhail, 379
Basehart, Richard, 214
Basie, Count, 378
Baum-Newborn Agency, 380
Baum, Martin, 2, 188, 225
Baxter, Anne, 178
Bayes, Nora, 5, 294
Bayless, Warren, 373
Bayne, Beverly, 35
Beatty, Clyde, 144, 149
Beatty, Warren, 376
Beckerman, Edith, 154
Beck, Martin, 10, 15
Beedle, Bill (See William Holden)
Beery, Wallace, 65
Begelman, David, 2, 212, 289, 305, 373, 375
Bego, Mark, 355
Behlmer, Rudy, 183
Belafonte, Harry, 278
Belasco, David, 5, 24
Bel Geddes, Barbara, 156
Bello, Mama Jean, 50, 51
Bello, Marino, 51
Benda, Marian, 119
Benji (Dog), 141
Bennett, Constance, 111, 331
Bennett, Joan, 175, 305-308, 330, 331
Bennett, Richard, 111
Benny, Jack, 121, 226, 300, 331
Benson, Edgar, 77

Benton, Robert, 344
Bercovici, Konrad, 282
Bergen, Edgar, 330
Bergen, Polly, 373, 374, 375
Berg, Gertrude, 197
Berg, Jeff, 249
Berg-Allenberg Agency, 160
Berg, Phil, 2, 160, 162, 297, 298
Bergman, Ingrid, 205, 210, 211, 212, 176-178, 223
Bergman, Ted, 362
Berkeley, Busby, 190
Berle, Milton, 6, 88, 128, 268, 300
Berlin, Kathy, 341
Bernhardt, Sarah, 6, 15, 292
Bernstein, Arthur L., 60-67
Biby, John, 66
Bierbower, Jenny, 25
Big Jim (Bear), 133, 134
Billings, Marion, 344
Birdwell, Russell, 320, 321
Bishop, Billy, 223
Black Jack (Horse), 143
Blakely, Barbara, 119
Blanchard, Nina, 2, 180
Block & Sully, 87
Blondell, Joan, 331
Blue, Monte, 210
Bogart, Humphrey, 101, 196, 325
Bonkers (Cat), 140
Borge, Victor, 156
Borgnine, Ernest, 134
Borie, Marsha, 380
Borzage, Frank, 238
Bowie, David, 191
Boyd, William, 148, 149, 160
Boyer, Charles, 223
Bradford, John, 242, 329
Brady, Bill, 5, 16
Brando, Marlon, 196
Brandt, Lou, 129
Brasselle, Keefe, 280
Brass, Kevin, 147
Brent, George, 161, 223
Brigham, Blanche C.,33
Brisson, Carl, 156, 169
Brisson, Frederick, 169, 170
Brokow, Norman, 239
Brolin, James, 368
Bronson, Charles, 282
Brook, Clive, 93
Brooks, Mel, 121

Brooks, Richard, 103
Brown, Jerry, Governor, 154
Brown, Joe E., 221, 238
Brown, Johnny Mack, 330-332
Brown, Johnny Mack, Mrs., 332
Brown, Kay, 176
Brown, Les, 153, 259, 261
Brown, Pat, Governor, 154
Brown, Peter H., 263
Brownlow, Kevin, 58
Bruce, Carol, 156
Brunton, Robert, 237
Brynner, Yul, 40, 208
Buchholtz, Horst, 366
Buchman, Sidney, 154, 155
Bullet (Dog), 141, 146
Burfield, Joan (See Joan Fontaine)
Burke, Billie, 174, 321, 333
Burnett, Carol, 49, 207
Burnett, W. R., 240
Burns and Allen, 86, 87, 90
Burns, George, 6, 86, 226, 358
Burton, Richard, 188
Bushman, Francis X., 35, 36
Butterfly, 43
Buttermilk (Horse), 146
Buttons, Red, 128
Byrd, Richard E., 279
Byrnes, Ed, 331

Caan, James, 339
Cabot, Ray, 149
Caesar, Sid, 128
Cage, Nicolas, 344-346
Cagney, James, 223, 228-231, 261
Cagney, Jeanne, 231
Cagney, William, 229-230, 231
Cagney, Willie, 230
Cahn, Sammy, 103, 279
Calhern, Louis, 240, 279
Calhoun, Rory, 212, 214, 218, 291
California Child Actors Bill 253
California Magazine, 249
Calloway, Cab, 270
Campbell, Glen, 216
Campbell, Mrs. Patrick, 116 117

Cannon, Dyan, 381
Cantor, Eddie, 255, 300
Capone, Al, 98
Capote, Truman, 102
Capra, Frank, 118, 160, 190, 242, 243, 245, 290, 297, 358
Capucine, 196
Carey, Harry, 351
Carillo, Leo, 222
Carmichael (Tarantula), 135
Carol, Sue, 164-168
Carpenter, Harlean (See Jean Harlow)
Carr, Alan, 248, 359
Carrells (Agent), 90
Carson, Jack, 260, 318
Carson, Johnny, 85, 88, 368
Carter, Jimmy, President, 154
Cassini, Oleg, 285
Cavett, Dick, 351
Chamberlin-Brown Agency, 168
Champion (Horse), 144, 145, 146
Champlin, Charles, 282
Chandler, Esmee, 317
Chandler, Raymond, 235, 236
Chaney, Lon, 6, 60
Channing, Carol, 330
Chaplin, Charlie, 6, 10, 18, 25, 26, 28, 47, 49, 56-60, 68, 188
Chapman, Marguerite, 202
Chase, Chevy, 141
Chasin, George, 162, 163, 173
Chasin-Park-Citron Agency, 379
Chatterton, Bob, 49
Chatterton, Ruth, 110
Chee Chee (Chimpanzee), 148
Cheta (Chimpanzee), 148
Churchill, Allen, 11, 12
Churchill, Pam, 127
C. J. (Orangutan), 142
Clarence (Lion), 133
Clark, Susan, 278
Clement, Renee, 282
Cohan, George M., 5, 223
Cohn, Harry, 95, 118, 154, 155, 189
Cohn, Sam, 249

Colbert, Claudette, 190
Coleman, Gary, 278
Colette, 102
Collier, Ruth, 159, 160
Collingswood, Charles, 379
Collins, Joan, 247, 284, 368
Collins, Joe, 284
Collins, Pauline, 284
Collins, Will, 284
Colman, Ronald, 178
Columbia Studios, 110, 117, 118, 154, 168, 189, 190, 192, 195, 196, 242, 282
Como, Perry, 300
Connolly, Mike, 242, 328, 329, 332
Coogan, Jack H., 55, 56, 60, 62, 64, 66
Coogan, Jackie, 55-68, 253, 254, 257
Coogan, Lillian R., 55-67
Coogan, Robert, 69
Cook, Anthony, 231
Cook, Fielder, 375
Coon Sanders' Kansas City Nighthawks, 81
Cooper, Gary, 191, 223, 268, 269
Cooper, Grant, 308
Cooper, Jackie, 68-70, 135
Coquelin, 5
Corday, Barbara, 351, 352
Costain, Thomas B., 188
Cotten, Joseph, 156, 205, 212
Cowan, Warren, 340, 341
Coward, Noel, 102
Cowl, Jane, 157, 294
Cox, Wally, 242
Crabtree, Lotta, 24
Crabtree, Mary Anne, 24
Crain, Jeanne, 282
Cramton, Raymond (See Chad Everett)
Crawford, Joan, 157, 169, 238, 247, 331, 340, 343
Creative Management Associates, 373
Cromwell, John, 16
Crosby, Bing, 136
Crosby, Bob, 153, 259
Crouse, Russell, 125
Crowther, Bosley, 97
Crutchfield, Bob, 347
Cruze, James, 143

Cukor, George, 173, 175, 176
Cummins, Bernie (Band), 100
Cunningham, Florence, 207
Curtis, Tony, 103

Daillard, Wayne, 300
Daisy (Dog), 141
D'Angelo, Bill, 278
Dandridge, Dorothy, 224
Daniels, Bebe, 49
Dantes, Edmund, 36
Darnell, Linda, 297
Darvi, Bella, 43
Davey, William, 49
David, Charles-Henri, 258
Davidson, Bill, 310, 312
Davies, Marion, 43, 299
Davis, Bette, 42, 156, 161, 165, 173, 191, 222, 223, 238, 257, 295, 343, 344, 368, 380
Davis, Roger, 239
Davis, Sammy, Jr., 128, 226
Daw, Marjorie, 93, 109
Day, Doris, 209, 259-264, 339
Dean, James, 208
DeCarlo, Yvonne, 282
de Cordova, Fred, 102, 103
Dee, Francis, 173
De Havilland, Olivia, 174, 211, 223, 298, 340
de la Coudraye, Marquis Le Bailly, 47, 49
Delon, Alain, 217
Del Rio, Dolores, 283
De Mille, Cecil B., 44-46, 49, 134, 238, 247
Denny, Reginald, 41
Derr, E. B., 47, 48
De Segruola, Andres, 258
Deutsch, Susan, 154
Devito, Danny, 347
Devol, Frank, 262
De Wilde, Brandon, 167
DeWitt, Joyce, 360, 362
Dietrich, Marlene, 190, 191, 343
Dileo, Frank M., 356, 357
Dillingham, Charles, 86, 87
Dillon, Josephine, 156-158, 163
Dix, Dorothea, 317

Donahue, Troy, 214, 217, 218
Donlon, Dolores, 291
Donohue, William F., 135
Dorsey, Tommy, 153, 239, 296
Dorso, Dick, 259
Douglas, Kirk, 208, 262, 340, 373, 377
Dressler, Marie, 57
Driscall, Hal, 141
Dudar, Helen, 341, 343
Duell, Charles H., 29-36
Duell, Colonel Holland, 30, 32, 34
Duffy, Father Francis, 223
Dufty, William, 49
Dugan, Johnny, 289, 305
Du Maurier, Daphne, 178
Dunaway, Faye, 376
Duncan, Leland, 136, 137, 140
Duncan Sisters, 96
Dunham, Katherine, 272
Dunne, Irene, 190, 247, 262, 330
Dunne, John Gregory, 148
Dunnock, Mildred, 156
Dupree, Minnie, 321
Durand, Harry, 40
Durante, Jimmy, 240
Durbin, Deanna, 144, 257-259, 282
Durbin, Edna Mae (See Deanna Durbin)
Durbin, James and Ada, 259
Durgin, Francis (See Rory Calhoun)
Durkin, Junior, 61
Dwan, Robert, 88, 119

Eastwood, Clint, 142, 247, 368
Ebony Magazine, 275
Ebsen, Buddy, 156
Eckstine, Billy, 128, 262
Edens, Roger, 272
Edington and Vincent Agency, 280
Egli, Joe, 164
Ehrlich, Stuart, 362
Einfeld, Charles, 221-224, 307, 324
Eisenhower, General, 294
Ekberg, Anita, 285
Ellington, Duke, 271
Elman, Ziggy, 100

Emerson, Faye, 300
Emerson, John, 369
Engels, Marty, 368
Engstead, John, 120
Enwall, Helmer, 176
Epstein, David, 351
Erlicht, Lewis, 278
Esmond, Jill, 174
Ettinger, Ruth, 230, 261
Evans, Dale, 146
Evans, Heidi, 247
Evans, Linda, 368
Everett, Chad, 217
Ewell, Tom, 196

Fadiman, William, 253
Fairbanks, Douglas, Sr., 23, 28, 47, 320, 321
Faith, William Robert, 122
Falkenburg, Jinx, 197
Falkin, Frederick, 257
Family Weekly Magazine, 366
Famous Artists Agency, 190, 195, 196, 212, 217, 312
Famous Players Corporation, 26, 27, 40, 41, 45, 378
Fantozzi, Tony, 239
Farr, Louise, 381
Farrell, Glenda, 222
Farrow, John, 297
Farrow, Mia, 283
Faye, Alice, 290
Feldman, Charles, 2, 176 189, 190, 191, 194-196 224, 291
Fell, Norman, 360
Ferber, Edna, 125, 127
Ferguson, Helen, 330-332
Fields, Freddie, 2, 212, 218 289, 373-379
Fields, Shep, 376
Fields, W. C., 221
Fifi (Poodle), 136
Fineman, Bernard, 96
Finley, Larry, 299, 300
First National Studios, 28, 56, 110, 116, 123, 237, 311
Fischer, Clifford C., 13
Fisher, Eddie, 128
Fiske, Dwight, 156
Fitzgerald, Barry, 206
Fitzgerald, Geraldine, 206
Fitzgerald, Roy (See Rock Hudson)

Fitzgerald, Walter, 206
Fitzpatrick, Tom, 87
Fleming, Karl, 196, 197
Fleming, Rhonda, 215
Flipper (Porpoise), 133
Flynn, Errol, 156, 161, 173, 174, 223
Fonda, Henry, 127, 283, 331, 343, 375, 377, 378
Fonda, Jane, 368
Fontaine, Joan, 136, 178, 179, 205, 211
Ford, Glenn, 242, 243
Ford, John, 188
Forman, Milos, 112, 231, 232
Forrest, Steve, 366
Fosse, Bob, 249
Fowler, Gene, 125, 184
Fox, William, 94, 95, 237
Fox Studios, 12, 94, 119
Fraganza, Trixie, 5, 90
Francis, Kaye, 110, 111
Francis (Mule), 147
Freddie Fields and Associates, 373
Fredricks, Pauline, 157
Freed, Arthur, 272
Freuler, John R., 26
Friedman, Rob, 347
Frings, Ketti, 329
Frings, Kurt, 329, 340
Fritz (Horse), 143
Frohman, Charles, 5
Frohman, Daniel, 36
Froman, Jane, 239
Frost, David, 101
Furry, Elda (See Hedda Hopper)
Furst, Renee, 348

Gable, Clark, 117, 120, 121, 156-163, 174-175, 297, 325
Gable, John Clark, 163
Gabor, Eva, 331
Gabor, Zsa Zsa, 262, 331
Gaines, John, 249
Gang, Martin, 145
Gansburg, Alan, 140
Garbo, Greta, 156, 188, 280, 283, 297, 325, 331, 335
Garceau, Jean, 121
Garfield, John, 156, 223, 294
Garland, Judy, 128, 258, 260, 290, 343, 373

Garner, James, 262
Garret, Kelly, 339
Garroway, Dave, 285
Garson, Greer, 161
Gaynor, Janet, 215, 321
Gelien, Art (See Tab Hunter)
General Amusement, 295, 296
General Artists Corporation (GAC), 378
Gentle Ben (Bear), 133
Gentry, Race, 217
George, Grace, 230
Gersch Brothers, 249
Gershwin, George, 102, 224, 225
Gibson, Hoot, 351
Giesler, Jerry, 308
Gilbert, Melissa, 279
Gish, Lillian, 22, 28, 29, 33, 34, 35, 39, 96
Gleason, Jimmy, 210
Gleason, Lucille, 210
Glick, Coulson, 135
Goddard, Paulette, 156
Godfrey, Arthur, 300
Goetz, William, 299
Goff, Ivan, 378
Goldfish, Samuel (See Samuel Goldwyn)
Gold, Sid, 256
Goldstone, Bernice, 205
Goldstone, Nat, 205
Goldwyn, Samuel, 95, 209 224-226
Goldwyn Studios, 122, 190, 191, 224
Goodale, George, 324
Goodheart, William, 2, 296, 297
Goodman, Benny, 100, 309, 378
Goodstadt, Oscar, 44
Gordean, Jack, 195
Gould, Charles (See Charles Feldman)
Gould, Elliott, 346
Grable, Betty, 62, 65, 67, 205, 290
Grade, Lew, 284
Gradle, Harry, 78, 80, 81
Graham, Barbara, 309
Graham, Sheilah, 327
Grant, Cary, 169, 262
Grant, Gogi, 262
Granville, Bonita, 65
Grauman, Sid, 117

Gray, Colleen, 214
Green, Abel, 10, 333
Green, Fitzhugh, 137
Green, Mitzi, 61
Gregory, Paul, 30
Griffin, Merv, 368
Griffith, Richard, 319
Griffith, D. W., 18, 23, 24, 28, 29, 40, 273
Grimaldi, Princess Grace, 5
Grushkopf, Mike, 373
Gub Gub (Pig), 148
Guinness, Alec, 195
Gumm, Harold, 271, 272
Gussow, Mel, 137
Guttman, Dick, 341
Gwenn, Edith, 339

Haber, Joyce, 51, 296, 327
Hackett, Hal, 289, 305
Hack, Richard, 248
Hagman, Larry, 368
Halmi, Robert, 231, 232
Hamel, Alan, 361-364
Hamilton, George, 262
Hammerstein, Oscar, 9
Hammett, Dashiell, 125
Hampton, Benjamin B., 26, 27
Hampton, Lionel, 153
Hand, Judge, 31
Haney, Carol, 203
Hardwicke, Sir Cedric, 117
Harlow, Jean, 49-51
Harmetz, Aljean, 249, 360, 361
Harmon, Estelle, 207
Harris, Mildred, 59
Harrison, Jenilee, 364
Harrison, Rex, 148-150
Harris, Richard, 262, 329, 330
Hart, William S., 143
Haskins, James, 273
Haver, Ronald, 94
Hawks, Howard, 127
Hawks, Kenneth, 41, 42
Hawn, Goldie, 249
Hays, Will, 46
Hayes, Helen, 243
Hayton, Lennie, 274-277
Hayward, Brooke, 123
Hayward-Deverich Agency, 297
Hayward, Leland, 2, 99, 123-128, 156, 291, 297, 298, 321
Hayward, Susan, 173, 196,
309
Hayward, Colonel William, 31
Hayworth, Rita, 240, 283, 305, 339
Hearn, George, 248
Hearst, William Randolph, 27, 43
Hecht, Ben, 117, 125, 173, 188, 238
Heisler, Stuart, 297
Heflin, Van, 167
Helen of Westmore's, 51
Helfer, Ralph, 142
Hellman, Lillian, 102, 117, 125
Hemingway, Ernest, 102, 125, 126, 297
Henie, Sonja, 43, 291
Henried, Paul, 379
Hepburn, Audrey, 340
Hepburn, Katherine, 126, 231, 351
Herbert, Hugh, 305
Herman, Woody, 378
Heston, Charlton, 173
Heyward, Dubose, 225
Heyward, Dorothy, 225
Hibbs, Gene, 51
Hildegarde, 156
Hiller, Arthur, 187
Hitchcock, Alfred, 93, 178 183, 311
Hoffman, Dustin, 210, 249
Hoffman, George Jerry, 326
Holden, William, 49, 194-196
Hollywood Reporter, The, 328, 329, 339, 346, 347
Holman, Leigh, 174
Holm, Eleanor, 222
Holtz, Lou, 122
Hope, Bob, 6, 122, 268, 299, 300
Hopkins, Miriam, 331
Hopper, Hedda, 326, 327, 329
Horne, Edna, 270
Horne, Lena, 270-277
Horner, Robert J., 61
Horton, Edward Everett, 41
Houseman, John, 351
Howard, Jean, 188
Howard, Leslie, 238
Howard, Sydney, 48
Hudson, Rochelle, 206
Hudson, Rock, 201, 205-209, 218, 261, 262, 299
Huff, Theodore, 56, 59
Hughes, Howard, 49, 50, 104, 105, 115, 116
Hunter, Ross, 262, 283
Hunter, Tab, 203, 204, 218
Hurrell, George, 284, 324, 332
Hurt, William, 344
Huston, John, 240, 283
Huston, Walter, 283
Hutton, Betty, 260, 330
Hyde, Johnny, 166, 240, 241, 242, 305
Hyman, Eliot, 188

International Creative Management (ICM), 378-379
International Famous Artists, 378

Jackson, Jermaine, 355
Jackson, Joseph, 355-358
Jackson, Marlon, 355, 357
Jackson, Michael, 277, 353-357, 368
Jackson, Tito, 355, 357
Jacobs, Arthur P., 148
Jaffe, Stanley, 344, 357
Jagger, Mick, 283
James, Harry, 100, 153, 200, 290, 378
Janis, Elsie, 25, 292
January, Lois, 222
Jewison, Norman, 227
Jip (Dog), 148
Johnson, Lyndon, 154
Johnson, Dean, 195
Johnson, Merle, Jr. (See Troy Donahue)
Johnson, Van, 156, 214, 262
Johnston, Alva, 134, 317, 321
Jolson, Al, 108, 228, 384
Jones, Buck, 120
Jones, Doris Cohen, 98
Jones, Charles H., 61
Jones, Edwin "Teddy," 271
Jones, Jennifer, 205, 208
Jones, Louis, 271
Jones, Shirley, 368
Jones, Spike, 301
Jordan, Bobby, 65
Jory, Victor, 156
Jourdan, Louis, 211

Joyce, Alice, 108, 119
Joyce, Frank, 108, 109, 116, 119, 122

Kael, Pauline, 120, 382
Kahn, E. J., Jr., 14, 293, 294
Kahn, Ivan, 201
Kamen, Stan, 239, 249, 285
Kane, Robert, 47
Kanin, Garson, 241
Kappelhof, Doris (See Doris Day)
Karloff, Boris, 210
Karras, Alex, 278
Katz, Charles J., 63
Katz, Ephraim, 192
Kaye, Danny, 197
Kaye, Sammy, 153
Keaton, Diane, 249
Keeler, Ruby, 222
Keeney Circuit, 10, 89
Keeshan, Robert (Captain Kangaroo), 379
Keith-Albee Circuit, 10, 89
Keith, B. F., 5, 10, 239
Keith, Brian, 262
Kellerman, Annette, 12, 55, 56
Kelly, Jack (See Orry-Kelly)
Kelly, Gene, 242
Kelly, Walter C., 6
Kennedy, Jack, 154
Kennedy, Jackie, 285, 328
Kennedy, Joseph P., 47, 48
Kennedy, Rose, 48
Kent, Barbara, 281
Kerr, John, 135
Khan, Prince Aly, 305
King, Alexander, 349
King, Claude, 210
King, Don, 356
King, John, 31
Kinski, Natassia, 344
Kirby and Degage, 339
Kirk, Phyllis, 141
Klaw and Erlanger, 5, 11, 12, 13, 15, 22
Klein, Calvin, 364, 365
Kline, Kevin, 344
Knight, Eric Mowbray, 141
Koehler, Bill, 141
Koehler, Ted, 271
Kohner, Fredrick, 283
Kohner, Pancho, 283

Kohner, Susan, 282-283
Kohner, Walter, 283
Kopoloff, Don, 373
Korda Brothers, 135
Korman, Tom, 380
Koster, Henry, 297
Krasna, Norman, 156
Krebs, Albin, 127
Knoll, Lucy, 243
Krupa, Gene, 100, 153
Kupcinet, Irv, 325
Kurnitz, Harry, 102

Ladd, Alan, 163-168, 299
Ladd, Alana, 166, 168
Ladd, Alan, Jr., 165, 166
Ladd, David, 166, 168
Laemmle, Carl, 95, 96, 281
Laemmle, Carl, Jr., 169
Lahr, Bert, 122
Lake, Arthur, 141
Lake, Veronica, 163, 164
Lamarr, Hedy, 161, 273
Lamour, Dorothy, 330
Lamphere, Dodie, 67, 68
Lancaster, Burt, 324
Lanchester, Elsa, 301
Landau, Arthur, 2, 50, 51
Landau, Joe, 368
Landon, Elizabeth, 347
Lane, Rocky, 143, 148
Lang, Fritz, 127, 189
Lange, Jessica, 279
Langham, Ria, 158
Langhanke, Lucille (See Mary Astor)
Langhanke, Otto Ludwig, 40, 41, 42
Lang, Jennings, 306-309, 341
Lang, June, 291
Lang, Pamela, 307-309
Langtry, Lily, 10, 22
Lansing, Sherry, 344, 345-346
Lantz, Robert, 21, 112, 188, 283
La Plante, Laura, 222
Larkin, Pete, 129
Lasky, Jesse L., 45, 46, 95, 134, 184, 211
Lassie (Dog), 142
Lastfogel, Abe, 2, 14, 101, 188, 243, 293, 294, 383, 384
Lauder, Sir Harry, 12, 13, 14, 15
Laughton, Charles, 300-

301
Laurie, Joe, Jr., 6, 7, 10, 11
Lawford, Peter, 141, 297
Lawrence, Gertrude, 106
Lawrence, Jerome, 238
Lazar, Irving (Swifty), 101-103, 289, 305
Lazar, Mary, 102
Leab, Daniel J., 273
Leavitt, Mike, 7
Lederer, Evelyn (See Sue Carol)
Lederer, Francis, 299
Lee, Gypsy Rose, 259
Lee, Tommy (Horse), 147
Lefkowitz, Julius, 196
Lefkowitz, Nat, 85, 196, 197
Le Gallienne, Eva, 280
Leif, Ronnie, 296
Leigh, Vivien, 161, 174-176, 178, 196, 205
Leipzig, Lloyd, 347
Lemaire, Rufus, 206
Leonard, Jack E., 128
LeRoy, Mervyn, 158, 159, 238
Lesser, Julian, 212
Lesser, Sol, 254
Lester, E. M., 98
Lester, Jerry, 156
Levee, M. C., 2, 188, 237, 238, 239
Levee, M. C., Jr., 373
Levine, Nat, 143, 144
Levy, Al, 259, 260
Levy, Louis S., 31, 32
Lewis, Emmanuel, 55, 278
Lewis, George, 281
Lewis, Marilyn (See Rhonda Fleming)
Lewis, Jerry, 128
Lewis, Ted, 40, 153
Liberace, 268
Lieberson, Sandy, 376
Liman, George, 7, 9
Lindley, Audra, 360
Lindsay, Howard, 125
Linet, Beverly, 165
Lloyd, Alice, 10
Lockhart's Elephants, 134
Loew, David, 223
Loew, Marcus, 15, 60
Logan, Josh, 127
Lombard, Carole, 119-121, 157, 161, 174, 178, 183, 321, 346
Lombardo, Carmen, 83

Lombardo, Guy Albert, 83, 84, 153
London International Agency, 378
London, Julie, 212
Long, Jimmy, 143
Loo, Bessie, 2
Loos, Anita, 368
Lopez, Vincent, 153
Loren, Sophia, 161
Lorie, Barry, 346
Louise, Anita, 173
Louis, Joe, 274
Love, Mike, 339
Loy, Myrna, 141, 156, 283
Luther, Lester, 207
Luxford, Captain, 134, 135
Lyons, Maidie, 333-335

MacDonald, Jeanette, 238, 331, 332
MacGraw, Ali, 341, 382
Mack, Judge, 33, 34
MacLaine, Shirley, 203
MacLane, Barton, 169
MacLeod, Gavin, 368
MacLean, Alistair, 102
MacRae, Gordon, 260, 262
Madison, Noel, 210
Madison, Guy, 216, 218
Mahoney, Jim, 341
Mahoney, Susan, (See Suzanne Somers)
Mahoney, Will, 87
Majors, Lee, 368
Malden, Karl, 196
Mamoulian, Rouben, 194, 225
Mankiewicz, Herman, 117, 189
Mankiewicz, Joseph L., 241, 297
Manners, Dorothy, 326
Mann, May, 24
Man o' War (Horse), 147
March, Fredric, 120, 156, 174, 321
Margulies, Lee, 352
Marion, Frances, 25
Marquand, John P., 188
Marriner, Edythe (See Susan Hayward)
Marshack, Laddie, 142
Marshall, Brenda, 194
Martin, Dean, 239, 242
Martin, Tony, 128

Marvin Josephson Associates, 378, 379
Marvin, Lee, 235
Marx, Chico, 118, 119
Marx, Groucho, 118, 119
Marx, Gummo, 118, 119, 201
Marx, Harpo, 118, 119
Marx, Timothy, 119
Marx, Zeppo, 118, 119, 201
Mayer, Louis B., 71, 95-97, 118, 127, 154, 155, 169, 209, 281, 298, 299, 383
Maynard, Ken, 143, 144
Mazursky, Paul, 344
McAdoo, William Gibbs, 321
McCarey, Leo, 176, 177
McCarthy, Kevin, 280
McCarthy, Neil, 104, 105
McCormack, Anne, 67
McCoy, Colonel Tim, 143
McCrary, Ted, 197
McCrea, Joel, 164
McCullough, Jimmy, 285
McDaniel, Hattie, 270
McDonald, Marie, 291
McDonald, Patricia, 347
McDowell, Malcolm, 283
McElwaine, Guy, 341
McEvoy, J. P., 65
McGovern, Elizabeth, 344-346
McGuire, Dorothy, 156, 211, 216
McLennan, Don, 149, 150
McLaglen, Victor, 240
McKean, Michael, 347
McMillan, Hazel, 255
McQueen, Steve, 368
Medavoy, Mike, 2, 373
Melcher, Martin, 259-264
Melcher, Terrence, 259, 262, 264
Melford, Frank, 212
Melnick, Al, 122
Menasco, Al, 162, 163
Mengers, Sue, 2, 373-383
Merman, Ethel, 111, 156, 207
Merrill, Dina, 331
Metro-Goldwyn-Mayer Studios (MGM), 28, 29, 36, 43, 50, 51, 61, 71, 97, 102, 105, 110, 118, 125, 127, 141, 142, 155, 156,

159, 160-162, 166, 169, 190, 240, 241, 257, 258, 272, 273, 275, 277, 279, 281, 298, 310, 317, 331, 332, 335, 340, 341, 376, 379
Meyerfield, Morris, Jr., 15
Meyer, Ron, 249
Middleton, Peggy (See Yvonne de Carlo)
Midler, Bette, 6
Mielziner, Jo, 127
Milestone, Lewis, 95, 96, 103-105
Millar, Mack, 122
Miller, Arthur, 162, 163
Miller, Arthur C., 35
Miller, Marilyn, 320
Mills, John, 366
Minnelli, Liza, 382
Minter, Mary Miles, 60
Mirisch, Harold, 242, 262
Mitchell, Thomas, 173
Mitchum, Robert, 297, 341, 368
Mix, Tom, 222, 256
Modern Screen magazine, 201, 325
Moller, Grace, 339
Monroe, Marilyn, 162, 163, 166, 188, 196, 240-242, 343
Monroe, Thomas, 297, 298
Montgomery, Baby Peggy, 254, 255
Moore, Dickie, 65
Moore, Dudley, 339, 347
Moore, Owen, 103
Moore, Victor, 122
Moorehead, Agnes, 279
Moreau, Jeanne, 283
Morgan, Dennis, 223
Morgan, Helen, 327
Morgan, Ralph, 210
Morris, William, Jr., 293, 294
Morris, William, Sr., 2, 5-17, 294
Morrison, Charlie, 203
Mosely, Robert (See Guy Madison)
Moss, Harry, 289, 305
Mostel, Zero, 128
Motion Picture Herald magazine, 256, 257
Motion Picture magazine, 325

Mowbray, Alan, 210
Mr. Ed (Horse), 147, 148
Ms magazine, 381
Muhl, Ed, 206
Muni, Paul, 238
Murphy, George, 122
Murray, George, 122
Murray, Ken, 122
Murray, Mae, 51, 52
Murray, William, 381
Murrow, Edward R., 300
Music Corporation of America (MCA), 75, 78-85, 98-100, 128, 153-156, 162, 167, 170, 205, 238, 239, 275, 289, 290, 292, 295-301, 309-313, 341, 373, 375, 376, 378, 380, 384
Myers, Julian, 348

Nabokov, Vladimir, 102
Naldi, Nita, 6
Nanette (Dog), 137
Nashua (Horse), 147
Natale, Richard, 277
Nathan, Robert, 216
National Vaudeville Association (NVA), 11
Neff, Wallace, 290
Negri, Pola, 283
Neilan, Marshall, 46
Nelson, Harmon Oscar, 155, 156
Nemy, Enid, 103
Newgass, George W., 33
Newman, Paul, 227, 334, 341, 377, 378
Newton-John, Olivia, 248
Niblo, Fred, 289, 290
Nicholl, Don, 363
Nicita, Nick, 249
Nidorf, Michael, 295
Nielson, Leslie, 187
Niessen, Gertrude, 190
Nipper (Dog), 136
Nissen, Greta, 50
Niven, David, 283
Nixon, Richard, 101
Norman, Barry, 162
North, Dorothy, 255
North, Jay, 255
North, Michael, 255
Novack, Joe, 129
Novak, Kim, 360

Oakie, Jack, 240
O'Brien, Margaret, 55, 290

O'Brien, Pat, 93, 116, 184, 228, 331
O'Connor, Donald, 147
Oberon, Merle, 126, 154, 174
Oliver, Maurine, 289
Olivier, Laurence, 174-176, 178, 208, 379
Olsson, Gustav, 358
Onassis, Aristotle, 359
O'Neill, James, 36
O'Neal, Ryan, 380
Orkin, Harvey, 376, 377
Orloff, Kathy, 347
Orsatti Agency, 290
Orsatti, Frank, 123, 281, 282, 290, 291
Orsatti, Morris, 290
Orsatti, Victor, 2, 123, 290, 291
Osborn, Fredrick H., 293
Osborne, Robert, 346
O'Shea, Dan, 183
O'Toole, Peter, 196, 283
Ovitz, Mike, 249

Paderewski, Jan, 170
Pal (Dog), 142
Palace Theater, 15, 26
Pantages, Alexander, 5
Paramount Studios, 61, 96 97, 110, 111, 117, 120, 122, 143, 145, 148, 156, 163-168, 179, 190, 191, 194, 195, 203, 211, 215, 224, 237, 238, 268, 310, 318, 345, 358
Park, Arthur, 261
Parton, Dolly, 368
Parsons, Louella, 39, 326, 329, 330
Paul, Les, and Mary Ford, 144
Pearson, Ben, 284
Peck, Gregory, 103, 211
Penn, Sean, 344-346
Perry, Al, 129
Pete (Dog), 135
Pete (Penguin), 135
Peters, Jane Alice (See Carole Lombard)
Peters, Jon, 379
Petrillo, James C., 292
Phillips, Stephanie, 373
Picker, David, 277
Pickford, Jack, 320
Pickford, Mary, 6, 22, 23,

24, 25, 26, 27, 28, 103, 238, 320
Pickford, "Maw," 24, 25, 28
Pine, Bill, 318, 319
Pinker-Morrison Agency, 111
Pitnof, Rose, 13
Plaskin, Glenn, 364, 365
Plummer, Christopher, 48
Poitier, Sidney, 224, 225, 267, 280
Poli Circuit, 9
Pollack, Sidney, 249
Polynesia (Parrot), 148
Pond, Steve, 357
Porter, Cole, 102
Post, Guy Bates, 5
Potts, Annie, 377
Powell, Dick, 222, 238
Powell, William, 110, 111, 141, 184
Preminger, Ingo, 226-228
Preminger, Otto, 225-228
Prima, Louis, 153
Proctor, F. F., 9, 10, 11
Proser, Monte, 260
Pryor, Richard, 277
Puck, Eva, 86
Pye, Michael, 16, 80

Raft, George, 190
Ragan, David, 258
Rainer, Luise, 283
Rains, Claude, 238
Rampling, Charlotte, 283
Ramsaye, Terry, 26
Randall, Bob, 147
Rapp, Charlie, 129
Raymond, Gene, 331, 332
Reagan, Ronald, 42, 154, 309
Redford, Robert, 249, 376
Redgrave, Vanessa, 283
Reed, Rex, 276, 277
Reeve, Christopher, 368
Reichenback, Harry, 5, 318
Remarque, Erich Maria, 223
Republic Studios, 43, 144, 145, 214
Reynolds, Burt, 347, 368, 381
Rhubarb (Cat), 133
Richmond, Harry, 239
Riklis, Meshulam, 43
Ringer, Judge, 368

Rin Tin Tin (Dog), 136, 137, 146
Rin Tin Tin, Jr. (Dog), 140
Ritter, John, 360
Ritter, Tex, 143
Ritz Brothers, 128
RKO Studios, 71, 111, 119, 126, 165, 166, 176, 177, 190, 191, 211, 215, 216, 228, 298, 320
Roach, Hal, 50, 68
Robards, Jason, 280, 375
Robert J. Woolf Associates, 379
Roberts, Ben, 378
Roberts, Ruth, 176
Robertson, Cliff, 196
Robinson, "Bojangles," 278
Robinson, Edward G., 212, 290, 297, 330
Rockford, Mickey, 77
Rodriguez, Miguel, 270
Rogers, Buddy, 24
Rogers, Ginger, 325
Rogers, Henry, 339, 340
Rogers, Roy, 141, 145, 146, 305
Rogers, Will, 143
Rolls, Ernest, 307
Roosevelt, Theodore, 29
Root, Elihu, 29
Rosenberg, Lee, 249
Rosenthal, Jerome, 262-264
Ross, Diana, 277, 381
Ross, Michael, 362, 363
Ross, Shirley, 222
Rowland, Richard, 28
Rowland, Roy, 279
Rowlands, Gena, 280
Rubenstein, Artur, 102
Rubenstein, Helena, 333, 365
Rush, Herman, 351
Russell, Ed, 347
Russell, Rosalind, 168-170, 340, 343, 358

Sabu, 35
Sam (Dog), 141
Sanders, George, 241
Saphier, Jimmy, 122
Sarnoff, David, 78, 97
Schary, Dore, 279
Schell, Maximilian, 191, 192
Schenck, Joseph, 237

Scherer, Harry, 347
Schertzinger, Victor, 268
Scheuer, Philip K., 279, 291
Schildkraut, Rudolph, 281
Schlesinger, Arthur, 102
Schmidt, Lars, 176
Schneider, Maria, 283
Schreiber, Lou. 241
Schreiber, Taft, 80, 82
Schroeder, Ricky, 55
Schulberg, B. P., 104
Schumann-Heink, Ernestine, 238, 257, 258
Schwartz, Tony, 361, 362
Schumach, Murray, 78, 313
Scott, Lizabeth, 188
Scorsese, Martin, 344
Segal, George, 346, 347
Segal, Maurice, 346

Seiter, William, 290
Selleck, Tom, 317, 368
Sellers, Peter, 196
Selznick, David O., 94-97, 110, 120, 173-183, 203-205, 208-212, 215, 216, 321
Selznick, Irene Mayer, 94, 97, 105, 109, 152, 178, 179, 183
Selznick-Joyce Agency, 109
Selznick, Lewis J., 94, 95, 109, 116, 182
Selznick, Myron, 2, 93-96, 103-119, 120, 154, 176, 204, 381
Selznick-Vanguard Productions, 201
Sennett, Mack, 56, 120
Shaw, Artie, 153
Shaw, Irwin, 102
Shearer, Norma, 169, 330
Shed, Bruce, 165
Sheedy Circuit, 9
Sheen, Martin, 283
Shepherd, Richard, 2, 373
Sheridan, Ann, 223
Sherrill, Jack, 257, 258
Shields, Brooke, 364-368
Shields, Frank, 365
Shields, Teri, 364
Shoemaker, Willie, 147
Shore, Dinah, 300
Shubert Brothers, 12
Shulman, Irving, 50
Schumacher, Augustus

(Dog), 140, 141
Shurr, Louis, 122, 272
Siegel, Moe, 144
Siegel, Herbert, 312
Siegel, Peggy, 344
Silbert, Harry, 147
Silvers, Phil, 242, 373
Silver, Stu, 278
Simon, Neil, 102
Simple Simon, 90
Sinatra, Frank, 119, 226, 239, 240, 242, 261, 295, 296, 300, 341
Sissle, Noble, and his orchestra, 271
Skelton, Red, 273
Slezak, Walter, 280
Sloman, Edward, 281
Slye, Leonard (See Roy Rogers)
Small, Edgar, 280
Small, Edward, 93, 94
Small, Lillian Schary, 2, 279, 280
Small, Paul, 279
Smight, Jack, 227
Smith, Albert E., 27
Smith, Boyce, 29, 33
Smith, Gladys (See Mary Pickford)
Smith, Jack, 24, 260
Smith, Jewel, 331
Smith, John, 214
Smith, Lois, 344
Smith, Lottie, 24
Smith, Maggie, 106
Smith, Pete, 61, 335
Smith, Roger, 358-360, 364
Snyder, Martin ("the Gimp"), 261
Somborn, Herbert, 45, 46, 87
Somers, Suzanne, 360-364
Sons of the Pioneers, 146
Sophie (Seal), 148
Sorrell, Helen, 207
Sothern, Ann, 273
Speck, Bobby, 202
Spigelgass, Leonard, 118, 119
Spitzer, Marian, 6
Spreckles, Kay Williams, 162
Springer, John, 343, 344
Stallone, Sylvester, 339, 368
Stander, Miles, 318

Stanwyck, Barbara, 160, 194, 223, 331, 359
Stark, Ray, 2, 188, 212
Stein, Doris, 170, 295, 384
Steiner, Ira, 378
Stein, Jules, 2, 5, 75-86, 98-101, 128, 153, 170, 205, 289, 290, 295-301, 305, 309, 313, 383, 384
Stein, Louis M., 75, 76
Stein, Milton, 351
Stein, Rosa Cohen, 75
Stein, William, 83-84, 154, 295
Stern, Isaac, 379
Steuer, Max D., 31, 33, 34
Stevens, Lee, 239
Stevens, Inger, 280
Stewart, Donald Ogden, 125
Stewart, James, 127, 142, 154, 281, 298, 299
Stewart, Nellie, 28
Stokey, Mike, 68
Stoller, Morris, 239
Stordahl, Axel, 296
Streep, Meryl, 249
Streisand, Barbra, 249, 279, 368, 378-381
Strickling, Howard, 105, 159, 317, 320, 335, 336
Stricklyn, Ray, 343
Sturges, Preston, 290
Stuart, Nick, 164
Styne, Jule, 77, 260
Sullavan, Margaret, 126, 127, 281
Sullivan, Ed, 257, 300, 301
Sullivan, Pat, 47
Sul-Te-Wan, Madame, 273
Sun, Gus, Circuit, 5
Sunderland, Ron, 362
Susskind, David, 259, 260
Sutherland, Donald, 361
Suttletones, 358
Swanson, Gloria, 6, 44-49, 300, 334
Swaps (Horse), 147
Sweig, Joe, 129
Swift and Kelly, 87
Swinburn Agency, 280
Sword Dancer (Horse), 147
Sydney, Sylvia, 230, 343
Syn (Cat), 141

Talbot, Lyle, 222
Tanguay, Eva, 5, 9
Tarzan (Horse), 143

Taurog, Norman, 68-70
Taylor, Elizabeth, 208, 283, 329, 340, 341, 343
Taylor, Robert, 283, 331
Taylor, Rod, 262
Taylor, Theodore, 77
Teagarden, Jack, 153
Temple, Shirley, 216, 278
Thalberg, Irving, 43, 50, 110, 117
This Week magazine, 374
Thomas, Bill, 318, 319
Thomas, Bob, 146, 195
Thomas, Marlo, 341
Thompson, J. Lee, 242
Thompson, Kenny, 210
Thorpe, Dr. Franklyn, 42
Tierney, Gene, 225
Tone, Franchot, 238
Tony (Horse), 143, 222
Topper (Horse), 143
Tornabene, Lynn, 160
Townley, Rod, 231
Tracy, Spencer, 126, 279
Tramont, Jean Paul, 382
Travolta, John, 248
Trevor, Claire, 340
Trigger (Horse), 146, 147
Trigger, Jr. (Horse), 146
Troulman, Jay, 361
Truman, Harry, President, 300
Tucker, Lillian, 29
Tucker, Richard, 210
Tucker, Sophie, 18, 190
Turan, Kenneth, 278, 359
Turner, Lana, 50, 173, 240, 285, 343
TV Guide magazine, 142
Twentieth Century-Fox Studios, 43, 110, 112, 148, 149, 161, 165, 196, 208, 214, 224, 225, 227, 230, 241, 251, 274, 326, 347
Twyeford, Curly, 135
Tynan, Kenneth, 102

Ullman, Liv, 283
Ufland, Marty, 373
United Artists, 47, 93, 110, 121, 123, 166, 196, 203, 212, 223, 229, 243
United Booking Office (UBO), 11, 14
United States Amusement Company, 12
Universal Studios, 96, 145, 190, 206-208, 211, 217,

248, 256, 258, 272, 281, 298, 309, 311, 313, 318, 320, 351, 376
Uno (Mule), 135

Valenti, Jack, 227
Valentino, Rudolph, 6
Van, Bobby, 214
Van Cleef, Lee, 214
Van Doren, Mamie, 214
Van Eyck, Peter, 214
Van Fleet, Jo, 214
Van Orden, Robert, 214
Van Patton, Dickie, 214
Van Sloan, Edward, 214
Van Zandt, Phillip, 214
Variety Club (Show business charity), 11
Variety, 10, 25, 239, 333
Variety, Daily, 227, 283, 328
Verdon, Gwen, 203, 204
Vereen, Ben, 278
Vickers, Judge, 257
Victoria, Vesta, 5, 10, 12
Vidor, Charles, 297
Vincent, Frank W., 170
von Stroheim, Erich, 40, 47, 49, 283
von Sydow, Max, 283

Walken, Christopher, 305
Wallis, Hal, 136, 201
Wallis, Minna, 2, 159-160, 161, 162
Walsh, Raoul, 206
Walt Disney Studios, 133, 227
Wanger, Walter, 306-309
Warfield, David, 15, 56
Warga, Wayne, 101
Warner, Albert, 95
Warner Bros. Studio, 96, 104, 108, 112, 136-138, 156, 159, 164, 173, 174, 190, 191, 195, 203, 206, 207, 211, 217, 221, 222, 223, 228, 238, 290, 295, 300, 311, 347, 375, 378
Warner Bros.-Seven Arts, 378
Warner, Harry, 95
Warner, H. B., 134, 257
Warner, Jack L., 95, 103, 104, 110, 111, 127, 136, 155, 159, 174, 209, 383
Warner, Rita Stanwood, 257
Warner, Sam, 95

Wasserman, Lew, 2, 153-155, 289, 296, 299-302, 305, 309
Waters, Ethel, 276
Wayne, John, 195
Weatherwax, Rudd, 141, 142
Webb, Clifton, 225
Weber and Fields, 5
Weber and Rush, 9
Weiss, Peter, 248
Weissmuller, Johnny, 135
Weitz, Barry J., 245
Welles, Sumner, 197
Wellman, William, 297
Werblin, David (Sonny), 2, 85, 99, 289, 305
West, Bernie, 362
West, Mae, 76, 145, 147, 190, 258, 299, 318-320, 333
Westmore, Perc, 332
Weston, Dick (See Leonard Slye)
Whale, James, 50
White Flash (Horse), 143
White, Sammy, 86, 318
White, Theodore, 102
Whitty, Dame May, 117, 156
Wiatt, Jim, 249
Wilcox, Fred, 141
Wile, Shelly, 373
Wilkenning, Cora Carrington, 25, 26, 27, 28

Wilkinson, June, 284-285
Wilkinson, Lily, 285
William Morris Agency, 85-100, 161, 196, 197, 226, 238-240, 242, 245, 247, 278, 293, 294, 297, 300-302, 310, 311, 378, 380, 382, 384
Williams, Andy, 284
Williams, Percy, 9, 11, 15
Williams, Tennessee, 379
Will Rogers Memorial Hospital, 11
Wills, Bob, 153
Willson, Henry, 2, 201-218, 164, 165, 378
Wilson, Dooley, 273
Wilson, Judge, 63, 67
Wilson, Howard, 164
Wilson, Marie, 217
Wilson, Teddy, 100
Winchell, Walter, 39, 60, 319
Winkler, Otto, 121
Winters, Shelley, 299
Wittles, David, 99
Wizen, Joe, 373
Wolders, Robert, 379
Wood, George, 5, 239, 240
Wood, Natalie, 55, 335
Woodward, Joanne, 339, 377, 378
Wyler, William, 127, 174, 281, 379, 380
Wyman, Jane, 156, 307,

310, 340, 368
Wynn, Ed, 90, 239
Wynters, Charlotte, 169
Wyse, Mike, 373

Yates, Herbert ("Papa"), 43, 144, 145
Young, Alan, 147
Young, Gig, 207
Young, Loretta, 178, 182, 195, 247, 297, 310, 331
Young, Margaret, 194
Young, Roland, 174, 321
Youngman, Henny, 129, 197
Yule, Joe, 256
Yule, Joe, Jr. (See Mickey Rooney)

Zadora, Pia, 44
Zanft, Major, 327
Zanuck, Darryl F., 28, 43, 136, 139, 159, 212, 241, 383
Zarem, Bobby, 344
Zeidman, Bennie, 95, 96
Ziegfeld, Flo, 333
Zifkin, Walter, 239
Zimmerman, Don, 231
Zimmerman, Marguerite (Marge), 231, 232
Zimmerman, Agnes Ethel (See Ethel Merman)
Zimmerman, Scott, 247
Zukor, Adolph, 25, 26, 46, 94, 95, 97